The Sicilian Puppet Theater of Agrippino Manteo (1884–1947)

The Sicilian Puppet Theater of Agrippino Manteo (1884–1947)

The Paladins of France in America

Jo Ann Cavallo

ANTHEM PRESS

Anthem Press
An imprint of Wimbledon Publishing Company
www.anthempress.com

This edition first published in UK and USA 2025
by ANTHEM PRESS
75–76 Blackfriars Road, London SE1 8HA, UK
or PO Box 9779, London SW19 7ZG, UK
and
244 Madison Ave #116, New York, NY 10016, USA

First published in the UK and USA by Anthem Press in 2023

Copyright © Jo Ann Cavallo 2025

The author asserts the moral right to be identified as the author of this work.

All rights reserved. Without limiting the rights under copyright reserved above, no part of this publication may be reproduced, stored or introduced into a retrieval system, or transmitted, in any form or by any means (electronic, mechanical, photocopying, recording or otherwise), without the prior written permission of both the copyright owner and the above publisher of this book.

British Library Cataloguing-in-Publication Data
A catalogue record for this book is available from the British Library.

Library of Congress Control Number: 2024944914

ISBN-13: 978-1-83999-394-7 (Pbk)
ISBN-10: 1-83999-394-4 (Pbk)

Cover image: Courtesy of Susie Bruno.

This title is also available as an e-book.

For Susie Bruno,
granddaughter of Agrippino Manteo

CONTENTS

List of Figures   ix

Acknowledgments   xiii

Foreword   xv

Preface   xix

Introduction   xxi

Part One   The Sicilian Puppet Theater of Agrippino Manteo and Family   1

1. The Puppeteers   3
2. The Scripts   39

Part Two   Select Plays from the Paladins of France Cycle   63

    Introduction   65

3. The Arrival of Angelica of Cathay in Paris (*sera* 152)   73
4. The Duel between Astolfo and Gradasso di Sericana (*sera* 159)   91
5. The Duel between Orlando and Agricane di Tartaria (*sera* 165)   111
6. The Grand Council of Agramante di Biserta (*sera* 170)   131
7. The Enamorment of Bradamante and Ruggiero (*sera* 182)   147
8. The Madness of Orlando (*sera* 198)   163
9. The Voyage of Astolfo to the Moon (*sera* 203)   179
10. The Battle of Three against Three in Lampedusa (*sera* 208)   193

Conclusion   213

Appendix 1: List of Characters 215

Appendix 2: Papa Manteo's Marionettes—Currently at IAM 219

Appendix 3: Extant Publications from the Library of Agrippino Manteo 221

Appendix 4: Paladins of France Scripts in the Handwriting of Agrippino Manteo 223

Appendix 5: Agrippino Manteo's Summaries of Plays in the Paladins of France Cycle 225

Appendix 6: Select Characters from the Paladins of France Cycle 285

Appendix 7: Manteo Family Genealogy 289

Works Cited 291

Index 297

LIST OF FIGURES

Cover: "Teatro Manteo. [Re]cuerdo a mi[s] queridos pri[mos]" (ca. 1930–1931). Back row: Caterina and Agrippino Manteo. Front row (left to right): daughter Ida Manteo, Mike's wife Mary Manteo, and Dominic's wife Frances Manteo. The marionettes may be the princess Angelica and the wizard Malagigi. The photo was addressed to Agrippino's cousins in Argentina. The handwriting is presumably that of one of Agrippino's children under his direction. Courtesy of Susie Bruno.

Figures

1.1	Members of the Manteo family (ca. 1916). The two women are Agrippino's sister Teresa (left) and wife Caterina (right). The children (left to right) are Mike, Dominic, Ritz, and Ida. Courtesy of Susie Bruno	8
1.2	Agrippino Manteo as an electrician (1922). Courtesy of Michael J. Manteo	9
1.3	The wedding of Mike and Mary Manteo (ca. 1930–1931). Front row (left to right): Johnny Manteo, Agrippino Manteo, Caterina Manteo, the bride Mary, the groom Mike, Rosina Manteo (wife of cousin Agrippino). Back row (left to right): Ritz, Ida, Dominic, and Agrippino Manteo (cousin). Courtesy of Michael J. Manteo	10
1.4	Agrippino Manteo's son Ritz (left) and another manipulator on the bridge with the youngest son Johnny in the wings (1920s). Courtesy of Susie Bruno	11
1.5	Agrippino Manteo's son Ritz (left) and another manipulator on the bridge, an unidentified older boy in the wings, and a young Orlando and princess on stage (1920s). Courtesy of Michael J. Manteo	11
1.6	Agrippino Manteo's four sons (from left to right) Mike, Dominic, Ritz, and Johnny on the bridge (ca. 1937–1938). Courtesy of Michael J. Manteo	12

1.7 Caterina Manteo collecting entrance fees at the 109 Mulberry Street theater (1928 or later). Courtesy of Susie Bruno 13
1.8 Agrippino Manteo reading directly from the script during a performance. Courtesy of Michael J. Manteo 14
1.9 Agrippino Manteo speaks the lines as Johnny reads the script and prompts him. Photograph from the documentary film by Tony De Nonno entitled *It's One Family, Knock on Wood* (1982). Courtesy of Tony De Nonno, De Nonno Productions, Incorporated 15
1.10 Agrippino Manteo and son Johnny discuss the script (ca. 1937–1939). Courtesy of Susie Bruno 15
1.11 Agrippino Manteo in Little Italy (ca. 1935–1937). Courtesy of Michael J. Manteo 19
1.12 Mike Manteo with two puppets (1985). Courtesy of Michael J. Manteo 23
1.13 Announcement of a performance by the Manteo family featuring a photo of the late Agrippino Manteo and his puppets (1950). On stage, Angelica is in the center surrounded by Orlando and Rinaldo. Courtesy of Susie Bruno 23
1.14 Mike Manteo improvises the dialogue while (left to right) Pino's nephew Michael Housen Manteo, Ida's husband Angelo Grillo, Mike's son Pino, and Dominic manipulate the puppets, at Symphony Space, New York City (1980s). Courtesy of Susie Bruno 24
1.15 Backstage during a performance, with Mike facing the stage, Ida at the piano, Ida's daughter Joanne Lauria standing behind her, and Ida's husband, Angelo Grillo, on the bridge with other manipulators, at Symphony Space, New York City (1980s). Photo by Martha Cooper. Courtesy of Michael J. Manteo 25
1.16 Papa Manteo's Life Size Marionettes at Symphony Space, New York City (early 1980s). Bottom (left to right): Ida and Mike Manteo with their puppets. Top (left to right): Susie Bruno, her husband Joe Bruno, Michael Housen Manteo, Derick Hunter, Frances Manteo, Dominic Manteo, Angelo Grillo, Pino Manteo, and his son Michael J. Manteo. Photo by Martha Cooper. Courtesy of Michael J. Manteo 26

LIST OF FIGURES

1.17	Susie Bruno and her husband, Joe Bruno, with the Balaheim puppet (1980s), described as a "mighty pagan giant, ruthless against all Christians" in the Manteo family's List of Characters (Appendix 1, #2). Courtesy of Susie Bruno	30
1.18	Performance at Symphony Space, New York City (1980s). The giant Mamalock (center right) wants to join the joust proclaimed by King Solatiello (left) to marry his daughter (far left). Courtesy of Susie Bruno	31
2.1	Agrippino Manteo backstage during a performance as fire burns center stage. Photo by William H. Field (circa 1935–1938). Courtesy of Michael J. Manteo	52
2.2	Mike Manteo's notebook 21, title page, note to his sister Ida. Courtesy of the Italian American Museum, New York City	60
3.1	Rinaldo (Appendix 1, #14). Manteo Family Marionettes, 1991. Collection of the Staten Island Museum	84
3.2	Carlomagno (Appendix 1, #78). Manteo Family Marionettes, 1991. Collection of the Staten Island Museum	89
4.1	Astolfo (Appendix 1, #12). Manteo Family Marionettes, 1991. Collection of the Staten Island Museum	92
5.1	Marfisa. Courtesy of Susie Bruno	123
6.1	Agramante (Appendix 1, #31). Manteo Family Marionettes, 1991. Collection of the Staten Island Museum	142
6.2	Rodomonte (Appendix 1, #50). Manteo Family Marionettes, 1991. Collection of the Staten Island Museum	143
6.3	Mandricardo (Appendix 1, #75). Manteo Family Marionettes, 1991. Collection of the Staten Island Museum	144
7.1	Bradamante (Appendix 1, #21). Manteo Family Marionettes, 1991. Collection of the Staten Island Museum	148
7.2	Ruggiero (Appendix 1, #52). Manteo Family Marionettes, 1991. Collection of the Staten Island Museum	148
7.3	The enamorment of Bradamante and Ruggiero in *sera* 182 (*Copione* 13). Courtesy of Michael J. Manteo	158

ACKNOWLEDGMENTS

First of all I would like to express my gratitude to Agrippino Manteo's descendants for the memories and materials they have shared with me through the years, especially his grandchildren Susie Bruno and the late Pino (Agrippino) Manteo and his great-grandchildren Michael J. Manteo, Catherine Bruno, and Thomas Bruno.

Given that the Manteo family donated most of their materials to the Italian American Museum of New York, I am likewise grateful to the museum's founder and president Joseph Scelsa who not only granted me access to Agrippino Manteo's scripts but also personally transported them to the Columbia University campus on several occasions beginning January 2015 and patiently waited while I scanned them page by page. He subsequently had several additional notebooks in Mike Manteo's handwriting scanned and sent to me so that I could complete the research for this book. I am also indebted to the Columbia University Digital Humanities Librarian Bob Scott and the Western European Humanities Librarian Meredith Levin for granting me exclusive use of the Digital Humanities Center's highest quality scanner for several hours at a time and for their invaluable guidance and support throughout the scanning process.

I owe a special debt of gratitude to Alessandro Napoli, preeminent scholar of Sicilian puppet theater and member of the Marionettistica dei Fratelli Napoli of Catania, not only for his generous foreword but also for his graciousness as an expert interlocutor on all things related to Catanese puppet theater.

I would also like to thank the friends and colleagues who provided feedback on Chapter 1, most notably Steve Abrams, Frank Proschan, Nancy Staub, and Anna Lomax Wood.

FOREWORD

Alessandro Napoli

"The curtain rises on a medieval courtyard. Two knights in shining armor are conversing in flamboyant Italian." These words open the chapter entitled "Orlando Furioso: The Flower of Chivalry," included in the now classic *Art of the Puppet* by Bil Baird published in 1965 for Macmillan in New York and translated into Italian as *Le marionette: Storia di uno spettacolo* (Milan: Arnoldo Mondadori Editore, 1966). Baird devotes this chapter to puppets that bring to life a chivalric repertory. To be more precise, however, the author focuses primarily on Catanese-style *Opera dei Pupi* as he came to know it in the New York theater of Agrippino Manteo and his family.

Baird's chapter—which I read while a university student writing my thesis, *La Marionettistica dei fratelli Napoli: permanenze e mutamenti nell'Opera dei Pupi di tradizione catanese*—marked my first encounter with the name and history of this Catanese puppeteer who immigrated to America. From that moment, there arose a long series of questions, many of which today are answered by the study that I have the honor and joy of presenting in this foreword. Baird's chapter title is placed at the bottom right of a double-page photograph featuring four puppets of the Manteo family: a Saracen, Ruggiero dell'Aquila Bianca, Bradamante, and Rinaldo. From a structural point of view, these puppets belong unequivocally to the Catanese tradition: most notably, they have rigid legs without knee joints as well as a fixed right-hand fist holding a sword, and they are meant to be manipulated by handlers (*manianti*) standing on a bridge (*'u scannappoggiu*) raised with respect to the puppet theater stage and hidden by the backdrop. Yet some details in the shape of the puppets' armor are very different from the typical Catanese shape codified by the great coppersmith masters Giuseppe *don Puddu* Maglia and Sebastiano *don Bastianu* Zappalà. The helmets without neck guards and the oval shields of Bradamante and Rinaldo with the lion insignia over an oblique bar, moreover, make those puppets look very much like the traditional puppets of Palermo. In short, Baird's chapter and the photographs published in it ignited in me a profound curiosity about Papa Agrippino Manteo and his puppets. And my curiosity only increased after learning that Agrippino was a disciple in Grammichele of the puppeteer Giuseppe Crimi, son and pupil in turn of Don Gaetano Crimi, the "founding father" (or "grande genitore" [great parent] as Bernadette Majorana rightly defines him) of Catanese puppet theater. What was the working hypothesis that made me want to learn more about the life and artistic career of Agrippino Manteo? I suspected that this Sicilian-born puppeteer, bringing to America what he learned at the school of Giuseppe Crimi, would have been a very important missing link to better understand what little is known and all that is still unknown about the puppet theater tradition of the founding father Don Gaetano and his children. Because, as Jo Ann Cavallo rightly notes in her study, the scripts of Agrippino's mentor, Giuseppe Crimi, and his father, Gaetano Crimi, are no longer extant.

This book, therefore, is important for the history of Catanese-style *Opera dei Pupi* for the following reasons. First of all, by supplying a human and artistic portrait on the basis of a meticulous examination of sources and documents, Jo Ann Cavallo restores to Agrippino Manteo the rightful place that he must occupy in the reconstruction of the history of this theatrical tradition. Second, it answers many of the questions that I tried to put on the table above. Finally, although it is not yet possible to give an account of some issues (such as the abovementioned difference in the shape of the armor compared to the traditional Catanese style), the book's inclusion of extensive photographs of the Manteo puppets paves the way for further investigation based on this newly available visual evidence.

The first great merit of this work is that of having conducted a careful and systematic analysis of a Sicilian puppet theater operating permanently outside Italy, that is, having described and explained the role of the puppeteer and the importance of the *Opera dei Pupi* tradition among diasporic communities, "bringing Italian immigrants across the globe together each evening to witness dramatizations of the same epic stories they knew and loved." From previous writings, we have news of some puppeteers who immigrated to America (such as Achille Greco in Brazil and Vito Cantone in Buenos Aires), but no prior publication has offered this kind of illuminating study illustrating the scope of the "double" reconfirmation that the vicissitudes of the paladins had for their traditional public: that is, the spectators' validation of their own literary models and cultural codes, reinforced and strengthened in a foreign land by the affirmation of their own group identity of belonging to a national heritage.

The second great merit of this work is to have indirectly corroborated, through the textual analysis of the scripts of Agrippino Manteo, the manner of *travagghiarisi 'i sirati* (structuring, composing, and performing the nightly plays) of his masters Giuseppe and Gaetano Crimi. As attested by the recollections handed down orally both within the family (along the genealogical axis of Raffaele Trombetta, Clementina Crimi, Pasquale Amico, Giuseppina Trombetta, and Nino Amico) and throughout the environment of Catanese puppet theater, as confirmed by the plays written by Don

Raffaele Trombetta (Gaetano Crimi's pupil and son-in-law), the Catanese manner of scripting plays inaugurated by the "grande genitore" went beyond stage directions for improvised action to include *parrati longhi* (long speeches). These extensive written parts, highly anticipated by the public, were considered a test of the mastery of the *parlatore* (speaker giving voice to the puppets) and were therefore necessarily composed in a more elaborate prose dependent upon elite literary sources. The erudite taste characterizing the work of Gaetano Crimi meant that all his students and successors paid particular attention to the literary and dramaturgical aspects of the dialogues of the puppets, in contrast to the more "popular" manner of Catanese *Opira* descended from the other great founder, Don Angelo Grasso. The taste for more refined and courtly language led Gaetano Crimi's descendants and disciples, both direct and indirect, to insert and recite particular moments of the chivalric cycle in *ottava rima* stanzas derived from the original poems. This practice was then also systematized in Giusto Lodico's *Storia dei Paladini di Francia* of 1858–1860, which likewise includes verses and stanzas derived from the original poems within a prose narrative. At least three important examples should be remembered of the "obligatory" use of verses derived from famous poems: the surrender of Mambriano to Rinaldo (from the *Mambriano* by Francesco Bello known as Il Cieco da Ferrara [24.75–76]), the speech of Angelica in Paris on the occasion of the Pasqua Rosata (from Boiardo's *Orlando Innamorato* [1.1.24–28]), and the reproach of the soul of Argalia to Ferraù for the failure to return his helmet (from Ariosto's *Orlando furioso* [1.27–28]). We also know from the poem in *ottava rima* entitled *Storia di Tullio di Russia*, composed by Giuseppe Crimi and published in Lentini in 1925, that Don Gaetano's sons themselves were used to composing original poetry to be inserted into their plays. This is not the place to evaluate the literary merit of these verses, but it is important to note the artistic intention of the puppeteers of the Crimi school, which was to ennoble the dramatic dialogue of the heroes by introducing parts in *puisia* (poetry), as they called it. As Jo Ann Cavallo has well demonstrated, especially in the second part of this study, the scripts of Agrippino Manteo, a worthy emulator of his teacher Giuseppe Crimi, stand out not only for their effective structural and dramaturgical cohesiveness but also for the particular attention paid to monologues and dialogues throughout the plays, to the stanzas chosen from Renaissance poems (extremely important is the knowledge of Papa Manteo, highlighted by the author, of the two redactions of the *Innamorato*, the original version by Boiardo and the *rifacimento* by Berni), and, finally, to the original stanzas composed by him on the basis of a remarkable familiarity with chivalric epic poetry. And in this regard, I would like to draw attention to the analysis conducted by the author on the episode of Angelica's arrival in Paris (Chapter 3). The language used by Manteo's puppets, literary and carefully crafted, is one of the first features that Baird alluded to in his reference to their "flamboyant Italian" at the opening of his chapter. This book, in sum, is packed with many new findings and starting points for further investigation in the field of Catanese *Opera dei Pupi*, as well as being a pleasure to read.

I want to conclude these notes with a personal memory, which also concerns Baird's chapter referenced at the outset. When I was a child, I used to eagerly listen to the stories of the puppets recounted by my uncle Pippo (i.e., Pippo Napoli, the elder brother of the second generation of the Marionettistica dei Fratelli Napoli of Catania, a company of Catanese puppeteers in activity since 1921 to which I am honored to belong). One summer evening when you could see Etna erupting, he began by telling me: "You know, Sandro, when we were doing the *Storia di Uzeta il Catanese*, there was an evening in which we brought down red rivers of lava from Etna in eruption." Uncle Pippo began to describe the preparation, telling me about the careful use of lighting, tissue paper construction, and both shifting and rotation movements. This evocative story remained locked in my childhood imagination until the way of realizing the scenic effect became clear to me by reading what Baird writes about the eruption of Vesuvius staged by the Manteo family in America. As Baird explains: "A smoky green light appears at the peak of Vesuvius and sparks and fire shoot into the sky. Lava erupts from the cone and begins to roll down the mountainside and over the grassy slopes. The bubbling, boiling lava advances, accompanied by the most ominous music [...]. The green fire in Vesuvius's top and the boiling lava [are] made by the turning of long scrolls placed in rising succession across the stage." Combining together my childhood memories of Uncle Pippo's story with this description of the staging by the Manteo family made it possible for me to operationally reconstruct the eruption of Etna with lava descending from the flanks of the volcano. We have restaged this eruption since 2013 in the play that I wrote together with my cousin Fiorenzo Napoli entitled *La passione di Agata*, dedicated to the vicissitudes of Catania's patron saint, Agatha. This scenotechnical effect, known and practiced by Catanese puppeteers on both sides of the ocean, once again attests to the discipleship and activity of Agrippino Manteo within the Crimi school of Catanese puppet theater. Uncle Pippo noted in his recollection that the family had staged the *Storia di Uzeta* for the last time in 1946 in the theater of Via Consolazione in Catania. The *Storia di Uzeta* had been invented in 1900 by Don Raffaele Trombetta, and in 1946 the *parlatori* of the Marionettistica dei Fratelli Napoli were Pasqualino Amico and Giuseppina Trombetta, the son-in-law and daughter of Don Raffaele, respectively. In America and in Catania, in short, the marionettes were given voice and the lava descended according to the great dramaturgical and scenotechnical lesson imparted by the "grande genitore" and his descendants.

PREFACE

> Intangible cultural heritage is an important factor in maintaining cultural diversity in the face of growing globalization.
> UNESCO (https://ich.unesco.org/en/what-is-intangible-heritage-00003)

Many will remember that *Opera dei Pupi* was designated by UNESCO as an "Oral and Intangible Masterpiece in the Heritage of Humanity" in 2001. It remains much less known, however, that this popular tradition also had an illustrious history in the United States, especially in New York City due largely to the passion and perseverance of the preeminent Catanese-American puppeteer Agrippino Manteo. In 2010, the Manteo family donated to the Italian American Museum of New York over thirty of their Catanese-style puppets and most of the family's extant scripts, along with Italian chivalric publications from Agrippino's library and painted backdrops used during performances.[1] This generous gift has in a real sense made *tangible* an extraordinary intangible cultural heritage.

The Italian American Museum of New York is scheduled to reopen in the fall of 2024 in a completely redesigned four-story building at 151 Mulberry Street—just down the block from the family's former marionette theater, *Teatro Manteo*, in Little Italy. In addition to a Manteo puppet display in the Museum's permanent exhibition, future plans include a full exhibit on the history of the Manteo family's puppet theater tradition featuring the marionettes donated by Agrippino's descendants.

At the time of this writing, I have scanned all of the extant notebooks in Agrippino Manteo's handwriting donated to the Italian American Museum as well as some additional privately owned scripts. The Museum, in turn, has scanned twenty-one notebooks from the Paladins

---

1 See Appendices 2–4 for a detailed account of the puppets, family library, and extant scripts in Agrippino's handwriting.

of France cycle copied by Agrippino's son Mike Manteo. These scripts will soon be made available on both the Museum's website and the eBOIARDO website.[2] While the Manteo Sicilian Marionette exhibit will give an idea of the artistic inspiration, cultural tradition, and artisanal craftsmanship at work in the construction of the wooden actors, the online scripts will give students, scholars, and the general public a unique window into an imaginative world that transcends the categories of elite and folk, Sicilian and American, and medieval and modern.

---

[2] As per written agreement, I will upload the scripts to the eBOIARDO website after they have been officially presented at the Italian American Museum and placed on the Museum's own website. See the eBOIARDO page dedicated to the Manteo family for updates (https://edblogs.columbia.edu/eboiardo/manteo-puppet-theater/).

INTRODUCTION

Although puppetry arts have existed since ancient times and can be found throughout the world from Southeast Asia to Northern Europe, Sicilian *opera dei pupi* has very distinct characteristics that set it apart from other forms of puppet theater.[1] Large wooden puppets with full metal armor, swords, and shields bring to life primarily epic narratives based on masterpieces of medieval and Renaissance Italian literature. This tradition of prose theater was the predominant form of nightly entertainment among working-class Sicilians from the early 1800s until the proliferation of television in the late 1950s.[2] *Opera dei pupi* also developed outside Italy among diasporic communities, especially in North and South America as well as North Africa, bringing Italian immigrants across the globe together each evening to witness dramatizations of the same epic stories they knew and loved.

Virtually all Sicilian puppeteers from the 1860s to the present have based their chivalric repertory on the prose compilation *Storia dei paladini di Francia*, first adapted from twenty Renaissance chivalric poems by Giusto Lodico in 1858–1860 and subsequently expanded by Giuseppe Leggio in an 1895–1896 edition. This monumental work provided puppeteers with the narrative material for a Paladins of France cycle consisting of well over 300 consecutive plays. The expanded fictional cycle stretched from before the birth of Charlemagne (740s) to the aftermath of the battle of Roncevaux (778). In addition, many puppeteers extended their chronological range even further by staging stories going back to the time of the emperor Constantine (reigned 306–337) and forward to the First Crusade (1096–1099) and beyond.

---

1 Although this popular tradition also flourished in southern and central Italy, it is commonly referred to as Sicilian given its once ubiquitous and still visible presence on the island.
2 The classic study of Sicilian puppet theater remains Antonio Pasqualino, *L'opera dei pupi*. For the Catanese tradition, see Alessandro Napoli, *Il racconto e i colori*, Bernadette Majorana, and Donata Amico. In English, see John McCormick's history of Italian puppet theater and Marcella Croce's study of Sicilian popular traditions, featuring storytelling, puppetry, and painted carts.

These stories, especially those concerning the Frankish paladins, were experienced as part of a shared history. After all, as emperor of the Holy Roman Empire, Charlemagne had presided over an extensive Christian realm to which the various Italian states had belonged. Some of the cycle's action, moreover, took place in Italy, such as Orlando's birth and childhood in Sutri, outside Rome, the invasion of Calabria by the North African king Agolante, and the epic battle of three-against-three on the island of Lampedusa that brought to a conclusion King Agramante of Biserta's invasion of France.

The handful of Sicilian puppet theater companies currently in existence, however, perform a very restricted repertory. Anyone who happens to see a performance today will most likely witness a version staged with elaborate battle scenes and limited dialogue for the benefit of tourists who are unfamiliar with the epic stories and who may not even understand the Italian language.[3] This contemporary reality could lead one to assume that the adaptation of chivalric literature in traditional Sicilian puppet theater consisted largely of a process of reduction and simplification. Yet nothing could be further from the truth. Puppet theater scripts bear testimony to the rich substance of the epic dramatizations that transpired night after night on the traditional *opera dei pupi* stage. Unfortunately, however, most of these invaluable documents have been lost, while the few sets still in existence are privately owned by the remaining puppeteer families or by collectors or are tucked away in the archives of Italian institutions.

This is where the Catanese-American puppeteer Agrippino Manteo (1884–1947) becomes of primary importance—not only for the history of Sicilian puppet theater in America, but for the understanding of this popular cultural tradition tout court. The notebooks containing his scripts reveal in painstaking detail the entire *opera dei pupi* repertory with the extensive Paladins of France cycle front and center. In addition to meticulous descriptions of the action to unfold onstage, there are elaborate prose dialogues (*parrati longhi*) with occasional *ottava rima* stanzas taken directly from the original Renaissance poems rather than from Agrippino's primary source, the nineteenth-century *Storia dei paladini*. The scripts even include original verses that appear to have been composed by the puppeteer himself.

Beyond their historical, cultural, and aesthetic value, the Manteo scripts invite us to relive the passion, heartbreak, excitement, and magic inherent

---

3 Among the notable exceptions, the Marionettistica dei Fratelli Napoli of Catania still performs puppet plays with very elaborate scripts. See, for example, their *Rinaldo, imperatore di Trebisonda* (2021), which is available for viewing online (https://edblogs.columbia.edu/worldepics/worldepicsinpuppettheater-italy/).

in the stories themselves. Reading through the plays, we encounter knights and damsels from around the globe—from Europe to North Africa to East Asia—who share the stage with a host of wizards, fairies, giants, and monsters, in alternating episodes of love, enchantment, adventure, and warfare. These stories are not only ultimately derived from masterpieces of Italian literature, but sometimes constitute meaningful rewritings of episodes from Homer, Virgil, Ovid, and other ancient classics that Italian medieval and Renaissance chivalric authors refashioned according to the technique of creative imitation. Some of these same stories circulated in both popular and elite culture for centuries, whether performed in opera and melodrama, recited by storytellers and street singers, or painted on palace walls, ceramics, and donkey carts. Yet in no other art form did they enjoy the sustained elaboration that they did in Sicilian puppet theater. Thanks to Agrippino Manteo's scripts, we can still enter a chivalric world that for nearly two decades this renowned puppeteer brought to life on a daily basis for Italian American immigrants and other enthusiasts of his art. It is a world that will not only move and delight us, but that additionally provokes us to think seriously about perennial core human concerns, such as justice, identity, duty, love, freedom, and virtue.

Part One of this study is comprised of two chapters. The first offers a history of the Manteo family across three generations of puppeteers, from Agrippino's birth and early years in Sicily to his celebrated theater in New York City's Little Italy, to the sustained efforts of his children and grandchildren to bring their theatrical tradition to new audiences beyond the original Italian American immigrant population. The chapter draws material from three main sources: scholarly studies in Italian on the Catanese puppet theater scene at the time of Agrippino's youth, with special attention to the famed Crimi family; scattered information found in newspaper and magazine articles and short book chapters throughout the decades of the family's theatrical activity; and the recollections of Agrippino's descendants themselves, primarily his granddaughter Susie Bruno.

The second chapter brings to light for the first time the contents of Agrippino Manteo's extensive notebooks, unraveling the tangled sets of scripts and reconstructing the order in which they were composed. After a brief introduction to the Renaissance works adapted in Giusto Lodico's nineteenth-century prose *Storia dei paladini*, the chapter examines the scripts containing Agrippino's Paladins of France cycle. Special attention is devoted to the relation of the scripts to the *Storia dei paladini*, the dates recorded in the scripts, and comments in the margins by Agrippino and his son Mike. The chapter concludes with attention to the scripts that Mike copied from the 1960s to the 1980s.

Part Two, the core of the book, presents the translation of eight plays in Agrippino's Paladins of France cycle, each accompanied by an introduction and a comparative analysis. These plays are based on the central portion of the *Storia dei paladini*, which in turn follows the plot of Matteo Maria Boiardo's *Orlando Innamorato* and Ludovico Ariosto's *Orlando Furioso*. While the selection—from the appearance of Angelica of Cathay in Paris to the final battle of three against three on the island of Lampedusa—was determined by the importance of these moments within the Paladins of France cycle, many of these episodes continue to be staged in Sicilian puppet theater today. The introductory section preceding each translated play provides the narrative background drawn from the original poems, while the comparative analysis closing each chapter moves from the *Innamorato* and the *Furioso* to the *Storia dei paladini* to Agrippino's scripts in order to examine in greater depth the creative process of meaning production in these literary and dramatic adaptations.

The appendices provide further relevant documentation pertaining to the Manteo family's collection of puppets, books, and scripts; characters from the Paladins of France cycle; and the Manteo family itself. More specifically, Appendices 1–4 list the marionettes possessed by the family in the 1980s as well as those donated to the Italian American Museum in 2010, extant chivalric publications from Agrippino's library, and Agrippino's extant handwritten scripts from the Paladins of France cycle. Appendix 5 offers a concrete manifestation of the vast traditional *opera dei pupi* repertory through a translation of all extant synopses in Agrippino's Paladins of France cycle. Appendix 6 identifies characters from the Paladins of France cycle that are featured in the eight translated plays. Appendix 7 lists Manteo family members mentioned in Chapter 1.

Unless otherwise noted, all translations of primary and secondary sources are my own.

Part One

THE SICILIAN PUPPET THEATER OF AGRIPPINO MANTEO AND FAMILY

Chapter 1

THE PUPPETEERS

Agrippino's Early Years in the Province of Catania[1]

Agrippino Manteo was born to Michele Manteo and Agata Tornello in the town of Grammichele, in the province of Catania, on April 1, 1884.[2] The dramatic and distant events of his childhood and early youth invite legendizing. He was orphaned at a very early age (possibly at four years old or even younger).[3] According to Agrippino's daughter Ida, "a stray bullet" killed her grandfather and a month later her grandmother died of "a broken heart" (Mandell). Agrippino and his older sister Teresa were subsequently relocated to their maternal grandmother's farm and put to work under very difficult conditions. Treated more like a child laborer than a grandchild, Agrippino often ran away due to his grandmother's harsh measures and the incessant farm chores.

Agrippino's passion for puppet theater, dating back to his early youth, is remembered by family members as an instance of love at first sight. When the puppeteer Giuseppe (Peppino, Peppe) Crimi (1854–1937) performed in Grammichele, the young Agrippino was so enthralled that he went backstage afterward. Finding out that the boy's last name was Manteo and that his father's first name had been Michele, Crimi informed him that his father had also been a puppeteer. Agrippino immediately asked Crimi to teach him

---

1 When no source is noted, I am reporting Agrippino's personal history as related to me by his granddaughter, Susie Bruno. Discrepancies between Susie's recollection and other accounts are outlined in the endnotes. The sparse and sometimes contradictory details in the following paragraphs convey the full extent of the information I encountered about the puppeteer's early life.
2 This information is taken from Agrippino's birth certificate, which his great-grandson Michael J. Manteo obtained in Grammichele and kindly shared with me.
3 The stated age of Agrippino upon losing his parents varies widely. The theater critic Lois Adler states in a 1976 review that Agrippino was orphaned at the age of eight but does not name the source of her information. In 1991, the journalist Jonathan Mandell reports Ida Manteo as saying that her father had been only three months old at the time.

the art as well. Since at the time traveling puppeteers remained for prolonged periods in the towns they visited in order to play out the cycle of the Paladins of France, Crimi took the boy under his wing and gave him a pair of puppets to practice on his own. According to another version of the story, Agrippino set out for Catania at the age of seventeen "to find his father's partners" and to learn the art of puppetry (Mandell, citing Ida Manteo). Regardless of how the encounter came about, Agrippino's foundational experience with Giuseppe Crimi set the stage for a life devoted to Sicilian puppet theater across three continents.

Agrippino's Apprenticeship in Catanese Puppet Theater and Dramatic Theater

The province of Catania was at the cutting edge of puppet theater during this period thanks primarily to Giuseppe Crimi's own father, Gaetano Crimi (1808–1873). The elder Crimi, in fact, is considered to be the primary founder and foremost early practitioner of puppet theater in eastern Sicily.[4] Some of the information we have about Gaetano's career comes from Giuseppe himself, who in his *Memorie* recounts that his father, in turn the son of a music and violin teacher, opened his first *teatrino* in Catania in 1835. He did not limit himself to puppetry arts, however, but staged classics of Greek and Italian literature, as well as comedies in dialect, with human actors.[5] In 1869, for example, Gaetano combined epic content and human actors in a production of Torquato Tasso's sixteenth-century heroic poem *Gerusalemme Liberata*. According to Giuseppe, the production was such a huge success that Gaetano followed the *Gerusalemme* with two more productions—*Caloandro e Leonilda* and the *Storia dei Paladini*—over the next three years. "The people of Catania," he wrote, "flocked to see the puppets of flesh and blood" (166).

Gaetano Crimi's staging of canonical epics and his move beyond puppetry arts to dramatic theater are linked to his pedagogical intentions. In an 1855 petition requesting authorization to direct "dramatic works staged by a group of young amateurs," Crimi specifies that he intends to produce "various educational and moral plays" (Majorana 94). Indeed, his theater would later be

---

[4] Bernadette Majorana calls Gaetano Crimi the "first and only puppeteer in the city" (89). For more precise information on Crimi's dates of birth and death, see Majorana 90n1.

[5] See Crimi, "Dalle *Memorie* di Giuseppe Crimi scritte intorno al 1924," in Li Gotti 161–67. Majorana refers to him as a "puppeteer in love with dramatic theater" (140).

characterized as embodying a "genuine classical and Arcadian-Enlightenment mould" (Majorana 110n74). The elder Crimi would be remembered by his son and grandson not only as a puppeteer and theater director, but also as a playwright, constructor of puppets, poet, and scenographer, as well as, in essence, "the only theatrical entrepreneur with his own headquarters, where he works on the stories that he is gradually inventing and subjects them to the test of the stage and the public" (Majorana 125–26).[6]

After Gaetano's death in 1874, his two sons took their puppet theaters to a succession of locations outside the urban center of Catania (Crimi 167). It could have been during this period of itinerant performances that Giuseppe arrived in Grammichele and sparked the lifelong passion of young Agrippino, thirty years his junior.[7] As a puppeteer, Giuseppe is remembered for having transformed wooden figures into "living and vibrant creatures filled with humanity" who "became emotions and ideas through the puppeteer's dramatic pathos" (Majorana 138). Giuseppe, moreover, was not exclusively a puppeteer, but referred to himself in his memoirs as his father's most passionate apprentice in staging performances with live actors.[8] In addition to inheriting his father's original stories, he invented some of his own "historical, patriotic, epic, tragic, and sacred narratives" (Majorana 137).

Giuseppe Crimi is not the only point of reference we have for Agrippino Manteo's early theatrical experiences in Catania, however. A note in the margin of one of Agrippino's scripts, presumably added by his son Mike, names in passing another protagonist of Catanese theater: Giovanni Grasso. The note reads: "Feraba's actions are boring and flat evenings. Therefore, it's not worth anything. These are the 'entrails' as Giovanni Grasso used to say."[9] The reference to Grasso as an authoritative presence and the use of

---

6 For an extensive account of Gaetano Crimi's activities and impact, see Majorana, especially the sections entitled "Pedagogical value of oratory and acting and the civilizing function of theater in Crimi's stage practice" and "His first relationships with young amateurs with a prestigious future" (89–110).

7 As noted earlier, Crimi was born in 1854 and Agrippino in 1884. Although Majorana does not mention Agrippino in this context, the inclusion of Grammichele in the list of Giuseppe Crimi's performance locations (137) indirectly corroborates Susie Bruno's account of the fateful encounter during Agrippino's boyhood referenced above.

8 Giuseppe Crimi writes of himself in the third person: "The first passionate apprentice of these great artists was Peppe Crimi di Gaetano who had the luxury of always being on the stage of the Arena Pacini to observe them at close range and to learn the art" (Crimi 165).

9 *Sera* 251 (*Copione* 18). The more precise definition of "quadume" is the tripe of cattle, which is soft and without color. The Italian is not that of a native speaker and shows some influence of Spanish.

the colloquial term "quadume" (which is the equivalent of "guts") give the impression of evoking one of Agrippino's personal recollections to his family.

Giovanni Grasso (1873–1930), grandson of a famed puppeteer also named Giovanni Grasso (ca. 1792–1863), initially collaborated with and subsequently competed against none other than Gaetano Crimi.[10] Giovanni's father, Angelo Grasso (1834–1888), was a puppeteer, *parlatore* (reciter of puppet voices), and actor who directly transmitted his skill and passion for both puppet theater and dramatic theater to his son. The younger Giovanni was performing as an actor as early as 1896 (Majorana 190–91). He is credited not only as "the most prominent bridge between the two theatrical universes" at the turn of the century, but also as "one of the most stunning and celebrated actors of the early twentieth century," even capturing the attention of the Catanese authors Nino Martoglio and Luigi Capuana.[11] The reference to Giovanni Grasso as a cultural authority while expressing a value judgment about a particular episode in the script suggests that Agrippino transmitted to his children the importance that this figure—and the Catanese theatrical culture he represented—continued to hold for him many years later and an ocean away.

Agrippino himself appears to have performed as an actor with Catanese theater companies during his youth. In a 1933 newspaper article, Mabel Greene reports that "twenty-five years ago Papa Manteo was an actor on the Sicilian stage, a member of the companies of such famous Italian stars as Giovanni Grasso and Cesare Rossi." The time frame cannot be correct given that twenty-five years earlier would have been 1908, and Agrippino left for Argentina in 1905, as discussed below. The substance of the statement nonetheless provides corroboration of Agrippino's theatrical experiences in Catania prior to his emigration from the island. Indeed, it would not have been surprising for a young puppeteer to have taken part in theatrical productions in early twentieth-century Catania given the involvement of the Crimi and Grasso families in both forms of dramatic arts. Giovanni Grasso obtained notable success with his theater company Città di Catania in 1901 (Majorana 192), when Agrippino would have been seventeen years old. The other name mentioned by Greene, Cesare Rossi, was another highly ranked actor who performed in Sicily at the turn of the century (Majorana 122).

Agrippino's mentors and models, the vanguard of Catanese culture at the time, were pioneers precisely in breaking down the barriers between puppet theater and dramatic theater. Their efforts and successes not only suggest

---

10 Majorana 143–44. See Majorana 144n4 for the elder Grasso's possible dates of birth.
11 Majorana 89. For a more complete picture, see 181–260.

a cross-pollination that could have served to enrich puppet theater moving forward, but also underscore the common components of both forms of theater. In this light, traditional Sicilian puppet theater, and particularly Catanese puppet theater, can be understood as a form of dramatic prose theater based on intricate interlacing plots and meaningful dialogue that could potentially be staged with human actors in place of wooden bodies. Agrippino's connection to the most prominent names in Catanese puppet theater and dramatic theater during his formative years can also help us understand the passion and theatrical notions that he brought to his career in puppetry arts, the high caliber of his productions that made his name stand out for decades, and even the underlying cultural-educational purpose that fed his inspiration.

Agrippino's Immigration to Argentina

Despite its thriving theatrical culture, early twentieth-century Catania did not offer many prospects for earning a living. Agrippino's older sister married and moved with her husband to Mendoza, Argentina, because there was no work to be had in Grammichele. In the meantime, Agrippino fell in love with his future wife, Caterina, who gave birth to their first child, Ida (née Agata, also known as Adelaida, Agatina, and Aida), on June 10, 1905. Although Agrippino initially worked on Caterina's family farm, he soon thereafter followed his sister's example and left for Mendoza to seek a better life for himself and his new family. Accompanying him at the time were only the two marionettes given to him by Crimi because his wife and their baby daughter did not join him until six months later.[12]

In Mendoza, Agrippino started a bakery specializing in Sicilian specialties and he also had outdoor ovens that the community used to bake their own bread. Yet given his experience in the world of Catanese theater, Agrippino could not have been expected to limit himself to culinary pursuits. He constructed marionettes in his free time, and he opened his first puppet theater in the New World as soon as he had amassed a sufficient number. In 1916, however, Agrippino was among the Italians abroad obligated to return to their homeland to fight in World War I. He was thus compelled to leave behind the growing number of marionettes

---

12 According to Adler, however, Agrippino took with him puppets he had inherited from his father. McPharlin writes that Agrippino first ran a puppet theater in Buenos Aires before moving to Mendoza, but the stated year of arrival (1896) does not match the family's accounts. McPharlin adds further background information uncorroborated elsewhere but said to have been supplied by Agrippino's son Ritz (*The Puppet Theater in America* 298).

as well as his wife, their daughter, and the three sons born in Argentina, Mike (Miguel, Michele, Michael), Dominic (Domingo, Domenic, Dom, Leo), and Ritz (Agrippino II, Pino).

Agrippino and His Family in New York City: The *Teatro Manteo*

Agrippino did not return to Argentina following the conclusion of the war; in June 1919, he sailed directly to New York City, where he also had relatives. He was soon thereafter joined by his wife and their four children (Figure 1.1). The couple's fifth child, Johnny, was born in New York City in June 1921. In order for Agrippino to open his puppet theater in Manhattan, he needed a full set of wooden actors. Lois Adler relates that since Caterina had brought with her from Argentina only about eighty of the original 300 puppets, Agrippino "had to start building puppets all over again to replenish the stock, which took more than two years."[13] This need to construct a new

Figure 1.1 Members of the Manteo family (ca. 1916). The two women are Agrippino's sister Teresa (left) and wife Caterina (right). The children (left to right) are Mike, Dominic, Ritz, and Ida. Courtesy of Susie Bruno.

---

13 Baird writes that Agrippino also acquired sixty additional figures from "an old player" (125).

series of marionettes could explain why Agrippino did not immediately open his puppet theater in New York. Moreover, according to his son Mike, from 1919, Agrippino was also at work composing the many notebooks of scripts that would constitute his repertory. In any event, by 1923, Agrippino, called Papa Manteo, opened his first New York City puppet theater at 76 Catherine Street on the Lower East Side.[14] In 1928, he moved his theater to 109 Mulberry Street, in the heart of Little Italy. During this time, he also ran an electrical contracting business by day (Figure 1.2).[15] His children, born in three different continents, would grow up and put down their roots in New York City (Figure 1.3).

Figure 1.2 Agrippino Manteo as an electrician (1922). Courtesy of Michael J. Manteo.

---

14 Baird 125. The year of 1921 is occasionally given for the opening of Agrippino's New York City puppet theater.
15 Having a full-time "day job" was not uncommon among traditional puppeteers in Sicily, either. As Carocci notes, puppeteers "often had—or were forced to have—another job" (*Il poema che cammina* 109).

Figure 1.3 The wedding of Mike and Mary Manteo (ca. 1930–1931). Front row (left to right): Johnny Manteo, Agrippino Manteo, Caterina Manteo, the bride Mary, the groom Mike, Rosina Manteo (wife of cousin Agrippino). Back row (left to right): Ritz, Ida, Dominic, and Agrippino Manteo (cousin). Courtesy of Michael J. Manteo.

All members of the family had a role in the puppet theater business according to their age and natural inclination. Agrippino spoke the parts of the male characters and constructed new puppets with the assistance of a sculptor who fashioned the heads. The task of his sons was to manipulate the puppets that—typical of the Catanese tradition—stood four- to five-feet tall and could weigh as much as 100 pounds or more (Figures 1.4–1.6).[16] Greene's 1933 article describes the three elder sons (at twenty-three, twenty-one, and seventeen years of age) handling the puppets on the bridge (the wooden scaffolding behind the stage) while the eleven-year-old Johnny "help[ed] with the props and stamp[ed] his feet when the followers of Charlemagne [were] engaged in particularly heavy fighting." A diary later penned by Mike Manteo also recalls his youngest brother selling soda, peanuts, and pumpkin seeds to the public (M. Manteo 11).

---

16 As Mike Manteo explained, "To put on a show, four people are needed on the bridge and two on either side to facilitate the change of marionettes for the manipulators" (Adler).

THE PUPPETEERS

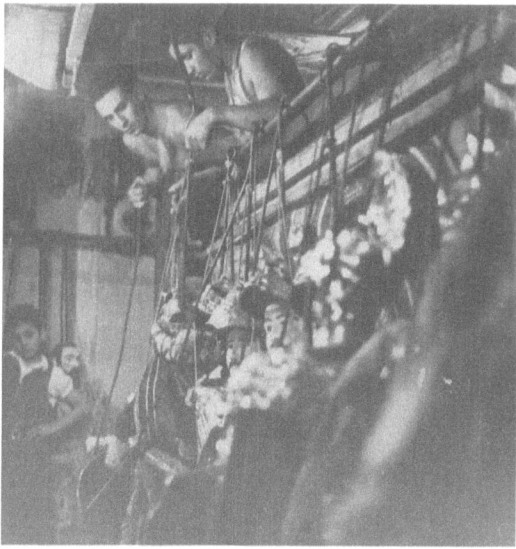

Figure 1.4 Agrippino Manteo's son Ritz (left) and another manipulator on the bridge with the youngest son Johnny in the wings (1920s). Courtesy of Susie Bruno.

Figure 1.5 Agrippino Manteo's son Ritz (left) and another manipulator on the bridge, an unidentified older boy in the wings, and a young Orlando and princess on stage (1920s). Courtesy of Michael J. Manteo.

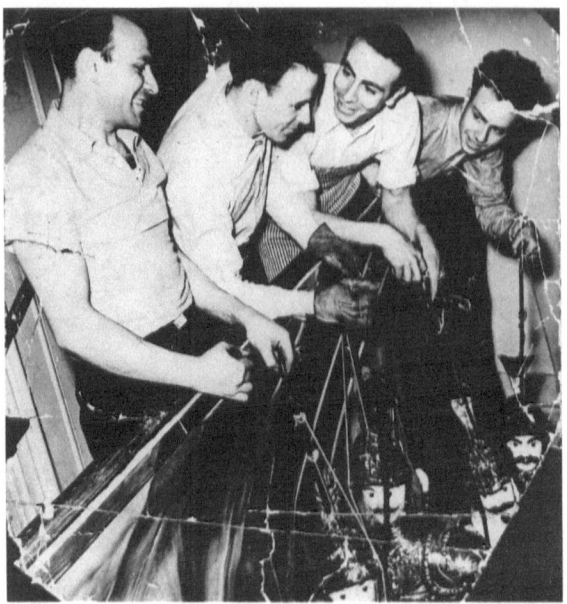

Figure 1.6 Agrippino Manteo's four sons (from left to right) Mike, Dominic, Ritz, and Johnny on the bridge (ca. 1937–1938). Courtesy of Michael J. Manteo.

The women in the family were no less active. Agrippino's wife Caterina sewed the costumes, spoke some of the female parts, and collected the entrance fees (Figure 1.7). She would also cook dinner before going to the theater so that the food would just need to be heated upon the family's return home. Ida had also learned from an early age to assist the production by sewing costumes, painting scenery, and playing the piano. When she was old enough, she provided voices for the female characters and sometimes manipulated the puppets as well.[17] Women giving voice to female characters was a characteristic of Catanese puppet theater going at least as far back as Gaetano Crimi (Majorana 90–91). Greene explains that Ida was "responsible for the countless painted back drops of garden scenes and Moorish palaces, as well as a fair share of the fine sewing on the costumes" and that she "now and then substitutes for her mother in the rare feminine lines of the performance." Noting Ida's impressive voice range decades later, Adler reports that "she could do the witches, old women and female warriors (the *guerriere*). For this reason, 'Papa' Manteo could hardly wait for her to be old enough to join the troupe."

---

17 There is some variance regarding the age at which Ida began to recite the female parts. Mike Manteo tells Susan Kalcik that Ida was not yet fifteen ("Old Ways in the New World" 12); Mandell later gives her age as eighteen.

THE PUPPETEERS 13

Figure 1.7 Caterina Manteo collecting entrance fees at the 109 Mulberry Street theater (1928 or later). Courtesy of Susie Bruno.

The *Teatro Manteo* was widely recognized for its dramatic intensity and artistic excellence. Bil Baird recalls having seen Agrippino perform: "Altogether it was a tremendous tour de force, and at the core of it were Agrippino Manteo's dramatic inventiveness and irreplaceable scripts" (125). Greene's description of the master puppeteer lending his voice to the characters from backstage gives a sense of his full psychological and physical engagement: "Today he is still an actor, clenching his fists and pounding his plump knees as he speaks the puppets' lines, his short squat figure and earnest red face an incomparable picture to the backstage visitor. Sometimes, when there is a fight in progress on the stage, he nearly falls off his chair." Mike Manteo later reflected on how both family members and the traditional public would experience intense emotions during the most dramatic scenes: "They may be marionettes, but when somebody died, and my father and my sister would put on a beautiful scene—with such sadness—my father crying, my sister crying, and the people—you could hear them sniffle, too" (quoted in Gold 72).

We may catch glimpses of Agrippino backstage during a performance thanks to a privately owned photograph and rare archival news footage. The photograph shows the puppeteer reading directly from the script as he speaks the lines (Figure 1.8).[18] In the newsreel, he is speaking the lines while Johnny sits at his side holding the script and prompting him (Figure 1.9).[19] Another photograph from many years later again shows father and son concentrating on the script, this time offstage in preparation for a performance (Figure 1.10).

Figure 1.8 Agrippino Manteo reading directly from the script during a performance. Courtesy of Michael J. Manteo.

---

18 According to Susie Bruno and Michael J. Manteo, respectively, the child in the photograph could be Agrippino's son Johnny, born in 1921, or his grandson Pino, born to Mike and Mary Manteo in 1932.

19 This archival footage was included in the documentary *It's One Family, Knock on Wood* (1982) directed by Tony De Nonno.

Figure 1.9 Agrippino Manteo speaks the lines as Johnny reads the script and prompts him. Photograph from the documentary film by Tony De Nonno entitled *It's One Family, Knock on Wood* (1982). Courtesy of Tony De Nonno, De Nonno Productions, Incorporated.

Figure 1.10 Agrippino Manteo and son Johnny discuss the script (ca. 1937–1939). Courtesy of Susie Bruno.

Habitual *opera dei pupi* spectators would have been fully familiar with Agrippino's cycle of plays based on the *Storia dei paladini*. Unfortunately, no ethnographer documented the traditional public's rapport with the *Teatro Manteo* as Antonio Pasqualino did for puppet theater in Sicily and Pietro Porta did for hand puppet theater in Northern Italy.[20] Nonetheless, we may glean some sense of Agrippino's Italian American audience from newspaper articles of the time. Noting that "many Italians in the neighborhood buy season tickets," Greene reported that Agrippino's theater goers "know every line of the play." Such a claim, which she attributes to Agrippino's son Ritz, could be misleading since much of the dialogue was improvised and the cycle contained not just one play but well over 300 plays. Nonetheless, her comment gives the impression of an intensely felt literary history shared by the Italian American immigrant community. In a *Harper's Weekly* article about Sicilian puppet theater in New York in 1908, Victor Rousseau had noted that the puppeteer Antonio Parisi's chivalric repertory aimed to satisfy audience demand: "Parisi presents the 'Paladins of France' because the people who go to the marionette theatre will listen to nothing else."[21] This popular cultural phenomenon might be envisioned as a sort of daily theatrical *Game of Thrones* or *Lord of the Rings* set to replay continuously at a time when there was no real competition from other forms of entertainment.

American journalists reporting on puppet theater among Italian American communities, however, sometimes conveyed a disparaging attitude that revealed their ignorance of both the literary masterpieces being staged and the illustrious theatrical tradition itself. A 1916 article in *The Cleveland Plain Dealer*, for example, employs the collectivist mindset at the root of racist labeling when referring to the Italian Americans attending Joseph Scionte's puppet theater as a "dark-eyed, pleasure loving race that works hard and plays hard" (Kelly). Conjuring up the vision of "whole families" who "come in droves to follow the fortunes of Angelica, Orlando, Charlemagne and the brave knights and ladies of his court," the reporter snidely remarks on the action: "Surely, more strenuous conflicts were never waged than the slaughter I witnessed on behalf of Angelica's wooden hand." Greene adopts an air of sophisticated superiority when calling the Manteo family's stage props "as primitive as the legendary drama they present."

---

20 For the traditional public of Sicilian puppet theater and Northern Italian hand puppet theater, see Pasqualino, *L'opera dei pupi*, and Porta, *Gente di Sarina*, respectively.

21 Incidentally, although Rousseau is one of the few American journalists to accurately report the source of Sicilian puppet theater as the *Paladins of France*, he mistakes it for the *Song of Roland* when he refers to it as "an old French epic poem of the eleventh century."

She acknowledges, nonetheless, the depth of the family's "historical" knowledge: "Each of them is fluently conversant with medieval history, and backstage the illusion of legendary antiquity is as thick as the dust on the floor" (Greene). More sympathetic to the social and working conditions of Italian American immigrants, Donna Lauren Gold reflects how "the immigrants would flock to the shows to watch the tales of their childhood, for the moment forgetting the confusing new world of sweatshops and tenements they had entered" (70).

Although the traditional public consisted primarily of the Italian diasporic community, John Bell notes that the Manteo family theater also attracted "a new generation of American puppeteers, including Remo Bufano and Bil Baird, who thrilled at the theatrical force of this powerful nineteenth-century puppet form" (33). Baird, who recalls being a spectator, remarks how "the artistry of the Manteos began to attract visitors from uptown, among them Tony Sarg" (125). Citing a *Theater Arts Monthly* piece from 1929, Mandell points out that the interest went beyond practitioners of puppet theater: "The uptown crowd took to it as well, with such theater lights as the Gish sisters dropping in." Gold, in fact, states that Dorothy Gish and Irving Thalberg "had made the little theater one of their highlights whenever they would go slumming" (71).[22] Greene's 1933 newspaper article indicates that Agrippino's theater also drew in students from uptown: "Weekdays the neighborhood and a few uptown students of the puppet art pay their 25-cent admission fee and sit goggle eyed between 8 and 10:30 P.M., watching the fortunes of Roland, Charlemagne and the twelve peers, and on Sundays they attend from 5 to 7 P.M."[23] Decades later, Agrippino's Mulberry Street theater would be remembered as "a neighborhood institution whose fame spread to nearby Greenwich Village and farther uptown" (Kline).

Agrippino's reputation led to invitations that brought his puppetry arts to venues outside the Italian American immigrant community. Bell relates that Agrippino was invited to perform at the Puppet Players Studio in Greenwich Village by New York University English professor Catherine Reighard, who also invited well-known puppeteers like Bufano and Sarg (65–66). Paul McPharlin reports that in March 1932, Agrippino Manteo took part in a festival of performances held at the New School for Social Research in New York along with Bufano, Sarg, and many others (*The Puppet Theater in America* 387). In a May 29, 1933, announcement about Papa Manteo's

---

22 Once again, however, discrimination against Italian Americans seeps through an apparent attestation of the Manteo family's broader appeal.
23 Adler, who gives the start time of the Sunday matinee as 2 pm, specifies that the nightly performances lasted two and a half hours, with ten-minute intermissions between acts.

marionette show at the Coney Island Luna Park, one columnist writes that an authority no less than Tony Sarg affirmed their excellence: "Papa Manteo's Marionettes [...] are coming to Luna Park, and Tony Sarge [sic] told me that these marionettes are as good as any he has ever seen. You know, Tony Sarge surely does know all about marionettes" (Jean). On June 7, 1933, the *Brooklyn Times Union* named "Manteo's Marionettes" as one of three new amusements at Luna Park that "fascinated the children" ("Luna Fascinates Children"). Such occasions may have also brought the general public's attention to Agrippino's Little Italy theater as well. A September 15, 1933, article in the *Brooklyn Daily Eagle* recommends "the beautiful story of Roland, re-enacted in Italian by Mr. Manteo, his children and their famous marionettes" at 109 Mulberry Street where "little Johnny [...] will take you backstage" (Fay).

Agrippino's connection to Brooklyn seems to have increased at the end of 1933. On December 30, 1933, the *Brooklyn Daily Eagle* announced the following:

> Signor Manteo will put on Brooklyn's opening marionette performance of "Tulio and Adelidia" in a former garage he has converted into a theater at 110 Starr St., near Wilson Ave. The marionette's run in this borough will be indefinite, possibly for years, Signor Manteo avers. The opening night's attendance will include a group of artists and writers, headed by Tony Sarg. ("Puppets in Garage")

It is not clear, however, how long the Brooklyn experience lasted. Newspaper articles from 1938 note that the Manteo family had been performing on Mulberry Street for the past several years ("Manteos Arrive on Broadway," Pollock, Walter), and Susie Bruno confirms that her grandfather continued to perform regularly on Mulberry Street in Little Italy throughout the 1930s (Figure 1.11).[24]

Agrippino also garnered notice in the press in 1938 performing outside Little Italy. The family staged a double feature at the Nora Bayes Theatre (44th Street Theatre rooftop): *Macbeth* and "part of the 'Orlando Furioso'." While Arthur Pollock's review from April 28, 1938, criticized the experiment that entailed American actors backstage

---

24 There is some variance in reports. In a 1939 publication, McPharlin states that the Manteo family had reopened a permanent theater in Brooklyn in October of the previous year (*Puppetry* 11). Yet Susie Bruno recalls that the rented basement that housed the puppets after performances ceased was right across the street from the family's Mulberry Street theater.

Figure 1.11 Agrippino Manteo in Little Italy (ca. 1935–1937). Courtesy of Michael J. Manteo.

reading Shakespeare's lines in English, it raved about the family's traditional *opera dei pupi* performance in Italian:

> Then Signor Manteo and his children put on one of their own shows, part of the "Orlando Furioso" they do down on Mulberry St., and things began to be really good. Let the Manteos alone and they know their stuff.
> The puppets took on quite a different air, began to prance gracefully, gallantly, and agilely about the place, a group of handsome, swashbuckling gentlemen in blazing armor and fair ladies in pretty distress, and duels came thick and fast. This time the Manteos did their own talking and the effect was three or four hundred percent better. They know how a puppet feels, their fluent voices have emotion in them and drama. Their "Orlando Furnioso" [sic] has elegance, a fine fury and sound by the earful.
> On their own the Manteos are splendid.

The same year, Agrippino Manteo's puppets were also shown at the First National Doll Show at the Spear Auditorium in Midtown Manhattan (Walker).

In 1939, Agrippino continued to reach wider audiences when the family performed at the American Puppetry Festival (organized by the Puppeteers of America) that took place in New York City from June 27 to 30. Their play, described by McPharlin as "a thrilling episode from the chivalrous cycle of Charlemagne dramas which they brought from Sicily," was staged in the auditorium of the New School. A photograph of Agrippino being introduced by Remo Bufano can be found in McPharlin's *Puppetry* (11).

Sadly, 1939 was also the year that the Manteo family theater under Agrippino's direction permanently closed due to a family tragedy. Eighteen-year-old Johnny, having just graduated from high school, contracted tuberculosis and died in July of that year.[25] According to Adler, Agrippino "never recovered from the shock of the premature death of his youngest son." In his diary written years later, Mike Manteo remembers (in English) that "for the next seven yrs / Dad was not the man that he was / His health was not good. / We all were worried" (13). Agrippino died on August 1, 1947. Considering that he is said to have offered shows on a daily basis from the early 1920s to the late 1930s—and had founded a puppet theater in Argentina prior to World War I—Agrippino may have staged well over 6,000 performances in the course of his career.

Agrippino Manteo's Legacy

Agrippino Manteo was initially one of a number of puppeteers who carried on the *opera dei pupi* tradition in the New World beginning with the large wave of Italian immigrants in the 1880s and 1890s. Susan Kalcik points to the existence of puppet theaters in Brooklyn, the Bronx, Manhattan, New Jersey, Chicago, San Francisco, and Cleveland, as well as Rio de Janeiro and Buenos Aires ("Old Ways in the New World" 13). In the 1908 *Harper's Weekly* article mentioned above, Antonio Parisi was heralded as the founder of Sicilian puppet theater in New York City and the most prominent among the five puppet theater companies operating there (Rousseau). Adler writes, however, that "by the time Manteo arrived, there were not many practitioners left." Within a short time, he "inherited the mantle of Parisi, becoming the most important Sicilian puppeteer of his generation."

---

25 Although Mike gives some contradictory indications regarding the family's performance activities in the margins of the scripts in later decades, his diary states that the theater on Mulberry Street, inaugurated in June 1928, remained in operation until the death of Johnny at the age of eighteen (M. Manteo 11–13).

As new generations of Italian Americans became increasingly less familiar with the Italian language and at the same time more interested in alternative forms of nightly entertainment, puppet theaters found themselves losing hold of their traditional audience. Gold writes that the Manteo family was "the last [puppet] theater running" in New York City (71). Agrippino would buy materials from puppeteers who were forced to close their doors. In 1933, Greene relates that he owned "over 400 different puppets, including a six-foot giant Ferragus." Mandell reports that at one time, Agrippino had amassed about 500 puppets (57).

In 1949, just two years after Agrippino's death, McPharlin reflects that stricter immigration measures limiting the arrival of Italians had dealt a death blow to Sicilian puppet theater in the United States: "It is possible that the Paladins could have survived without artificial stimulus if severe immigration measures had not been adopted both by the United States and Italy at this time." He goes on to bemoan the fate especially of the famed Manteo puppets: "Now even the Manteo puppets, hung away in a damp cellar, are succumbing to decay and rust. Perhaps something will bring them out to be refurbished once more. It is cordially hoped so" (*The Puppet Theater in America* 302).

Accounts differ as to the ultimate fate of Agrippino's marionettes. A January 21, 1963, newspaper article reports that the original marionettes had recently been "dusted off; the heroines of the medieval epic about Roland and Charlemagne got new gowns, and the knights' armor was refurbished" (Kline). Yet a March 17, 1997, *Oggi* article maintains instead that many of Agrippino's puppets were eventually thrown away by the landlord of the warehouse where they were being stored while the rest were destroyed by rodents (Caparrotti 7). There are occasional references to Agrippino's original puppets among descriptions of the family's collection. A November 21, 1979, article, for example, states that four of the 150 puppets in the Manteo collection at that time had been constructed by Agrippino (LaRosa). At least one Manteo puppet from the 1920s appears to have survived to the present day. A Morgante puppet is described as "original, made in 1923" in a List of Characters compiled by the Manteo family (Appendix 1, #9) and listed among those donated to the Italian American Museum (Appendix 2, #9).[26]

---

26 In addition, the five-foot Orlando puppet donated by Mike Manteo to the National Museum of American History of the Smithsonian Institute is said to have been constructed between 1928 and 1935—albeit by Mike himself rather than Agrippino. Although the puppet is not currently on display, it can be viewed online at https://americanhistory.si.edu/collections/search/object/nmah_670131.

The Manteo Sicilian Marionette Theater: The Next Generation

In a recent study of Sicilian puppet theater and its literary sources, Anna Carocci maintains that two traits characterized the great Sicilian puppeteers of the past: first, an "in-depth, targeted knowledge of chivalric stories [...] that is not limited to the narrative repertoire (the plots), but extends to the collection and reading of books and the writing of scripts," and, second, "a love for chivalric stories so strong that it was even obsessive, and in fact became the dominant passion in the life of these individuals" (*Il poema che cammina* 108–9). Agrippino Manteo can certainly be considered among this elite group on both counts. Moreover, he passed on his intense devotion to the art of Sicilian puppetry to his children even though they grew up in Argentina and New York rather than Catania. Susie Bruno recalls her family's constant focus on the puppets: "That's all they've ever done. At gatherings they talk marionettes, my uncle's always cleaning the marionettes, my mother's always sewing …" (Kalcik, "Old Ways in the New World" 14).

The Manteo family's passionate involvement naturally extended to the characters and stories as well. Affirming the centrality that the *Storia dei paladini* had for Agrippino and the rest of the family when she was young, Susie Bruno recalls: "My grandfather would study it. [...] This was like their Bible. They would sit down and look at the book and they would play games, like to say 'Who did this and who did that?' because they were so into it."[27] The book in question was Leggio's expanded version that is still in the family's possession today.

Agrippino's passion for staging the chivalric stories was so contagious that for decades after his death his children were determined to keep the family's puppet theater alive despite all obstacles and against all odds. His son Mike (b. September 2, 1909), in particular, having learned the craft at a young age from his father, worked tenaciously to refurbish the existing marionettes and construct new ones. With the concrete help and enthusiastic moral support of his brothers Dominic and Ritz as well as his sister Ida, her husband, and other family members, Mike set the family's marionette theater back in motion. Affectionately dubbed Papa Manteo II by the rest of the family, Mike would strive to carry on his father's legacy for the next four decades (Figure 1.12).

Susie Bruno recalls that the first performance the family staged after Agrippino's death in 1947 was an afterschool show for the benefit of the James Children Center and the Children's Aid Society in New York City in 1950. The flyer for the event features a photograph of the late patriarch standing below his puppets who line the stage (Figure 1.13). According to

---

27 Her interview is on the eBOIARDO website (https://edblogs.columbia.edu/eboiardo/manteo-puppet-theater).

Figure 1.12 Mike Manteo with two puppets (1985). Courtesy of Michael J. Manteo.

Figure 1.13 Announcement of a performance by the Manteo family featuring a photo of the late Agrippino Manteo and his puppets (1950). On stage, Angelica is in the center surrounded by Orlando and Rinaldo. Courtesy of Susie Bruno.

Adler, that year the Manteo heirs "re-opened the theatre with a production of *The Life of Genovefa*."[28] Gold also notes that the family "occasionally perform[ed] in schools and churches for the Italian community" (71).

While Mike remained the point of reference for Papa Manteo's Sicilian Marionettes, other family members were equally essential components of the troupe. During performances, while Mike lent his voice to the male characters, his male relatives manipulated the puppets from the bridge and Ida provided the female voices and played the piano (Figures 1.14 and 1.15). Ida also designed and sewed the costumes as well as painted the scenery. In her free time, moreover, she carried on her father's legacy of participating in live theater: in addition to acting and singing in local shows for the Italian

Figure 1.14 Mike Manteo improvises the dialogue while (left to right) Pino's nephew Michael Housen Manteo, Ida's husband Angelo Grillo, Mike's son Pino, and Dominic manipulate the puppets, at Symphony Space, New York City (1980s). Courtesy of Susie Bruno.

---

28 This hagiographic tale about a chaste and brave woman unjustly accused of infidelity by her husband due to the evil machinations of a third party is in the repertory of various traditional Sicilian puppet theater companies.

Figure 1.15 Backstage during a performance, with Mike facing the stage, Ida at the piano, Ida's daughter Joanne Lauria standing behind her, and Ida's husband, Angelo Grillo, on the bridge with other manipulators, at Symphony Space, New York City (1980s). Photo by Martha Cooper. Courtesy of Michael J. Manteo.

community, she performed with the well-known actor and director Sandrino Giglio (1906–1987) as far as Pennsylvania and upstate New York.

Just as Agrippino had regularly involved his wife and children in different tasks, now his children also involved their spouses as well as sons and daughters (along with *their* eventual spouses) as their various ages and competencies permitted. Adler's 1976 article notes that "Today Ida Manteo is no longer the only woman in the troupe. Often her two daughters do female parts. The troupe is still a family affair. It is comprised of four of the older generation; Ida, Mike, Dom and Grillo (Pino is dead). The rest include Mike Manteo's son Agrippino [Pino], Ida's daughters Joan and Suzy, Joan's husband [Vinni] and [Susie's] husband, Joe. With the exception of Joan and Suzy and occasionally Agrippino who take roles, all are manipulators."

Although the actors were all wooden puppets, staging a play required numerous collaborators (Figure 1.16). In addition to Mike's relatives noted above, there were two other members of the troupe. The first

Figure 1.16 Papa Manteo's Life Size Marionettes at Symphony Space, New York City (early 1980s). Bottom (left to right): Ida and Mike Manteo with their puppets. Top (left to right): Susie Bruno, her husband Joe Bruno, Michael Housen Manteo, Derick Hunter, Frances Manteo, Dominic Manteo, Angelo Grillo, Pino Manteo, and his son Michael J. Manteo. Photo by Martha Cooper. Courtesy of Michael J. Manteo.

was Mr. Aiello, the pianist who had previously worked with Agrippino.[29] The second was Derick Hunter, a student who had first seen the Manteo family perform at his junior high school in Brooklyn. After accepting Mike's invitation to visit his workshop, Derick ended up collaborating with the family for eight years as one of the manipulators who handled the puppets from the bridge. Derick later acknowledged the impact of that experience on his future life choices: "It shaped me, more or less. It got me away from negative things, like crime. I was young and black in Brooklyn; I had a lot of energy. This took up a lot of it. I don't think I'd be as creative now" (Mandell 73).

Whereas Agrippino had generally performed for fellow immigrants in an Italian American neighborhood, the family now reached a culturally and

---

29 Baird remarks that in Agrippino's day "there was only one outsider, Mr. Aiello, who played piano in the pit during scene changes, or whenever Papa, sitting in the wings, gave him his cue by ringing a little bell" (125). Adler notes that Mr. Aiello usually played "a mixture of his own tunes; always lively and suited to the action—loud and crashing for a battle, sad if someone died" (26).

socially diverse audience in a variety of performance spaces. Most of this new public was introduced to Sicilian puppet theater for the first time thanks to the Manteo family revival. Yet Mike Manteo also received a nostalgic letter from someone who had been a spectator at Agrippino's plays decades earlier. Upon hearing about an upcoming show, Hartwell M. Webb wrote a letter dated June 24, 1975, from a Washington, DC, address to reminisce about his puppet theater experience and to share Mabel Greene's newspaper article that he had kept all those years. His letter reads as follows:

> Dear Mr. Manteo,
> I cut the story out of the New York Times about 42 years ago. I thought you might like to have it. You don't remember me I am sure, but about 1930 I used to go down from Columbia University to Mulberry Street every few weeks to watch the great show. I can remember your father and mother very well. They used to let me go back stage and up in the loft. It was a treat I have always remembered with pleasure. All good luck to you and your family and the show.[30]

This former Columbia University student was likely one of those mentioned by Greene who traveled regularly to the puppet theater from uptown Manhattan.

The Manteo family launched their "comeback" (Clinton) in earnest at the beginning of 1963 with regularly scheduled performances at Brooklyn's Old Bay Ridge Theater. A January 21, 1963, article in *The Brooklyn Daily Eagle* reports that for the previous three weekends, the Manteo "actors" had given children's matinee performances in English, "each time to a larger audience," and that the family had added shows in Italian for adults on Saturday and Sunday evenings (Kline). Although no titles are given, we are told that forty almost life-sized marionettes "fill the stage with romances and resounding battles from the legends of Charlemagne and Roland." A July 21, 1963, *Daily News* article about weekly matinees for children in English indicates that the family was still routinely performing in that venue during the summer (Milburn).

---

30 "New York Times 1933" is handwritten at the top of the article, but the newspaper's name and date are not shown printed in the clipping. Mario Maffi gives the newspaper as the *New York Sun*, with the date of February 14, 1933, in his bibliography. Meredith Levin, Western Europe Humanities Librarian at Columbia University, has confirmed in a personal correspondence that the article was not in the *New York Times* and further noted that during this period the *New York Sun* was titled *The Sun*.

The Manteo family occasionally performed elsewhere in the course of the 1960s.[31] In June 1963, they were included in the program of the Puppeteers of America Festival in Hurleyville, New York, co-directed by Jim Henson.[32] In October 1964, they opened and closed a program that included twelve puppet theater companies in the context of Columbus Day and the Puppet Guild of Greater New York Day at the New York World's Fair (McPharlin, *The Puppet Theater in America* 548). In March 1969, they performed a play for children entitled *Roland and His Friends* at Nathan's Famous Playhouse. On this occasion, we are told, "Noble bearded Roman kings in flowing velvet robes argue passionately with fierce moustached knights in full armor" and "beautiful painted ladies flirt with love-struck court jesters against a backdrop of clowns, wizards, witches, soothsayers and snorting dragons" ("Knights of Old Find Modern Audience").

Various newspaper pieces from the 1970s indicate that the Manteo family persevered to keep their tradition alive throughout the decade. In the summer of 1975, they performed for six days at the Festival of American Folklife at the Smithsonian Institute in Washington, DC. Susan Kalcik, who was working with the Smithsonian Folklife Program at the time, reported that the Manteo plays were "an immense favorite with the crowds who came to see the 'Old Ways in the New World' section of the Festival" ("Old Ways in the New World" 12). A June 15, 1976, *Star-Gazette* article announces a benefit variety show at the Elmira Free Academy to help preserve the Manteo's marionette theater (Crooks). The event was spearheaded by a local resident who sought to raise money for the puppeteers after viewing a television news program about them on a New York City station. A September 24, 1977, *Newsday* article refers to the Manteo family's performance of "excerpts from 'Orlando Furioso'" (mistakenly called "a medieval drama based on 'Song of Roland'") as a "highlight" in a week-long "festival of all things Italian" at Bloomingdale's in Manhasset, New York ("Festival Italiano"). The Manteo family's puppet theater also appeared in a scene in Francis Ford Coppola's *The Godfather: Part II* (1974): during a festival in Little Italy, a Mafia boss briefly stops in front of an outdoor puppet performance in which two knights oppose each other while an elegant damsel looks on.

Mike Manteo frequently brought his puppet theater to schools and universities during this period, including the University of Rhode Island

---

31 The events discussed below from the 1960s through 1980s do not represent an exhaustive list of the Manteo family's performances, but constitute rather the highlights based on publications, printed programs, and the family's personal recollections.

32 I thank Nancy Staub for sharing this program with me. The title of the play is not specified.

and Columbia University. An April 24, 1979, *Daily Item* article reports that in the early 1970s, Mike "received a grant from the Brooklyn Arts and Cultural Association which allowed him to take on student apprentices to teach the operation of a puppet theater" and that he also performed at Lincoln Center, Fordham University, and New York University, as well as a number of city high schools, thanks to State Council on the Arts grants (McMahon). A March 29, 1979, *Daily News* article announcing a Manteo performance at a high school in Bensonhurst also noted Mike Manteo's additional activities, which included giving "presentations of the medieval spectacle, 'Orlando Furioso'," "helping youngsters produce their own puppet play version of 'Pinocchio'," and hosting visits to the Manteo workshop in Brooklyn (Kramer). A November 21, 1979, article notes that funding from the Italian Cultural Institute would be used to stage a free show at a public school in Bensonhurst the following April (LaRosa). This initiative was said to have come in the wake of a performance the previous May in which the family had drawn a standing-room only crowd of 800.

But what was the substance of the family's performances under Mike's direction? Some idea of their repertory can be gleaned from newspaper and magazine articles. A February 18, 1963, *Newsday* article about the family's shows at the Bay Ridge Theater reports that the family had replaced the original cycle, described as "a running account of the centuries old legends of Charlemagne," with a new "little play" featuring Roland (Clinton). According to Mrs. Rick Amoriello (Dominic's daughter Dolores), cited in the piece, the character of Roland was "so popular we had to write a little play to bring him back even though it doesn't follow the story. We've changed the title to Adventures of Roland." The March 1969 article announcing the play *Roland and His Friends* anticipates that "Roland, the enchanted knight, will wield his lance once again against Mandrecardo, the evil six-foot giant, who will die in a gush of red blood, as he has for nearly 300 years" ("Knights of Old Find Modern Audience"). In actuality, Mandricardo di Tartaria is a Mongol khan invented by Boiardo who sets out to kill Orlando to avenge his father Agricane's death and whose eventual battle against Orlando in Ariosto's poem is interrupted and then permanently suspended due to the paladin's madness (see Chapters 7 and 8). The fact that Agrippino's descendants reimagined this character as an evil giant who is killed by Orlando suggests a rewriting of the traditional stories to reach contemporary audiences unfamiliar with the Paladins of France cycle.

In addition to evoking familiar names in new story lines, the family also invented two new protagonists. A September 17, 1979, *New Yorker Magazine* article reports that the family's current play, entitled *Great Tournament in Damascus*, features the giant Balahim based on Ariosto's *Orlando Furioso*

Figure 1.17 Susie Bruno and her husband, Joe Bruno, with the Balaheim puppet (1980s), described as a "mighty pagan giant, ruthless against all Christians" in the Manteo family's List of Characters (Appendix 1, #2). Courtesy of Susie Bruno.

(Singer 154). While there is no Balahim in Ariosto's poem, a "Balaheim" is listed as a "mighty pagan giant, ruthless against all Christians" in the Manteo family's List of Characters (in Appendix 1, #2; Figure 1.17). Alessandro Napoli has identified two different uses of the name Balaìm:

> "Balaim" (with its graphic variants) is one of the many blasphemes uttered by Saracens in the pagan polytheism of Catanese puppet theater. "Pig of Balahim" and "For god Astrakain" are formulas that I myself remember hearing as a child from the *parlatore* Rosario Mannino, who came from the school of Raffaele Trombetta. Then, in the *Storia di Guido di Santa Croce*, there is the Saracen king Alì Balaim of Cairo, who is killed in a duel by Corradino, son of Guido di Santa Croce.[33]

Thus, the choice of this name by Agrippino's descendants could have been based on the blasphemous phrase or the Egyptian king in the *Storia di Guido*

---

33 Personal communication, June 15, 2022. For the story of Alì Balaim in the *Storia di Guido di Santa Croce*, see Napoli, *Il racconto e i colori* 235–36.

di Santa Croce (1904)—or both. In either case, it is noteworthy that family members would have chosen a name not from the *Orlando Furioso* or even the *Storia dei paladini*, but from the Catanese popular chivalric tradition.[34]

The second protagonist—or rather antagonist—invented by the family is another menacing Saracen giant. A January 20, 1984, *New York Times* article announcing a Manteo family performance describes the fight between Orlando and "the mighty warrior Mammaloc" as the play's most noteworthy duel (Schonberg). A puppet named "Mamalock" is present in the Manteo family's List of Characters as a "pagan giant in the court of King Solatiello" (Appendix 1, #4; Figure 1.18).[35] The character's name sounds similar to Mameluke, the term for Christians and, more generally,

Figure 1.18 Performance at Symphony Space, New York City (1980s). The giant Mamalock (center right) wants to join the joust proclaimed by King Solatiello (left) to marry his daughter (far left). Courtesy of Susie Bruno.

---

34 The name Balahìm, of unknown origin, was also diffused in the popular culture of northern Italy. Pietro Porta cites Augusto Monti's historical novel *I Sanssòssì* (1929) in which dogs were given the name "Balaìm" and also recalls boys in the streets of Tortona shouting "Balaìm, balaìm!" as they pretended to be Saracen troops in retreat (*Gente di Sarina* 140n and 162).

35 This latter name recalls that of the African king Salatiello, who appears in the *Storia dei paladini* thanks to Lodico's rewriting of Lodovico Dolce's *Prime imprese di Orlando* (1572).

non-Arabs abducted in childhood and raised as slaves in the Muslim world to carry out military and administrative duties. The corresponding term in Italian, *mammalucco*, which had come figuratively to mean a foolish and clumsy person, is even closer to Mammaloc.[36] According to Susie Bruno, it was Dominic's daughter Dolores who gave the giant this name.

Fortunately, we do not need to rely solely on newspaper articles to reconstruct the Manteo family's repertory during this period. Five programs from the early 1980s preserved by family members provide detailed information about two plays featuring a Balahiem and a Mammaloc, respectively. Even though the title of both plays is *Un'avventura d'Orlando Furioso*, given in English alternately as "An Adventure of *Orlando Furioso*" and "The Adventures of Roland," the two synopses, lists of characters, and summaries of individual scenes indicate that neither play is based on Ariosto's romance epic.

Programs for the first play, subtitled bilingually as "L'Amore di Viviana e Alessandro" and "Romance of Viviana & Alexander," correspond to performances at St. Finbar's Center in Brooklyn (December 13, 1981), the American Museum of Natural History (May 16, 1982), and Symphony Space (January 20–23, 1983). The synopsis reads as follows:

> Roland the Furious is a knight in service to King Charlemagne's court. Travelling in a seemingly endless search for his true love Angelica, Roland meets a fellow Christian knight Alexander. Alexander has been rendered unconscious by the giant pagan Balahiem, who abducted Alexander's beloved Viviana and forced Alexander to flee. Viviana is a princess, daughter of the King Soriano of Damascus.
>
> Roland champions the cause of God, country, and chivalry. He vows to reunite the lovers Alexander and Viviana at any cost, and then to continue his endless search for his own beloved, the elusive Angelica.[37]

Although Orlando's stated love for Angelica evokes both the *Orlando Innamorato* and the *Orlando Furioso*, the play centers instead around the paladin's heroic fight against an evil opponent on behalf of others in need. Balahim is also the featured

---

36 See https://www.treccani.it/vocabolario/mammalucco/.
37 This synopsis, along with a list of characters and summary of the six scenes, is provided in both English and Italian in all three programs, although the text of the latter two programs is slightly updated with respect to the 1981 version. Another difference is that for the third event, at Symphony Space, the program states that the narration was written and performed by Isaiah Sheffer, the venue's founder and artistic director. Susie Bruno confirmed that Sheffer, dressed in a long robe and hat, introduced the events in verse before each scene in order to help viewers understand the play, which was in Italian.

antagonist in a fifteen-minute version of the same basic plot with different character names (Riccardo and Fiordiligi), performed in Washington, DC, in 1980.[38]

The second play, performed at the Ethnic Folk Arts Center in co-sponsorship with Sloop Clearwater (June 18–19, 1983) and at Symphony Space (January 19–22, 1984), is subtitled bilingually "L'Amore di Isabella e Zervino" and "The Romance of Isabella and Zervino." The overall plot loosely evokes the *Orlando Furioso* episode of Isabella and Zerbino (see Chapter 8) to the extent that Orlando here also saves a knight by that name from execution and unites two lovers. Nonetheless, as the synopsis demonstrates, the story line does not correspond to the *Furioso* episode but is instead a revised rendition of the family's previous play with new character and place names:

> Orlando Furioso is the greatest Christian knight in service to King Charlemagne's court. He is traveling in a seemingly endless search for his true love Angelica.
>
> Zervino is traveling home through pagan territory most hostile to Christian knights. He saves the beautiful Princess Isabella, daughter of the pagan King Salatiello of the Kingdom of San Marchan, from pirates who are abducting her.
>
> Zervino and Princess Isabella fall in love. The giant knight Mammaloc, a traitor who is a strong, cunning and ruthless leader at King Salatiello's court, intends to make the kingdom his own, as well as the most beautiful Princess Isabella.
>
> Orlando, the champion of God, country, and chivalry, frees Zervino from his unjust imprisonment and execution, rids the kingdom of the evil of Mammaloc, returns the kingdom to King Salatiello, reunites the lovers Zervino and Isabella, and continues the search for his own beloved Angelica.[39]

---

38 One video recording, held at the Museo Internazionale delle Marionette Antonio Pasqualino in Palermo, Italy, contains two performances (with variations) of this play under the title of *Riccardo D'Alessandria e Orlando* (F-60). A second recording, shot as part of the footage for Jim Henson's *Here Come the Puppets* (1981), contains one performance along with footage of preparations, post-performance interviews with Mike Manteo and his family, and the donation of an Agricane di Tartaria puppet to the Smithsonian Institute. I am grateful to the Museo Internazionale delle Marionette and to Nancy Staub for making it possible for me to view these respective recordings.

39 The wording of this synopsis, from the Symphony Space program, differs slightly from that of the Ethnic Folk Arts Center program.

In 1963, Dominic's daughter Dolores had already explained the family's practice of fashioning new narrative material for performances that featured Roland (Clinton), and in 1976, Adler commended Ida for her skill in "creating scenes that can be included in the Orlando tale—scenes that are geared to contemporary audiences." Susie Bruno has confirmed that her mother constructed the plots of these two plays. On the one hand, the *Storia dei paladini*—at one time the indispensable puppeteers' Bible—seems to have been set aside in the family's repertory except for the use of Orlando's infatuation with Angelica as a frame. On the other hand, however, both plays foreground the heroic imperative to fight against injustice for the sake of others—whether damsels or fellow knights in distress—that is at the core of the Paladins of France cycle. This elaboration of a new plot based on quintessential chivalric themes indicates, moreover, that the family's efforts were not a static reenactment of an inherited tradition, but rather a living elaboration of that tradition in the present.[40]

Numerous newspaper articles during the 1980s document the continued activity of the Manteo family in many different venues—from local Italian American street festivals to the most prestigious elite performance spaces in New York and Washington, DC. An event especially worthy of note was the 1980 combined World Puppetry Festival and the XIII Congress of UNIMA.[41] In charge of this historic collaboration were Vincent Anthony and Nancy Staub, President and Executive Director of Puppeteers of America, respectively, and Jim Henson, President of UNIMA-USA. According to the program book, Papa Manteo's Sicilian Marionettes staged two performances of a play that "tells of Orlando's distress because of his frustrated love for Angelica and involves such other characters as Rinaldo, Orlando's cousin, and Bradamante, Rinaldo's sister."

The Manteo family's participation at the 1980 festival brought their brand of Sicilian puppet theater to the attention of puppeteers and researchers who arrived in Washington, DC, from across the United States and beyond. In at least one case, moreover, they had an impact on American puppet theater when they directly influenced the puppeteers Stephen and Chris Carter.

---

40 A description of the Manteo play "The Romance of Gilda and Polindo" found in a 1987 newspaper article relates the same basic plot outline despite the new title: "Orlando's dogged search for the elusive Angelica brings him to Damascus where he battles thieves and later, the giant Balahiem, eventually reuniting the knight Polindo and his beloved Gilda, before continuing his quest for Angelica" (Fressola).

41 Sponsored by the US Commission for UNESCO, the combined Festival and Congress took place at the Kennedy Center for the Performing Arts in Washington, DC, from June 8 to 15.

As Luman Coad explains: "The Manteo Marionettes' use of traditional Sicilian rod marionettes was an inspiration. Unlike all-string marionettes which are easily tangled and difficult to control during rapid, repeated actions, the rods to the head and right arm (used for sword fighting) allow the manipulator to have precise control over the puppet. This is the style of marionette the Carters adopted for many, if not most, of their productions."[42]

Another defining moment for the Manteo family was Tony De Nonno's *It's One Family, Knock on Wood* (1982), which details the family's multigenerational devotion to Sicilian puppet theater both on and off stage. This twenty-four-minute documentary features conversations with Mike, Ida, and other family members; rehearsals and performances; Mike constructing a puppet in his workshop; and Ida playing the piano, sewing costumes with her daughter Susie, and playfully engaging with both Mike and her grandchildren through puppetry. In addition, archival news footage shows Agrippino performing to a packed crowd, with unique shots of the puppet master behind the scenes giving voice to the male characters while his youngest son serves as prompter and his four elder children (including daughter Ida) manipulate the puppets from the bridge.

The Manteo family's puppet theater garnered further recognition and various arts awards in the course of the decade, including Mike Manteo's National Heritage Fellowship from the National Endowment for the Arts for his outstanding contribution to American culture (1983), a Mayor's Award for Art and Culture (1986), and a Governor's Arts Award (1986).[43] When Mike received the National Heritage Fellowship, one of his puppets was displayed in the corollary exhibition at the Smithsonian National Museum of American History (Colford).[44] The Manteo family also performed at a prestigious new venue in upstate New York, The Egg in Albany, in 1989 (Mandell 73).

Performing in diverse venues not only entailed transporting multiple heavy puppets, some of which weighed up to 100 pounds, and accompanying materials, but also required assembling and disassembling the bridge before

---

42 Coad 2. For photographs from the Carter Family Puppet Theater production of Caccini's *Liberation of Ruggiero from the Island of Alcina*, see https://edblogs.columbia.edu/eboiardo/carter-family-marionettes.

43 See https://www.arts.gov/honors/heritage/mike-manteo.

44 A cover story on the family in the August 1983 issue of the *Smithsonian* magazine refers to this puppet as "one of Charlemagne's knights called Agricane di Taria" (Gold 72). Although the identification and provenance are incorrect, the name "Agricane" nonetheless allows us to identify the puppet as the one that Mike Manteo donated to the Smithsonian Institute when he was in Washington, DC, in 1980. Agricane di Tartaria, a Mongol khan invented by Boiardo, is featured in Chapter 5.

and after each event. Throughout the years, Mike Manteo expressed his dream to reestablish a permanent theater company, including in the following poem:

> If my unlucky star
> stops being against me
> my wish is to have my
> small permanent theater and stage
> nightly performances ... starting
> with Costantino, up to Roncisvalle.[45]

Mike's dream edged closer to a reality in 1986 when over 100 Manteo puppets were relocated to the Staten Island Institute of Arts and Sciences (SIIAS).[46] In *Daily News* articles from February 8 and April 1, 1987, Mary Engels reports that the Manteo Family Sicilian Marionette Theater had embarked on a pilot educational program for students under the auspices of the Institute ("Manteo Puppets Come to Isle," "Hart Hails Puppet Theater at Reception"). Having a "home" through the SIIAS meant that the marionettes were accessible to a larger public, including puppeteers and researchers. Nancy Staub writes about her visit to the workshop for a personal guided tour and interview with Mike Manteo in 1988, when plans were underway to recreate the Manteo family's original Catherine Street theater (Staub). A September 17, 1989, *Daily News* article announces that the Institute's new extension would permanently house the Manteo Family Sicilian Marionette Theater, including "a classroom surrounded by a stage and more than 80 near-life-sized marionettes dressed in medieval splendor" and a backstage workshop "where the 'performers' are created and repaired" (Engels, "Museum's annex making history").

In the end, however, Mike Manteo's dream of a permanent puppet theater under his direction was not to be realized. On September 13, 1989, just a few days before the above-mentioned article went to print, Mike passed away at the age of 80. Without his leadership, the arrangement with the SIIAS proved to be short-lived. In 1991, the Manteo family was asked to retrieve the marionettes to free up the space. They were subsequently stored by Mike's son Pino in his garage until 2010 when many of them found a new home at the Italian American Museum, as noted earlier.

---

45 This poem, dated March 3, 1982, follows *serata* 193 on the final page of Mike Manteo's notebook 16 (see Chapter 2).
46 Newspaper articles commonly refer to 200 puppets. The List of Characters made during this period, however, notes 115 pieces, including complete puppets, bodies, and heads.

Although Mike Manteo never traveled to Sicily, he dedicated his life to learning, cherishing, and maintaining the tradition of Sicilian puppetry that his father had carried in his heart when he left the island in the early 1900s. Having absorbed the stories night after night during his childhood and performed them for years as a manipulator during his youth, he kept the family's theater active from the 1950s through the 1980s thanks to his unwavering determination, the unconditional support of his family, and sheer hard work.

Mike Manteo's additional dream, looking to the future, was the preservation and valorization of his father's scripts. In the front inner cover of the last notebook of scripts from the Paladins of France cycle, he expressed (in English) his tenacious hope amidst disappointment that one day the cultural and literary worth of the scripts would be recognized:

> I tried to explain the value of these manuscripts but to no avail. People with an education and culture and understanding of what art is are the only ones who know its value.
>   a chaser of rain[bows]
> Miguel Manteo
> p.s. My dreams never came t[rue]
> Maybe someone else might be
> more luckier than I am.
>
> (Copione 23)

Thinking ahead to the day in which Sicilian puppet theater would no longer be performed, McPharlin lamented that the "blank countenances [of puppets in museum cases] cannot tell the frenzy of action that pulverized the boards, the excitement of the audience that shook the rafters, and the heartache that they deadened" (*The Puppet Theater in America* 303). Although the Manteo puppets will no longer be brought to life on stage, the scripts nevertheless provide an extraordinary window into the intricate, authentic, and frenzied narrative world of the Paladins of France. Chapter 2 delves into various aspects of the Manteo family scripts, including the division into different sets, the relation of the scripts to the prose *Storia dei paladini*, the structure of the individual plays, the dates scattered throughout the pages of the notebooks, and the comments in the margins.

Chapter 2
THE SCRIPTS

Sources of the Paladins of France Cycle

Giusto Lodico's *Storia dei paladini* (1858–1860) weaves together in chronological fashion episodes from both canonical and lesser-known fifteenth- and sixteenth-century poems to arrive at almost 3,000 pages of prose.[1] This monumental compilation quickly became the undisputed source of Sicilian puppet theater and was commonly referred to as the puppeteers' Bible or simply "the book." Following the publication of Giuseppe Leggio's expanded edition in 1895–1896, puppeteers increasingly adopted this more extensive and readily available version even while invariably citing Lodico as the sole author. Leggio's version, printed frequently in the following decades, also became the basis of all successive editions.[2] A perusal of Agrippino's scripts confirms that he likewise drew from Leggio's expanded version rather than Lodico's original narrative. Indeed, a copy of the 1909 edition published by Bideri in Naples is still in the family's possession today (Appendix 3).

Anyone interested in reading the prose source of the stories staged in Agrippino's Paladins of France cycle can find Leggio's expanded version of the *Storia dei paladini* most recently published in 13 volumes between 1993 and 2000. For those who do not read Italian, there are excellent English translations of the most famous Renaissance poems refashioned by Lodico, namely Torquato Tasso's *Rinaldo* (1562), Matteo Maria Boiardo's *Orlando Innamorato* (ca. 1483, 1495), Ludovico Ariosto's *Orlando Furioso* (1516, 1532) and *Cinque canti* (published posthumously in 1545), and Luigi Pulci's *Morgante* (ca. 1478, 1483). These five poems take the reader from Rinaldo's initiation

---

1 See Carocci, *Il poema che cammina* 50, for a list of the twenty chivalric poems used by Lodico, in whole or in part, to compose the *Storia dei paladini*, including sources that she newly identified.
2 For a detailed examination of Lodico's and Leggio's relation to each other as well as to their sources and to select *opera dei pupi* scripts, see Pasqualino, *Rerum palatinorum fragmenta*, and Carocci, *Il poema che cammina* 29–103.

into knighthood (Tasso) to his departure from the Frankish court following his heroic exploits at Roncevaux (Pulci), and include the central episodes of Orlando's enamorment of the princess Angelica (Boiardo), descent into madness, and miraculous recovery (Ariosto).

Using the *Storia dei paladini* as his direct source, Agrippino painstakingly transformed the third-person prose adaptation into intricate scripts. Each play consists of three acts, with each act generally divided into various scenes with detailed stage instructions. Substantial dialogues (and monologues) are written out in full while the less notable exchanges would have been improvised during the performance. In the absence of an audio or video recording of the Paladins of France cycle, these scripts provide the only indication we have of the speech and action that occurred in each evening's play.

Despite their unique importance, Agrippino's scripts have received scant attention. Although Bil Baird refers to the scripts as "irreplaceable," he directs his gaze to their material state which exhibited traces of untold battle scenes:

> I have seen these scripts, all in Papa's handwriting. They are written in a small mountain of copybooks, each containing a bare outline of the action, plus certain key lines and poems transcribed in full. They all bear the marks of battle. Here there is a thumb print red with the blood of a giant (beet juice in an eggshell that broke when the sword hit), there a tear occasioned when some unlucky foot soldier's head flew too far. (125)

When it comes to identifying the actual narrative, however, Baird mistakes both the number of plays and the literary source, referring to "the five hundred plays that constitute the Sicilian marionette epic, *Orlando Furioso*" (118).

Nor do other mentions of the scripts in newspaper and magazine articles provide accurate information about their substance. The theater critic Lois Adler, with much less imagination than Baird, recalls the quantity of the scripts along with the quality of Agrippino's penmanship in her 1976 article: "They are to be found in several stacks on one of the tables. Actually, they are composition books in which Manteo wrote in a small neat hand" (27). She then underestimates the amount of written dialogue in the scripts when positing their "striking" resemblance to *commedia dell'arte* plays and she disregards the titles on the notebook covers when asserting that the scripts are "taken directly from Ariosto" (27).

Regarding the actual content of Agrippino's scripts, Greene had made the same error back in 1933 when attempting to identify the source of the plays. She wrote that it took thirteen months to complete a play titled

"The Adventures of Orlando Furioso." She confused the matter further later in the article by naming Ariosto as the author of *I Paladini di Francia*: "The play, which is being produced for the fourth consecutive time in six years, is an adaptation of the legend of the French epic hero, Roland, taken from Ariosto's *I Paladini di Francia*." Virtually every subsequent English-language publication I've found referring to Agrippino Manteo's repertory repeats the same claim that his plays were based on the *Orlando Furioso*.³

It would be logical to attribute this misunderstanding to the authors of the publications since American journalists and puppeteers could not be expected to know the long textual history behind the scripts. Yet Adler goes on to cite Mike Manteo on the subject: "Mike Manteo says: 'Sure, Ariosto wrote in cantos but who's gonna listen to poetry? The common people on Mulberry Street, they want to see action. My father used the exact plot and characters from Ariosto; we never recited it as poetry'" (27). Is it possible that Mike Manteo himself did not realize that his father's scripts were taken from the nineteenth-century prose *Storia dei paladini*? After all, in the same quotation, he goes on to tell Adler that he did not need to consult even the scripts since he knew the stories by heart exclusively through the repeated performances: "Actually, we know it by heart; we don't even have to look at the script, understand? WE NEVER REHEARSED. We learned by going on, knowing the action" (emphasis in the original). Mike Manteo explains this same hands-on approach to Bil Baird: "'We never rehearsed at any time,' said Mike, 'By looking at my father we got the inspiration'" (126). In a 1979 interview, he emphatically told a newspaper reporter, "I don't NEED a script" (Lagnado, emphasis in the original).

Knowledge of the *opera dei pupi* repertory based exclusively on performance without attention to the written narrative source was not, in fact, unusual among *figli d'arte* (sons of puppeteers) in the past. The Palermitan puppeteer Enzo Mancuso, for example, explained to me that initially his knowledge of the episodes was based on his father's performances and retellings of the stories and not on any reading of the texts.⁴ In popular theatrical traditions, moreover, documenting the original source is generally not deemed essential since attention is focused on the shared effort of

---

3 Gold, for example, writes that Agrippino Manteo improvised from Ariosto's text (69) and that "the Manteos' version of *Orlando Furioso* lasted 394 episodes" (70).
4 For Enzo Mancuso's remark, see the interview clip "On his sources of knowledge of the chivalric narratives" on the eBOIARDO website (https://edblogs.columbia.edu/eboiardo/sicilian-puppet-theater/interviews/nino-and-enzo-mancuso/).

staging a work in the present for which the script is but the vehicle.[5] Mike Manteo's emphasis on performance-based learning over reading might help explain why he does not correctly identify the source of his father's chivalric repertory. If he first learned the stories not by perusing the texts but by watching and later participating in the nightly performances, it stands to reason that his primary connection was to the staged action and the spoken dialogue rather than to words written on the page—whether the *Storia dei paladini* or the scripts themselves.

Mike's remarks reported in the above quotations do not tell the whole story, however. First of all, Mike's comments at various places in the margins of Agrippino's scripts demonstrate that he had the full written repertory at his fingertips. Second, Mike himself patiently recopied his father's scripts by hand between 1962 and 1986. Mike's twenty-three notebooks covering the *Reali di Francia* and *Paladini di Francia* cycles (discussed below) reproduce the names of both source texts on the respective covers.

In a 1976 interview, moreover, Mike (Papa) and Ida give a clear indication of the extent of Agrippino's chivalric repertory:

> PAPA--I don't know if you ever read medieval stories, about Constantine the Great. He started the Christian faith; and then, generation, generation, it came to Charlemagne. From Charlemagne came his son and two more generations. That ends the story. Then the sequel.
> IDA--It's like the Bible, just like the Bible.
> PAPA--See the end of the Paladin, then the sequel; there's the story of Guido Santo. Then how long does Guido Santo last?
> Ida--About three months.
> PAPA--So Guido Santo dies. Now we have another sequel which is two brothers [i.e., a sister and brother], Dolores and Strenero [i.e., Straniero]. That lasts about three months. This story has two brothers [i.e., siblings] unknown to each other. So after that comes, what my sister says, the Crusaders. That's just the last. (Kalcik, "Old Ways in the New World" 13)

While not distinguishing between history and fiction or between earlier Italian chivalric epics and nineteenth-century Sicilian epigones, Mike and Ida nonetheless demonstrate an awareness that their father's repertory

---

5 In the epic Maggio tradition of the Tuscan-Emilian Apennines, for example, many of the extant chivalric plays come down to us without the original author's name but rather with the name of the company that staged them and that of the company's director who last revised them.

stretched from Constantine the Great to characters featured in late nineteenth-century prose sequels published in Sicily.

Given their intimate familiarity with their father's scripts, why would Mike and his siblings have nevertheless referred to the *Orlando Furioso* instead of the *Storia dei paladini* as the source of the Paladins of France cycle? This is all the more striking because traditional puppeteers operating in Sicily customarily did the opposite, referring exclusively to Lodico as the foundation of their repertory without mentioning the Renaissance sources behind the *Storia dei paladini*. Perhaps the answer lies in the Manteo family's consideration of their interlocutors' lack of familiarity with the material. Although the traditional Sicilian puppet theater audience who knew the stories as well as the puppeteers would have immediately understood a reference to Lodico or Leggio, the names of these Sicilian authors would not have meant anything to a local newspaper reporter or to the American public at large. Anyone with even a cursory knowledge of the Italian literary canon, however, would most likely have heard of Ariosto's *Orlando Furioso* and would have therefore needed no further explanation. In this light, the use of Ariosto's name would have immediately signaled that behind what one reporter had dismissively called the "primitive" legends staged by Agrippino was nothing less than an acclaimed masterpiece of Italian Renaissance literature. No other name or title would have functioned quite as effectively in this regard. Consequently, even though Ariosto was only one of several authors whose work had been refashioned in the *Storia dei paladini*, naming the *Orlando Furioso* would have conveyed the excellence and essence of Sicilian puppet theater's chivalric matter to the outside world in the most economical and effective way possible. In this light, then, one could consider this designation as a synecdoche rather than an error.

Whatever the reason for the oft-repeated misidentification of Agrippino Manteo's main source as the *Orlando Furioso* rather than the *Storia dei paladini*, the accessibility of his scripts means that his actual repertory can now be read and studied in as much depth as anyone cares to delve. This chapter provides the first concrete account of Agrippino's Paladins of France cycle based on an extensive examination of the handwritten notebooks.

Scripts Containing the Paladins of France Cycle

In the inner front cover of Agrippino's *Libro* 1, Mike Manteo states (in English): "Written by my father 'Papa Manteo' at the theater 76 Catherine St N.Y. year 1919. Finished his writing at 1935. All this time his work never ended" (signed "Miguel Manteo"). If the scripts were written in 1919 and would have had to be complete in order for Agrippino to perform the cycle beginning in the early 1920s, why does Mike say that his father only finished writing in 1935, a full sixteen years later? A closer look at the scripts themselves can provide at least a partial answer.

While scanning Agrippino's many unordered notebooks over the course of the spring 2015 semester, I assumed that the Paladins of France cycle would be contained in one complete set that I could reassemble like the pieces of a puzzle. Yet when I examined the scanned documents more carefully and arranged the notebooks in order according to the sequencing of the plays, it was rather like trying to sort out a pile of pieces from various incomplete puzzles. To complicate matters even further, I found that some pieces could fit two puzzles at the same time. It slowly emerged that there are three partial—and partially overlapping—sets with a complex and still not fully discernible relationship to each other.[6]

We may, therefore, understand Mike's comment about the scripts' sixteen-year composition period to refer to an ongoing process of revision and rewriting between 1919 and 1935 on the part of his father. It may be that the original scripts required recopying because they became worn out or damaged. After all, the photocopier was only invented in 1938 and did not become commercially available until over a decade later. Pages in some of the notebooks are, in fact, loose and tattered. Agrippino did not simply copy the plays verbatim, however, but he modified them in the process. Comparing the sets of scripts in Agrippino's handwriting reveals both changes within the plays and the rearrangement of narrative material across plays. In addition, within each set of scripts, there are amendments noted with various colored pencils in different handwriting. These additional changes reveal a constant reassessment of the dramatic presentation in the course of the nightly performances.

Of the extant scripts handwritten by Agrippino that comprise the Paladins of France cycle, the most complete set consists of seventeen notebooks numbered 3 to 23 (with 15–17 and 20 missing). I have tentatively labeled this set *Copioni* (Scripts) because the word is written prominently on the front covers. The set contains a total of 265 extant plays ranging from *sera* 1 in *Copione* 3 to *sera* 330 in *Copione* 23.[7]

---

6 The below description of the sets supersedes the one I provided in "The Catanese-American Puppeteer Agrippino Manteo," published before additional notebooks had been located.

7 Occasional anomalies in the numbering are indicated next to the corresponding translated summaries of plays in Appendix 5. There are, moreover, more summaries than extant plays.

I am tentatively calling the second set *Libri* (Books) because the number of each notebook is preceded by the word *Libro*. There are two versions of *Libro* 1: the first, in Agrippino's hand, has a very worn front cover and tape holding together its initial and final pages; the second, in markedly better condition, is a copy transcribed by Agrippino's son Johnny with slight variations and increased use of punctuation. Whereas Agrippino's *Libro Primo* was apparently retired since "EXTRA" is written on the cover in block letters, Johnny's notebook was given a new cover and repurposed as *Copione* 3. *Libro* 2 likewise received a new cover and was repurposed as *Copione* 4. The other three extant notebooks in the set, however, *Libri* 5, 6, and 7, exist independently of the *Copioni* set. The substantial wear and tear on these notebooks may have been what prompted Agrippino to rewrite the scripts by hand rather than to simply replace the covers.

A third extant set in Agrippino's hand, like the *Libri* set, consists of some notebooks that were incorporated into the *Copioni* set as well as other notebooks that remain independent of it. I am tentatively calling this set *Paladini* because this word is prominently written on the cover of some of the notebooks. The first one, *Paladini* 1, exists independently of the *Copioni* set. The next three, however, *Paladini* 2–4, were repurposed as *Copioni* 5–7. The following three, *Paladini* 6–8, exist independently, and the 76 plays contained therein correspond to plays found in *Copioni* 9–13.[8] The final three extant notebooks, *Paladini* 9, 13, and 14, were repurposed as *Copioni* 14, 18, and 19.

Although both the *Libri* and the *Paladini* notebooks were composed earlier than the *Copioni* set, they cannot be considered as part of the same set because *Libri* 5, 6, and 7 exist independently of *Paladini* 6, 7, and 8. All *Libri* and *Paladini* notebooks that were not incorporated into the *Copioni* set contain plays that are near duplicates of the latter set. This means that for at least part of the cycle, there are three separate sets of scripts.

The relation of both the *Libri* and the *Paladini* notebooks to the *Copioni* set is undoubtedly more conspicuous because of the partial repurposing. Nonetheless, a correspondence between the *Libri* and *Paladini* sets themselves can also be noted in at least one notebook. The cover of *Libro* 6 contains the number 4 and the word PALADINI written in block letters. A comparison of *Libro* 6 and *Paladini* 4 (*Copione* 7) indeed confirms that the *serate* in both

---

8 The plays of the *Paladini* set closely match (within a number or two) those of the *Copioni* set. The numbers of the notebooks diverge substantially, however, because the *Paladini* notebooks contain many more pages. A comparison of the variations confirms that *Paladini* is the earlier set.

notebooks overlap.[9] Thus, the writing of "PALADINI 4" on the cover of *Libro* 6 may have facilitated consultation across the sets by keeping the correspondences readily visible.

A listing in separate columns of the notebooks comprising the three sets may help visualize the comprehensive situation (gray with an arrow for the *Libri* and *Paladini* sets indicates notebooks repurposed in the *Copioni* set while gray in brackets for the *Copioni* set indicates missing notebooks):

Libro 1 >	*Paladini* 1	*Copione* 3
Libro 2 >		*Copione* 4
	Paladini 2 >	*Copione* 5
Libri 5 and 6	*Paladini* 3 >	*Copione* 6
Libri 6 and 7	*Paladini* 4 >	*Copione* 7
		Copione 8
	Paladini 6	*Copione* 9
	Paladini 6 and 7	*Copione* 10
	Paladini 7	*Copione* 11
	Paladini 7 and 8	*Copione* 12
	Paladini 8	*Copione* 13
	Paladini 9 >	*Copione* 14
		[*Copioni* 15–17]
	Paladini 13 >	*Copione* 18
	Paladini 14 >	*Copione* 19
		[*Copione* 20]
		Copione 21
		Copione 22
		Copione 23

It is possible that the *Libri* and *Paladini* notebooks never existed as complete sets; in that case, the number of missing notebooks would be fewer. However, it is also worth noting that *Libro* 7, the last extant notebook of that set, has "Vintaggia 1923" written on the inner cover, suggesting that notebooks from this set may have been for sale as "vintage" at a much later date. If any

---

9 To be precise, the plays in *Libro* 6, *serate* 64–79, fall largely within the same range as the *serate* 69–92 found in *Paladini* 4 (*Copione* 7).

missing notebooks eventually come to light, they will no doubt provide crucial pieces to this incomplete tripartite puzzle.

There are indications, moreover, that all three sets were preceded by an even older set that served as a reference point. This may be surmised by a jump in numbering near the same play in both *Libro* 6 and *Paladini* 4 (*Copione* 7). In the case of *Libro* 6, a note at the end of *sera* 76 explains that the jump from *sera* 76 to *sera* 80 was deliberate so that the sequence of plays could fall in line with another script: "After this evening N. 76 there follows N. 80 of the other script." Yet the script in question cannot be *Paladini* 4 (*Copione* 7) since that notebook's *sera* 80 corresponds to the earlier *sera* 75 of *Libro* 6; conversely, *sera* 76 of *Libro* 6 already corresponds to *sera* 81 of *Paladini* 4 (*Copione* 7). Therefore, the note about *sera* 76 being followed by *sera* 80 in "the other script" must be referring to a different set altogether.

The jump occurring in *Paladini* 4 (*Copione* 7) is of an entirely different nature. In this case, the page following Act 3, scene 5, of *sera* 81 jumps to the end of Act 2 (partially crossed out) and Act 3, scenes 1–4, of *sera* 83. Since pages have not been physically torn out, there must have been a glitch in copying from another set: pages from an earlier script corresponding to all of *sera* 82 and part of *sera* 83 could have been missing or accidentally skipped over. That presumed earlier script, however, cannot be from the *Libri* set. Although the narrative roughly corresponds in both notebooks, there are also substantial differences in the arrangement of the episodes and the details. In short, the inadvertent omission of text between *sera* 81 and the middle of *sera* 83 in *Paladini* 4 (*Copione* 7), like the deliberate skipping of *serate* 77–79 in *Libro* 6, seems to indicate that there was yet another set of scripts that served as a point of reference.

Additional Scripts from the Paladins of France Cycle Composed by Agrippino

There are two additional notebooks in Agrippino's handwriting that correspond to episodes from the Paladins of France cycle. One of these contains three plays (numbered 326–28) from the climactic Battle of Roncevaux. The title on the cover written in block letters, presumably by Mike Manteo, reads *La morte dei Paladini nella Roncisvalle*. The other notebook contains ten consecutive plays with episodes numbered 1–10, giving the impression of a ten-part mini-series that could have been performed as an autonomous unit. There is no title because the cover is missing, but the plays dramatize material originally from Ariosto's *Orlando Furioso*: from Pinabello's attempt to murder Bradamante to the *guerriera*'s later killing of him in revenge. Even in this case, however, Agrippino follows the *Storia dei paladini* rather than Ariosto's poem.

The Relation of the Paladins of France Scripts to the *Storia dei paladini di Francia*

Sera 1 of *Libro* 1 (*Copione* 3) begins with the advisors of Pipino (Pippin III), king of the Franks, exhorting him to marry in order to produce an heir. This episode, which eventually leads to the birth of the future Frankish emperor Carlomagno, corresponds to the opening chapter of Leggio's expanded version of the *Storia dei paladini*.[10] Yet there is no reference to the source text until the end of *Copione* 8's *sera* 104, where Agrippino writes "End of the first volume," followed by "Second volume" above "*sera* 105" on the next page. This indicates retrospectively that the first 104 plays in the *Copioni* set are based on the 82 chapters of Leggio's first volume.

For the plays based on the second and third volume of the *Storia dei paladini*, however, Agrippino regularly provides consecutive numbers to the right of the number of the play. For Volume Two, the numbering extends from 1 next to *sera* 105 (*Copione* 8) to 91 next to *sera* 195 (*Copione* 13). The conclusion of *sera* 195, in fact, is marked by a note regarding the shift to Volume Three. The numbering resumes with the number 7 appearing to the right of *sera* 204 (*Copione* 14), and continues consecutively until the number 133, which accompanies the final play of the cycle, *sera* 330 (*Copione* 23). Nonetheless, the correspondence between Agrippino's plays and the *Storia dei paladini*'s chapters does not continue for long after the opening of the second and third volumes. Indeed, as occurred for the first volume, in this case as well there are substantially more plays than chapters: to be precise, the 145 chapters in the latter two volumes (76 and 69, respectively) give rise to 226 plays (*serate* 105–330).[11]

It is also worth noting that the synopses preceding the plays in the scripts do not generally replicate the language of the chapter summaries of the *Storia dei paladini*. Not only are the sentences often phrased differently even when recounting the same action, but the substance of the synopses also demonstrates the extent to which Agrippino reordered and revised the plotlines. This is yet another area that invites further research.

---

10 When referring to the Italian literary tradition and Agrippino's scripts, from this point forward, I use Charlemagne's Italian names "Carlo" and "Carlomagno" in order to keep present that we are dealing with a fictionalized character rather than the historical figure.

11 I derive the number of chapters from Alessandro Napoli's corrections of the numbering for the three volumes (Pasqualino, *Rerum palatinorum fragmenta* 362–97).

Composition of the Scripts

Agrippino's notebooks are representative of traditional Catanese puppet scripts, which historically tended to be more developed than those from the Palermitan area.[12] The number of each play is almost always preceded by *sera* or *serata* (evening), indicating that the plays were intended to be performed on a nightly basis.[13] Each play begins with a synopsis summarizing the events and a Cast of Characters (and, occasionally, props). While the location of these synopses within the scripts would have no doubt allowed Agrippino to quickly see the action to be performed that evening, summaries also typically served as announcements to alert and entice the public. As Alessandro Napoli explains, in the Catanese tradition, written summaries, referred to as *ricordini*, were attached to the painted posters (*cartelli*) advertising upcoming shows.[14]

The plays are structurally divided into three Acts that would have allowed for two intermissions during performances. With rare exceptions, the Acts are further broken down into various scenes that note the location next to the scene number (such as the name of a city or a generic place like "forest," "castle, or "battlefield"). During performances, the change of location would have been rendered primarily by the lowering of a different painted backdrop. As noted above, the plays contain not only precise stage directions with a detailed description of the action but also extensive dialogues, speeches, and monologues, with occasional stanzas of *ottava rima* poetry.

Occasional recourse to poetry was part of the *opera dei pupi* tradition. Lodico had inserted a small number of verses and *ottava rima* stanzas from the poems that he refashioned in his prose compilation, and Carocci notes that some puppeteers transcribed these stanzas in their scripts (*Il poema che cammina* 142). According to Alessandro Napoli, moreover, Gaetano Crimi had a particular

---

12 Napoli also notes that the Catanese tradition is "much freer than the Palermitan one in adapting the original literary source for performances" ("Immaginare Ariosto in Sicilia" 15).
13 When providing the summaries in Appendix 5, I use *sera*, *serata*, or no word at all preceding the number of the play, exactly as I find it in Agrippino's script. In the course of my study, however, for the sake of consistency, I use *sera* when referring to Agrippino's script and *serata* when referring to plays copied by Mike Manteo since these are the most frequent terms used by each. For multiple plays I simply use the plural term *serate*.
14 Summaries of the following evening's performance were also customarily provided orally by the puppeteer to the public between the second and third acts. Napoli, *Il racconto e i colori* 23 and 302n.

penchant for citing poetry directly from the original poems.¹⁵ Agrippino Manteo shares this predilection, adding *ottava rima* stanzas not found in the *Storia dei paladini*. Some of these are copied from the chivalric poems that were rendered into prose, yet there are also *ottava rima* stanzas in his scripts that I have not encountered elsewhere (see Chapters 3–5).

The inclusion of poetry in these scripts indicates that Agrippino not only expected his audience to understand and enjoy the verses, but also that he had either familiarity with the original Italian poems or access to previous scripts that implemented this procedure. As far as I know, the scripts of Agrippino's mentor, Giuseppe Crimi, and of the latter's father, Gaetano Crimi, are not extant. It is therefore not possible to ascertain with absolute certainty the extent of Agrippino's originality in this regard.¹⁶ Since, however, there is no mention of the Catanese immigrant carrying scripts with him to the New World, my working assumption is that the poetry with no known source was composed by Agrippino himself. His granddaughter Susie Bruno has confirmed, moreover, that he did also write poetry.

Agrippino's Comments in the Margins of His Scripts

The notebooks not only reveal the substance of the nightly performances, but they can also provide insight into the puppeteer as an artist. Agrippino was sparing in his comments about the action at hand. Nevertheless, the few notes and reflections that he does interject offer clues to his artistic vision. In particular, four comments written between *serate* 320 and 328 (*Copione* 23) give a sense of his emotional engagement with the material, his commitment to excellence, and his heartfelt tension between adhering to "the book" and innovating for emotional effect and poetic justice.

In the course of *sera* 320, twenty-two kings from the eastern Mediterranean travel to Paris on behalf of Rinaldo—earlier banished by Carlomagno and then proclaimed the king of Trebisonda (Trebizond)—in order to plead for the release of Rinaldo's wife and two sons from prison. After the Frankish

---

15 Cited in Carocci, *Il poema che cammina* 154n. Donata Amico notes that another early Catanese puppeteer, Raffaele Trombetta (active 1882–1928), Gaetano Crimi's son-in-law and protégé, also inserted stanzas from the *Furioso*, *Innamorato*, and *Morgante*, as well as other chivalric poems, into his improvised dialogues (87–88).

16 I have not had the opportunity to examine the extant scripts of Raffaele Trombetta preserved in Palermo. However, when comparing Agrippino's notebooks and specific references to Trombetta's scripts in Amico, Carocci (*Il poema che cammina*), Napoli (*Il racconto e i colori*), and Pasqualino (*Rerum palatinorum fragmenta*), I did not encounter convergences in the scripts of the two puppeteers.

emperor adamantly refuses to free the hostages, the rulers visit Clarice in her cell and witness her death. Agrippino's emotional engagement with the narrative and his desire to stage for his public a performance worthy of the tragic occasion come through in the final two sentences of the play's synopsis: "Clarice's death and a great funeral with a monumental scene with a deep stage never done before in Marionette theaters. Come and you will see for yourselves."[17]

Agrippino's following three comments occur in plays that bring us to the climactic battle of Roncevaux that Lodico drew from Pulci's late fifteenth-century *Morgante* rather than from the medieval French *chanson de geste* cycle. The most striking difference in Pulci's version is the presence of Rinaldo as the hero who both avenges the death of his companions vis-à-vis the Saracens and revindicates his honor vis-à-vis his own king.[18] In *sera* 321, Rinaldo sets off as a pilgrim after hearing the news of Clarice's death while Gano di Magonza sends out his men to murder the grieving paladin. When Guidone is assaulted by the Magonza clan, Perinda (Marfisa's daughter) comes to his rescue by defeating the assailants. The two youths subsequently fall in love. When they arrive in Babilonia, they are attacked by the fierce woman warrior Antea who, after a long battle, succumbs to Perinda's sword. Agrippino adds a note following the Cast of Characters that signals the strong dramatic impact of the play and instructs the female reader how to effectively convey the range of emotions demonstrated by the two opposing female knights:

> N.B. This is a beautiful evening, please study it well and it will have a great effect, just as the fire in the middle of the room has a great effect because nobody does it, so that even though it may seem that they don't say anything, the public is moved by it. I ask the young lady to devote her attention to Antea and Perinda. Anger, laughter, and calm give a beautiful color and also create a portrait; my congratulations if it succeeds, and that of the public, accept my sincerity.[19]

---

17 Napoli refers to the deep stage ("scena in fondo") as "that particular stagecraft procedure that amplified the depth of the stage space for puppet action on important occasions" (Pasqualino, *Rerum palatinorum fragmenta* 177n). The address to the public here recalls the function of these summaries as announcements, as noted above.

18 For a comparative analysis of this episode from Pulci's *Morgante* to Sicilian puppet theater today, see Cavallo, "The Ideological Battle of Roncevaux."

19 Since extant documentation indicates that only Agrippino's wife and daughter read the part of the female characters, the use of the formal term "young lady" (*signorina*) here is puzzling.

Figure 2.1 Agrippino Manteo backstage during a performance as fire burns center stage. Photo by William H. Field (circa 1935–1938). Courtesy of Michael J. Manteo.

In addition, Agrippino's satisfaction over the impact of fire burning center stage reveals his attention to spectacularity as well. This particular special effect may be seen in a rare photograph of Agrippino during a performance (Figure 2.1).

Agrippino intervenes again in *sera* 323 in another episode involving Rinaldo. After an unidentified pilgrim is killed by a wild lion, some members of the Magonza clan believe the corpse to be that of Rinaldo and they transport it to Paris. Among other vicissitudes, Orlando arrests Gano and an enraged populace forces Carlo to free Rinaldo's sons. In addition, after repeated entreaties by foreign kings friendly to Rinaldo and eventually the rebellion of his own paladins, the emperor is finally compelled to permit the rebuilding of the castle of Montalbano which he had razed to the ground in the persecution of Rinaldo and his family. Between the initial paragraph summarizing the action and the Cast of Characters, Agrippino writes a note advising brevity in the dialogue and the reduction of repetitious scenes regarding the rebuilding of the castle of Montalbano. His concern to avoid repetition shows his attention to the pacing of the drama so as to maintain a high level of audience interest. It is also a reminder of the flexibility inherent in the nightly performances.

Agrippino's comment in *sera* 328 is instead a more personal reflection on his own *modus operandi* as playwright and theater director. The play dramatizes the culminating moments in the battle of Roncevaux, itself the tragic climax of the entire Paladins of France cycle. Orlando bleeds after blowing his olifant for the second and third time, and he will die by the end of the evening. Carlo orders the arrest of Gano and returns to the valley. In the meantime, Rinaldo returns from exile with his brother Ricciardetto and turns the tide of the battle, defeating the remaining Saracens and chasing the Spanish king Marsilio from the field. Agrippino explains in a note following the Cast of Characters that he inserted an invented scene in the midst of these events, one in which Rinaldo embraces his two sons before they die. Yet within the same sentence, he also acknowledges that it would be more correct to simply adhere to the *Storia dei paladini*'s rendition of events.[20] With the freedom afforded him as a playwright in charge of the action, Agrippino chose to modify the plot in the script in order to give his hero a final moment reunited with his children after all the unspeakable suffering that Carlo had afflicted upon them. Nonetheless, his stated unease with regard to this deviation from the *Storia dei paladini*'s plotline suggests that in principle he aimed to faithfully dramatize events as he found them in the prose compilation. In fact, although Rinaldo does indeed embrace his sons in the course of this play (Act 2, scene 4), in the version of *sera* 328 found in the independent *Roncisvalle* notebook, Agrippino writes that the scene must be staged according to the book: "N.B. Rinaldo's children die before his arrival, as the book says."

Mike's Comments in the Margins of Agrippino's Scripts

There are various additional comments in the margins of Agrippino's scripts signed by Mike Manteo and others apparently written by the same hand. While Mike occasionally remarks on either the quality of a performance or

---

[20] Napoli notes that in the Catanese tradition, puppeteers staged a heartbreaking episode in which Olivero's sons die in his arms and then duplicated the episode by having Rinaldo's two sons die in his arms as well (in Pasqualino, *Rerum palatinorum fragmenta* 323n).

the nature of a scene, most of his statements appear to have been written in later years because they are tinged with nostalgia. The following comment, for example, both extols his father's craft and expresses his goal to carry on his father's legacy:

> Time only knows how many times these pages were turned in the theatres that our Papa, gave his best shows par to no one. He was the best. With the help of his proud family. He was the best. "He is gone" and still is the best. I do my best—but! not the best. Like Papá. "Mike." (Inner front cover, *Libro* 6, in English)

Mike's conviction that Agrippino would remain unsurpassed is counterbalanced by an unwavering determination to follow in his footsteps.

Mike's comments in the margins of his father's scripts are also a reminder of the multicultural and multilingual upbringing of Agrippino's children. Mike spent the first decade of his life in Argentina before the family relocated to New York City. Although clearly more accustomed to speaking and writing in Spanish and subsequently in English, he nonetheless wrote most of his notes in the margins of the scripts in Italian with occasional phrases in Spanish and only resorted to English in certain reflections about the trajectory of his family. Given the often imprecise grammatical constructions, it is clear that Italian was not the language that came most naturally to him. On the contrary, he seems to have made a considerable effort to express himself in the same language as his chivalric heroes and the theatrical tradition he so cherished.

Dates Recorded in Agrippino's Paladins of France Scripts

The temporal annotations in the notebooks in relation to the sequence of plays may reveal some information regarding the composition and performance history. Unfortunately, Agrippino did not supply composition dates in any of the notebooks he composed. The only dates that correspond with any certainty to the composition of the Paladins of France cycle during Agrippino's lifetime were those provided by his son Johnny on the first and last page of the notebook he copied from *Libro* 1: April 7, 1933, and November 30, 1934, respectively. According to these two dates, Johnny (who refers to himself on the title page by the Italian name Giovanni) would have taken over a year and a half to copy a single notebook of fourteen complete plays and the beginning of a fifteenth one. Such an extended timeframe indicates that he must have worked on the project only intermittently.

The earliest temporal indication recorded in any of the notebooks is "VINTAGGIA 1923" written in thick black block letters on the inner cover of *Libro* 7. As noted above, however, the year would have logically been written long after the fact for this notebook to have been considered "vintage." Although the date is therefore not reliable as a date of composition, it is perhaps not coincidental that Agrippino is said to have begun performing in New York City precisely in 1923. The plays contained in that notebook would likely have been composed by that year—if not earlier.

Leaving aside this later reference to the year 1923, the oldest date appearing in any of the notebooks occurs in a loose page inserted within *Libro* 6. Just prior to *sera* 64 is the announcement of a contest for schoolchildren with a deadline of October 10, 1931. In addition, *Copione* 12 appears to have the year 1932 written very faintly on the label pasted to the inner cover. Apart from these two dates, all the remaining references to time recorded in the Paladins of France notebooks appear to be performance dates (and days of the week) entered sporadically in handwriting other than Agrippino's, presumably that of Mike and his siblings. In considering below the instances of dating that I came across in Agrippino's scripts, I also include the various enigmas I encountered in the hope that further study may bring ever greater clarity.

The earliest dates that appear connected to performances are three references to 1932 found within the pages of the *Copioni* set. The first is that of Sunday, January 24, 1932, recorded in *sera* 143 (*Copione* 10) as "Domenica 24 genaro 1932."[21] The next is May 26, 1932, recorded in *sera* 288 (*Copione* 21) as "Mayo 26 giovedì 1932." This date combines the month written in Spanish and the day of the week in Italian, with the month preceding the date according to the style of notation adopted in the United States. This mixing of language systems is another reminder that the Manteo children were polyglots with a different degree and manner of instruction in the various languages. The third date from 1932 is "sabato 5, 1932," followed by what looks to be "junio," in *sera* 299 (*Copione* 22).[22]

The earliest temporal indications recorded in the pages of the *Libri* set, found in *Libro* 2 (*Copione* 4), pertain to the year of 1933. The first, appearing

---

21 The spelling of the month may be a combination of the Spanish "enero" and Italian "gennaio" or was possibly influenced by the Sicilian ending for the month, "-aru."

22 June 5 fell on a Sunday, not Saturday, in 1932. Nonetheless, the ten days between these two dates fit the number of plays between 288 and 299. On the other hand, however, the 124 days between the first two dates are not sufficient to accommodate daily performances of the 145 plays between *serate* 143 and 288.

at *sera* 22, gives the date as "Enero 12 1933." Two additional dates accompany *sera* 26, but they seem to be at odds with each other. The first, "enero 1933," is in line with the January 12, 1933, date recorded four plays earlier. The second date, however, written at the bottom of the page, is "Novembre 15 - 1933." This date possibly refers to a mock battle among family members with fasola beans reported under the Cast of Characters on this page.[23] It is not clear, however, why that playful family encounter would have been recorded on that particular page if it had not occurred the same day as the performance.

The only other two dates found in the *Libri* set pertain to the year of 1935. The first of these, also in *Libro* 2 (*Copione* 4), is "Marzo 8, 1935," written on the penultimate page of the notebook. We cannot link this date to the surrounding performances with any degree of certainty, however, since the page, which had become loose and was inverted when taped, was originally the final blank page of the notebook where the date could have been added for any number of reasons.[24] The other date in the *Libri* set, written on the first page of *Libro* 7, is April 14, 1935.

The *Copioni* notebooks occasionally contain additional dates between 1933 and 1935. Given the overlapping of these years in both sets, we may compare the dates to see what they might reveal about Agrippino's usage of the two sets. Setting the date of April 14, 1935 (*sera* 81, *Libro* 7), alongside that of August 19, 1935 (*sera* 96, *Copione* 8), however, only raises a new question. *Sera* 96 is only 15 plays later than *sera* 81, and yet four months are said to have passed. This discrepancy may indicate a possible pause in performances in the intervening months. However, the full annotation of the second date, "agosto 19 – 1,935 / 3$ che fenomemo," suggests that it was written to draw attention to the amount of money taken in that evening rather than to signal a previous interruption in performances.[25]

---

23 "Combat between Pino and Domingo, Bill and Michele with the strokes of fasola beans—the end of the fasola beans."

24 Below the date, in fact, is the address of a transportation company in New York City.

25 Decades later, Mike wrote the following comment (in English) on the same page: "As of this day – Dec 24 1978 This inscription above – states – Aug 19, 1935 – We took in $3.00 – and says what! A fenomenon – on a good night – we took at least $27.00, and it supposed to be good." Accounting for the inflation of the money supply under the Federal Reserve banking system, $3 in 1935 would be the equivalent to the purchasing power of about $62.13 in 2022 (CPI Inflation Calculator at https://www.in2013dollars.com/us/inflation).

Another instance of dating in *Libro* 7 is even more inexplicable. A note at *sera* 87 would at first glance appear to refer to the year 1947: "Domenica 13 Dicembre 47."[26] However, Agrippino ceased to perform in 1939 and died in August 1947. Furthermore, December 13 of that year fell on a Saturday, not a Sunday. Compounding the mystery is the fact that the day of the week and the month are again noted only four plays later, at *sera* 91, the final play in this last extant notebook of the set. This time, Thursday, December 18 ("giovedì 18 Dicembre") actually does correspond to the year 1947. This second date, at such a short interval after the first, suggests in any case that the plays 87 through 91 were performed consecutively within the space of a week even if the year is uncertain.

Apart from the 1931 contest announcement, all the dates I found in the Paladins of France notebooks written during Agrippino's lifetime are between 1932 and 1935. Chronologically, they are as follows:

January 24, 1932 (*sera* 143, *Copione* 10)
May 26, 1932 (*sera* 288, *Copione* 21)
June 5, 1932 (*sera* 299, *Copione* 22)
January 12, 1933 (*sera* 22, *Libro* 2 [*Copione* 4])
January 1933 (*sera* 26, *Libro* 2 [*Copione* 4])
April 11, 1933 (*sera* 129, inner cover, *Copione* 10)
November 15, 1933 (*sera* 26, *Libro* 2 [*Copione* 4])
January 31, 1935 (*sera* 297, *Copione* 22)
March 8, 1935 (*Libro* 2 [*Copione* 4], loose page at the end of the notebook)
Aprile 14, 1935 (*sera* 81, *Libro* 7)
August 19, 1935 (*sera* 96, *Copione* 8)

It remains unclear why during these few years Agrippino or his children had a sporadic interest in documenting performance dates. At the same time, however, it is striking that all the dates noted in the margins—with just one exception—are either in the *Copioni* set or in a repurposed *Copioni* notebook. Most notably, these handwritten dates indicate that the *Copioni* set was being used as early as January 1932. In addition, *Libro* 2 would appear to have been repurposed as *Copione* 4 by 1933. The 1935 date in *Libro* 7 suggests, however, that the *Libri* set was still near at hand.

We may also gather some indication of performance history from the days of the week frequently noted above the synopses. These are always written by

---

26 Both numbers appear in boxes, with 13 above the day of the week and month, and 47 underneath.

a hand other than Agrippino's and usually in blue- or orange-colored pencil. When the days of the week are noted in sequence over the course of several plays, as sometimes happens, we can see that in those cases the plays were indeed performed seven days a week.

Before the Paladins of France: *I reali di Francia*

As noted above, the first play of *Libro* 1 corresponds to the first chapter of Leggio's extended version of the *Storia dei paladini*. How, then, did this notebook become the third rather than the first in a new set of scripts? As it turns out, *Libro* 1 was repurposed as *Copione* 3 because Agrippino prefaced the Paladins of France cycle with two notebooks of scripts dramatizing the *Reali di Francia* (Royals of France) cycle. The title refers to the prose epic *I reali di Francia* by Andrea da Barberino (c. 1370–1431) that narrates the Matter of France from Constantine to Charlemagne.[27] Leggio had already opened his extended *Storia dei paladini* with the latter part of this work, more precisely, the events surrounding Pipino's marriage to Berta. Yet Sicilian puppeteers often went beyond Leggio to dramatize earlier episodes from the *Reali di Francia* as a prequel to the Paladins of France cycle. Agrippino is no exception in this regard. His 51 handwritten plays in the Royals of France cycle likewise begin with the Roman emperor Constantine. We have confirmation, moreover, that these plays were staged: Baird provides a first-hand recollection of Agrippino's play in which Constantine is cured of leprosy upon converting to Christianity (125).

The two notebooks containing the *Reali di Francia* cycle have new covers with the following titles in Mike Manteo's handwriting: "Storia dei / Reali di Francia / Copione 1 / Le quattro / Battaglia di Rizieri / M. Manteo 1923" and "Storia dei / Reali di Francia / Fioravante e Rizieri / Volume 2 / Michele Manteo."[28] The second notebook's final play, *sera* 51, is designated as the final play of the entire cycle, and is followed by instructions in Mike's handwriting to pick up with "Copione 1" and "Copione 3," both of which refer to *Libro* 1

---

27 A late nineteenth-century critical edition of *I reali di Francia* (1872–1900), with an introductory essay by Pio Rajna, can be found online. Substantial selections translated by Max Wickert with the title *The Royal House of France* are also currently available online. For a brief introduction to Andrea da Barberino's life and works, see Allaire 5–13.

28 Although the cover of the first notebook gives the year as 1923, the inner cover, also in Mike's handwriting, says that it was written on April 27, 1935. That date is then repeated in another hand on the first page, followed by the date of October 9, 1939.

(*Copione* 3). Confirmation is provided by a description of the action beginning with the marriage of Pipino and Berta.

A third notebook in Agrippino's handwriting pertaining to the *Reali di Francia* cycle contains *serate* 1–23. It is missing the cover and initial pages, and thus opens with Act 1, scene 5 of *sera* 1, the play devoted to Constantine's conversion. The final pages are also missing, leaving off at Act 3, scene 1, of *sera* 23. Thus, it seems that this cycle preceding the Paladins of France was staged frequently enough that at least the first notebook warranted recopying due to wear and tear.[29]

Scripts Copied by Mike Manteo in Later Decades

Mike Manteo copied the Royals of France and Paladins of France cycles by hand in twenty-three notebooks from the 1960s to the 1980s. Unlike Agrippino, Mike documented the dates at various moments during his composition: the starting date of the Royals of France cycle is given as September 2, 1962 (inner cover of notebook 1), and the completion date of the Paladins of France cycle is recorded as March 1, 1986 (following *serata* 330 in notebook 23). Since Mike was not rewriting the plays in order to stage the cycle, this massive undertaking was a sheer labor of love. As he wrote to his sister Ida in a comment dated March 2, 1986, that is, the day following the recorded completion date of the cycle, he was very happy to copy the scripts even though he did not expect to see the plays ever performed again (notebook 21; Figure 2.2). He also occasionally supplied brief English translations that he appears to have authored himself.

The first five notebooks copied by Mike incorporate the 51 plays contained in Agrippino's two *Reali di Francia* notebooks, while notebooks 6–23 contain the Paladins of France cycle. Since Mike numbered his pages consecutively across the twenty-three notebooks, we can observe that the Royals of France cycle comprises pages 1–356 and the Paladins of France cycle extends from page 357 (notebook 6) to page 2,355 (notebook 23).[30]

---

29 These three notebooks, privately owned, have not been scanned to date. There are additional notebooks dramatizing chivalric narratives that are likewise privately owned and unscanned. Although they do not figure into the present study devoted specifically to the Paladins of France cycle, I hope to be able to devote attention to them in the future.

30 The remainder of notebook 23 contains the beginning of the *Guido Santo* cycle (pages 2,356–63), which then continues in typed notebooks. These latter notebooks, not yet scanned, are privately owned.

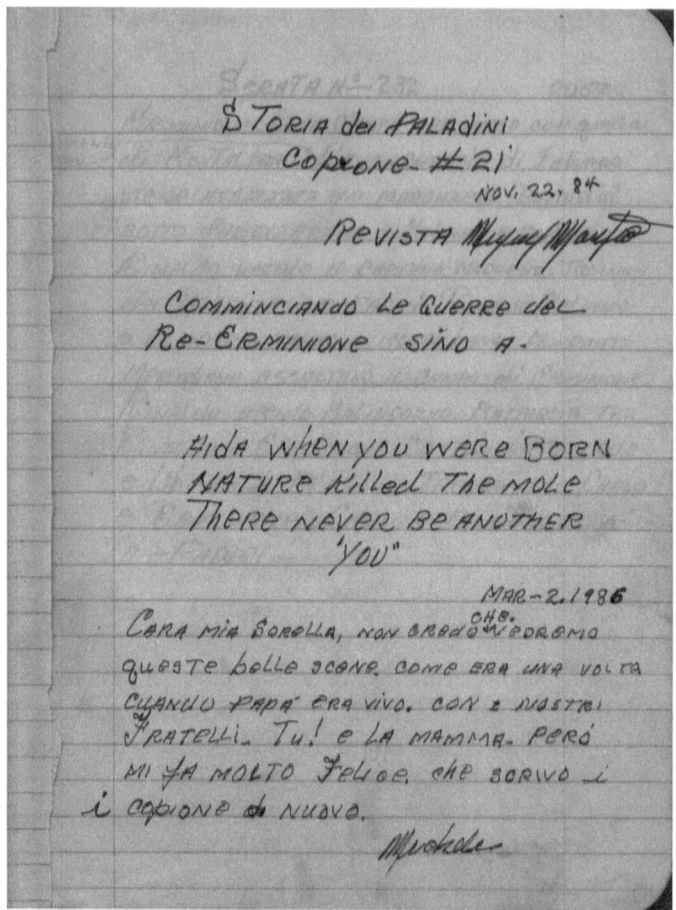

Figure 2.2 Mike Manteo's notebook 21, title page, note to his sister Ida. Courtesy of the Italian American Museum, New York City.

Although Mike's scripts can give us some idea of the full Paladins of France repertory, they cannot be taken as a substitute for the missing *Copioni* notebooks. First of all, Mike freely skips over material that he finds monotonous, as he acknowledges at the end of notebook 10.[31] On one occasion, he explains his criteria with reference to specific episodes: "I had to skip several chapters.

---

31 As he writes: "A bit of time that I steal / every evening after dinner / to write the new revision / of the Paladins of France - / and to remove many scenes / that are too monotonous. / You have to add the sauce / And eliminate the dregs. / Miguel Manteo."

Finding them very flat and monotonous, and I am not writing for the benefit of the public, I begin with the deeds of Angelica in the enchantment of Alcina" (first page of notebook 19).[32] Mike's set is incomplete not only because he intentionally skipped over plays, however, but also because he apparently needed to jump ahead due to missing source notebooks. In the midst of notebook 22, he jumps from *serata* 249 to *serata* 319 without explanation. The crossing out of the summary of *serata* 250 on the page in-between the two plays suggests that this summary was located at the end of the corresponding source notebook but that the subsequent source notebooks containing *serate* 250–318 were not available for Mike to copy.

Mike speaks not only of reducing but also of revising his father's scripts. On the first page of the first notebook, in fact, he announces that the material is "Revista da Michele Manteo" (also written elsewhere as "rivista" and "rivistata"). My comparison of a sampling of plays confirms that the phrasing often does not match that of Agrippino's extant notebooks. Some of the changes where the grammar is not that of a native speaker of Italian were presumably made by Mike himself since they are comparable to his comments in the margins.

The biggest surprise to me when examining Mike's notebooks was that he did not copy (or revise) the plays from the *Copioni* set (or from either of the other two partial sets, for that matter). For example, after the summary of *serata* 224 in the middle of notebook 19, Mike writes "Manuscript #19" and explains that he is picking up from "the next manuscript, which is No 20" (note inserted on an unnumbered page between pages 1,962 and 1,963). This Manuscript #19 cannot be from the *Copioni* set because the corresponding plays would have been located in the missing *Copione* 15. While beyond the scope of this study, the contents of Mike Manteo's notebooks and their relation to Agrippino's extant scripts merit further attention.

At the conclusion of the Paladins of France cycle at *serata* 330, Mike expressly bequeaths the scripts to his son Pino (in English): "Take them. If you show them to the right people—they could be priceless" (page 2,355, notebook 23). The originals, he goes on to say, are even more valuable because they date back to 1923. Mike concludes his note to his son by underscoring the uniqueness of the scripts: "You're the only one in the U.S.A. with these documents."

---

32 In this case, Mike skipped over the material corresponding to Ariosto's *Cinque canti*, included in the *Storia dei paladini*, and jumped ahead to episodes derived from Vincenzo Brusantini's *Angelica innamorata* (1550).

Part Two

SELECT PLAYS FROM THE PALADINS OF FRANCE CYCLE

INTRODUCTION

The *Storia dei paladini di Francia*, as noted earlier, combines several Renaissance chivalric works into a single continuous narrative of interlacing episodes. Lodico wove together stories in chronological order, supplied additional background and explanatory details to fill in narrative gaps and smooth out contradictions among the source texts, and sometimes related new adventures to further develop the plot. Despite the resulting sense of both cohesiveness and comprehensiveness, the many source texts incorporated into this massive prose compilation were written in different geopolitical environments and convey distinct ideological perspectives. Thus, the worldview of any particular episode inevitably takes its starting point from the source text.

The eight plays presented in Part Two—from the appearance of Angelica of Cathay in Paris to the final battle of three against three on the island of Lampedusa—are drawn from the central portion of the *Storia dei paladini* which follows the plot of Boiardo's *Orlando Innamorato* and Ariosto's *Orlando Furioso*. These two source texts have a prominent place in the cycle as a whole. As Carocci has pointed out, the entire repertory of the *Storia dei paladini* is constructed around the nucleus of the "'beautiful story' of Orlando in love and then furious" (*Il poema che cammina* 51). What is announced by Boiardo as an embarrassing parenthesis in Orlando's heroic trajectory—that is, the paladin's enamorment of Angelica of Cathay and subsequent disregard of his duty to king and *patria*—becomes in Lodico's hands "the pivotal point around which the rest of the narrative revolves: the heart and nerve center of the story" (51). In the process, "whereas many other poems are shattered, dismembered and modified, the Boiardo-Ariosto core is faithfully reproduced in its entirety and right down to the details, following the particular narrative arrangement of spacetime of the authors without modifications, displacements, or cuts" (51).

Boiardo's late fifteenth-century *Orlando Innamorato* created a literary sensation by purportedly exposing a scandalous history: the hitherto stalwart Frankish paladin actually deserted both the emperor Carlo and his own wife Alda to traverse the globe as a would-be Arthurian knight errant seeking to win the affection of the beautiful princess of Cathay. The *Innamorato*'s interlacing narrative also introduces new characters from Asia, Africa, the Middle East, and Europe who interact in myriad ways, from armed conflict to friendship and romance. Although Boiardo does not refute the eventual tragic fate of Carlo's rearguard at the battle of Roncevaux, he provides an alternative vision in which knights and damsels undertake adventures across the entire stretch of the known world motivated not by religious or ethnic difference but by universal impulses such as love, ambition, and empathy, and by the desire for glory, honor, justice, or revenge.[1] The Frankish emperor is involved exclusively in defensive warfare: from sending allied troops to assist the Saracen king Marsilio in the defense of Spain from the East Asian king Gradasso of Sericana to defending his own kingdom against both Gradasso and the North African emperor Agramante of Biserta. Warfare is no longer envisioned as a civilizational clash between Christians and Saracens as in the quintessential Carolingian epic, but is caused by the limitless desires of overreaching sovereigns.[2]

Ludovico Ariosto was not the only author who set out to continue the poem left unfinished with Boiardo's death in 1494.[3] He was, however, the only one to write a masterpiece that for several centuries overshadowed that of his predecessor. Revising a claim made by the *Innamorato*'s narrator to recount "the largest and the fiercest fight, / [...] / that verse or prose have ever told" (*OI* 2.30.1), Ariosto opens his poem asserting that "of Orlando I will also tell / Things unattempted yet in prose or rhyme" (*OF* 1.2). Indeed, as indicated by the modified title, in Ariosto's hands, Orlando goes from being hopelessly in love (*innamorato*) to being stark raving mad (*furioso*). Stunned that Angelica has ceded her virginity to another man, the jealous Orlando loses not only his mind and his identity as a Frankish paladin, but sheds his very humanity in the process and wanders across distant lands

---

[1] For the record, Boiardo refutes the veracity of the battle of Roncevaux in his *Historia imperiale* by adhering to Einhard's account in which the Frankish rearguard was routed by local Basques rather than Saracens.

[2] Following the terminology of the time period, I employ the term "Saracen" when referring to literary characters rather than historical Muslims. The words "Islam" and "Muslim" were virtually unknown in western European languages prior to the sixteenth century (Tolan, xv).

[3] The *Orlando Innamorato* was an instant success, leading not only to frequent reprintings but also to five continuations by three different authors (not counting Ariosto) with only one definitely appearing after the first edition of the *Orlando Furioso*. For the publication history of Boiardo's poem, see Harris, *Bibliografia dell'Orlando innamorato* and "L'avventura editoriale dell'*Orlando innamorato*."

like a ferocious beast wreaking havoc upon anyone and anything in his path. He only regains his sanity with the help of his friends, primarily Astolfo, and God, who, as we subsequently discover, had caused the paladin's insanity as punishment for his errant ways. Orlando's recovery makes possible the definitive victory of Carlo's Christian forces over the allied invaders from Africa and Asia in a war that increasingly takes on the tenor of a religious crusade.

Agrippino's traditional public had an advantage over most contemporary readers beyond the immersive experience of the actual puppet plays with all the performative elements that letters on a page cannot replicate. The intimate knowledge of the stories that they brought to every performance allowed them to understand each word and action within a vast web of meaning. Today, by contrast, no one can attend the Paladins of France cycle in its entirety since even in Sicily the *opera dei pupi* repertory is very limited, and few will have had the occasion to read the multivolume *Storia dei paladini* or the Renaissance chivalric works upon which this prose adaptation is based.

The critical apparatus that accompanies the eight selected plays aims to provide the essential literary context as well as to investigate the process of adaptation stretching from the Renaissance poems to the dramatic scripts. While the introductions preceding each translation are primarily concerned with the immediate narrative background, the comparative analyses that follow delve more deeply into the transformation of the stories as they pass from Boiardo's and Ariosto's poetry to Lodico's prose and subsequently to Agrippino's theatrical adaptation. Given that Agrippino diverged from "il libro" with reluctance, as we saw in his hesitancy to rewrite the death of Rinaldo's sons at Roncevaux, the scenes in which he does refashion the narrative take on added significance. Since transformation is an integral part of the process of retelling epic stories throughout the centuries, of interest is not the variation per se but rather the ways in which the change affects the meaning conveyed.

Locating Boiardan and Ariostan Material in Agrippino's Scripts

The plays dramatizing episodes from the *Storia dei paladini* based on the *Orlando Innamorato* are centrally located in notebooks 11 to 13 of the *Copioni* set. The Boiardan material ranges from *sera* 151 (*Copione* 11) to the first scene of *sera* 184 (*Copione* 13). The total number of full plays corresponding to Boiardo's poem is thus 33 (*serate* 151–183), exactly one-tenth of the total Paladins of France cycle consisting of 330 plays.

Plays ultimately derived from the *Orlando Furioso* begin near the end of *sera* 183 (*Copione* 13) and continue to *sera* 210 (the final play of *Copione* 14). Since *Copione* 15 is missing, the number of extant full plays corresponding to Ariosto's poem is 27 (*serate* 184–210). Given that the contents of *sera* 210 bring us almost to the end of the material derived from the *Orlando Furioso*, the total number of plays corresponding to the *Orlando Furioso* in the *Copioni* set can be estimated to be just under 30. Together, then, Boiardo and Ariosto (via the *Storia dei Paladini*) would have provided the narrative for almost one-fifth of Agrippino's Paladins of France cycle.[4]

Plays corresponding to the Boiardan and Ariostan sections of the *Storia dei paladini* can also be found in Agrippino's handwriting in *Paladini* 7 and 8. This set contains the *Orlando Innamorato* material in its entirety, ranging from *sera* 153 in *Paladini* 7 to *sera* 185 in *Paladini* 8. The latter notebook also contains 11 plays derived from the *Orlando Furioso* (*serate* 185–195).

Agrippino's Recourse to Poetry from the *Orlando Innamorato* and *Orlando Furioso*

In the plays translated below, Agrippino turns to Boiardo's original poem on various occasions to render the dialogue in *ottava rima* stanzas rather than following Lodico's prose (see Chapters 3–5). For the plays ultimately derived from the *Furioso*, however, Agrippino only resorts to poetry on the one occasion in which he already finds the verses in the *Storia dei paladini* (see Chapter 8). Since the eight plays presented in this volume are only a fraction of the 33 plays corresponding to the *Innamorato* and 27 extant plays corresponding to the *Furioso*, it is worth examining Agrippino's recourse to poetry in the full Boiardan-Ariostan sequence for greater context.

There are three ways in which Agrippino inserts poetry into his prose plays. The first, and the most conservative, is to reproduce it where he finds it in the *Storia dei paladini*. Lodico typically copies verses from the original poems when the characters are portrayed reading text in various formats. On these occasions, Agrippino adheres closely to the passages as quoted in his nineteenth-century source. For the *Innamorato*, this includes the following:

- Five stanzas from the book that Orlando consults during an adventure devised by Morgana in Act 1, scenes 1 and 3, of *sera* 168 (*Copione* 12), corresponding to *OI* 1.24.28–29 and 46–48.

---

4 This is a general estimate. A more precise ratio would have to take into account additional scenes within these plays (corresponding to episodes inserted into the *Storia dei paladini*) not based on the Renaissance poems.

- The six-verse inscription and four-verse warning during Brandimarte's adventure in Febosilla's palace in Act 1, scenes 4 and 5, of *sera* 178 (*Copione* 12), corresponding to *OI* 2.25.56 and 2.26.6 (4–8).
- The two-verse warning to Mandricardo about Hector's shield at the Fonte della Fata in Act 2, scene 1, of *sera* 179 (*Copione* 12), corresponding to *OI* 3.2.8 (7–8).

For the *Furioso*, Agrippino appears to be following the *Storia dei paladini* with minor variations in spelling in the case of Medoro's two-stanza poem celebrating his love for Angelica in *sera* 198 (*Copione* 14), discussed in Chapter 8.

On other occasions, Agrippino departs from the prose *Storia dei paladini* to quote directly from the original poems. This occurs relatively frequently in the plays based on the *Innamorato*:

- Rinaldo's one-stanza response to Balugante's interpreter and five stanzas of Angelica's speech during her conversation with Carlo in *sera* 152 (*Copione* 11), discussed in Chapter 3.
- Astolfo's speeches regarding Gano (one stanza) and the Magonza clan (four verses) in Act 2, scene 5, of *sera* 154 (*Copione* 11), corresponding to *OI* 1.3.13 and 19 (4–8).
- The conversation of five stanzas and six verses between Rinaldo and Gradasso concerning a proposed single combat in Act 2, scene 6, of *sera* 156 (*Copione* 11), corresponding to *OI* 1.5.7–12.
- Rinaldo's four-stanza speech relaying his desperation at sea in Act 1, scene 7, of *sera* 157 (*Copione* 11), corresponding to *OI* 1.5.48–50, 52.
- The conversation between Astolfo and Gradasso (three and a half stanzas) prior to their single combat in *sera* 159 (*Copione* 11), discussed in Chapter 4.
- The conversation between Orlando and Agricane (twenty stanzas) during their combat in *sera* 165 (*Copione* 12), discussed in Chapter 5.
- The debate between Orlando and Rinaldo (nine and a half stanzas) at Albracca in Act 3, scene 3, of *sera* 168 (*Copione* 12). These stanzas, not presented in order but recombined into a new sequence, correspond to *OI* 1.26.61, 1.27.16–19, 1.26.63, 1.27.31–32, 33 (1–4), and 34.

By contrast, Agrippino directly quotes Ariosto in only one of the extant plays corresponding to the *Furioso*:

- Two verses when a messenger (here, Fiordispina) tells Sacripante the identity of the knight who bested him (Act 1, scene 3), six verses when Rinaldo confronts Sacripante (Act 1, scene 3), and two stanzas plus three verses when Argalia chastizes Ferraù (Act 1, scene 6), in *sera* 184 (*Copione* 13), corresponding to *OF* 1.69 (7–8), 2.3, and 1.26 (6–8)–28.

Agrippino's most inventive use of *ottava rima* stanzas is original poetry inserted as dialogue to fit the surrounding action. This occurs on two occasions when elaborating scenes based on the *Innamorato*:

- Angelica's conversation with Carlo following her appearance in *sera* 152 (*Copione* 11). This exchange not only contains five stanzas reproduced from the *Innamorato*, as noted above, but also interweaves six and a half stanzas with no known antecedent, as discussed in Chapter 3.
- The first-person speech by a demon (here, Nucalone) to Malagigi explaining the scheme set in motion by Angelica's father in Act 1, scene 2, of *sera* 153 (*Copione* 11). In this case, Agrippino devises five original stanzas elaborating on Boiardo's third-person account (*OI* 1.1.36–40).

There are no occurrences of this practice in the extant scripts derived from the *Furioso* narrative.

In the cases outlined above, most of the plays that incorporate verses not found in the *Storia dei paladini* correspond to *Innamorato* episodes. These are generally moments that warrant heightened attention, such as conversations between adversaries that reveal aspects of each combatant's character. The exceptional recourse to original poetry serves to further develop one of the high points of the entire Paladins of France cycle: the dramatic entrance of Angelica in the Parisian court and the ensuing revelation of her father's plot.[5]

Editions of the *Orlando Innamorato*, *Orlando Furioso*, and *Storia dei paladini* Used in the Comparative Analyses

As noted above, we have the good fortune of knowing that Agrippino used Leggio's expanded version of the *Storia dei paladini* printed in Naples by Bideri in 1909 (Appendix 3). The fragile state of the bound three-volume book in the family's possession, however, precludes frequent handling. Given the conformity across the many successive editions of Leggio's version, I based my comparative analysis on the recent 1993–2000 edition.[6] Unless otherwise

---

5 For the record, Agrippino does not limit his recourse to poetry to the parts of the script ultimately derived from Boiardo and Ariosto. His selective incorporation of poetry throughout the scripts is another area that invites future research.

6 Napoli indicates that this conformity includes the Bideri 1909 edition and the Celebes 1971–72 edition upon which the 1993–2000 edition is based (Pasqualino, *Rerum palatinorum fragmenta* 19n). I also verified that the passages I cited from the 1993–2000 edition were likewise present in the Bideri 1909 edition. The single discrepancy I found (beyond minor variations in spelling or punctuation) is noted in the course of my analysis.

stated, all citations are from this readily available edition. For the chapters under discussion, I also compared Leggio's expanded version to Lodico's original 1858–1860 edition. In the rare cases in which there were divergences, I distinguish between the two authors. Where Leggio simply reproduced Lodico's wording, I refer to Lodico as the author following common practice.

Agrippino's extant library does not include a copy of either the *Orlando Innamorato* or *Orlando Furioso*, thus making it impossible to know which editions of the poems he used when incorporating verses into his scripts. When citing from these two poems, I generally use the modern translations of Charles S. Ross and Barbara Reynolds, respectively. For the comparative analyses, however, I also reference two earlier Italian editions of the *Innamorato* for reasons that warrant a brief explanation.

Lodico based his prose adaptation not on Boiardo's original poem but on Francesco Berni's sixteenth-century *rifacimento*, a Tuscan rewriting that had become the only version published for centuries until Antonio Panizzi sought to recuperate Boiardo's poem in 1830–1831. I generally leave aside Berni's *rifacimento* in order not to introduce another layer of rewriting for each episode before arriving at an analysis of Agrippino's scripts. For instances in which Lodico's text was based on a variation in Berni, however, I point this out in the course of the discussion.

When Agrippino reproduces stanzas from the *Innamorato* that are not present in the *Storia dei paladini*, he draws alternately from both Boiardo's poem and Berni's *rifacimento* (as discussed in Chapters 3–5). It seemed critical, therefore, to consult editions of both that predated his composition. I have opted to cite from two early nineteenth-century editions that are readily available online: Antonio Panizzi's 1830–1831 edition and an 1806 edition of Berni's *rifacimento*.[7]

My Translation, Formatting, and Editorial Choices

In translating the plays into English, I aimed to convey the original meaning as closely and clearly as possible. I therefore provide a literal rendering whenever feasible, with occasional recourse to idiomatic expressions in English that capture nuances of meaning that would have been lost in a word-for-word translation.

Regarding punctuation, I took a practical approach. Since the original script served as a blueprint for the recitation, it has sparse and inconsistent

---

[7] The links to both editions are provided in the Works Cited. For the record, Panizzi's edition of the *Innamorato* comprises the second through fifth volume of a nine-volume publication that includes the *Orlando Furioso* and extends to 1834.

punctuation. I inserted commas and periods where this would lead to more immediate comprehension. However, I avoided adding punctuation to every sentence which would have, in my view, transformed the script from a vehicle for oral performance to a sanitized academic document. Anyone wishing to read and study the handwritten originals will soon be able to consult the notebooks online.

The formatting of the translation attempts to evoke the look of the original pages rather than following the current standard formatting for a dramatic script. At the same time, however, the arrangement of the text on the printed page is but an approximation. There is also an aesthetic quality to the handwritten manuscripts that cannot be replicated in typewritten form.

I would also like to note that there is some variation in the names of characters and places referred to in the Renaissance epics, the *Storia dei paladini*, and Agrippino's scripts (for example, Ranaldo and Rinaldo, Maganzesi and Magonzesi, Albraca and Albracca). In my comparative analyses, I therefore adhere to the variant used in the particular passage under discussion without drawing attention to the different spellings unless a shift of meaning is involved.

Finally, I have used three different forms of typographical emphasis for poetic passages in plays based on the *Orlando Innamorato*. Text not present in either Boiardo's poem or Berni's *rifacimento* (from single words to full stanzas) is highlighted in bold font to draw attention to Agrippino's own contribution. For stanzas that combine wording from both sources, where Berni's rewriting diverges from Boiardo's precedent, I have placed in italics the words corresponding to Berni and have underlined those corresponding to Boiardo in order to make evident the puppeteer's lexical choices. Since the actual editions used by Agrippino are presently unknown, this highlighting is intended only as a suggestive indication of his *modus operandi*.

Chapter 3

THE ARRIVAL OF ANGELICA OF CATHAY IN PARIS (*SERA* 152)[1]

Introduction

Boiardo's *Orlando Innamorato* begins with two East Asian rulers threatening Carlo's Frankish realm. The first to be announced—although his arrival is long postponed—is King Gradasso who ventures all the way from Sericana (southeast Asia) to France in order to acquire Orlando's sword Durlindana and Ranaldo's horse Baiardo. This impetuous acquisitive desire prompts the author's opening reflection on very powerful rulers who crave what they do not possess: "The greater obstacles there are / to reaching what they would obtain / the more they jeopardize their realms, / and what they want, they cannot gain" (*OI* 1.1.5). The second ruler, King Galafrone, has sent his daughter Angelica and son Argalia from Cathay (China) to France to challenge all the knights present at Carlo's international tournament to undertake a new joust with the princess herself as the prize. Since Argalia possesses an enchanted lance that knocks his opponent from the saddle at the slightest touch, the proposed contest is simply a ruse to lead the unwary knights, both Christian and Saracen, back to Cathay as prisoners. Although Galafrone's scheme will not go as planned, Angelica's presence in Paris and sudden departure nonetheless have the effect of shifting the conceptual frame of the poem from Carolingian epic to Arthurian romance in its opening canto.

The contemporary Sicilian puppeteer Mimmo Cuticchio asserts that "the Arrival of Angelica is one of the traditional public's most loved episodes because the most beautiful stories, interlaced with love, duels, and enchantments, begin from this point" (50). The episode is also one of the most iconic moments in Italian literary history. It was subject to creative imitation in subsequent fiction, such as the entrance of Armida in Torquato Tasso's epic *Gerusalemme Liberata* and,

---

1 The play translated and discussed in this chapter is found in *Copione* 11. To compare versions, see the plays 153 and 154 in *Paladini* 7 and *serata* 166 in Mike Manteo's notebook 14.

extending into the novel, that of characters named Angelica in Giuseppe Tomasi di Lampedusa's *The Leopard* and, beyond the Italian tradition, Salman Rushdie's *The Enchantress of Florence*. The episode remains one of the most frequently staged plays in Sicilian puppet theater today.[2] As we shall see below, Agrippino endeavored to make his theatrical version particularly memorable. After interweaving Gradasso's exploits and the interactions between the Christian Franks and Saracen Spaniards in Acts 1 and 2, the puppeteer devotes all of Act 3 to elaborating the arrival of Angelica in ways that go well beyond the *Storia dei paladini*'s prose adaptation.

Translation

Evening 152[3]

Gradasso at the enchantment of Sibilla fights four giants, cuts down the tree, attains Samson's armor, and vows to attain Durlindana and Baiardo. The Spaniards arrive in Paris and attempt to mock Rinaldo, who gives a worthy answer. Angelica arrives in Paris. Great *scena in fondo* (deep stage). Orlando and others fall in love with Angelica. Gradasso gathers his troops in order to have Baiardo and Durlindana.

Characters
4 giants for the enchantment
Sibilla [Sibyl] sorceress
Tree with armor
Gradasso later with Samson's armor
Rosetta
Old baron and captain for Gradasso
Angelica dressed in luxurious clothing
A dragoman (interpreter) for the Spaniards
Grandonio
Serpentino della Stella, son of Balugante
4 giants for Angelica (if they don't fit in the deep stage, they can be done tomorrow)

---

2 For videotaped examples of this episode in Sicilian *opera dei pupi* and other forms of theater, see the "Arrival of Angelica" page on the eBOIARDO website (https://edblogs.columbia.edu/eboiardo/authors/boiardo/angelica).

3 "Domenica" is written in pencil to the left of "Sera 152," and "Dom" is written in orange to the right, suggesting that on separate occasions the performance was scheduled to take place on a Sunday.

Act 1°

1 Paris

Carlo   has not let up in his preparations to hold a grandiose celebration

2 Walls

Gradasso   This is the castle of enchantment, I will enter
Four giants try to prevent him, he chases them away, the walls change into a garden, he sees the armor, he approaches

3 Garden

Tree with armor hanging from it
Gradasso   cuts down the tree, Sibilla approaches
Sibilla   Oh arrogant one, you believe you have won, whereas two things are missing here, Durlindana and Baiardo, and their masters sell their wares at a high price, and just as you cut down the tree in one fell swoop, in the same way your own head will fall
Gradasso   I am not afraid and I vow to attain Durlindana and Baiardo

4 Zaragoza

Marsilio   Having learned about the tournament in Paris, he departs with his brothers and Ferraù, Grandonio, and Serpentino, son of Balugante, in order to shame Carlo

5 Trebisonda

Malaguerra and Rosana
Who are happy in their own realm[4]

---

[4] Malaguerra, a character invented by Lodico to be Rinaldo's adopted son, is destined in the *Storia dei paladini* to be murdered by neighboring kings soon after his marriage (which in Agrippino's dramatic adaptation took place the previous evening, *sera* 151). Agrippino's inserted scene makes a point to evoke instead Malaguerra's happiness as a newlywed even as the main focus of events shifts elsewhere. Carocci explores additional alternative endings to his story in traditional puppet theater in "Metamorfosi del tema dell'esilio." For more on this character, see Carocci, *Il poema che cammina* 44–48, and Cavallo, "Malaguerra".

6 Siricana

Gradasso	with the armor of Samson, and Rosetta, to whom he narrates his attainment of the armor. But it is still not everything; for now, Rosetta, it is necessary for me to rest

7 Paris

Carlo	with the paladins, arrival of the Spaniards
Carlo	honors them

8 Siricana

Gradasso, Rosetta, Captain, and an old baron

Gradasso	My barons, as you well know, I attained this armor from the enchantment of Sibilla, but this armor, which belonged to Samson, is not complete without Baiardo and Durlindana, and I want to win them as well
Old Man	points out the greatness of Carlo and the valor of Orlando and Rinaldo
Gradasso	To defeat those two I alone suffice
Rosetta	You forget that a single knight bested you
Gradasso	Luck is not always the same, and, moreover, I will bring 50,000 men with me[5]
Knight	That is not enough to fight Carlo
Gradasso	Put him in prison. He begins to gather troops, he sends for the giant Alfrera, and his first goal is Spain in order to clear the route [to France]

Act 2

1 Paris

Gano with the Spaniards

Gano	Faithful friends, I am happy to see you. You did not come for the festivities but to shame Carlo and perhaps we will have the opportunity
Balugante	I would like to laugh at Rinaldo since, being poor, he cannot compete with us. I will send over a dragoman, which means interpreter, to say that since we are foreigners and we don't know the customs, we

---

5 In Boiardo's original and Lodico's prose compilation, the number is 150,000.

THE ARRIVAL OF ANGELICA OF CATHAY IN PARIS (*SERA* 152)

Gano	want to know whether the poor man or the rich man is honored here. If he says the poor man, we will scorn Carlo who invited us, if he says the rich man, then we will hold Rinaldo in contempt
Gano	Bravo, great idea, send him immediately
Balugante	Michele, come forward
Michele	arrives
Balugante	You who are a polyglot, that is, a connoisseur of many languages, you shall go to Rinaldo and ask in my name if here the poor or the rich are honored, since as a foreigner I do not know the custom (Michele leaves)
Marsilio	We will wait for the answer

2 Room

Rinaldo	I saw the Spaniards laughing, scoundrels, we'll see who knows how to hold his own in the joust
Dragoman	Sir, I am sent to you by Balugante, who is unfamiliar with the customs of France and wants to know whether the poor or the rich are honored
Rinaldo	laughing, **I answer you** with a **serene face and therefore say to you, Sir**, <u>report</u> to Balugante and *tell him that I told you that, if I have studied well our customs,* gluttons at the table and *women* in bed <u>are on many occasions caressed by us,</u> but where it is necessary to demonstrate valor according to his merit each one is honored

3 Paris

Gano	and the Spaniards, return of the dragoman, he reports the answer
Marsilio	The thief is bold, he does not give in to anyone

4 Room

Orlando	has seen the Spaniards bantering, he calls Rinaldo and tells him to make sure the festivities are a success and to not let anyone upset him (they go to the court)

5 Paris

Carlo	with everyone, he orders that dinner be served, inviting all the nobles

Act 3 a single scene

A deep stage

Everyone seated at the table

Carlo
This is a day of great celebration and festivities
Today for me and for my empire
Today my sad court rejoices
Today brings to each of us joy and jubilation
(voices, long live the foreigner)

Carlo inquires, and learns about the arrival of a knight and a woman with four giants who want to introduce themselves (Angelica and Argalia on their knees)

Carlo
Please do rise, damsel and knight,
Who with your presence honor my court,
The one with a dignified and proud bearing
The other with her magical beauty
Tell me who you are, handsome warrior,
And you, damsel, what is your name?
Say who you are and why you have come here
And we will listen to you attentively and in silence

Angelica
Magnanimous lord, your virtue
And the exploits of your paladins,
Which *have already come to everyone's ear,*
Indeed, they have crossed the confines of the sea,
Make me hope that the hardships
Of *these* pilgrims – having come from the ends of the earth
Filled with a passionate and joyful desire for honor –
Will not be in vain.
And so that I make manifest to you,
As briefly as possible, the reason
That **compelled me** *to witness* your celebration,
Know that this is Uberto of the Lion,
Of noble birth and heroic deeds,
Banished from his kingdom without reason.
I, who was driven out together with him,
Am his sister. Angelica is my name.
A two-hundred-day journey beyond the Don River,
Where *our home used to be,*
The news *reached* us
About the preparations for this tournament,

THE ARRIVAL OF ANGELICA OF CATHAY IN PARIS (SERA 152)   79

Whence we passed through many provinces
Only to **arrive** *into your presence*
And to attain, if possible, the prize
That has been proclaimed, made of roses
Which is certainly much more pleasing
Than any expensive gift whatsoever
Because to a magnanimous heart enough is given
If it attains the mere title of honor.
For this reason my brother is prepared
To give everyone an account of his valor,
And no matter whether you are Christian or Saracen
He will wait for you at the Rock of Merlin
The battle shall be with this condition:
All who want to enter it should know
That anyone who is thrown from the saddle
Cannot undertake any other defense
And, without uttering another word, will remain a prisoner.
But whoever *will succeed in* unhorsing Uberto
As a reward will attain my person
And he will depart along with his giants. [cfr. *OI* 1.1.24.28]

Carlo **Thank you first of all for the homage**
You paid to my entire court,
Counts, knights, valets, and pages,
To whom you gave the label of valorous,
Courtesy is part of your birthright
And you deserve a better fate,
You, Angelica, and Uberto del Leone,
Who is worthy of comparison to you.
It does not surprise me that my great fame
And that of my paladins have reached you
Because each of us has a strong desire
To immortalize his name,
And girding the great branch of the oak
Makes every one of us immensely happy.
We do not seek anything other than justifying
That renown that makes us famous.
Therefore I see my knights almost making a sign
To accept the challenge you've just announced
Because, as everyone knows, in my realm
A challenge has never been refused.

	It is not for the reward of having you as a prize,

It is not for the reward of having you as a prize,
But to respond to the invitation,
And it seems they are urging me to let them measure themselves
against the knight who today has come to challenge us.
And so I accept your challenge, damsel,
In the name of the warriors here present,
And we hope that fortune comes to them
And that they may warrant the fame spread to the winds
That throughout the whole world and everywhere shouts out
That Carlo and his men are very powerful.
Now I invite you both to stay with me
Or, if you prefer, you may go.

Angelica I render my thanks, oh great emperor,
For the courtesy you have now granted me.
And it will be my great and immense honor
to give myself to Uberto's victor.
Let everyone therefore demonstrate his valor,
Since you all have excellence reflected in your faces.
Now it is time for me to take my leave,
So peace and farewell to each of you
(They depart)

Orlando in love, wants to be the first
Ferraù wants to go
Carlo also wants to try, everyone wants to go
Carlo Let's all go into the hall and there we shall decide

Comparative Analysis

Act I (scenes 2, 3, 6, 8): "Gradasso at the enchantment of Sibilla, fights four giants, cuts down the tree, attains Samson's armor and vows to attain Durlindana and Baiardo."

Gradasso di Sericana appears for the first time in the *Orlando Innamorato* as a sovereign reigning in the Far East who is "so powerful in wealth and state / and so impressive in his strength" that "he held the world of no account" (*OI* 1.1.4). Even if his stated goal is to acquire through his valor a very particular sword and horse, the king's ambition and destructive force are potentially limitless. In fact, he is so confident in his own valor that he believes he can single-handedly "conquer and destroy / all the sun sees, all sea surrounds" (*OI* 1.1.7).

While the *Orlando Innamorato* does not supply any specific motivation for Gradasso's plan beyond his hubris and overreaching personality, the *Storia dei paladini* elaborates a backstory set in Asia. Taking his cue from Boiardo's remark that Gradasso's armor once belonged to the Herculean figure Samson (*OI* 1.4.71), Lodico devises a new adventure in which the king of Sericana attains the armor of the Biblical hero in an enchanted garden presided over by a fairy named Sibilla (7: 71). Yet Gradasso finds that his triumph is not complete when Sibilla promptly informs him of the existence of the famous sword and horse. The fairy's subsequent assertion that Gradasso is not up to the task only serves to fuel the king's desire to prove himself. This new episode thus ties together in one storyline three quintessential symbols of chivalry (armor, horse, and sword) as it establishes Gradasso's pedigree as a romance hero prior to his departure for Europe.[6]

Agrippino dramatizes the backstory invented by Lodico. In Act I, moreover, he alternates Gradasso's exploits leading up to his invasion of France (scenes 2, 3, 6, and 8) with a succession of events taking place in Europe: (1) in scene 1, Carlo discusses the preparations for an international tournament in Paris; (2) in scene 4, the Spanish Saracen king Marsilio states his intention to shame the French emperor at the upcoming joust—a motivation not stated in Boiardo's poem, where we first encounter Marsilio already at the Parisian banquet—and then leaves Zaragoza with his entourage; and (3) in scene 7, Carlo honors Marsilio in Paris.

Agrippino's use of interlacing, a hallmark of Boiardo's poem that was adopted in the successive romance epic tradition as well as in the *Storia dei paladini*, increases the play's dramatic tension.[7] The alternating between scenes taking place at opposite ends of the globe (Sericana and Spain) creates the sense of parallel threats to Carlo's Frankish realm on the part of aggressive sovereigns to the east and south. In addition, Agrippino's attribution of hostile intentions to Marsilio, even though in the context of a joust, reinforces the sense of real danger ensuing from Gradasso's departure from Sericana with 50,000 troops. Thus, Act I sets up a situation of impending peril descending upon France even before we learn of the king of Cathay's duplicitous use of his two children to capture all the knights gathered at the Parisian tournament.

---

6 For a more detailed analysis of Gradasso's introduction in the *Storia dei paladini* in relation to Boiardo's original, see Cavallo, "Boiardo's Eastern Protagonists in Giusto Lodico's *Storia dei paladini di Francia*" 150–57.

7 See Praloran for Boiardo's innovative use of interlacing with respect to the previous chivalric tradition.

Act II (all five scenes): "The Spaniards arrive in Paris and attempt to mock Rinaldo, who gives a worthy answer."

The action of the *Orlando Innamorato* begins with "numberless people" arriving in Paris "from every region, every nation" (*OI* 1.1.9) for a tournament proclaimed by Carlomagno. Surprisingly, King Marsilio's Spanish Saracens, the perennial enemies of the Frankish Christians in the Carolingian epic tradition, are prominent among the invited guests at the opening banquet. Yet the fact that Boiardo brings these two traditionally hostile groups together to break bread rather than cross swords does not mean that the poet feigns ignorance of their conflictual history. The narrative of their encounter, oscillating between mistaken assumptions and shared understanding, moves away from religious difference and places the focus instead on both the challenges and the possibilities of interacting across linguistic and cultural divides.

In an atmosphere of potential ill feeling due to different social customs (*OI* 1.1.13), Marsilio's brother Balugante initiates a conversation (via an interpreter) with the Christian knight Ranaldo over the ways of the Frankish court. The Spanish Saracen is somewhat disingenuous, however, since he approaches Ranaldo with a provocative question after noticing that Carlo's advisor Gano di Maganza and his clan had enraged the paladin by mocking him for the poverty of his clothing. Invited to explain whether in the French court honor is won by wealth or by valor (*OI* 1.1.17), Ranaldo laughingly deflects the provocation through an off-color but effectual remark equating the Maganzesi with gluttons and prostitutes: "Whores in bed and, at dinner, gluttons / most often get endearments from us, / but when our valor is on view, / let each receive the honor due" (*OI* 1.1.18). In essence, Ranaldo's retort unequivocally affirms his society's adherence to a code of chivalry despite Gano's apparent threat to such values. Moreover, as Charles Ross points out, Ranaldo "does not merely give his own opinion but, recognizing Balugante's ability to read behind the signs, says that Balugante will be able to induce from what he will witness in the upcoming tournament that valor is the ultimate value in Paris."[8] Thus, the first dialogue in the poem—and the only one preceding the appearance of Angelica—turns a potentially confrontational situation into an occasion to affirm a chivalric ethos that can be shared across national, ethnic, cultural, and religious borders.

The *Storia dei paladini*'s prose adaptation of the scene brings its latent hostility to the surface. First, Lodico takes care to shield Rinaldo in the readers' eyes

---

8 Ross, "Boiardo and the Derangement of Epic" liv.

from the brunt of the Magonzesi's mockery by first asserting that the knight scorned ostentation: "Rinaldo, however, who had little esteem for pomp, was secretly mocked by those of Pontieri because he did not dress as splendidly as they did" (7: 75). Bolugante, for his part, is now found together with the Magonzesi (7: 75), suggesting that his baiting question no longer results from an autonomous observation of Rinaldo's state of mind but instead is prompted by his complicity with Gano's treacherous clan. Indeed, whereas in the *Innamorato* Balugante was so perceptive that he "practically divined his thoughts" (*OI* 1.1.17) by simply observing Ranaldo's face, now he intervenes only after witnessing a less self-controlled—albeit more dramatically expressive—Rinaldo "murmuring out loud" as he "displayed his irritation at being derided." The Saracen Spaniard's question about the Frankish court's value scale no longer concerns the abstract nouns "wealth" and "valor," but, in this case, following Berni's *rifacimento*, is rephrased to contrast two distinct groups of people. Yet whereas Berni had pit "the rich" against "the good" (1.20), Lodico makes his opposition between "the rich" and "the poor."

Lodico adds a conflictual tone to the interaction as well. In the *Innamorato*, Ranaldo's witty response to the provocation follows immediately and, by implication, effortlessly. In the *Storia dei paladini*, however, Lodico focuses on Rinaldo's motivation before the knight opens his mouth to speak, revealing that his seemingly cheerful manner is a conscious effort to restrain himself in deference to the explicit request of his cousin Orlando: "Rinaldo wanted to be on good behavior because his cousin Orlando had pleaded with him not to show offense at any remarks and to suffer in silence for his sake" (7: 75–76). Lodico's Rinaldo, now only smiling rather than genuinely laughing, prefaces his reply by stating that if Bolugante "has studied the ceremonies well, he must certainly already know" what is about to be explained to him.[9] Rinaldo's allusion to his interlocutor's critical acumen now concerns the past rather than the upcoming joust, thereby implying that the latter's question is superfluous and thus in bad faith.

Despite this increased underlying hostility, Lodico concludes the exchange with a comparable reaffirmation of courtly values. He follows Berni in replacing Ranaldo's reference to "whores in bed" (*OI* 1.1.18) with the tamer "women" and also substitutes "gluttons" with "those who enjoy themselves at the table." This bowdlerization does not, however, alter the gist of the punchline that true

---

[9] Berni's Rinaldo had introduced the phrase "if I have studied the ceremonies well" (1.21), but Lodico's shift of the verb from the first to the second person turns the focus to Balugante's feigned ignorance of Frankish custom.

valor is what matters at the end of the day. As in the *Innamorato*, moreover, the conversation between the two knights is interrupted by music in the hall signaling the onset of the banquet.

Agrippino, as noted above, has already introduced a more confrontational tone on the part of Marsilio in Act I via the king's stated antagonistic reasons for attending Carlo's joust (scene 4). The puppeteer then devotes the entirety of Act 2 to the relations between the Frankish Christians and Spanish Saracens as well as among the knightly contingents in Carlo's court, developing the action on both external and domestic fronts beyond what is presented in either the *Innamorato* or the *Storia dei paladini*.

Regarding international relations, the composition of the group ridiculing Rinaldo (Figure 3.1) undergoes a further transformation. If in the *Innamorato* the "traitors" who "mocked him and laughed among themselves" (*OI* 1.1.15) were exclusively Gano and the Maganza clan, and in the *Storia dei paladini* Bolugante is in their company, in Agrippino's refashioning it is now Gano who stands together with a group of Saracen Spaniards throughout the episode. Indeed, Act II opens announcing the association of "Gano with the Spaniards" and proceeds with a lengthy speech in which Gano first confirms that they

Figure 3.1 Rinaldo (Appendix 1, #14). Manteo Family Marionettes, 1991. Collection of the Staten Island Museum.

all share the same goal of shaming Carlo and then hopes for their success. This serves not only to reinforce Gano's treacherous nature and foreshadow the nefarious alliance with Marsilio that will lead to the fatal ambush of the Frankish rearguard at Roncevaux, but it also leads to Balugante's subsequent provocation of Rinaldo in a more direct way than the simple mention of his physical proximity to the Magonzese clan in the *Storia dei paladini*. With Gano in the midst of the Spaniards, Balugante becomes almost a mere instrument of the Magonzese's machinations. Indeed, Gano immediately supports Balugante's impulse by praising him for the plan and instructing him to dispatch his interpreter to Rinaldo without delay ("Bravo, great idea, send him immediately").

Given this new configuration, Agrippino makes a point to show that the object of Rinaldo's indignation has also shifted: "I saw the Spaniards laughing, scoundrels, we'll see who knows how to hold his own in the joust." Since in this refashioning Rinaldo reacts to being taunted not by Gano's clan but by the Spaniards, the situation is more dramatically conflictual when someone from that latter group has his interpreter approach the angry paladin. This also serves to underscore the self-discipline exercised by Rinaldo since his unflappable response will now be knowingly directed at one of the derisive instigators.

Agrippino also further elaborates the dialogue between Balugante's interpreter and Rinaldo. First, Balugante explicitly acknowledges that he wants to laugh at Rinaldo's expense and that his question regarding the treatment of the rich and the poor at the Frankish court is a trap intended to force the paladin to bring the Spaniards' scorn either upon himself for his relative poverty or upon Carlo for the emperor's implied disregard of magnificence. In formulating Rinaldo's reply, Agrippino does not use Lodico's paraphrase but goes back to Boiardo's original poem to produce an *ottava rima* stanza almost verbatim.[10] The rhyme and rhythm of the eight verses in the midst of a prose drama lends greater importance to the moment and increases the effect of Rinaldo's quick thinking and verbal bravura.

While Balugante is engaged in this vocal confrontation, Agrippino shows Gano in cahoots with Marsilio as they wait together in the wings for the outcome. Rinaldo's declaration that everyone is honored according to his merit is therefore a response not just to Balugante but to Gano and the group of Saracen Spaniards as well. Accordingly, whereas Agrippino's

---

10 In *Sera* 152 of *Copione* 11, following Berni and Lodico, Agrippino uses "women" (Act 2, scene 2). In *sera* 154 of *Paladini* 7, however, he reproduces the brashness of Boiardo's original reply in his verse "gluttons at the table and whores in bed" (Act 1, scene 6).

sources break off the conversation immediately following Rinaldo's reply, the puppeteer continues the scene by having the interpreter report back to Gano and the Spaniards. Marsilio's begrudging acknowledgement that "the thief" has gained the upper hand in this battle of wits reveals a certain admiration for Rinaldo's ever-present resourcefulness: "The thief is daring, he does not give in to anyone."

Orlando also plays a revised part in Agrippino's scene. Whereas in the *Storia dei paladini* we are told that Orlando had previously beseeched Rinaldo to behave wisely, as mentioned above, Agrippino directly stages the paladin's plea to Rinaldo to prevent a potential escalation of the tensions in order to guarantee the success of the festivities. This not only reinforces Orlando's good judgment, political acumen, and public diplomacy just as he is about to lose it all upon Angelica's entrance, but it also reminds us of the habitual solidarity between the cousins when external forces do not set them at odds. The Act concludes with Carlo inviting everyone to the banquet.

The entire second Act, then, carefully develops a balance between the sinister complicity of a malicious Gano and the Spanish Saracens, on the one hand, and the level-headed control of the situation by Rinaldo (with the support of Orlando) on the other. The addition of inimical forces prompting Balugante's provocative question serves to darken the moments preceding Angelica's entrance by underscoring the domestic threat at the heart of Carlo's court together with an undercurrent of external hostility from Saracen Spain—both of which will ultimately lead to the battle of Roncevaux, the climactic tragic moment of the Paladins of France cycle. Yet such concerns are swept aside when a more immediate and unprecedented danger presents itself.

Act III (single scene): "Angelica arrives in Paris. Great deep-set stage. Orlando and others fall in love with Angelica."

The *Innamorato*'s opening dialogue between Ranaldo and Balugante already revealed that alliances and hostilities among Franks and Spaniards are not necessarily determined by group identity. The arrival of a character from outside the Carolingian epic sphere will change the focus of the entire poem and show that the world extends far beyond the homeland of the characters heretofore gathered in Paris. As the feast is about to begin in the banquet hall, the narrator announces the imminent arrival of something new that will astound everyone: "But there appeared a prodigy / that left him − with the rest − amazed" (*OI* 1.1.20). That "prodigy" is the princess Angelica who, collapsing the customary framework of Carolingian geography, arrives in Paris from the "ends of earth" (*OI* 1.1.24), referred to in travel time as a two-hundred-day journey beyond the Don, the river traditionally considered the dividing line between Europe and Asia.

Boiardo does not distinguish Angelica by any exotic features in appearance or dress, but simply states that her superlative beauty diminishes that of all the other women in the room (*OI* 1.1.21).[11] Every knight without exception falls in love with her in one fell swoop, thereby providing the first concrete example of the poem's opening assertion of love's universal power (*OI* 1.1.2). This simultaneous collective enamorment nullifies any perceived territorial, cultural, or religious distinctions among those present. Angelica thus brings the amorous and magical world of Arthurian romance crashing into the Carolingian epic universe, thereby enacting "Boiardo's well-known operation of converting Carolingian heroes to Breton values."[12]

At the same time, however, Angelica's mission, like Gradasso's announced quest, poses an existential threat to the Frankish realm. Although the princess hides that menace by proposing a joust in which the victor will win her as a prize, the Christian wizard Malagise soon learns that King Galafrone plans to capture the knights present at Carlo's tournament and then transport them to Cathay as prisoners, eventually bringing about the death of the Frankish emperor and destruction of his kingdom (*OI* 1.1.36). Even though this plan is thwarted, Angelica's intervention will nonetheless draw Carlo's foremost paladins from Latin Christendom across the expanse of Asia, leaving the Frankish realm vulnerable to attack from all sides for the remainder of the poem.

Although the *Storia dei paladini* introduces minor variations that subtly temper the agency of the princess and enhance the portrayal of her brother, Lodico's rendition of Angelica's arrival in Paris follows the *Innamorato* narrative fairly closely.[13] Agrippino adheres to the original poem even more strictly since he leaves aside the *Storia dei paladini*'s exclusive prose narrative and draws directly from Boiardo's *ottava rima* stanzas. The switch to poetry occurs only exceptionally in Agrippino's scripts, as noted previously, signaling the heightened importance of the matter at hand. The centrality of this dramatic moment is also underscored by two additional factors:

---

11 As Sharon Kinoshita notes, "In the conventional language of epic [...] the Saracen queen is indistinguishable from any beautiful woman of high station" (184). See Marco Villoresi for Angelica in relation to previous Saracen females in fifteenth-century Italian literature.

12 The quotation reports the words of Simona Cremante (5).

13 For differences in the treatment of Angelica in the *Storia dei paladini* with respect to the opening of the *Orlando Innamorato* in both Boiardo's original and Berni's *rifacimento*, see Cavallo, "Boiardo's Eastern Protagonists in Giusto Lodico's *Storia dei paladini di Francia*" 141–50.

this single scene occupies all of Act 3 and it employs the rarely used deep stage that suggests momentous action through greater depth of field and the potential to present more characters together.

Agrippino had already established Angelica's primacy in the previous evening's play when preparing her departure from Cathay. In Act 3 of *sera* 151, when King Galafrone instructs his two children to travel to France accompanied by four giants, he first addresses his daughter. His speech emphasizes that it is precisely Angelica's beauty that will make it possible for him to put his plan in motion: "Your beauty provides the opportunity for me to adorn my kingdom with the armor stripped from the paladins, you will leave with Argalia who will bring the enchanted lance, to you a ring that will vanish all enchantment" (*sera* 151, Act 3, scene 2).

Agrippino's direct use of Boiardo's verses in *sera* 152 is not unprecedented. Carocci notes that Catanese puppeteers—whose scripts included poetry in *ottava rima* to a greater extent than those of their Palermitan counterparts—likewise inserted Angelica's speech directly from *Orlando Innamorato* 1.1.24–28 rather than paraphrasing Lodico's prose version.[14] Nonetheless, a close examination of the dialogue in Act 3 reveals some unique features, beginning with the fact that Angelica's words combine both Boiardo's original (*OI* 1.1.24–28) and Francesco Berni's Tuscan rewriting (1.27–31)—sometimes interwoven within the same stanza. Such an *ars combinatoria* would have required not only close attention to two different versions of the *Orlando Innamorato* but also a discriminating literary and dramatic sensibility.

Agrippino's most remarkable creative innovation in Act 3, however, is that he did not limit himself to the *Innamorato*'s five stanzas when devising this scene, but inserted an additional six and a half *ottava rima* stanzas not found in Boiardo's poem. Moreover, the stanzas in Act 3 do not commence with the citation of Angelica's verses but rather with a new speech that Carlomagno (Figure 3.2) pronounces to his guests:

This is a day of great celebration and festivities
Today for me and for my empire
Today my sad court rejoices
Today brings to each of us joy and jubilation

Whereas earlier Agrippino had added initial verses to Rinaldo's abovementioned retort in order to reach the full eight verses required of

---

14 *Il poema che cammina* 148. She points out, moreover, that Gaetano Crimi's son-in-law Raffaele Trombetta copied the stanzas from Boiardo's original poem rather than from Francesco Berni's *rifacimento* (154).

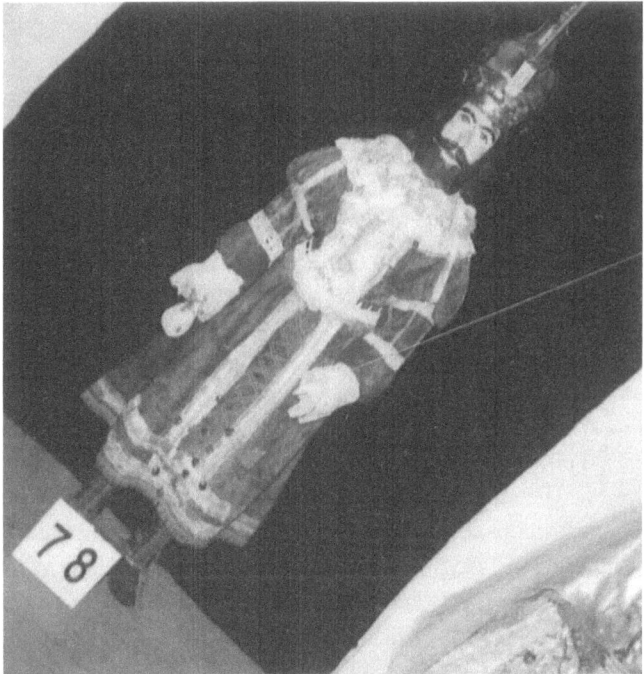

Figure 3.2 Carlomagno (Appendix 1, #78). Manteo Family Marionettes, 1991. Collection of the Staten Island Museum.

an *ottava rima* stanza, here he purposefully cuts off Carlo at the midpoint of this opening stanza, leaving the listener with an aural sense of rhythmic incompleteness.

Voices shouting "Long live the foreign woman!" interrupt the emperor's speech as a knight, a damsel, and four giants appear on stage. When Carlo resumes speaking, he now addresses the pair kneeling before him with a full *ottava rima* stanza. Although the welcome speech is addressed to both newcomers, it is only Angelica who replies, thus maintaining her prominence as in Boiardo's original. Agrippino replays her entire speech in five full *ottava rima* stanzas that, as noted above, intricately combine the wording of Boiardo's original and Berni's *rifacimento*.

In the *Orlando Innamorato*, Angelica's direct discourse is followed by the narrator's third-person description of Carlo's response without any part of the emperor's long-winded speech cited directly:

In a long speech, King Charles the Great
offered the damsel his response.
He spoke for as long as possible.
He talked, he stared; he stared, he spoke;

he granted everything she wished.
He sealed each one of her requests
and swore his service on the Bible.
Then she, her brother, and the giants left.

(*OI* 1.1.35)

Agrippino, by contrast, stages Carlo's reply to Angelica in a first-person *ottava rima* speech that serves to counterbalance Angelica's declaration. Although Carlo is a misguided and even tyrannical ruler elsewhere in the *Storia dei paladini*, the sentiments he expresses in this scene bring to the fore the chivalric values that were expected of the Frankish court. Additionally, fashioning Carlo as a counterpart to Angelica in the poetic verse form of Boiardo's poem serves to further develop the scene's poetic, theatrical, and emotional impact.

Carlo is not the only character for whom Agrippino provides original *ottava rima* stanzas in this scene, however. Not only does the puppeteer reproduce all five stanzas from Angelica's speech, but he concludes her exchange with Carlo by attributing to her a sixth stanza not found in the *Innamorato*. In this way, the Cathayan princess not only has the last word prior to her departure, but she also regains her verbal primacy over Carlo who had spoken for a total of only five and a half stanzas. After the almost hypnotic eleven-and-a-half stanza exchange between the two protagonists, the play ends with an eruption of voices of those who want to vie for the princess in the joust.

Chapter 4

THE DUEL BETWEEN ASTOLFO AND GRADASSO DI SERICANA (*SERA* 159)[1]

Introduction

Following Angelica's sudden departure from France (discussed below), Astolfo of England wins the Parisian tournament initially proclaimed by the emperor thanks to his serendipitous acquisition of Argalia's lance whose magical property remains unknown to him. Yet rather than receiving recognition for his victory, Astolfo is wounded from behind "with / much treachery and false deceit" (*OI* 1.3.21) and then slandered by Gano and the Maganzese clan. In response to the resulting scuffle, the gullible emperor precipitously orders Astolfo's arrest rather than duly honoring him as the champion. After languishing in prison for months, the English knight is released only after Gradasso's army (having passed through Spain) wages a direct assault on Paris and overcomes Carlo's forces. With the fate of Christendom in the balance, the newly freed Astolfo courageously challenges the king of Sericana to single combat. Following his unexpected defeat of Gradasso, Astolfo also gains a moral victory over Carlo by censuring the emperor's poor judgment and departing from his realm (*OI* 1.7.37–71).

Most of the action in *sera* 159 concerns the vicissitudes taking place in Paris: from Gradasso's conquest of the city in the absence of Orlando and Rinaldo to its liberation at the hands of Astolfo (Figure 4.1). In addition, however, Agrippino also weaves in the romance adventures undertaken by both Orlando and Rinaldo far beyond Europe while Paris is under siege. The play's interlaced episodes not only thereby take place in three very disparate regions of the globe, but they also contrast the actions and mindset of the three paladins: (1) Astolfo, after single-handedly saving France, remonstrates with Carlo for having acted against justice; (2) Orlando, having deserted the emperor (and his own wife Alda) out of love for Angelica, falls under the spell of a fairy

---

1 The play translated and discussed in this chapter is found in *Copione* 11. To compare versions, see plays 160 and 161 in *Paladini* 7 and *serata* 173 in Mike Manteo's notebook 15.

Figure 4.1 Astolfo (Appendix 1, #12). Manteo Family Marionettes, 1991. Collection of the Staten Island Museum.

in the Caucasus region and thereby loses his identity; and (3) Rinaldo, having been whisked away against his will on the morning of a scheduled duel against Gradasso in Spain, arrives on an island in the Indian Ocean where he resists the allure of an enchanted site whose construction is attributed to Angelica.

Translation

Evening 159[2]

The battle outside Paris continues. Gradasso returns to the battle and takes Oliviero and Ugiero prisoner. Astolfo, freed by the people, challenges Gradasso with Argalia's lance and defeats him. Liberation of

---

[2] Although the day of the week is not marked at the beginning of this play, the subsequent play, *sera* 160, has "Lunedì" (Monday) written next to it in orange pencil. Since *sera* 152 had also been scheduled for a Sunday, this is a further indication that during this period the plays were performed seven days a week.

the paladins. Orlando falls victim to the spell of Drogantina. Rinaldo, invited to Angelica's garden, flees in order not to hear her.

Characters
1 Jailer
Lance for Gradasso
Christian and pagan captains
1 Woman or even Nucalone himself
Drogantina with a glass

Act 1°

1 Field

Gradasso	has bandaged his wounds from Baiardo, returns to battle[3]

2 Battle

Gradasso	takes prisoner Oliviero and Ricciardetto and other paladins. Grandonio and Ferraù are engaged in a massacre

3 Paris

Galerana	weeps over Carlo's imprisonment and continues to follow the battle on the field
Ugiero	arrives and, upon hearing the danger, goes back down to fight even though he is wounded

4 Battle

Gradasso	takes Ugiero prisoner, night falls, he retreats

5 Prison

Astolfo	complains about his imprisonment
Jailer	Don't you know that Paris is besieged by Gradasso who has a giant called Alfrera? There are also the Spaniards
Astolfo	If I had been free, I would have gained victory
Jailer	I'll discuss it and we'll see how to set you free

---

3 Rinaldo's very intelligent horse Baiardo had previously given Gradasso a couple of swift kicks when the usurper attempted to grab his bridle (see also *OI* 1.7.25–27 and *Storia dei paladini* 7: 156), thus demonstrating that he was perfectly capable of defending himself from Gradasso in Rinaldo's absence.

6 Field

Gradasso	commands that Carlo be brought to his presence (they bring Carlo)
Gradasso	Do not believe, oh Carlo, that the desire for empire drove me here; it was rather for Baiardo that Rinaldo promised to me before he fled. If you give me Baiardo, I will set everyone free
Carlo	Bring Ricciardetto to me (they bring Ricciardetto)[4]
Carlo	This fellow, oh Ricciardetto, will free us in exchange for Baiardo. Go into the city and take hold of him and then bring him to the field

Ricciardetto goes

7 Paris

Galerana	cries (voices of the people, that Astolfo be set free)
Galerana	has Astolfo released and entrusts the people [to him]
Astolfo	goes into the square and gathers together the people in order to go into battle (he leaves)
Galerana	prays for victory

8 Square

Ricciardetto, having arrived to take Baiardo, sees Astolfo assembling the people (Astolfo arrives)

Astolfo	What are you doing here?
Ricciardetto	Carlo sent me to take Baiardo and give him to Gradasso
Astolfo	By what right does Carlo want to give away Baiardo? Now I will go down and you'll see what I shall do
Ricciardetto	I must obey Carlo
Astolfo	Hey there, soldiers, put this disobedient one in prison! (The soldiers arrest Ricciardetto)
Astolfo	has the people go out and sends a messenger to challenge Gradasso to a duel by lance

9 Field

Gradasso	receives the messenger, goes to see the prisoners to find out who is this Astolfo fellow

---

4 Agrippino changes the name of the knight to Ricciardetto.

Act 2°

1 Pavilion

	Carlo with all the imprisoned paladins
Gradasso	Astolfo sent me a challenge, who is he?
Gano	A buffoon not worth anything
Oliviero	He won the latest joust
Gradasso	to Gano, you call the winner of a joust a buffoon? Guards, beat this fellow with rods
Ugiero	Actually, Astolfo is a valorous knight and very graceful; in addition, he is a great lord and very modest
Gradasso	However he may be, I will take my lance and accept the challenge

2 Walls[5]

Astolfo	blows his horn and then shouts
	Come here, **Gradasso**, and whoever is at your command,
	I want to make a mountain of you all!
	Bring that favorite of yours, Alfrera,
	And, if you like, a host of a thousand
	Bring Marsilio and bring Balugante
	And Serpentin with them and Falsirone
	And that Grandonio who is such a great giant
	That another time I treated him like a castrated horse,
	Bring that Ferraù, who is so arrogant
	Contrary to the custom of his nation,
	And finally bring everyone under your command,
	Let all of you be **united** and I alone shall stand!
Gradasso	**The emperor** Gradasso **comes before you**
	Given that I don't know who you are
	But asking about your status
	Gano **told** me you're a buffoon
	Others told me that you're a **forthright** lord,
	Graceful, well-built, courteous and modest
	And that you are imbued with courage and valor.

---

5 For the stanzas copied directly from the *Orlando Innamorato* in this scene, see Berni's *rifacimento* (7.59–63), in turn drawn from Boiardo's original (*OI* 1.7.50–54).

	Whatever the case may be, I have no interest in this;
	Instead, I'm here to honor you always
	But let me make it perfectly clear and evident
	What I aim to take from you (and you may, if you will, be valorous)
	I want Baiardo and nothing else
Astolfo	**One** who pays the bill without the innkeeper
	(**I say to you**) will come back to pay it again.
	I thank you for your proposals
	And because you know how to speak with such courtesy
	I don't want your fall to cost you anything
	Other than releasing the prisoners
	And I will let you go free
	To respond to courtesy with courtesy
	(they pledge their word and engage in combat)
Gradasso	defeated, he declares himself a captive and invites Astolfo to the field to release the prisoners
Astolfo	I accept, we will go among the prisoners and do not say that you were beaten by me because I want to have some fun (they leave)

3 Pavilion

	The imprisoned paladins
	Astolfo arrives with Gradasso
Astolfo	You see, oh Carlo, where you find yourself for having listened to Gano, and tomorrow you will be hanged. I gave Baiardo to Gradasso and I am in his service since I was wrongly kept in prison
Carlo	You disobeyed me
Astolfo	Enough, you are all free, I won, only Gano will remain a prisoner. He recounts Gano's vileness to Gradasso
Carlo	beseeches Astolfo to free him
Astolfo	I will free him as long as he goes back to prison when I say the word
Carlo	promises
Gradasso	releases his army and the Spaniards
Carlo	enters Paris

4 Forest

Orlando	sees a bridge, blows his horn, Drogantina arrives
Drogantina	Nobody can pass without drinking this water (offers a glass)
Orlando	drinks and gives himself over to love for Drogantina

5 Forest

Malagigi	makes a garden appear in order to attract Rinaldo and take him to the enamored Angelica, and he sends Nucalone in the form of a woman to incite him

6 Forest

Rinaldo	I don't know where I am anymore since I left that damned ship (he sees a woman)
Lady	Knight, if you want to come, I invite you to enter the fortress surrounded by a beautiful garden, the fortress is called joyous
Rinaldo	accepts and they leave

Act 3°

1 Paris

Carlo	holds festivities in honor of Astolfo and gives the island of Ireland to him as a gift

2 Garden

Rinaldo	and the woman, he admires that place, asks to whom it belongs
Woman	To a woman who is crazy about you, she is Angelica
Rinaldo	hears Angelica's name and flees

3 Zaragoza

Marsilio	cannot figure out how Gradasso was defeated
Balugante	Brother, I heard that Poliso, the prisoner left by Gradasso, seduced my daughter, and I sent messengers to beseech Drogantina to trap them in her enchantment and make them suffer[6]

4 Forest

Rinaldo	runs away in order not to hear the name of Angelica

---

[6] For the use by Lodico (following Bernardo Tasso) of Boiardo's Dragontina in an episode not derived from the *Innamorato*, see Napoli (in Pasqualino, *Rerum palatinorum fragmenta* 161n).

Comparative Analysis

Act I (scenes 1–9): "The battle outside Paris continues. Gradasso returns to the battle and takes Oliviero and Ugiero prisoner."

Act II (scenes 1–3); Act 3 (scene 1): "Astolfo, freed by the people, challenges Gradasso with Argalia's lance and wins. Release of the paladins."

In the *Orlando Innamorato*, after overpowering Carlo's remaining defenders and conquering Paris, Gradasso confirms that his ultimate goal is not to occupy foreign lands but only to attain Baiardo and Durlindana (*OI* 1.7.42–43). His captive Carlo is ready to cede Rinaldo's horse to him in the absence of its owner and promises to seek Orlando's sword as well. Astolfo, however, has other ideas.

After having been forgotten by virtually everybody, Astolfo is finally released when all the prisons are opened in the wake of Gradasso's occupation of Paris (*OI* 1.7.37–38). Ironically, therefore, it is only thanks to the king of Sericana's victory over Carlo that the maligned English prince regains his freedom. Having "assumed the royal staff" upon his release, Astolfo promptly has Ricardo arrested when the latter comes to seize Baiardo (*OI* 1.7.44). He then challenges Gradasso to a duel since Carlo "did not own the steed" and therefore cannot cede the horse to anyone else (*OI* 1.7.45).

When Gradasso asks Carlo about his challenger, Gano immediately follows the emperor's statement about Astolfo's high social status with a disparaging description of him as a jester who merely entertains the court and who should therefore be disregarded. Although the king of Sericana concedes that Gano has expressed himself adroitly ("You speak well"), he chooses to base his judgment on the current situation in which Astolfo is prepared to single-handedly face an opponent who has already bested the entire Christian army (*OI* 1.7.46–47). Carlo's hasty arrest of Astolfo after the Parisian joust appears even more culpable when compared to Gradasso's ability to intuit the valor of the English prince despite Gano's deprecation of him.

Both Gradasso and Astolfo observe a universal code of chivalry throughout their encounter, beginning with the mutual courtesy they show each other as they negotiate the conditions of the battle. After Astolfo unhorses his opponent against all odds, Gradasso could have easily refused to concede defeat, especially given the fact that his forces had already overpowered those of Spain and France. Yet as soon as he rises to his feet, the East Asian king nobly declares Astolfo the victor and releases all the Frankish prisoners to him in accordance with their prior agreement (*OI* 1.7.57).

While Astolfo's valorous action has "saved / the emperor and the Christian faith" (*OI* 1.7.69), of even greater dramatic interest is the scene that ensues after his victory. With Gradasso's complicity, the English prince plays a trick on Carlo by temporarily pretending that he lost the duel, converted to Islam, and agreed to head East to serve as Gradasso's court jester thanks to Gano's recommendation (*OI* 1.7.61). The rest of the Franks, moreover, have been assigned to serve Gradasso in various other capacities: "He wants Ogieri waiter, Charles / dispenser, Olivieri cook!" (*OI* 1.7.61).

Although Astolfo is angry that the emperor had "usurped" Baiardo and "wrongly" imprisoned him (*OI* 1.7.59–60), he does not let the joke go on for too long (*OI* 1.7.64). Disclosing his victory to his dismayed compatriots, he asks the king's pardon for his impudence. He even frees Gano of his own accord with the provision that the latter will become his prisoner for four days whenever he should so wish. Astolfo does not cease speaking truth to power, however: following the reconciliation, he announces his plan to leave the court permanently—"I'll never come to court again"—and to set out in search of his cousins Ranaldo and Orlando (*OI* 1.7.65). Even though Carlo tries to bribe him by promising him sovereignty over the Irish—something English rulers historically coveted—Astolfo refuses to take the bait.

With respect to the exchange between Ranaldo and Balugante discussed in the previous chapter, the level of both internal criticism and external solidarity has increased. Gano and his clan are the catalyst for the injustice committed in both instances; however, while their initial mockery of Ranaldo's attire merely incited the paladin's momentary irritation, their treacherous treatment of Astolfo following the joust leads to the latter's lengthy imprisonment. If in the first case Carlo appeared simply oblivious to the Maganzese clan's offensive behavior, in the second he is directly responsible for a grievous injustice. Indeed, the emperor's arrest of Astolfo demonstrates that Ranaldo's confidence in the primacy of chivalric valor had been overly optimistic: despite Astolfo's victory in the very joust in which Ranaldo had hoped to get the better of Gano's clan, Carlo not only fails to reward the English prince but imprisons him indefinitely on false charges and is subsequently willing to cede Ranaldo's horse to Gradasso.

The *Storia dei paladini* refashions the episode of Astolfo's release from prison and liberation of Paris to underscore the heroism of the unjustly treated paladin and the ignominy of Carlo's evil counselor as well as to give more agency to the citizenry. Indeed, whereas Boiardo describes the populace "in flight" and "running wild" (*OI* 1.7.29) and all the prisons opened randomly—even using the passive tense in "the prisons [were] emptied" (*OI* 1.7.37)—Lodico depicts the population actively seeking out Astolfo:

> Grief, fear, and pity kept the population of Paris awake all that night, which came to the attention of Astolfo, who made known that if he had been free, Carlo with his people would not have been in such dire straits. Those people who had no longer remembered the Englishman's imprisonment, once they became aware of it, went to release him and each voluntarily submitted to his command, whereby Astolfo comforted those citizens, asserting that the new day would make the pagan repent of having dared so much; he then went to comfort the empress. (7: 157).[7]

Lodico thus creates a symbiotic relationship between the people who purposefully free Astolfo and the paladin who in turn comforts them and vows to save them from Gradasso.

Whereas in the *Innamorato*, moreover, Astolfo simply assumes command in light of the power vacuum (*OI* 1.7.44), Lodico has the people expressly place themselves under the paladin's leadership. Astolfo is thus not a self-declared authority but the people's chosen ruler when he comes upon Riccardo intending to seize Baiardo and "has him put in prison" on the grounds that Carlo did not have the authority to dispose of the horse. The English paladin, in fact, categorically states: "Carlo is not the owner of Baiardo."[8] This utterance in direct discourse underscores the inviolability of private property rights even under monarchical rule.

The *Storia dei paladini* likewise elaborates the ensuing scene in which Gradasso inquires about Astolfo's identity. Here Gano is the first to reply, calling Astolfo a "charlatan" and "court jester."[9] When Gradasso pursues the matter further, Carlo not only tells him that Astolfo is the son of the king of England, but also mentions in passing that he was imprisoned since the day he won the joust. When the envious Gano immediately chimes in to

---

[7] In Boiardo's poem, Astolfo makes a similar claim only after having been freed along with everyone else upon the opening of the prisons.

[8] I quote above the statement as found in Lodico's original (vol. 3, libro 7, ch. XI, 87) and Leggio's expanded edition used by Agrippino (vol. 2, ch. XXXVIII, 308). Interestingly, a subsequent editor, as evidenced by the most recent edition, reinforced the legal connotations of the principle by inserting the adjective "legitimate": "Carlo is not the legitimate owner of Baiardo" (7: 158).

[9] Berni had, on the contrary, reduced the scene so that Gano was not simply the first but also the only one to respond to Gradasso (7.55).

denigrate Astolfo yet again as "without worth," Gradasso promptly replies that he does not give credence to Gano's words. Astolfo, he argues, could not be "of little worth" since "your lord calls him the winner of the joust" (7: 159). In this way, Lodico not only depicts Gradasso refusing to believe Gano's slander but also calls to mind Astolfo's previous victory rather than simply his present courage.

The scene following Astolfo's defeat of Gradasso is developed even further. Whereas in the *Innamorato* Carlo was purportedly destined to be employed as a steward at Gradasso's court, Lodico's Astolfo imagines a far more drastic fate for him: "Tomorrow you will have the honor of being hanged in sight of your people with all of your men" (7: 160). Astolfo explicitly states, moreover, that it was Carlo's mistreatment of him that led him to enter Gradasso's service: "I have placed myself in his service, since you despise my service and have kept me a long time in prison" (7: 160).

Although here, too, Astolfo does not let much time go by before revealing the truth and asking Carlo's pardon for his behavior (7: 161), he is not quite as forbearing when it comes to Gano. Whereas in the *Innamorato* Astolfo's clemency toward Gano was unsolicited, here Gano is shown on his knees begging the forgiveness of Carlo before Astolfo agrees to free him. The terms, moreover, are not as favorable. Omitting Boiardo's reference to four days, Astolfo simply states that he will free Gano only "on the condition that however many times he asked for him to be imprisoned, Carlo would have to hand him over to him" (7: 161). Furthermore, Astolfo's motivation in freeing Gano is no longer his love for Carlo, but rather his desire to further humiliate the evil counselor.

A final modification deserves mention before we turn to Agrippino's dramatic and narrative choices. Since Carlo had publicly condemned Astolfo to prison, he now wants to publicly honor him. In this context, the offer of rulership over Ireland is no longer an unsuccessful attempt at bribery but rather a reward bestowed for exemplary service. Carlo is depicted "investing him with the lordship of all Ireland, acknowledging verbally and in writing that Paris had been freed from the cruelest enemy thanks to Astolfo" (7: 161). There is no mention of Astolfo's departure from France until later, where it is motivated solely by his desire to locate "his beloved cousin" (7: 173). Thus, even though Lodico develops the episode to accentuate Carlo's and especially Gano's culpability, he concludes with a reconciliation between the Frankish emperor and the English prince in which the latter's past service is abundantly remunerated.

Agrippino refashions the episode even beyond the details added in the *Storia dei paladini*. To begin, the play opens with four successive scenes reinforcing the desperate circumstances in which the Franks find themselves:

Gradasso and his allies carry out a massacre and take captive Carlo's most stalwart defenders. Agrippino also lends a greater epic quality and pathos to the drama by bringing to the stage the emperor's wife Galerana as she "weeps over Carlo's imprisonment and continues to follow the battle on the field" (Act 1, scene 3).

These initial scenes demonstrating Gradasso's complete victory over the totality of Carlo's available forces and the ensuing despair on the part of Galerana preface Astolfo's release from prison. Yet rather than simply reporting the paladin's liberation, Agrippino devises a new succession of scenes. He begins with a dialogue between Astolfo and his jailor in which the captive prince laments his imprisonment and asserts that he would have defeated Gradasso had he been free. The jailor's reply that "I'll discuss it and we'll see how to set you free" shows both his willingness to actively help Astolfo and his lack of agency to unlock the paladin's cell on his own initiative (Act 1, scene 5).

The second scene in the staging of Astolfo's release devotes additional attention to the citizenry. Whereas in the *Storia dei paladini* it was the people who, upon remembering Astolfo's imprisonment, "went to release him," in Agrippino's play the general public does not have the physical means to liberate the knight. Not only are they outside the structures of power, but they are quite literally outside the space of action since they do not physically appear on stage. Nonetheless, it is the people who set in motion Astolfo's release through the strength of their voices. The stage directions indicate that there is clamoring for the paladin's liberation: "voices of the people, let Astolfo go free" (Act 1, scene 7). In such choral moments which still occur in Sicilian puppet theater, the spectators hear multiple voices offstage repeatedly shouting the same phrase. This technique gives the impression of a large crowd without the need to assemble multiple puppets. The subsequent enactment of Astolfo's release in the same scene reveals that it is the people's raised voices rather than the jailor's efforts that provide the catalyst. But if the people do not directly free Astolfo, as in the *Storia dei paladini*, who does?

Whereas both Boiardo and Lodico envision a power vacuum in the city brought about by Carlo's capture, Agrippino brings another figure to centerstage: the empress Galerana. Carlo's wife was entirely absent from this episode in the *Orlando Innamorato* and only mentioned briefly as having been comforted by Astolfo following his release in the *Storia dei paladini*. Her onstage presence in Agrippino's play gives new importance to her role on both a thematic and practical level. As noted above, she was already introduced into the action in Act 1, scene 3, as she observed the battle and wept over Carlo's imprisonment. At the moment in which the people's voices are heard offstage calling for Astolfo's release, it is none other than Galerana who is once again onstage and who is therefore shown to be the privileged recipient of their plea. When Act 1, scene 7, opens, the stage directions indicate that the empress is alone and weeping, thus inviting spectators to emotionally identify with her distress. Upon hearing the people's voices, however, she immediately orders Astolfo's liberation and places the population under his care. The scene thus enacts the transformation of Galerana's role from that of Carlo's helplessly distraught wife to that of an acting sovereign responsible for the well-being of her people. In this way, moreover, Astolfo is granted his authority by no less than the empress herself. His first action upon his release is to gather the people and set out to confront Gradasso. Whereas the scene begins with Galerana weeping, it concludes with her praying for victory, thus foreshadowing the positive outcome made possible by a combination of the people's voices, her own decision-making, and Astolfo's fortitude.

This refashioning of Astolfo's release also colors his ensuing encounter with Ricciardetto (previously, Riccardo). Whereas the *Storia dei paladini*'s prose version had largely paraphrased Boiardo's account of the action (7: 158), Agrippino devises a verbal exchange to play out the conflict between Carlo's royal power and the paladins' right to their own property:

Astolfo   By what right does Carlo want to give away Baiardo? Now I will go down and you'll see what I shall do.
Ricciardetto I must obey Carlo
Astolfo   Hey there, soldiers, put this disobedient one in prison! (The soldiers arrest Ricciardetto)

(Act 1, scene 8)

Agrippino's staging of the moment in which Astolfo prevents Ricciardetto's seizure of Baiardo under Carlo's orders not only exploits the dramatic potential of the scene but also renders the political significance even more explicit. Astolfo's rhetorical question establishes that the issue at stake is one of rights. In his reply, Ricciardetto eschews the question of rights and shifts the discourse to one of obedience to political rule. Consequently, Astolfo, having been (temporarily) granted by Galerana the executive power of the dethroned emperor, uses Ricciardetto's own reasoning against him by accusing him precisely of disobedience at the present moment. This gives further credibility to the arrest of Ricciardetto by the soldiers despite Carlo's express wishes.

The dramatic refashioning continues in the following scene in which Gradasso, having learned of the new challenge, inquires about the identity of Astolfo:

Gradasso	Astolfo sent me a challenge, who is he?
Gano	A buffoon not worth anything
Oliviero	He won the latest joust
Gradasso	to Gano, you call the winner of a joust a buffoon? Guards, beat this fellow with rods
Ugiero	Actually, Astolfo is a valorous knight and very graceful; in addition, he is a great lord and very modest
Gradasso	However he may be, I will take my lance and accept the challenge

(Act 2, scene 1)

Gradasso's skepticism over Gano's assertion that Astolfo was a buffoon in the *Orlando Innamorato* had already passed to outright disbelief in the *Storia dei paladini*. Agrippino further develops the scene beyond his sources in order to stage the punishment of the evil counselor for his malicious impudence. Although Gano is the first to reply, he is prevented from uttering any further falsehoods as his statement is forcefully countered by two of Carlo's most stalwart knights. Here, in fact, it is Oliviero rather than Carlo who informs Gradasso of Astolfo's victory at the tournament. Gradasso, for his part, does not simply chastise Gano verbally but orders the guards to beat him with rods as well. This visually dramatic rendition gives the puppeteer the occasion to castigate Gano not only for his most recent defamation of Astolfo's character, but also implicitly for his earlier treachery that led to Astolfo's imprisonment in the first place. This added beating was no doubt to the liking of the traditional public who despised Gano for his repeated nefarious actions culminating in the betrayal that led to the battle of Roncevaux. Indeed, Manteo family members recall an incident during Agrippino's time in which an audience member shot Gano with a pistol and they had to suspend the performance and evacuate the theater.[10]

For the critical moment of the encounter between Astolfo and Gradasso, Agrippino leaves aside the *Storia dei paladini*'s prose narrative and draws directly from the *Orlando Innamorato* in an exchange of three and a half

---

10 Anecdotes abound regarding spectators' violent reactions to the Gano puppet in Sicilian *opera di pupi* (Napoli, "The Fratelli Napoli" 233; Pasqualino, *L'opera dei pupi* 114–15). For the customary, even ritualistic, burning of Gano following the battle of Roncevaux in the hand puppet tradition of Northern Italy, see Porta, *Gente di Sarina* 55–62 and "Riti e miti del Gano."

ottava rima stanzas. Astolfo's speech frames the interaction, with one full stanza at the beginning and conclusion, while Gradasso speaks for a stanza and a half in-between (Act 2, scene 2). This poetic rendition, adhering almost verbatim to the source, underscores the centrality of the scene through its rhythmic musicality. Where there is a discrepancy between Boiardo and Berni, Agrippino here follows the latter's *rifacimento*. The only meaningful lexical deviation from the poem is Gradasso's addition of the term "forthright" to describe Astolfo in the line "Others have told me that you are a forthright lord," thus subtly reinforcing the paladin's worthiness in the estimation of his peers.

Although Astolfo's defeat of Gradasso is prodigious in that it saves the entire Frankish realm, the most memorable moment of the play—as it was in the sources—is the verbal exchange initiated by the English prince in the wake of his victory to express his indignation. Following the *Innamorato* and the *Storia dei paladini*, *sera* 159 depicts the still enraged Astolfo playing a joke on Carlo by claiming to have lost the joust—thus purportedly leaving the Frankish court at Gradasso's mercy—and rebuking the emperor for his previous misconduct. Although Agrippino leaves out Astolfo's claim to have converted to Islam, perhaps too overtly sacrilegious for his audience, he retains the intensity of the political protest when describing Carlo's anticipated fate. Following Lodico, in fact, he announces the emperor's imminent execution by hanging:

Astolfo   You see, oh Carlo, where you find yourself for having listened to Gano, and tomorrow you will be hanged. I gave Baiardo to Gradasso and I am in his service since I was wrongly kept in prison
(Act 2, scene 3)

Such a drastic announcement could have sounded excessive in the context of Boiardo's original poem, but it is perfectly fitting in the context of the Paladins of France cycle where Carlo is constantly duped by Gano and even willing to execute his trusty paladins under the evil counselor's pernicious influence. Indeed, in a later episode based on Pulci's *Morgante*, Carlo orders Astolfo's death by hanging and it is none other than Gano who drags him to the scaffold.[11] Perhaps it is precisely in anticipation of this harrowing experience that Lodico and Agrippino envision the reversal of roles in Astolfo's imagination.

---

11 Astolfo is rescued at the last minute by Rinaldo. For a discussion of this episode in Pulci's *Morgante*, the *Storia dei paladini*, and Sicilian puppet theater, see Cavallo, "The Ideological Battle of Roncevaux."

Agrippino departs from both his sources, however, when staging the liberation of Gano. Whereas in the *Innamorato* Astolfo acts spontaneously for the sake of Carlo and in the *Storia dei paladini* he is prompted by Gano's pleading, here it is the emperor himself who beseeches Astolfo to free his brother-in-law. This request reinforces the sense of Carlo's unrelenting support of the treacherous Gano over the pursuit of justice. As in the *Storia dei paladini*, Astolfo will release Gano only on the condition of his indefinite imprisonment at any time in the future: "I will free him as long as he goes back to prison when I say the word" (Act 2, scene 3).

The conclusion of the episode in Act 3, scene 1, follows the *Storia dei paladini* in depicting the emperor's celebration and remuneration of Astolfo: "Carlo holds festivities in honor of Astolfo and gives the island of Ireland to him as a gift." Accordingly, the paladin's departure is postponed to a later evening where it is motivated solely by his desire to seek his cousin Orlando. Thus, despite Agrippino's aggressive treatment of Gano (the beating ordered by Gradasso, his future indefinite imprisonment to be determined by Astolfo) and equally harsh treatment of Carlo (his purported impending execution, his need to plead on Gano's behalf), the puppeteer nevertheless concludes with a public reconciliation between the Frankish emperor and the English prince. As the traditional audience would have known, however, there would be plenty of future occasions for tensions to flare up again within the Frankish court.

Act II, scene 4: "Orlando falls victim to the spell of Drogantina."

Orlando was so thunderstruck by Angelica upon her entrance into the banquet hall that when he hears of her disappearance after her proposed joust has gone awry, he sneaks out of Paris in disguise in order to seek her in the East. As he heads through the Caucasus region, he learns that Angelica has already returned to Cathay where she is besieged at the fortress of Albraca by the Mongol khan Agricane (discussed in Chapter 5). Yet as soon as the paladin sets off to her rescue, he encounters the fairy Dragontina who tells him that he must follow the custom of drinking from a crystal chalice she holds out to passersby. The magic beverage causes total forgetfulness of one's history and identity as it instills a state of passive worship and unconditional obedience. The unsuspecting Orlando thus becomes utterly subjected to the fairy's every whim and remains trapped in her garden without any recollection of his beloved Angelica, his ruler Carlo, his wife Alda, or even his own self: "He did not know how, why, or when / he'd come or if he was the Count" (*OI* 1.6.45). His loss of identity is combined with complete stasis, a pitiful situation for a knight who defines himself through his exploits.

In the *Storia dei paladini*—and consequently in Sicilian puppet theater— the fairy is renamed Drogantina to bring out the drug-like qualities of her potion rather than the dragon-like connotations of her nature. Lodico alters minor details of scenography (e.g., the crystal chalice becomes a cup of gold) and provides more descriptive narrative action. Orlando's drinking of the liquid, for example, is depicted with greater emphasis as he "ran to the goblet and guzzled down with great thirst all that was contained in that cup" (7: 147). Nonetheless, the plot basically follows that of the *Orlando Innamorato*.

In Agrippino's play, the subjection of Orlando to Drogantina is one of the instances in which most of the dialogue is left to improvisation. The scene reported in the script is comprised of just two lines of stage directions and a single line of dialogue in which Drogantina states her demand:

Orlando	sees a bridge, blows his horn, Drogantina arrives
Drogantina	Nobody can pass without drinking this water (offers a goblet)
Orlando	drinks and gives himself over to the love of Drogantina

(Act 2, scene 4)

Not only is any dialogue surrounding Drogantina's invitation left to be improvised, but the final line denoting Orlando's sudden enamorment does not indicate how his psychological transformation would have been expressed on the puppet theater stage.

Regardless of how the scene was played out in performance, spectators would have witnessed the shocking fact that Orlando—whose overwhelming desire for Angelica had propelled him from Paris across Eurasia in search of her—falls just as instantly and hopelessly in love with another female character. This adventure thus reinforces the depiction of love as an irrational force that—like a magic potion—can remove agency and self-possession from any character under its spell. Even though the object of desire may be interchangeable, its power certainly seems irresistible.

The episode at Drogantina's garden will extend across various plays. Astolfo eventually reaches Orlando but fails to rescue him and is instead compelled to flee the site to save himself from his cousin's attack. Ironically, it will take nothing less than Angelica to free Orlando from his subjection to the fairy (discussed in Chapter 5).

Act II (scenes 5 and 6) and Act III (scenes 2 and 4): "Rinaldo, invited to Angelica's garden, runs away in order not to hear her."

In the meantime, Angelica's proposed joust was derailed when the Spanish Saracen Feraguto refused to accept defeat upon being unhorsed and continued to attack Argalia on foot. As Angelica fled through the Arden Wood, she inadvertently drank from the Fountain of Love when she stopped to quench her thirst and subsequently fell desperately in love with Ranaldo. The latter, however, thanks to the nearby magical Fountain of Merlin, was not only released from erotic desire in general but was fated to detest the next person he encountered—by unhappy coincidence, Angelica. These twin fountains with opposite effects—reminiscent of Cupid's twin arrows in Ovid's *Metamorphoses*—set up a situation in which the enamored princess will relentlessly pursue her intractable Prince Charming and will seemingly stop at nothing to win his love—albeit, all in vain.

Compelled to assist Angelica, the Christian wizard Malagise has Ranaldo whisked away on an unmanned boat the morning of a decisive battle against Gradasso that was scheduled to take place in Spain before the king of Sericana ever crossed onto Frankish soil. (Ranaldo's sudden disappearance on that occasion explains why Gradasso felt entitled to Baiardo after conquering Paris.) The boat eventually leads the despairing paladin to the Palazzo Gioioso (Pleasure Palace), on an island in the middle of the Indian Ocean, where alluring maidens offer him hospitality. Although Ranaldo initially accepts the gracious reception, he chooses to depart as soon as he hears that the site was constructed by Angelica for him alone. The maidens claim that he is a prisoner powerless to escape, but he proves them wrong by fleeing the island (*OI* 1.8.1–15).

In the *Orlando Innamorato*, the Pleasure Palace and Dragontina episodes are presented as occurring simultaneously through interlacing. This allows the reader to contrast Orlando's hopeless amorous entrapment with Ranaldo's ability to leave a magical palace through his own volition.[12] The *Storia dei paladini* further develops the parallels between the two adventures. Rinaldo is likewise "led to the garden" where initially "forgetting everything he put his mind to the beauty of that place" (7: 162). Lodico even tells us that Rinaldo, after eating and drinking from "cups of very fine gold," was "inebriated from the pleasure he felt in the food and wine, and more so from the dance of those ladies" to the point that he "had forgotten all his past" (7: 162). This description seems to bring him close

---

12 For a more detailed comparison of these two episodes, as well as their classical precedents, see Cavallo, *Boiardo's* Orlando Innamorato 42–53.

to the state in which Orlando finds himself in Drogantina's garden, yet the contrast between the two knights soon becomes apparent. Despite the "great pleasure" that Rinaldo feels at this moment, he is still mindful that Malagigi had warned him he would play a trick on him for having refused Angelica.[13] It is Rinaldo's palpable diffidence that leads one of the maidens to claim that the palace was constructed by a lady enamored of him named Angelica.

Agrippino stages the Palazzo Gioioso episode in four scenes, adopting the technique of interlacing in order to juxtapose Rinaldo's actions with those of his cousins Astolfo and Orlando. Of the four scenes, the first is not found in either the *Orlando Innamorato* or the *Storia dei paladini*. In Act 2, scene 5, Agrippino's Malagigi, having been unsuccessful in bringing Rinaldo to Angelica voluntarily, "makes a garden appear in order to attract Rinaldo and take him to the enamored Angelica, and he sends Nucalone in the form of a woman to incite him." This description of the action contains two innovations. First, in the *Orlando Innamorato*, Angelica's maidens declare to Rinaldo that Angelica herself created the Pleasure Palace through her magic. Here, the construction of the site is credited to Malagigi. It is not only more congruous for Malagigi to undertake such a feat since he is a wizard after all, but the effect of this change is to keep Angelica well within the human realm rather than temporarily take on the aura of a sorceress. The second novelty is that Malagigi has enlisted the demon Nucalone in his efforts. Whereas the group of maidens on site described by Boiardo and Lodico had been presented as nothing more than attractive maidservants of Angelica invested in the success of her plan, Agrippino's Rinaldo finds himself facing a demonic spirit in disguise rather than actual human beings. The Cast of Characters, in fact, lists the corresponding marionette as "1 Woman or even Nucalone himself." The addition of Nucalone—who can be represented either in his own form or in that of a female puppet—underscores both the theme of deceptive appearances and the association of the garden with diabolical magic.

Like Orlando in Drogantina's garden, Rinaldo initially accepts the deceptive invitation (Act 2, scene 6). He remains in control of his mind, however, even once within the garden. While both Boiardo and Lodico describe Rinaldo's impressions and reactions, from amazement in the first case, to inebriation and then diffidence in the second, only Agrippino's Rinaldo takes the initiative in asking the identity of the palace's proprietor

---

13 For the record, the only added detail in this scene anticipated by Berni is the mention of Rinaldo's wariness of Malagigi (8.17).

(Act 3, scene 2).[14] It is not possible to know whether the revelation of Angelica's name was followed by an improvised dialogue along the lines of the heated exchange reported in Boiardo and Lodico in which the maidens insist on the impossibility of leaving the island. The script, as it is written, underscores instead the indisputable agency of Rinaldo in effecting an immediate departure:

Rinaldo   and the woman; he admires that place, asks to whom it belongs
Woman   To a woman who is crazy about you, she is Angelica
Rinaldo   hears the name of Angelica and flees
(Act 3, scene 2)

Two scenes later, Rinaldo appears back on stage still fleeing "in order not to hear Angelica's name." In addition to providing a transition to Rinaldo's next adventure, this dramatization of his ongoing flight reinforces the contrast with respect to Orlando's confinement in a state of stasis without any self-determination.

---

14 Lodico's Rinaldo earlier asks the name of the castle, but the reply of "Gioioso" does not elicit a reaction on his part (7: 162).

Chapter 5

THE DUEL BETWEEN ORLANDO AND AGRICANE DI TARTARIA (*SERA* 165)[1]

Introduction

Although Roland/Orlando had an extensive literary history as the character passed from medieval France to Renaissance Italy, Agricane di Tartaria is, like Angelica and Gradasso, an invention of Boiardo.[2] The great khan is imagined as another powerful ruler who covets a prize he cannot attain. Like those gathered in Paris for the opening joust, moreover, he too has fallen under the spell of the princess of Cathay:

> One single thought consumes his heart.
> He wants to win that damsel fair;
> kingdoms and crowns are not his care.
>
> (*OI* 1.10.14)

Agricane's words and actions on the battlefield offer a complex portrait despite his single-minded focus. Unlike the would-be Arthurian lover Orlando who intends to "win" Angelica through valiant deeds on her behalf, Agricane is unrelenting in his goal to gain possession of the princess through military force. Nevertheless, he abides by an international code of chivalry that places honorable behavior above victory at all costs. Accordingly, he not only dismounts from his horse in order to fight an opponent without an unfair advantage (*OI* 1.11.22–23) but he also refuses to conquer through treachery when offered the opportunity (*OI* 1.14.55).

Agricane's battle against Orlando near the fortress of Albraca is not only one of the *Innamorato* episodes most commonly included in Italian literature

---

1 The play translated and discussed in this chapter is found in *Copione* 12. To compare versions, see play 166 in *Paladini* 7 and *serata* 178 of Mike Manteo's notebook 15.
2 For a succinct account of Orlando's various permutations from the *Chanson de Roland* to Ariosto's *Orlando Furioso*, see Morgan. For Agricane in the *Orlando Innamorato*, see Cavallo, *The World beyond Europe* 45–61; for the latter's characterization in the *Storia dei paladini* and Sicilian puppet theater, see Cavallo, "Six Characters in Search of a Puppeteer" 133–38.

anthologies, but it also continues to be prominent in contemporary Sicilian puppet theater.³ The episode stands out not so much for the martial combat, but rather because of the philosophical dialogue between the two opponents as they lie down next to each other under a starry night sky. In Agrippino's play, the battle between Agricane and Orlando extends across all three Acts and their famous conversation occupies most of Act 3.

Sera 165 also interweaves the exploits of another Eastern character invented by Boiardo—the indomitable female warrior Marfisa. In the *Orlando Innamorato*, she is both a queen and the greatest warrior in "all the East" who arrives in Albraca as an ally of Angelica's father Galafrone against Agricane (*OI* 1.16.28). She is not originally associated with any specific region, but in Niccolò degli Agostini's continuation of the poem (and subsequently in the *Orlando Furioso*, the *Storia dei paladini*, and Sicilian puppet theater) she is the twin sister of Ruggiero, an exemplary knight of mixed heritage designated by Boiardo to become the cofounder of the family dynasty of his patron, Ercole I d'Este (discussed in Chapter 7).

Translation

Evening 165

Gandellino is taken prisoner by Archeloro. Orlando challenges Agricane. King Galafro, along with many troops commanded by Marfisa and a giant, arrives at Albracca and engages in battle. A truce between Orlando and Agricane. Orlando scatters the Tartar army. Agricane with a simulated flight lures Orlando to a distant spot where they fight until nightfall. Each knight recounts his love for Angelica. Out of jealousy they return to fighting. Agricane's death.

Characters
Captains
Kings or knights
1 Giant
Fountain
Baiardo

---

3 In 1969, Antonio Pasqualino noted that in Sicilian puppet theater, the battle between Orlando and Agricane—with titles such as *Il gran duello di Orlando e Agricane per amore di Angelica*, *Il duello di Agricane e Orlando*, and *La morte di Agricane*—was one of the best loved of the cycle's famous duels, playing in the Catania area the same predominant role that the duel between Orlando and Rinaldo over Angelica did in Palermo ("Il repertorio epico dell'opera dei pupi" 102). For videoclips of more recent examples, see "Agricane at Albraca" on the eBOIARDO website (https://edblogs.columbia.edu/eboiardo/authors/boiardo/albraca/agricane).

Act 1º

Scene 1º

Castle

Archeloro   wants to force himself on Alda, he hears a trumpet, goes down to see who it is

2 Walls

Gandellino fights the giant, who flees; he pursues him

3 Room

Gandellino falls into the trap

4 Walls

Silvanella   cannot understand how they are captured and taken inside, she goes in search of the others

5 Fortress

Orlando   asks Angelica's permission, then goes to challenge Agricane

6 Castle

Archeloro	wants to have Gandellino killed
Alda	with sweet words makes him change his mind
Archeloro	wants to possess her
Alda	When you take Orlando prisoner, I will be yours
Archeloro	accepts and waits

7 Field

Agricane	hears a trumpet (a soldier arrives)
Soldier	(frightened) Lord, the knight who demonstrated so much valor challenges you
Agricane	One knight makes you so afraid, I will go fight him

8 Forest

Marfisa, Galafro, and the giant Archilao [Archiloro] in sight of the Tartar camp

Marfisa   Here we are in sight of the enemy and I will immediately create three divisions in order to attack. You, Archilao, will take the first, Galafro the second, and I will take the third. Go with the two

	divisions, you will attack and I will stay here to swoop down when it becomes necessary
Galafro and Archilao go to attack	
Marfisa	(alone) Alone I want to destroy Agricane, then Gradasso, and finally Carlo. That's why I decided to enter last

9 Walls

Orlando and Agricane encounter each other. They fight after exchanging courtesies, they enter fighting

Act 2

1 Field

Uldano and Poliferno hear about the attack by the new army, they run

2 Battle in the forest

Archiloro	chases away Uldano and Poliferno
Galafro	fights
Captain	sees the danger because Agricane is engaged elsewhere, goes to notify him

3 Walls

	The battle between Orlando and Agricane continues
	They strike each other down in turn
Captain	stops the battle and says that the army is in danger because new forces have arrived and it is not known to whom they belong
Agricane	Knight, as you have heard, my men are in danger, I ask you for a truce
Orlando	I agree to the truce and offer you my assistance
Agricane	Thank you, courteous and valiant knight (departs)
Orlando	enters Albracca

4 Forest Battle

Agricane	kills the giant and chases away the others

5 Fortress

Angelica	sees her father's people fighting (Orlando arrives). Why are you here while my father's people will be destroyed?

Orlando	I didn't know. He goes down to the battlefield with Grifone, Aquilante, and Brandimarte

6 Battle

Agricane	chases away Grifone and Aquilante
Orlando	fights
Agricane	reproaches him for having broken the truce
Orlando	You are right, but the men you are fighting were coming in my defense
Agricane	I need to pretend I am fleeing so as to lead him far from here, and when I kill him the victory will be mine. They fight and he flees
Orlando	pursues him

Act 3° single scene[4]

Forest, there is a fountain

Agricane	arrives riding Baiardo and waits, he sees Orlando
Orlando	How much shame you can withstand
	To have run away from a single knight
	Maybe you believed you would escape death
	But you see that your plan has failed
	Those who can die with honor must be prepared to die
	Since it often happens, and easily,
	That in order to remain alive in this sad life
	One attains at once both shame and death.
	[*OI* 1.18.33]
Agricane	For certain you are the most stalwart knight
	I have ever encountered in my life
	Thus let the cause of your release
	Be **that valor** and that courtesy
	You showed me today on the field
	when I went to give succor to my men
	[*OI* 1.18.34.3–8]
	Therefore I want to let you live,
	But you must never return to hinder me.

---

4 Since the twenty stanzas taken from the *Innamorato* in this scene are not consecutive, I have indicated the corresponding stanzas in brackets.

	This is what made me simulate an escape,
	Nor is there any other way out.
	If you still want to fight against me
	You will remain dead upon this field
	But may my witnesses be the sky and sun,
	Killing you brings me sorrow and pain.
	[*OI* 1.18.35]
Orlando	**I answer you in a** very humane way
	Because I already **have** compassion for **you**.
	The more forthright and outstanding **you** are
	The more I regret, in truth,
	That you will die and you are not a Christian,
	And you will go among the damned souls.
	But if you want to save your body and your soul,
	Receive baptism and I will let you go.
	[*OI* 1.18.36]
Agricane	**Let me take a good look at** your face,
	If you are a Christian, you're Orlando.
	I would prefer to measure myself against you
	Than to be crowned the king of Paradise.
	But from this moment on I remind and warn you
	Not to speak to me about the affairs of the gods
	Because you would be preaching in vain.
	Let each defend himself with sword in hand.
	[*OI* 1.18.37]
	(they fight, night falls)
Orlando	**You see** that the sun has already passed beyond the mountain
	And stars are beginning to fill the sky.
	Listen to what a count **says to you,**
	What will we do **now** that the day is gone?
	[*OI* 1.18.39.1–4]
Agricane	**I answer you** straight away
	The two of us will lie down upon this field
	And tomorrow morning at the break of dawn
	Together we'll resume our fight.
	[*OI* 1.18.39.5–8]
	(They sit down)
Orlando	**Look at the path across the sky**.
	What we see is a beautiful creation
	Produced by the divine monarch.
	The silver moon and the golden stars

	And the light of day and the shining sun,
	God created all of this for everyone.
	[*OI* 1.18.41.3–8]
Agricane	**Valorous knight**, I certainly recognize
	That you want to discuss religious faith.
	I am not an expert in any science,
	Nor did I ever want to learn as a boy
	And I broke my teacher's head for his efforts.
	Then a replacement could not be found
	Who would show me a text or a tome,
	So frightened of me was everyone.
	[*OI* 1.18.42]
	And so I spent my childhood
	In hunting, in military exercises, and in horseback riding.
	Nor does it seem to me fitting for a nobleman
	To spend the whole day with his head in the books and thinking,
	But it is appropriate for a knight to improve
	the strength of his body and his dexterity.
	Doctrine is fine for the doctor and the priest,
	I know just as much as is suiting to me.
	[*OI* 1.18.43]
Orlando	**Listen**, I'm in complete agreement
	That arms are a man's first **love**,[5]
	But book learning is no less worthy.
	Indeed, the one adorns the other like flowers in a field
	And whoever does not think about the eternal creator
	Is similar to an ox, a stone, a piece of wood.
	Nor without learning can one **ever** think
	About the lofty and divine High Majesty.
	[*OI* 1.18.44]
Agricane	**I reply to you that** it is highly discourteous
	To insist on debating with an advantage.
	I disclosed to you my nature
	And I know that you are learned and wise.
	If you speak any further, I will not answer.
	If you'd like to sleep, then you may sleep unperturbed,
	But if you want to talk to me some more,
	Speak to me only of love and war.
	[*OI* 1.18.45]

---

5 Boiardo's original verse has "honor" instead of "love."

| | Now I beseech you to respond to what I ask,
As a gentleman tell me the truth on your honor,
Whether you are really that Orlando
Who is famous throughout the world,
And why you came here and how and when
And if you ever were enamored
Because every knight who is without love,
Even if he breathes, lives without a heart. |
|---|---|

[*OI* 1.18.46]

Orlando **Oh great monarch**, I am that Orlando
Who killed Almonte and his brother Troiano.
Love has led me to abandon all else
And has brought me to this foreign place,
And to explain to you something more,
I want you to know that my heart is in the hands
Of King Galafrone's daughter
Who dwells within Albracca's walls.

[*OI* 1.18.47]

You are waging war against her father
To take over his country and his fortress,
And I was led here out of **honor**[6]
And to please that lovely damsel.
Many times I have fought on horseback
For my honor and religious faith.
Now it is only to attain this maiden so fair
That I fight, and I have no other care.

[*OI* 1.18.48]

Agricane **Dear Orlando**, you must realize
That as the new day dawns
We must wield arms against each other
And one of us will remain dead on the field.
Now I want to make just one request:
That until we arrive at that moment
You agree to abandon and leave to me
The thought of the damsel your heart desires.

[*OI* 1.18.50]

---

6 Boiardo's original verse has "love" instead of "honor." If not an oversight ("onore" is in fact used again later in the stanza), this substitution could serve to suggest Orlando's sense of the honorableness of his undertaking even as he aims to "please the damsel."

While I'm alive, I cannot suffer
That anyone but me should love that fair countenance.
One of us will be completely deprived
Of both life and the lady when the new day arrives.
No one will ever know except for this stream
And this forest that surrounds us
That you renounced her in this place
And at this moment, which will be brief.
[*OI* 1.18.51]

Orlando **I tell you that** all my promises,
as many as I've ever made, I have kept,
But if I promise to do what you ask of me now
I couldn't keep it even if I were to take a vow.
Relinquishing my love for Angelica
Would be like yanking off my limbs
Or gouging my eyes out of my face
And living without a soul or heart.
[*OI* 1.18.52]

Agricane **See here, I am burning** beyond measure
And I **cannot** accept such an answer.
Although it's in the middle of a dark night
I want to bring an ending to this fight.
Even though my victory is not assured
I want to challenge **you, take the field**!
I tell you, knight, you must leave aside the lady,
You must either let her be or get ready to fight against me.
[*OI* 1.18.53]

They get up and fight
Orlando knocked down many times, gets angry
Orlando I have already been here for two days
In order to defeat a single knight
And I still find myself face to face with him,
Nor do I have any more advantage than on the first day.
But if I prolong the battle for another hour
I will abandon my weapons and inside a monastery
Will become a friar, and I will call myself damned
If evermore a sword at my side is seen.
[*OI* 1.19.9]

(He knocks down Agricane, who is almost dead)

Agricane	Baptize me, baron, at the fountain Before I completely lose my speech And if my life has been iniquitous and strange Let not my **soul** rebel against God. He who came to save the human race May he raise up my poor soul. **I** confess that I have sinned greatly But ever so boundless is his mercy. [*OI* 1.19.13]
Orlando	takes the helmet and fills it
N.B.	Agricane falls down in such a way that the helmet can be removed to fill it with water
Orlando	Confess your sins to God, even your sinful thoughts
Agricane	I confess
Orl	Do you believe in God?
Agr.	I believe
Orl	Do you believe in three divine persons in one God?
Agricane	I believe
Orl	I baptize you in the name of the father, the son, and the holy spirit (he pours water)
Agricane	I feel reborn, what a sweet sound I hear, mixed with a celestial melody. God, I thank you. My vision is blurred …. I'm losing my energy … My strength is failing … God, welcome my soul (he expires)
Orlando	sees Baiardo and does not know how the pagan gained possession of him. He takes him and departs

Comparative Analysis

Act 1 (scenes 1–4, 6): "Gandellino is taken prisoner by Archeloro."

This episode does not occur in the *Orlando Innamorato* but is inserted into the *Storia dei paladini* by Giusto Lodico.[7] Agrippino's choice to begin a play featuring Orlando's exploits in the distant East on behalf of Angelica with

---

7 Pasqualino and Napoli discuss the details of this story, noting aspects drawn from Bernardo Tasso's *Amadigi*, in *Rerum palatinorum fragmenta* (149–52 and 163n–167n, respectively).

the dangers facing a defenseless Alda back home at the hands of the giant Archeloro brings to the fore the paladin's negligence of his duty to protect and honor his wife.

Act 1 (scenes 5, 7, 9): "Orlando challenges Agricane."

The morning after his entrance into the fortress of Albraca with Angelica and his fellow former prisoners of Dragontina's garden, Orlando blows his horn to challenge Agricane (*OI* 15.55). Yet after hearing Agricane's horn blast in response, the paladin does not proceed to think about the battle at hand. Instead, in recognition of the Tartar king's valor, he "asks Jesus Christ if by His grace / he might convert him to His faith" (*OI* 1.16.9). This sudden and anomalous proselytizing impulse on the part of Boiardo's Orlando foreshadows the conversation between the two opponents the following night.

In replaying Orlando's challenge, the *Storia dei paladini* does not include the paladin's prayer for the conversion of Agricane prior to the battle. Instead, Lodico imagines Orlando taking leave of his beloved Angelica before he heads out of the fortress to face Agricane (7: 238). The prose adaptation also makes a point to underscore the absence of any dialogue between the two opponents before they cross swords: "The Tartar lord [...], without deigning to open his mouth, signalled to the count to take his distance" (7: 239).

Agrippino's play builds up dramatic tension by prefacing the onset of this battle between Orlando and Agricane with two scenes that foreground each knight's mindset. In Act 1, scene 5, Orlando's thoughts are directed to his beloved's approval rather than Agricane's salvation. The stage directions indicate that he seeks Angelica's authorization within the fortress before heading out to confront Agricane: "Orlando asks Angelica's permission, then goes to challenge Agricane." Compared to the *Storia dei paladini*'s statement that Orlando, "having asked farewell from that face, had the bridge lowered and went out to the field" (7: 238), Agrippino's phrasing accentuates the paladin's obedience and subservience to Angelica. Agricane, for his part, is characterized by resoluteness as he awaits his opponent on the field (Act 1, scene 7). In response to a frightened soldier (rather than a herald, as in the *Storia dei paladini*, and thus a stand-in for the entire terrified army), the Tartar king succinctly conveys his readiness to prove his martial superiority (Act 1, scene 7).

When the two knights meet on the field, Agrippino imagines that they exchange courtesies ("cortesie") before initiating their combat (Act 1, scene 9). This is a departure from both the *Innamorato* and the *Storia dei paladini* where no speech occurs. Like the wish for Agricane's conversion on the part of

Boiardo's Orlando, this exchange of courtesies anticipates later developments in the encounter. Yet whereas the Renaissance poet foreshadowed the theme of spiritual deliverance that concludes the episode, the Sicilian puppeteer prepares spectators instead for the civility that exemplifies the knights' extensive conversation prior to the denouement.

Act 1 (scene 8): "King Galafro, along with many people commanded by Marfisa and a giant, arrives at Albracca and engages in battle."

In the *Orlando Innamorato*, Galafrone's forces are divided into three lines of defense: the first led by the giant Archiloro, the second by the Eastern queen Marfisa, and the third by the Cathayan king himself, each with successively greater numerical forces (*OI* 1.16.27–28).[8] When Boiardo introduces Marfisa as "bold—as bold as she was lovely" (*OI* 1.16.28), he alerts us to the fact that she has vowed not to remove her "hauberk, plate, and mail" until defeating Gradasso, Agricane, and Carlomagno in battle (*OI* 1.16.29–30). Yet Boiardo is in no rush to tell her story: "I'll say nothing else for now" (*OI* 1.16.30). As we later find out, it was Marfisa herself who was in no rush to jump into the fray. She is so relaxed, in fact, that she actually takes a nap at a certain distance from the battlefield. She does not intend to take action until all is lost since, as she explains to her maidservant, "I'm all we need for victory" (*OI* 1.16.56). Although Marfisa will easily lose her temper when provoked, especially in cases that touch upon questions of chivalric honor, Boiardo takes pains here to balance her explosive martial intentions with a controlled self-confidence that matches the mix of boldness and beauty in her face.

In the *Storia dei paladini*, echoing Berni's *rifacimento*, Lodico emphasizes instead Marfisa's ferocity, presenting her in this scene as "the most harsh, brutal, and savage creature in the world (7: 241)."[9] After the explanation that the three divisions are headed by Archiloro, Marfisa, and Galafrone, Lodico's use of the third person plural ("they attacked the Tartars") gives the impression that all three act in unison (7: 241). As we hear about the actions of Archiloro on the field, we may wonder what has happened to Marfisa. Only subsequently do we learn that this allegedly wild creature

---

8 Despite the similarity of name and gigantic stature, Galafrone's ally Archiloro is not to be confused with Aldabella's abductor Archeloro back in France.

9 Although Berni reiterates Boiardo's description of Marfisa as bold and lovely (16.27), he then goes on to claim that she is "the most desperate, / harsh, brutal, savage, ungodly girl, / Who I believe will ever be or ever was" (16.28).

is taking a nap prior to engaging in combat because "she alone was enough to defeat her arrogant foe" (7: 243). Lodico's mixed signals miss the balance that characterized Marfisa's introduction in Boiardo's original poem.[10]

Agrippino has his own plans for Marfisa as he revises the scene in a way that places her at the forefront of the action even when she is not fighting. First of all, the warrior maiden's facial features, albeit wooden, would have directly attested to the boldness and beauty visible in Boiardo's character rather than the crudeness and savagery introduced by Lodico via Berni (Figure 5.1).[11] And whereas Lodico creates confusion by omitting Boiardo's temporary transition away from Marfisa and initially gives the impression that she is mixed in with the others, Agrippino not only brings greater clarity but actually puts Marfisa in charge of both the narrative progression and the battle plans. Whereas previously one could have assumed that Galafrone determined the three divisions as both the defending king and the one with the greatest number of troops (*OI* 1.16.27–28), here Marfisa is the one deciding

Figure 5.1 Marfisa. Courtesy of Susie Bruno.

---

10 For more on Marfisa in the *Storia dei paladini*, see Cavallo, "Boiardo's Eastern Protagonists" 157–62.
11 In traditional Sicilian puppet theater, Marfisa's face was generally depicted as bold and beautiful rather than crude and savage. See, for example, figures 3 and 25 in Pasqualino, *L'opera dei pupi*.

upon the threefold formation as well as the plan of attack. As Act 1, scene 8, opens, Marfisa is shown to be giving instructions to both Archilao and Galafro to attack first while she will enter the battle last. And so as to not leave any room for misunderstanding, Agrippino has Marfisa explain in a subsequent aside to the audience that her delayed entrance into the battle is in order to attain the victory alone. As in Boiardo, she assumes that Agricane will defeat the combined forces of her allies and that her own prowess will suffice to prevail. Now, however, her boundless self-assurance is further supported by her directives to the other kings as though she were in command of the entire military operation.

Act 2 (scenes 1–6): "A truce between Orlando and Agricane. Orlando scatters the Tartar camp."

In the course of the battle, Boiardo devises a scene in which Orlando's love for Angelica leads to an incongruous situation. Agricane asks Orlando with courteous words to suspend their combat so that he may defend his troops from Archiloro's ferocious massacre (*OI* 1.16.36–37). He even offers to bestow the entire realm of Russia upon the cavalier in return for his consideration. Yet it is not the allure of a vast northern kingdom that prompts Orlando to acquiesce to Agricane's plea; rather, it is his love for Angelica: "He could not scorn the king's request. / A gentleman, *innamorato*, / may never fail at courtesy" (*OI* 1.16.43). Indeed, Orlando not only accepts a truce but even "offered him his aid." Had Agricane accepted such an offer, Orlando—Angelica's most ardent defender—would have found himself fighting on behalf of her fiercest assailant.

When Angelica sees her father in "great mortal peril," she sends a messenger to the field asking for Orlando's assistance (*OI* 1.16.58). The enamored paladin immediately complies with her wishes and—forgetting his previous agreement with Agricane—resumes battle against the Tartars. Agricane has apparently forgotten as well, since he does not take offense when he sees his opponent back on the field. Indeed, when the knights later converse, Agricane refers to "the ability and courtesy / you showed me in the field today / when I was forced to help my army" (*OI* 1.18.34).

Lodico further develops the interactions between Orlando and Agricane. Rather than attempting to reconcile the paladin's contradictory actions, however, he adds a further incongruity into the mix. In addition to his willingness to give Orlando rule over the territory from Moscow to the Russian Sea, Agricane also inexplicably offers his opponent Angelica herself: "I give you the beautiful woman and allow you to enjoy her" (7: 242). Apart from the fact that Angelica was not his to give away (the entire war was undertaken in order to possess her, after all), it is inconceivable that Agricane would so lightly relinquish the very woman he is going to such extreme measures to conquer. Such an over-the-top proposition (albeit ignored by Orlando) makes the paladin's subsequent offer to assist his rival in battle appear a bit less extreme.

As in Boiardo's poem, Orlando immediately reenters the battles when Angelica asks for his help (7: 243). Now, however, Agricane is no longer mindless of Orlando's broken promise and instead takes him to task for his inconstancy:

> Agricane's entire army was already seen in a rout. Imagining that this disaster was due to the valor of the one who had fought him at the fortress, the khan went to face him flushed with anger, saying: "So this is how a knight keeps his word? While I asked you for time to help my people, you came to take away my victory! But if Macone is not a liar, I hope to humiliate your pride." (7: 258–59)

Despite the extensive dialogue between the two knights both before and after this moment, Orlando has nothing to say for himself here. Instead, Lodico expressly informs us that "the count gave no indication of having heard him and rained down a blow upon the pagan's helmet that made himself known for the force that he was" (7: 259). In this way, Orlando's contradictory actions are explicitly underscored but left unresolved.

Agrippino refashions the episode in a manner that both reduces and works through the incongruities. When recounting Agricane's plea for a truce to succor his men, Boiardo included the incentive of land and Lodico added that of the princess herself to boot. Agrippino's Agricane, by contrast, does not offer an enticement of any kind, thus avoiding both the contractual and the hyperbolic aspects of the request. After Orlando agreed to the truce and offered his help, Boiardo's Agricane explicitly departed in silence (*OI* 1.16.44) while Lodico's character, following Berni's *rifacimento* (16.43), thanked the paladin before leaving (7: 242). Agrippino, having just diverged from his precedents through omission, here modifies the scene by accretion. Before departing, the Tartar khan replies to Orlando in the following manner: "Thank you, courteous and valiant knight." In this way, Agrippino not only tempers the incongruity of the episode (at least as far as Agricane is concerned) but also foregrounds the Tartar khan's esteem for his opponent prior to their nighttime conversation.

Whereas both Boiardo and Lodico recount that Angelica sends word to Orlando on the field, Agrippino renders more concrete the paladin's withdrawal from the battle by depicting him actually back inside the fortress.

In the earlier renditions, moreover, Angelica simply spurred her defender back to battle by calling upon his love for her and reminding him that she would be observing his valor from her tower. In Agrippino's play, by contrast, she outright accuses him of negligence: "Why are you here while my father's people will be destroyed?" (Act 2, scene 5). Her rhetorical question thus lays bare the incongruity of Orlando's acquiescence to Agricane's request. In the *Innamorato* and the *Storia dei paladini* Orlando reacts by departing silently—Lodico even specifies that Orlando "did not reply" (7: 243). Agrippino, however, brings to the fore the paladin's lapse of judgment by including a response to Angelica. Orlando acknowledges, in fact, that he had not understood the implications of his retreat from the field: "I didn't know." Thus, rather than seemingly ignore the incongruity of Orlando's actions (Boiardo)—or soften them by imagining an even greater incongruity on Agricane's part (Lodico)—Agrippino makes this part of the dialogue between the paladin and his lady.

Given Agrippino's close attention to Orlando's behavior in his dealings with Agricane thus far, it is not surprising that the continuation of the episode both incorporates and departs from the earlier versions discussed above. After Orlando returns to fight, Agrippino's Agricane initially follows the *Storia dei paladini* and "reproaches him for having broken the truce." But rather than repeating the reaction of Lodico's Orlando and immediately attacking as his only response, Agrippino's more thoughtful character acknowledges the validity of Agricane's reprimand and then goes on to explain his predicament to his opponent: "You are right, but the men you are fighting were coming in my defense." Orlando's greater communication not only serves to deal straightforwardly with his perplexing actions but also anticipates the later dialogue between the two knights that will occupy most of Act 3.

Act 3 (single scene): "Agricane with a simulated flight takes Orlando to a distant spot where they fight until nightfall. Each knight recounts his love for Angelica. Out of jealousy they engage in a new battle. Agricane's death."

In the course of the battle, Agricane decides to lure Orlando to a secluded spot where he thinks he can quickly dispatch with him and then rejoin the combat to turn the tide in his favor. Boiardo notes that his ploy is the result of a thought process (*OI* 1.18.29–30). Reflective thinking, in fact, rather than military action, will take centerstage when Orlando and Agricane suspend their battle at nightfall and engage in a conversation about what gives meaning to life. Turning to a higher concern, Orlando points to the beauty of the cosmos and seeks to reach agreement at the most basic level—namely the existence of a divine creator. He refrains from restricting his discourse to any particular belief system and includes all of humanity, rather than just one chosen people, as beneficiaries of the heavenly monarch's creative outpouring. Not wanting to discuss religion or science on any level, Agricane prefers to focus exclusively on military endeavors. Although Orlando expresses his agreement on the primacy of arms, he nonetheless maintains that education enhances an individual just as flowers adorn a field (*OI* 1.18.44). His defense of learning brings him back to his original reflection, and he goes on to assert that without study one cannot begin to understand the mysteries of the universe. Orlando's speech essentially argues for the fundamental role of reading in the formation of a fully developed human being capable of spiritual contemplation. Contesting his opponent's unfair advantage due to intellectual training, Agricane refuses to discuss metaphysical issues and proposes instead the topic of love. Although the knights are in agreement about the importance of love, the problem arises from the fact that they are both enamored of the same woman. Ironically, whereas the conversation between the two knights was not impeded by religious or cultural differences, their love for Angelica propels them to precipitously resume their battle in the middle of the night.

In refashioning the episode, Lodico depicts Agricane more under the sway of wrath than guided by a thought process. When pretending to flee the battlefield, he is "all fired up with fury." Upon learning of his opponent's identity, he himself states his unstoppable vehemence: "Even if you were Hector, Hercules, or Antaeus, you would not be able to survive my fury" (7: 259). By contrast, Boiardo's Agricane had been delighted by the prospect of measuring himself against Orlando: "I would prefer to fight you than / to be the king of Paradise!" (*OI* 1.18.37). In addition, Boiardo's subsequent return to action with the narrator's interjection "No more words" (*OI* 1.18.38), omitted by Berni, is replaced here by Agricane's deliberate act of stopping Orlando's attempt to engage in further dialogue by immediately landing a blow with his sword while cursing (7: 259).

Agrippino, having focused on Orlando and Agricane increasingly through Acts 1 and 2, devotes the entirety of Act 3 to their culminating confrontation. Near the end of Act 2, Agrippino has Agricane explain his decision to pretend to flee the battle without any reference to the irate emotional state the character exhibited in the *Storia dei paladini*. As Act 3 opens, we find that Agrippino's Agricane not only follows the behavior and mindset of Boiardo's rather than Lodico's character, but that he also speaks the same words found in the *Innamorato*'s *ottava rima* verses. Indeed, the puppeteer offered to his audience the full philosophical dialogue that transpired between the two knights in Boiardo's poem.

Whereas for Angelica's opening speech (*sera* 152) Agrippino combined the wording of Boiardo and Berni, and for the conversation between Astolfo and Gradasso (*sera* 159) he drew from the latter's *rifacimento*, he now adheres exclusively to Boiardo's original poem. Dividing the stanzas by speaker, we find that Orlando speaks for eight stanzas, Agricane for eleven, and the two knights share an additional stanza with four verses each.[12] Tellingly, this shared stanza marks the moment in which nightfall is approaching and the warriors agree to cease their fighting and rest alongside each other for the night. In the original stanza, Boiardo had given one line to Orlando's question and three to Agricane's response (*OI* 1.18.39). In turning the stanza into first-person speech, Agrippino distributes the verses in equal measure.

Despite Agrippino's close adherence to the *Innamorato* during the nighttime conversation, his conclusion of the episode, specifically the conversion and death of Agricane, departs substantially from both Boiardo and Lodico. Indeed, the divergences across all three versions merit particular attention for the overall vision of humanity they convey. Boiardo's Agricane, upon finding himself mortally wounded, spontaneously expresses his belief in the Christian God and asks Orlando to baptize him on the spot (*OI* 1.19.12). Rather than the victory of one belief system over another, as in the Carolingian epic tradition, Agricane's detailed reasoning reveals a mental shift from a secular to a spiritual mindset. The God that he evokes in his request for baptism is not a promoter of religious warfare but a compassionate and benevolent deity who demonstrated love for all humanity through the Incarnation and Crucifixion. This attitude is only possible because the preceding combat was not motivated by religious difference.

Much later in the poem, Boiardo will allude to Agricane's salvation when Orlando's friend Brandimarte chances upon the khan "whose handsome looks had not decayed" (*OI* 2.19.28). At the moment, however, Boiardo turns his focus from Agricane to Orlando, who asks his former opponent's forgiveness and performs the baptism:

His eyes were filled with tears as he
Dismounted to the level field.
He took the gored king in his arms
And set him on the marble by

---

12 One of each of their stanzas consists of six rather than eight verses, but this does not affect the ratio. In Boiardo's poem, allowing for some narrative mixed with the direct speech, Agricane likewise speaks more than Orlando, with approximately twelve stanzas compared to Orlando's approximate eight.

The fountain, weeping with him while
He asked for pardon for his deeds
Then baptized him with fountain water.
He joined his hands and prayed to God.

(*OI* 1.19.16)

In contrast to the *Innamorato*'s three-and-a-half stanza description of Agricane's spiritual awakening (*OI* 1.19.12–15), the *Storia dei paladini* devotes less than a sentence to the khan's change of heart: "falling, he recognized the fateful hour of his death, so he suddenly turned his thoughts to the count and asked him to baptize him" (7: 262). This restricted account not only omits Agricane's stated motivation for his conversion but also leaves out the references to divine benevolence highlighted in Boiardo's precedent. What Lodico focuses on instead is Orlando's intense emotional engagement as well as his plea for Agricane's forgiveness as the paladin holds the dying man in his arms. All of the attention thus falls on Orlando's regret for the violence that led to Agricane's death at his hand rather than on the khan's newfound spirituality.

Agrippino's citation of Boiardo's poetry throughout the dialogue does not carry over to the moment of Agricane's conversion and death. The puppeteer does not, however, return to Lodico's prose adaptation, but instead develops his conclusion in a new direction. Eschewing any reference to Orlando's feelings of pain and remorse (the main aspect that Boiardo and Lodico had in common), Agrippino concentrates instead on the doctrinal aspect of baptism and Agricane's salvation. The description of the rite summarized in the final two verses of Boiardo's above-cited stanza is here transformed into a precise dialogue of the utmost religious solemnity:

Orlando	takes the helmet and fills it
N.B.	Agricane falls down in such a way that the helmet can be removed to fill it with water
Orlando	Confess your sins to God, even your sinful thoughts
Agricane	I confess
Orl	Do you believe in God?
Agr.	I believe
Orl	Do you believe in three divine persons in one God?
Agricane	I believe
Orl	I baptize you in the name of the father, the son, and the holy spirit (he pours water)

For both Boiardo and Lodico, Agricane draws his final breath immediately following the baptism. This is not the case, however, in Agrippino's script.

The Tartar khan is now given the opportunity to express his sensations and confirm his grace as a Christian neophyte:

Agricane I feel reborn, what a sweet sound I hear, mixed with a celestial melody. God, I thank you. My vision is blurred .... I'm losing my energy .... My strength is failing ... God, welcome my soul (he expires)[13]

Orlando's recourse to liturgical language at the moment of the baptism is thus reinforced by Agricane's awareness of heavenly music and the offering of his soul to God. These additions all seem designed not only to assure spectators of the Tartar khan's salvation but also to make them direct witnesses of it.

---

13 The moment of Agricane's death is more developed here than in the version of the play contained in *Paladini* 7. In *sera* 166 of that earlier script, Agricane is limited to saying: "I feel reborn. My eyesight is becoming dimmer".

Chapter 6

THE GRAND COUNCIL OF AGRAMANTE DI BISERTA (*SERA* 170)[1]

Introduction

In Book One of the *Orlando Innamorato*, King Galafone of Cathay sent his daughter Angelica to Paris in a scheme to capture the international array of knights gathered at Carlo's court, King Gradasso of Sericana crossed the globe in order to attain a famous horse and sword, and King Agricane of Tartaria waged a large-scale war back in Cathay to possess none other than Angelica. As we have seen in the previous chapters, all three undertakings ended in failure. At the opening canto of Book Two, King Agramante of Biserta (Bizerte, in today's Tunisia) has a more grandiose and openly territorial goal: the conquest of Carlo's entire Frankish realm. Yet no earthly kingdom can contain his ambition since he boasts that after subjugating France he intends to assault the heavens themselves (*OI* 2.1.64). His ally Rodamonte, king of Sarza (Chercel, in today's Algeria), aims to surpass him in his vertical extension, declaring that he is ready to follow—or lead—Agramante equally into the heavens or the *inferno* (*OI* 2.1.65). Agramante's most trusted advisors, however, are against such a foolhardy undertaking, thus setting the stage for a heated debate at the pan-African council held in Biserta.[2]

As this impending threat to Carlo's realm arises from the south, newsworthy occurrences continue in various other regions of the globe. Agricane's son Mandricardo leaves Tartaria to invade Circassia (Caucasia), where he will wreak havoc in the region in the absence of its ruler Sacripante who is off fighting in Cathay on behalf of Angelica. The war in Albraca, in fact, rages on despite Agricane's death as though it had taken on a life of its own.

---

1 The play translated and discussed in this chapter is found in *Copione* 12. To compare versions, see play 171 in *Paladini* 7 and *serata* 182 in Mike Manteo's notebook 16.
2 For more on Agramante's invasion of France in the *Orlando Innamorato* and the war's conclusion in the *Orlando Furioso*, see Cavallo, *The World beyond Europe*, in particular, the chapters "Agramante of Biserta (Tunisia)," "Rugiero (Atlas Mountains, Northern Africa)," "Rodamonte of Sarza (Algeria)," and "The Destruction of Biserta."

Orlando is absent, however, because Angelica has sent him to the fairy Falerina's enchanted garden in Orgagna in order to prevent him from killing the recently arrived Ranaldo. Along the way, Orlando meets an even more deceitful damsel, named Origille, who beguiles him. If earlier Orlando's subjection to Dragontina was the result of a magic beverage, the paladin has no such excuse when he is smitten with the perfidious but fully human Origille and (temporarily, at least) forgets all about Angelica. Origille abandons Orlando after stealing his horse and sword, but the paladin later encounters her in the company of the brothers Grifone and Aquilante at the Bridge of Roses. This site, as it turns out, is part of a vast network designed to ensnare travelers who are then transported to their death at the garden of Orgagna, Orlando's destination.

Sera 170 is most memorable for the two council scenes in Biserta that lead to Agramante's invasion of France. Agrippino's juxtaposition of these North African gatherings with happenings in Albracca, Tartaria, and Paris, as well as at the abovementioned Bridge of Roses, makes for a very eventful evening elaborating both epic and romance themes in original ways.

Translation

Evening 170

A grand council held by Agramante to defeat Carlo. Grifone and Aquilante are taken prisoner at the Bridge of Roses. Mandricardo goes to Circassia to avenge his father. Rodomonte refutes the king of Garamanta's speech. The latter, before dying, instructs how to find Ruggiero. Orlando frees Grifone and Aquilante, kills a giant, and heads for the enchantment of Falerina.

Characters
King Fizzano
Garamanta
Subrino
Branzardo
Malabuferso
Brunello
Mandricardo (without the eagle until he acquires Hector's armor)
King of Fiessa
Dardanello with eagle
Other kings for the council
two women

1 Castellan
1 Giant
Rodomonte
Pinadoro |
Alzirdo | for the council
Manilardo |

Act 1

1 Biserta

          Agramante's Council
          Agramante, King of Garamanta, Branzardo, Dardanello, Subrino, Rodomonte, Fizzano, Malabuferso, King of Fiessa, and others

Agramante   I am pleased that you have come in response to my call. Know that it is my wish that this love of yours will last until my goal is accomplished. I have no other desire than love and glory to make our virtues shine forth. It is sufficiently known to you what Alexander the Great attained and the things he accomplished, it is enough to tell you only that they were the splendor of my family. It is not necessary to tell you how many flags were lowered in the presence of my father Troiano because in part you remember. Now so much love did not come to them while feasting but rather while fighting on the battlefield. What will we do to acquire such fame?
          Bonfires and tournaments will not lead us to such heights, but we must employ our swords in faraway countries where our enemies are more formidable. You are aware that the Christians shower us with insults and shame, but our strength will be sufficient to mitigate their pride and to avenge my father Troiano. How many of you don't nourish the same desire? France should therefore be our crowning achievement and when we have destroyed it, we will raise our gaze majestically to the sky.

Branzardo di Bugia asks to speak
          Sir, three approaches are necessary to convincingly persuade: reason, example, and experience; therefore, to state my opinion, I say that the war against Carlo will be harmful to you, not to say disastrous. The reason for this is because that lord has valorous and proud men, trained in warfare and who

know how to fight in the rigors of winter and in sweet spring and who never fear danger. You have nothing but crude and cowardly men who cannot compete with them. I could draw the example from your ancestor Alexander when he went to Persia with few men and King Darius went to meet him with a large army, but because the king was unskilled and not used to war, he was deprived of his life and his kingdom. You can draw the experience from many accounts of war but, to be brief, I'll just tell you to remember Caroggieri, a descendant of your great-grandfather, who, sending many warriors to Italy, remained a prisoner with all of his men, as well as Almonte and Troiano who were the mirror of chivalry throughout the world. They found their grave with Agolante where they believed they would be achieving victory. Therefore, my lord, put such a thought to rest because against Carlo you cannot have the advantage and believe me that the harm that will come to you is weighing a lot on me because I have loved you since you were a child.

Subrino — I am that Subrino who never wavered while assisting your grandfather Agolante, and I still have not lost that courage even though I have lost some of my strength. Now if you wish to have news of that land where by treading it you will find the blood of our relatives, I can satisfy you because while young I traveled around those lands as an explorer and I still tremble thinking of Ruggiero whom I found inside Reggio Calabria. Do not believe that out of cowardice I advise against this undertaking because I understand that my life is short and more pleasing to me on the battlefield than in a soft featherbed.

You can reach France in two different ways, one of which is through Aigues-Mortes, which I deem to be inopportune because you will find the Christians at the shoreline who will make a valiant defense and ten of them are worth a hundred of our men. In the other direction there is the Strait of Gibraltar, where Marsilio will not deny you help, and with brave men continue to France through Gascony, but we will have to contend with that damned Montalbano castle where Rinaldo stands guard, and if by luck he is not there, then Bradamante will be there to keep your army at bay until Carlo arrives with his men, among whom it is enough to name Ugiero, Oliviero,

	Agolaccio, and woe to us if in the midst of them is Orlando who carries the weapons and sword of Almonte. Therefore, if I have to give my advice, it is to leave them alone …
Rodomonte	You have forgotten that we did not come here to give advice but to receive the commands of the emperor; therefore, it is necessary to put our forces into action and whoever refuses to do this is a traitor
Garamanta	Gentlemen, this foolish person wants to speak when everyone is silent, but I will tell you what Apollino imparts to me. All those who pass into France will be sliced by the blade of the sword and Rodomonte, who now displays so much brilliance, will remain there as a meal for the crows
Rodomonte	While we are here I take pleasure in your predictions, but when we have reached enemy territory and set Paris on fire and burned down Rome with the pope, you will see the flames from here, and do not stand around with your prophecies because I will give you a sword blow atop your head, since I have little—that is, no—faith in your babble
	Some older people advise against it, some young people want war
Agramante	Let nobody be dismayed, because I will not call myself Troiano's son if Carlo and his men are not brought to Africa weighed down by chains
	(Viva Agramante)
Garamanta	Since you despise your empire and leave aside the good to embrace its opposite, accept my last piece of advice. Know that on Mount Carena there is a valiant young man, his name is Ruggiero like his father, he is your relative because he is the son of Galiacella. It is our good fortune that he was born a pagan and was raised by a necromancer named Atlante, your friend and subject, and because the young man craves to exercise the profession of Mars, the wizard has instructed him well. Now if you ever manage to take him to France, you can have hope for some positive outcomes
Agramante	sends Malabuferso to Mount Carena and dissolves the council

2 Field

Marfisa and Torindo send for men and Sebasti, Bursia, Smirne, and Scandeloro to reinforce the field

3 Fortress

Grifone and Aquilante depart, leaving the pagans

4 Forest

Malabuferso sees nothing other than wolves, returns to Biserta

5 Fortress

Angelica is pained that Orlando is not present
Sacripante comforts her

6 Tartary

Mandricardo blames Sacripante for the death of his father Agricane, and he leaves with his army to lay siege to Circassia

Act 2º

1 Biserta

      Agramante's second council
      Agramante awaits the arrival of Malabuferso to have news about Ruggiero
Malabuferso arrives and says he has found only wolves
Malabuferso Tell the king of Garamanta that he should learn how to prophesize better and, if his knowledge is equal to what he predicted, I assure you that there is not a more miserable liar. I understand that, being old, he yearns more for peace than for war
Rodomonte Agramante, unfortunately you will be mocked, and one who has faith in those who want to foretell the future is poorly advised. I hanged many in my kingdom who wanted to predict the future and whether a woman should find a good husband or remain a virgin. You, my lord, will be considered a child if you believe the king of Garamanta, since last year he prophesized that—Mars being unarmed—leeks would be sprouting low and potatoes would be selling at a bargain, and the poor people found themselves deceived, and if you listen to him then don't talk about war, but stay at home scratching your belly
Garamanta Don't listen to this man who is devoid of reason, and this will be proven in France when he finds a shameful grave. I said that Ruggiero is on Mount Carena and I affirm it, but where

	he lives is well guarded by a strong enchantment, and finding him will require a ring that Angelica has on her finger that dispels every enchantment. I therefore repeat to you: Do not leave without Ruggiero
Rodomonte	You predict everything except your own death
Garamanta	It is not far off. In a few minutes the sun will enter Cancer and I will no longer exist. Look at the solar ray, as it passes across that window I will die (the ray appears and Garamanta falls dead as it disappears)
Agramante	He is a saint
Rodomonte	What saint? He was full of diseases, that's why he died, but since I see that you are afraid, I am enough to defeat the Christians (he departs)
Everyone	We want Ruggiero
King of Fiessa	I have a servant called Brunello, an expert thief
Agramante	Bring him here
King of Fiessa	leaves and returns with Brunello
Agramante	Are you confident that you can steal a ring from Angelica in Cathay? I will make you a king
Brunello	promises and departs
Everyone	leaves to gather troops

2 Forest

Grifone	and Aquilante see a bridge, they see a woman and ask [information]
Woman	This is the Bridge of Roses where by order of the king of Orgagna every knight is honored. Therefore, you are invited
Grifone	We accept (Origilla arrives)
Grifone	This is Orlando's horse
Origilla	Its owner is dead. They all go to the bridge

3 Forest

Orlando	blames all women (then regrets it) Only Angelica is sincere. He looks for Origilla

4 Castle

Governor	who arrests those who happen to arrive in order to send them to the garden of Falerina (Grifone, Aquilante, and Origilla arrive)
Governor	honors them and then has them arrested

Act 3°

1 Forest

Orlando	But where do I go to find her? (a woman arrives)
Woman	Sir, change your direction because you are near Falerina's garden
Orlando	That is what I am seeking
Woman	Yesterday Falerina finished constructing a sword to kill Orlando, the one who will destroy her enchantment
Orlando	I am willing to go
Woman	I give you a book. You must wait for daybreak and then enter the garden, the book will explain everything to you

2 Paris

Carlo	has learned about Agramante's military preparations. He sends Dudone in search of Orlando and Rinaldo

3 Forest

	Grifone, Aquilante, and Origilla in chains, led by a giant
Orlando	kills the giant and liberates them, sees Origilla
Grifone	in love with Origilla, he says that he believed Orlando to be dead
Orlando	realizes that Grifone loves her and says: I have to go on an undertaking and I want to be alone. I will take Origilla with me.
Grifone	sorrowful, he departs with his brother

Comparative Analysis

Act 1 (scene 1): "A grand council held by Agramante to defeat Carlo."

Act 1 (scene 4), Act 2 (scene 1), Act 3 (scene 2): "Rodomonte refutes the king of Garamanta's speech. The latter, before dying, explains how to find Ruggiero."

Book Two of Boiardo's *Orlando Innamorato* opens with a council in which the twenty-two-year-old King Agramante of Biserta announces his plan to conquer France (*OI* 2.1.18–77). This newly invented character's projected military invasion evokes both the historical attacks and the occupation of various parts of southern Europe by North African forces beginning in the eighth century and, in turn, the fictional invasion of southern Italy by King Agolante of Africa recounted in the medieval epic *Aspramonte*.³ At the same time, Agramante aims to emulate a more distant ancestor. Like his purported grandfather Agolante, Agramante claims descent from that most relentless of would-be world conquerors, Alexander of Macedonia. In his council speech, in fact, he devotes much more attention to his ancient Macedonian predecessor than to his North African relatives.⁴ For the better part of three stanzas, Agramante urges his fellow kings to win renown in the manner of Alexander, whereas the aim of extending Mohammad's law, so central to Agolante's war, is simply tacked on in the final verse (*OI* 2.1.35–37).⁵

The reaction of Agramante's fellow kings and advisors shines the spotlight on the limits and possibilities of deliberation when the power to go to war resides in the hands of the ruler. Three prominent figures—King Branzardo, King Sobrino, and the king of Garamanta—draw upon reason, experience, historical example, and astrology to argue against the invasion. The overreaching and impetuous King Rodamonte of Sarza, however, aims to squelch debate by denigrating those who disagree with him. Rather than offering arguments on Agramante's behalf, the king of Sarza maintains that they were convened to demonstrate unconditional support and not to voice their opinion (*OI* 2.1.55). Nevertheless, the king of Garamanta continues to speak his mind and a discussion then ensues between the eager youths and the disinclined veterans until Agramante silences the hall and declares his intention to move forward with his plan (*OI* 2.1.63).

Although Agramante will not be dissuaded from his reckless enterprise, he does agree to delay his departure until the incomparable Rugiero can be located and recruited since, according to the wise astrologer king of Garamanta, it is only this youth's presence that will bring some measure of success to the African army. The initial search for Rugiero, however, comes up empty. At a second gathering, therefore, Rodamonte disparages Agramante for heeding another's advice and decides to leave to invade France

---

3 For Boiardo's use of historical and fictional figures in his depiction of Agramante, see Cavallo, *The World beyond Europe* 85–94. There are fifteenth-century Italian versions of the *Aspramonte* (based on the Old French *Aspremont*) in both *ottava rima* verse and in the prose of Andrea da Barberino. See Villoresi, *La letteratura cavalleresca* 65–69.

4 The scene's classical allusions go beyond the explicit references to Alexander of Macedonia. Giovanni Ponte (81) and Michael Murrin (59–63) have pointed out that the council recalls parallel episodes in both Herodotus and Livy, and Cristina Zampese (193–99) has noted links to Statius's *Thebaid* as well.

5 Berni, for his part, will replace this casual reference to Mohammad's law with an allusion to revenge that evokes longstanding hostilities: "To avenge our ancient injuries / From those people so hostile to us" (30.44).

with his own army (*OI* 2.3.36). Thus, the figure who initially fashioned himself as an enforcer of the king's commands—and labelled as traitorous those who would profess anything less than blind obedience—demonstrates that his prior attempts to suppress discussion were merely a cover for his own boundless ambition.

The *Storia dei paladini* provides new biographical details concerning Agramante's childhood to further develop his character. Whereas Boiardo noted he assumed the crown as a seven-year-old orphan, Lodico also imagines that he was raised personally by the king of Garamanta from that time forward. This creates the sense of a long-standing special bond between Agramante, here twenty-three years old, and the wise astrologer king. Nonetheless, as we are shown, nurture was unable to counteract nature. Despite his guardian's best attempts to "restrain that pride that was growing in Agramante," all the same "the little monarch developed the nature of his ancestors" (8: 45).

Lodico, moreover, combines the overreaching typical of "great lords" that Boiardo warned about at the opening of the *Innamorato* (*OI* 1.1.5) with the overtones of religious warfare typical of the Carolingian epic. Even prior to the council scene we are told that Agramante "turned his thoughts to attacking France in order to destroy the Christians and the Church" (8: 45). This expression of hostility toward Christianity accords with both the increasingly religious connotations that Agramante's invasion assumes in the course of Ariosto's *Orlando Furioso* and the habitual aggression on the part of Saracen rulers found throughout the *Storia dei paladini*. In addition, the plan to destroy Christendom is given an explicitly global scope from the outset when Lodico adds that the council brings to Biserta "infinite troops" not only from Africa but from Asia as well (8: 45).

Lodico also subtly develops the despotic connotations of Agramante's rule. Whereas Boiardo's Agramante "waited for response" (*OI* 2.1.38) and those present at the council readily expressed their views, in the *Storia dei paladini* there is an initial silence before the first reply due to the danger involved in voicing independent judgment: "No one at the council gave any indication of answering because contradicting a statement made by the emperor was considered a crime" (8: 47). This reference to the lack of freedom of expression underscores the courage of the three wise men who will subsequently speak their mind despite the prohibition.

The *Storia dei paladini*'s ensuing discussion between the three advisors and the overbearing Rodomonte closely follows Boiardo's original scene, but once again a religious motivation is added. In this case, it is Leggio who adds the holy war rhetoric. Whereas Boiardo's Rodamonte had spoken of ruining France with sword and fire (*OI* 2.1.61) and Lodico's character had planned to set fire to Paris and see Italy in flames (3: 29 in the 1858–60 edition),

Leggio specifies that the king of Sarza imagines having "set Paris on fire and burned down Rome with the Christian pope" (8: 49). In shifting the focus to religious hostility, Leggio's phrasing nonetheless accords with Lodico's earlier assertion that Agramante had convened the council because he wanted to destroy the Church by waging war against the Christians (3: 26 in the 1858–60 edition).

The second council, which takes place in the following chapter, while also closely following the *Innamorato*, emphasizes even more the hold that the king of Garamanta has over Agramante and the other kings, on the one hand, and Rodomonte's irreverence, on the other. When the astrologer king predicts his own imminent death and then falls dead in the midst of the gathering, Boiardo's Agramante had been astonished ("sbigotito") and "everyone there received a fright" (*OI* 2.3.33). Lodico intensifies everyone's reaction. The other kings are now said to be astonished ("si sbigottirono"), while Agramante is shown to actually tremble (8: 61). As in the *Innamorato*, whoever had earlier demonstrated bravado has a change of heart and asserts that the king of Garamanta had spoken the truth. Now, however, their assertion is accompanied by the physical reaction of their faces changing color (8: 61). Rodomonte, for his part, not only dismisses the king of Garamanta's sudden death as a consequence of sickness and old age, but belittles those present. In the *Innamorato*, Rodomonte had already sarcastically contrasted the stasis of those present with his own desire for action: "Stay then—don't anybody move!" (*OI* 2.3.35). Now, however, he adds insult to injury by calling them faint-hearted, frightened, and unwilling to undertake a revenge he claims is expected of them by their fathers: "Since you look at him timidly and fear has entered each of your chests, I tell you that I am strong enough to place the crown of France upon my head and undertake that vengeance that your parents hoped in vain from you" (8: 61).

Whereas Agramante's two councils occur in two separate cantos of the *Innamorato* (2.1.18–77 and 2.3.16–45) and two separate chapters of the *Storia dei paladini* (8: 45–50 and 59–62), Agrippino stages both councils within the space of *sera* 170. Indeed, their placement at the opening of Act 1 and Act 2, respectively, treats them as parallel scenes that create a structural symmetry within the play.[6] Both councils closely follow the *Storia dei paladini*'s paraphrasing—even copying substantial material from the speeches verbatim.

---

6 *Sera* 171 in *Paladini* 7 underscores the importance of the opening council scene by specifying that it is staged with a *scena in fondo* (deep stage). Alessandro Napoli notes that in the Catanese puppet theater tradition, this scene was always set up with a deep stage (Napoli in Pasqualino, *Rerum palatinorum fragmenta* 177n).

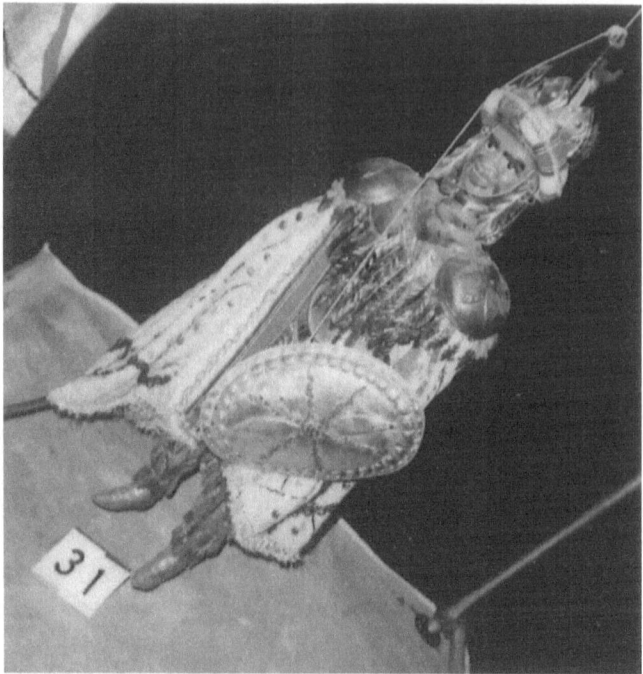

Figure 6.1 Agramante (Appendix 1, #31). Manteo Family Marionettes, 1991. Collection of the Staten Island Museum.

As a result, Agrippino incorporates the new emphasis on religious warfare, including, for example, Rodomonte's threat to burn Rome with the pope (Act 1, scene 1).

Agrippino is also attentive in accentuating the contrast between Agramante (Figure 6.1) and his fellow kings, on the one hand, and Rodomonte (Figure 6.2), on the other.[7] In the *Innamorato* and the *Storia dei paladini*, the king of Garamanta spontaneously predicts his own death in the course of his speech near the end of the second council. Agrippino, by contrast, has Rodomonte interrupt the astrologer king to sarcastically quip "You predict everything except your own death" (Act 2, scene 1). It is this interjection that leads to the astrologer king's prediction and instantaneous demise. Agrippino next intensifies Agramante's reaction even more than Lodico did by having him exclaim that the king of Garamanta "is a saint." Such a pronouncement combines faith in the astrologer's predictions, already in Boiardo and Lodico, with a sense of religious awe for the figure himself. In this context,

---

7 For another example of a Rodomonte puppet, see the one constructed by Nino Canino in Amico 22.

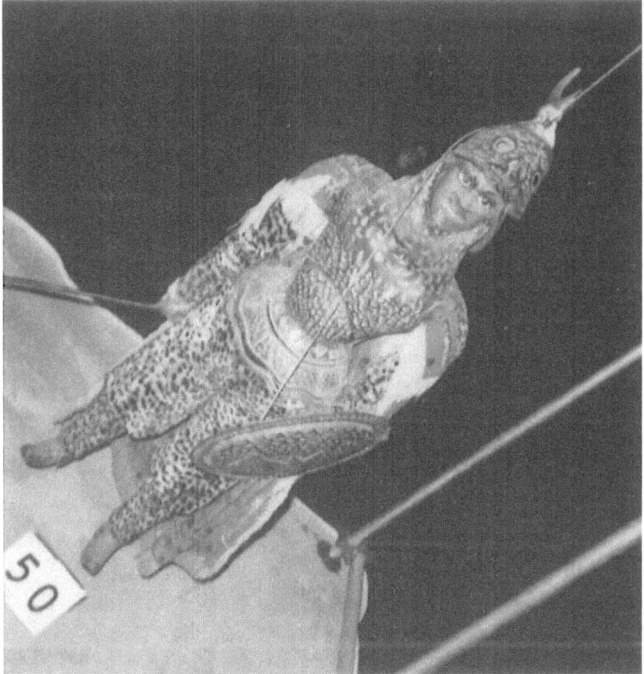

Figure 6.2 Rodomonte (Appendix 1, #50). Manteo Family Marionettes, 1991. Collection of the Staten Island Museum.

Rodomonte's dismissive remark about the astrologer king's ill health, while echoing Agrippino's sources, becomes a response not only to the occurrence itself but also to Agramante's belief in the king's saintliness. Rodomonte's open derision of the king of Biserta's assertion directly anticipates the contempt he will show soon thereafter by precipitously walking out of the council and preparing to invade France on his own.

Act 1 (scenes 2, 5, 6): "Mandricardo goes to Circassia to avenge his father."

In the meantime, the war at Albraca rages on even after Agricane's death. By this time, the protagonists are Marfisa (who has changed sides due to a perceived offense from her erstwhile ally Galafrone) and Sacripante (the king of Circassia who is also in love with Angelica). Even the news that Agricane's son Mandricardo is laying waste to vast areas of Circassia and has murdered Sacripante's own brother does not induce the Circassian king to leave Albraca because Marfisa will not agree to a mutual retreat (*OI* 2.3.13). According to Boiardo, Mandricardo set his sights on neighboring Circassia after hearing rumors of Sacripante's demise (*OI* 2.3.9).

Refashioning this episode in the *Storia dei paladini*, Lodico attributes Mandricardo's sudden invasion of Circassia to the mistaken belief that Sacripante was responsible for Agricane's death (8: 57). Mandricardo's motivation is thus recast as filial piety rather than opportunistic ambition and his destruction of Circassian territories is due to uncontrolled rage in seeking revenge rather than an excess of gratuitous violence. This new twist also creates a foreshadowing of Mandricardo's subsequent journey westward in search of Orlando when he learns that it was the Frankish paladin who killed his father.

Agrippino includes three scenes related to Albracca in *sera* 170 ensuring that his spectators would have kept the ongoing war in mind. The first two take place directly at Albracca: on the part of the assailants, Marfisa and her Turkish ally send for reinforcements (Act 2, scene 2); on the part of the defendants, Sacripante comforts Angelica as she laments Orlando's absence even though, as we recall, it was she who sent him away (Act 2, scene 5). The third scene takes us to Tartaria where, following the *Storia dei paladini*, Mandricardo (Figure 6.3) holds Sacripante responsible for the death of his father and leaves with his army to lay siege to Circassia (Act 2, scene 6).

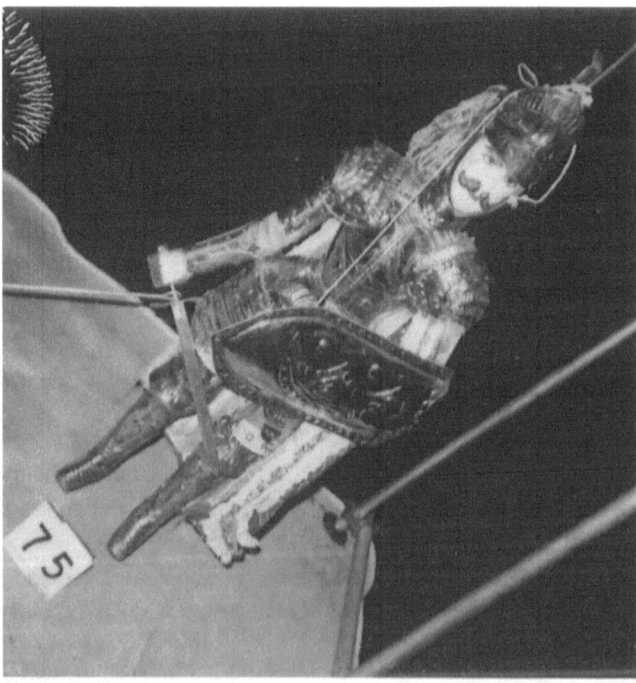

Figure 6.3 Mandricardo (Appendix 1, #75). Manteo Family Marionettes, 1991. Collection of the Staten Island Museum.

Act 1 (scene 3); Act 2 (scene 2): "Grifone and Aquilante are taken prisoner at the Bridge of Roses."

Act 2 (scenes 3 and 4) and Act 3 (scenes 1 and 3): "Orlando frees Grifone and Aquilante, kills a giant, and heads for the enchantment of Falerina."

As Orlando heads to the Garden of Falerina in Orgagna following Angelica's command, Boiardo alerts us to the fact that the danger of this death trap extends to the surrounding area. Travelers who arrive at the nearby Bridge of Roses, on the Caspian Sea (*OI* 2.2.39), are first graciously entertained and then captured in their sleep and taken to Orgagna to be fed to the serpent monster who guards the garden gate. The brothers Grifone and Aquilante, who earlier found themselves fighting on the side of Orlando at Albraca, as well as Origille, who arrives after having stolen Orlando's steed, fall victim to this trap (*OI* 2.2.37–51). Fortunately for them, Orlando arrives in time to rescue them before they become a meal for the serpent. Grifone is not entirely happy about the outcome, however. Since he had in the meantime fallen in love with Origille, he is sorry to be deprived of her presence when Orlando takes her with him on his journey to the garden of Orgagna (*OI* 2.3.48–65).

Lodico alters several details of the Bridge of Roses episode in the *Storia dei paladini*. For example, the Caspian Sea becomes a river, making it easier to visualize the palace across a bridge, and Boiardo's "flowering field" (*OI* 2.2.37) is complemented by roses and other plants decorating the building's entrance, thus rendering more apposite the name of the site (8: 53). In addition, the imposition of one night's lodging in order to pass the bridge is turned into a supposed stay of three nights required by local law (8: 53). The narrative, however, remains likewise divided into two parts (8: 53–54 and 62–64).

Agrippino's intervention is not so much in the details (which are sparse) but rather in the division of the material. What had been narrated in two segments in two different *canti* of the *Innamorato* and chapters of the *Storia dei paladini* is divided by Agrippino into six separate scenes all within the span of a single evening. The fact, moreover, that the scenes run across all three Acts—with only the three central ones staged consecutively—gives a sense of greater development and suspense to the episode while at the same time juxtaposing it throughout with the epic themes of the play's main events.

The first scene depicts Grifone and Aquilante leaving the fortress of Albracca (Act 1, scene 3). The intervening scenes take us from the forest outside Biserta to Albracca to Tartaria and then back to Biserta proper before the two knights arrive at the Bridge of Roses in Act 2, scene 2. This gives a sense of time having passed and therefore of distance having been traveled. For the next two scenes, which follow consecutively, Agrippino reorders the narrative. In the *Innamorato* and *Storia dei paladini*, Orlando's monologue complaining of the treachery of Origille (and, for a brief moment, of all women) immediately precedes his encounter with the three prisoners (cfr. *OI* 2.3.46–47 and 8: 62). Agrippino, however, inserts the speech in-between the brothers' arrival at the Bridge of Roses and their apprehension during the night (Act 2, scene 3). This once again gives a sense of time passing since we may imagine that the brothers continue to be entertained as Orlando grumbles to himself. Moreover, this narrative reordering also reintroduces the theme of deceit with the intent to harm, thus preparing the audience for the next scene in which the lord of the castle first honors the knights and then traitorously has them apprehended in their asleep (Act 2, scene 4).

The Bridge of Roses episode is continued in the first and third scenes of Act 3. In the intervening scene, Agrippino takes us to Paris where Orlando's absence is felt in the light of Agramante's upcoming military invasion of France. The fact that Carlo "sends Dudone in search of Orlando and Rinaldo" reminds us once again that while Orlando succumbs to one amorous illusion after another, he is derelict in his duty to his homeland which is facing imminent attack (Act 3, scene 2). The first scene in which a woman warns Orlando to stay away from Falerina's garden and then gives him a book to help him achieve victory is likewise moved up with respect to Boiardo's poem (where it occurs only when the paladin is about to enter the garden), but this time it is the *Storia dei paladini* that first enacts the narrative shift. The sixth scene of the sequence—and the final scene of the entire play—brings all the components together on stage in a dramatic finale. Orlando kills the giant leading Grifone, Aquilante, and Origilla to their death, thus providing some of the agonistic action for which *opera dei pupi* is famous. The brothers are then summarily dismissed by the knight who is once again under the sway of Origilla. *Sera* 170's final scene thus leaves spectators with both a satisfying conclusion to the Bridge of Roses episode in which Orlando saves the day by defending victims from a death trap and, at the same time, a sense of anticipation regarding his upcoming adventure in the traitorous garden that has already killed so many travelers before him.

Orlando will go on to destroy the garden of Orgagna only because he (temporarily) puts aside his infatuation with deceitful women and uses both the gift of the book of answers and his own critical thinking to overcome the garden's deathly traps. But at present we leave behind Orlando and his vain unrequited desire as we shift focus in the following chapter to a case of enduring reciprocal love between two exemplary characters.

Chapter 7

THE ENAMORMENT OF BRADAMANTE AND RUGGIERO (*SERA* 182)[1]

Introduction

By this point in the *Orlando Innamorato*, the North African invasion of Carlo's realm is well under way. Although Rugiero's wizard guardian Atalante had been sheltering him in the Atlas Mountains in the Maghreb to protect him from his destined early death by betrayal, the youth was lured out by a ruse and he subsequently joined Agramante's expedition as it followed Rodamonte to France. In the meantime, Gradasso has undertaken another journey from the Far East to France to attain Durlindana and Baiardo. Along the way, he teams up with Mandricardo, who has set out from Tartaria to avenge the death of Agricane by killing Orlando. As the two new companions head westward, the narrator remarks that "such a valiant pair / was not then found in pagan lands" (*OI* 3.2.39). The two warrior kings will eventually join the allied Saracen forces closing in on the Christian Franks. Nonetheless, as we find out in *sera* 182, they do not hesitate to fight each other over the right to possess Orlando's sword.

In the midst of the invasion of France, a battlefield love story arises between the Saracen Rugiero and the Christian Bradamante that goes against the "us" versus "them" mentality characteristic of war. Although the two are technically enemy combatants when they meet, they treat each other first and foremost as individuals deserving of respect. Their encounter is not a minor diversion from the martial exploits but rather the most crucial moment of the *Innamorato* given that Boiardo imagines the North African Rugiero and the Frankish Bradamante to be the progenitors of the Estense dynasty of Ferrara, currently headed by the poem's dedicatee, Duke Ercole I d'Este.

The core of *sera* 182 dramatizes the fateful encounter of Bradamante (Figure 7.1) and Ruggiero (Figure 7.2) leading to their enamorment.

---

[1] The play translated and discussed in this chapter is found in *Copione* 13. To compare versions, see play 183 in *Paladini* 8 and *serata* 190 in Mike Manteo's notebook 16.

Figure 7.1 Bradamante (Appendix 1, #21). Manteo Family Marionettes, 1991. Collection of the Staten Island Museum.

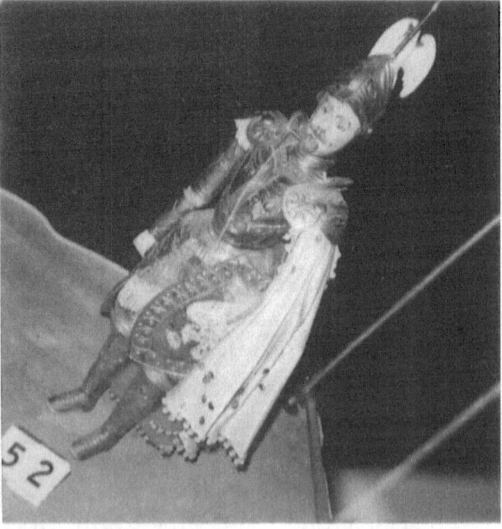

Figure 7.2 Ruggiero (Appendix 1, #52). Manteo Family Marionettes, 1991. Collection of the Staten Island Museum.

The growing bond between the two courteous knights provides a contrast to the animosity surrounding them on both a grand scale (the pan-African invasion of France serving as frame in Acts 1 and 3) and at an individual level (Rodomonte's discourtesy in Act 1, scene 5; the ambush in Act 2, scenes 2 and 3; and the dispute between Mandricardo and Gradasso over Orlando's sword in Act 3, scene 4).

Translation

Evening 182

The battle near Montalbano continues. Arrival of Gradasso and Mandricardo. Defeat of the Christians. Ruggiero fights against Rodomonte in defense of Bradamante. Enamorment of Ruggiero and Bradamante. Martasino treacherously injures Bradamante. Ruggiero defends her. Battle between Mandricardo and Gradasso. Brandimarte separates them.

Characters
two hermits
Grifone di Magonza
Martasino
Daniforte
Barrigano
Captains
Knights

Act 1

1 Field

Carlo	The Christians are in danger. Where are Orlando and Rinaldo? He orders Turpino to go out with all the reserves

2 Forest

Gradasso and Mandricardo, having landed at the Port of the Frog in Aigues-Mortes and traveled through the territory of France, approach Montalbano. They see the battle and decide to fight against the Christians

3 Battle

Gandellino	knocks down Ruggiero and is then chased
Cladinoro	stuns Agramante
Ruggiero	stuns Oliviero and Uggiero
Grifone di Magonza treacherously wounds Ruggiero	
Ruggiero	pursues him
Rinaldo	fights, arrival (of Grifone)
Grifone	Rinaldo, save me from that man who treacherously wounded me
Rinaldo	attacks Ruggiero, they fight
Ruggiero	sees his men in danger, leaves Rinaldo and rushes to them
Rinaldo	goes to fight elsewhere
Mandricardo		

Gradasso	| they have entered the fray
Agramante	orders ambushes to slaughter the Christians
Carlo	orders a retreat
Ruggiero	takes Oliviero and Ottone prisoner
Turpino	fights, Ruggiero arrives
Ruggiero	Sir, flee, I offer you my horse
Turpino	Your kindness tells me that you were not born a pagan, but I do not want what is not mine, thank you (he departs)
Gradasso and Mandricardo	We have arrived late, let's retire to the mountain to watch the conclusion of the battle (they depart)
Baiardo	runs away, Rinaldo pursues him

4 Forest

Rinaldo	pursues Baiardo

5 Battle

The battle between Bradamante and Rodomonte continues

Ruggiero	stops the battle, informs Bradamante that Carlo has fled, so it is useless to fight
Bradamante to Rodomonte	Let me join my liege
Rodomonte	You're raving mad, here you must die
Ruggiero	You're discourteous. Knight, go join Carlo and I will take care of this
Bradamante	departs
Rodomonte	attacks Ruggiero, they enter fighting

6 Forest

Bradamante	Carlo has fled and I left alone the knight who may be in danger because he took up my defense. It is necessary for me to return for the sake of my honor and to defend him (she departs)

7 Forest

The battle between Rodomonte and Ruggiero continues. Rodomonte stunned

Ruggiero	waits for him to regain consciousness (Bradamante arrives)
Bradamante	Forgive me, oh knight, if I was discourteous to leave you in the hands of that warrior, now leave this battle to me
Rodomonte	regains his senses, sees the two knights, understands the danger,

THE ENAMORMENT OF BRADAMANTE AND RUGGIERO 151

	and says to Ruggiero: You have defeated me both in valor and in courtesy, and given that the two armies have divided I will return to Marsilio since I was fighting on his behalf (he departs)
Bradamante	Since the enemy has departed, I will leave as well
Ruggiero	I will accompany you given that there are traps all around us; you will not be in danger if you are with me. They depart

8 Forest

	Fiordiligi and Brandimarte, who are traveling through Christian lands, see a hermit
Hermit	You go in search of Orlando. He is to be found at the enchantment of the Naiads, but you can't go alone; others are needed but there must be an odd number
Brandimarte	seeks companions
Hermit	calls Fiordiligi, gives her a garland and says to give it to Brandimarte because it will break every enchantment

Act 2

1 Forest

Ruggiero and Bradamante exchange kind words

Bradamante	Tell me your name, o courteous knight
Ruggiero	My origin comes from Troy Page 498
	It would take a long time to relate it to you. My father was Ruggiero, son of Rampaldo di Risa, killed treacherously by Beltramo. My mother Galiacella, daughter of Agolante, died in giving birth to me, and I was raised by a wizard. And who are you?
Bradamante	I am the sister of Rinaldo. (They lift their visors, they fall in love.) Tell me, your father was a Christian, why don't you follow his example?
Martasino	wounds Bradamante by treachery
Bradamante	kills Martasino (Pinadoro arrives)
Ruggiero	confronts him
Pinadoro	You are disloyal to Agramante
Ruggiero	stuns him
Daniforte	treacherously wounds Ruggiero and flees
Bradamante	pursues him
Ruggiero	kills Barrigano; Pinadoro regains consciousness and then is killed; he goes in search of Bradamante

2 Forest

Bradamante	reaches Daniforte and kills him, and then leaves to tend to her wound

3 Forest

Angelica	has fled due to the destruction of Carlo's camp

4 Forest

Ruggiero	in search of Bradamante, he remains pensive; Gradasso and Mandricardo arrive and greet him
Ruggiero	does not answer
Mandricardo	Uncouth knight, we greeted you!
Ruggiero	Forgive me, love has taken away my faculty of reason
Mandricardo	You have a noble spirit, if you need help we are at your disposal
Ruggiero	Thank you
Mandricardo	Tell me, what right do you have to wear that insignia without having first proven that you are worthy of it?
Ruggiero	I did not notice this before. Where did you acquire this insignia? I do not permit you to wear it
Mandricardo	I acquired it in Asia
Ruggiero	This is my family's insignia
Mandricardo	No more words, en garde!
Ruggiero	You have no sword
Mandricardo	I cannot carry any sword if it's not Durlindana which is now held by Orlando
Gradasso	Slow down there, Durlindana is mine!
Mandricardo	Durlindana must be joined to Hector's armor
Gradasso	I don't want to hear any discussion, en garde!
Ruggiero	walks away laughing

Gradasso and Mandricardo fight, they enter fighting

5 Forest

Ruggiero	Those two want the sword but Orlando will sell it at a high price He sees a knight and a lady, he recognizes them from having seen them in Africa, they are Bramadoro and Fiordiligi.[2] Brandimarte and Fiordiligi arrive and greet Ruggiero

---

2 Bramadoro is the original name of Brandimarte.

Ruggiero	relates that two knights are fighting over Durlindana and he could not pacify them
Brandimarte	Let's go together

Act 3

1 Forest

	The battle between Gradasso and Mandricardo continues
Brandimarte	stops them and says, you are fighting over Durlindana while I, coming from Africa, learned from a soothsayer that Orlando is under a spell. I alone cannot liberate him, we will all go together, and then we'll see who will attain the sword
All	depart, in agreement
Brandimarte	One moment, we are four, but the number of knights must be uneven, so one of us will have to leave. There are many stones over there, whoever gets the black stone will have to leave. (They go)
Mandricardo	gets the black one and departs

Ruggiero, Gradasso, and Brandimarte head toward the enchantment

2 Forest

Bradamante, without a helmet, sees a hermitage and calls out	
Hermit	sees that a woman has arrived, says Go away, Satan!
Bradamante	I am a Christian
Hermit	leads her away to tend to her wounds

3 Field

Agramante has joined forces with the Spaniards; Rodomonte arrives and recounts his adventure at Monaco.[3] Mandricardo arrives, and they march toward Paris

4 Forest

Cladinoro and Carinda go to join Carlo in Paris

---

[3] The adventure is the shipwreck of Rodomonte's fleet on the coast of southern France after sailing from North Africa. Boiardo locates Monaco at the border of Provence (*OI* 2.6.37).

Comparative Analysis

Act 1 (scenes 1–3): "The battle under Montalbano continues."

Rugiero was introduced at the conclusion of Book One of the *Orlando Innamorato* as a knight "blessed with all virtues, who surpassed / all other men the world has known" (*OI* 1.29.56). Such an assertion effectively places his virtue above that of every other character in the poem, including Carlo's famous paladins. The participation of Rugiero in Agramante's invasion of France gives Boiardo the occasion to demonstrate the knight's praiseworthiness through actions undertaken prior to his encounter with Bradamante. In the course of a fierce battle in southern France, the warrior bishop Turpino appropriates Rugiero's horse and then falls into a swamp while trying to flee. Rugiero not only saves Turpino from drowning in the stagnant water, but then also offers him his horse (*OI* 3.4.43–44). Rugiero's extraordinary kindness to an enemy may echo the exceptional courtesy that Orlando and Agricane showed each other on the battlefield of Albraca (discussed in Chapter 5), but it has greater ramifications because his genealogical line is purported to lead us out of the fiction of the poem and into the historical present of the Estense family. Rugiero's other-regarding action prompts Turpino to exclaim: "You were not born a Saracen" (*OI* 3.4.44). Tellingly, the Christian connotations that Turpino intuits in Rugiero's character are not connected to fighting the enemies of one's faith but rather to showing unconditional benevolence—even toward those who have done one harm.

In the *Storia dei paladini*, Ruggiero likewise saves Turpino from drowning after chasing after him, but his subsequent offer of his horse to the enemy who had just been fleeing from him is now given a context that motivates his action. It is in looking into Turpino's "venerable face" that Ruggiero feels compassion and declares: "Since this horse can be more useful to an older man than to a younger one, take it if you need it" (8: 220). Turpino's reply not only hypothesizes Ruggiero's Christian origins but also obliquely foreshadows his future conversion: "May heaven always guide you toward your greater good" (8: 221).

Agrippino follows suit in showcasing Ruggiero's courtesy and valor on the battlefield in the course of the war. His dramatization, however, refrains from denigrating Turpino in the process. In Act 1, scene 4, the bishop is still actively fighting even after Carlo has ordered a retreat. Seeing this, Ruggiero spontaneously offers Turpino his horse on his own initiative so that the Christian warrior may follow his king. The elimination of Turpino's attempt to usurp Ruggiero's horse and the latter's hot pursuit of him not only spares Turpino from cutting a less than ideal figure but also makes the courteous offer seem more plausible. In this way, too, Ruggiero's new motivation for his gesture, that is, so that a Frankish knight may follow the retreating emperor, anticipates his subsequent interruption of a one-on-one battle for the same reason.

Act 1 (scenes 5–7); Act 2 (scenes 1 and 2): "Defeat of the Christians. Ruggiero fights against Rodomonte in defense of Bradamante. Enamorment of Ruggiero and Bradamante. Martasino treacherously injures Bradamante. Ruggiero defends her."

In the *Innamorato*, as the combined Spanish and African armies compel Carlo's forces to flee northward toward Paris, Rugiero comes upon Rodamonte engaged in a battle against a Frankish paladin. Little does he know at the time that the latter is actually the female warrior Bradamante who is destined to become his wife. Rugiero is the first to act courteously when he offers to take Bradamante's place after Rodamonte refuses to give her leave to follow Carlo's retreating army. Although Bradamante initially accepts his offer and departs, she subsequently regrets having left a stranger to guard her back with his front (*OI* 3.5.7). She thus declares that she would have to return to see the courteous knight even if she were to encounter "King Charles and all / his soldiers dead and captured." Her reasoning reveals that she places herself and her honor above her duty to Carlo on her value scale: "I'm bound to my high emperor, / but to myself and honor more."

The episode further develops the exemplarity of Rugiero's courtesy that does not distinguish between friend and foe. When Bradamante returns to the battle, she finds him waiting for his opponent Rodamonte to recover from a stunning blow rather than capitalizing on his advantage. After a humbled Rodamonte departs having declared Rugiero the victor in both arms and courtesy, the latter offers to accompany the Frankish knight to safety even though they are on opposite sides of the war. Bradamante admires Rugiero because of his courteous actions and she accepts his kind offer without any concern over his identity as a North African Saracen. The purported future founders of Ferrara's ruling family are thus able to form a bond because both have placed universal codes of chivalry and individual honor above the interests of their political leaders.

Although belonging to two distinct groups in conflict with each other, Rugiero and Bradamante develop a friendship that quickly turns into reciprocal love. As the episode unfolds, moreover, it is the Frankish Christian female who first feels both admiration and physical attraction toward the North African Saracen male. Indeed, Bradamante is so attracted to the handsome figure in front of her that she pays no attention to the extensive (twenty-stanza) family history he is relating to her (*OI* 3.5.18–37). An entire stanza is devoted to her physical and psychological reaction: while, on the one hand, she holds her breath, on the other, her wandering eyes take in Ruggiero's physique a thousand times from his crest to his stirrups. Playfully bordering on the sacrilegious, Boiardo tells us that Bradamante can think of nothing else and that she is more desirous to see his face than to catch a glimpse of Paradise (*OI* 3.5.38).

Unlike Bradamante, the reader is expected to pay close attention to the knight's genealogy. Rugiero's family is highly heterogamous: his mother was the intrepid knight Galaciella, born of an Amazon warrior and the North African king Agolante (descended from Alexander of Macedonia, as noted above), while his father Rugiero di Risa (descended from Hector of Troy) was one of the Christians defending Calabria during Agolante's invasion. The fact that his parents belonged to different sides of that conflict did not prevent them from falling in love and marrying. Their union was short-lived, however, because the treacherous alliance between the brothers of each led to the murder of Rugiero and the capture of Reggio Calabria. The widowed Galaciella escaped by sea and gave birth on the shores of North Africa before expiring (*OI* 3.5.34).[4]

Despite its close adherence to Boiardo's original, the *Storia dei paladini* nevertheless contains variations in the dialogue that affect our perception of the characters and our understanding of the action. To begin, Rodomonte's negative characteristics are intensified. When Bradamante asks him leave to follow her ruler, Rodomonte adds an insult to his discourteous refusal ("You're raving" [8: 221]). Later in the episode, after he has been bested by Ruggiero, Rodomonte minimizes his stated debt toward his valorous opponent. While likewise declaring himself "defeated in courtesy," he no longer offers his services unconditionally to Ruggiero as he did in the *Innamorato* ("Anywhere you see fit you may / order my services—always. / Masters command subordinates" [*OI* 3.5.13]). Instead, he simply declares his departure: "So I want to leave you in peace" (8: 223).

The *Storia dei paladini*'s Bradamante undergoes a more pronounced transformation that diminishes the uncompromising independence and iconoclasm of Boiardo's character. First of all, her reasoning process before returning to the site of the combat no longer places her own honor above her duty to the emperor on a comparative value scale. Instead, it is now Carlo's honor that she deems equally worthy as the defense of her own person: "If for the honor of my lord it is necessary for me to shed blood, when must I not

---

4 Although the North African invasion of Calabria is recounted in the twelfth-century Old French epic *Aspremont*, believed to have been written by a Norman author in Sicily (Sunderland 228), the love story is found only in Italian rewritings. For the fictional and historical precedents of Rugiero and Bradamante, see Cavallo, *The World beyond Europe* 95–111.

shed it for myself?" (8: 222). With the emperor's honor now stated to have the same value as her selfhood, Bradamante must somehow tip the scales to justify her return to resume her interrupted duel with Rodomonte. She does so by declaring that Carlo's retreat to safety has eliminated his need of her: "He has fled and has no more use of my sword, so I must use it for my honor" (8: 222). Such an explanation would have been superfluous in the original poem where Bradamante had made an unequivocal choice to place her own honor above her duty to the emperor.

The *Storia dei paladini* also tames Bradamante's unconventionality as she falls in love with Ruggiero. Whereas Boiardo's character had paid no heed to the courteous knight's religion during their interaction, now the female warrior brings up the youth's religious alterity early on as a factor that conditions her estimation of him: "If he did not adore Mohammad, I would hold him to be the best knight in the world, his courtesy is not a bit less than his valor" (8: 222). While anticipating the conversion that the *Furioso*'s Bradamante will require of her beloved prior to their marriage, Lodico's character no doubt also thereby conformed to the expectations of nineteenth-century Sicilian Christian readers.

The *Storia dei paladini* continues to temper Bradamante's character as the two knights converse. No longer distracted by Ruggiero's physical attributes, Bradamante now listens to his lengthy genealogical trajectory so attentively that "she did not lose one word of the story" (8: 226). The attention shifts from her attraction to the physical body of the knight in front of her to her purported recollection of Carlo's praise for Ruggiero's father: "Often from the lips of Carlo she had heard praise of the famous name of Ruggiero di Risa" (8: 226).

These changes are further developed in the maiden's response. Boiardo's Bradamante is "on fire with love" and remains "silent" until asked by Ruggiero to share her own name and history (*OI* 3.5.39). Lodico's Bradamante responds immediately and is characterized by courtesy ("cortesia") rather than desire. In keeping with the shift from sensual to sacramental, she picks up on a detail from Ruggiero's family history in order to bring to the fore his Christian origin (and thus also point toward his future conversion): "You are therefore the son of Ruggiero; he was a Christian and subject of my lord Carlo, and you differ in nothing from your father" (8: 226).

To relate Ruggiero's account of his family history, Agrippino uncharacteristically refers back to the relevant page number in the *Storia dei paladini* (Figure 7.3).[5] Although it is impossible to know if any of the lengthy

---

5 Agrippino's personal copy of the 1909 edition, in fact, has a large "X" in orange pencil at the top of this page.

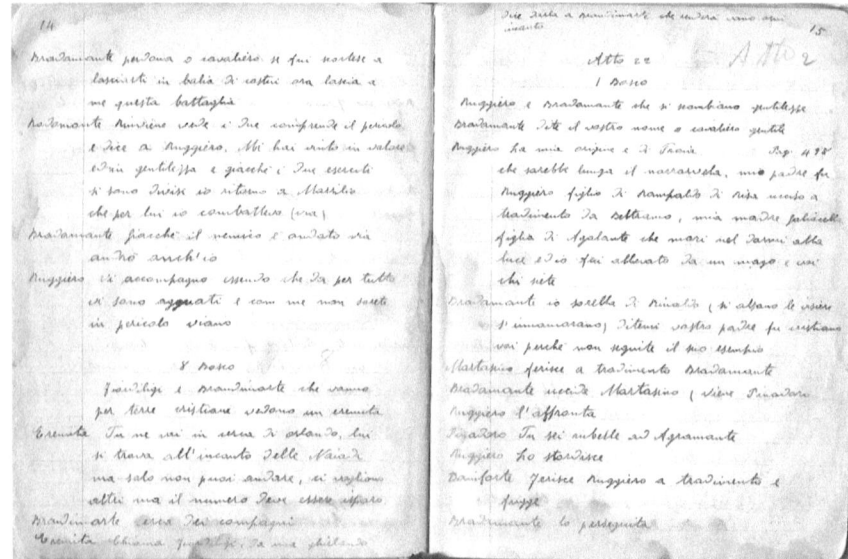

Figure 7.3 The enamorment of Bradamante and Ruggiero in *sera* 182 (*Copione* 13). Courtesy of Michael J. Manteo.

excursus was recited verbatim during performances, the page number of the source suggests that Ruggiero's ancient Trojan and more recent southern Italian genealogy were considered important enough to warrant reporting accurately and in detail. Agrippino could have expected his traditional public to be especially interested in Ruggiero's family history due to the prominence of Sicily—the Isle of Fire (*OI* 3.5.21)—and southern Italy in the story.[6] Ruggiero's family history specifically mentions Mount Etna, Messina, Siracusa, and Agrigento, in addition to nearby Reggio Calabria. It may be that Agrippino wanted to easily consult this page of the *Storia dei paladini* not only to underscore Ruggiero's remarkable chivalric pedigree but also to ensure the inclusion of place names familiar to his audience.

In staging the moment of Ruggiero and Bradamante's enamorment, Agrippino refashions the story in meaningful ways (Act 2, scene 1). First, whereas Boiardo and Lodico both relate that Bradamante is the first to feel the stirrings of attraction, Agrippino stages a double *coup de foudre* in which both knights lift their visors and simultaneously fall in love with each other. In a fictional world fraught with endless examples of unrequited desire, this case

---

6 Indeed, Lodico's original edition of the *Storia dei paladini* identifies the Isle of Fire in a footnote to be sure that it is not missed by readers: "This is how Sicily was called in the past because of the flames thrown by Mount Etna" (3: 400n).

of reciprocal love at first sight offers a memorable exception and places both knights on a symmetrical and even plane. In addition, whereas Boiardo had made religious difference irrelevant to the couple's enamorment, and Lodico, on the contrary, made Bradamante's appraisal of Ruggiero qualified by religious difference, Agrippino finds a way to resolve both perspectives. Following Boiardo, he depicts Bradamante and Ruggiero falling in love regardless of their different religious affiliations while, at the same time, following Lodico, he acknowledges the importance of the Christian faith by having Bradamante suggest straightaway to Ruggiero that he follow the religion of his father: "Tell me, your father was a Christian. Why don't you follow his example?"

The couple's conversation is interrupted when they are attacked by a group of Saracens and separated during the ensuing combat. The wounded Bradamante will eventually be cared for by a hermit in Act 3, scene 1, but Agrippino first turns his attention to Ruggiero's encounter with Gradasso and Mandricardo.

Act 2 (scenes 4 and 5); Act 3 (scene 1): "Battle between Mandricardo and Gradasso. Brandimarte separates them."

In the *Innamorato*, Gradasso and Mandricardo greet Rugiero courteously ("de animo perfetto") and show their adherence to the code of courtly love by telling him that his enamorment is proof of his gentility ("gentilezza") and by offering their assistance (*OI* 3.6.34–36). Yet their budding friendship is disturbed shortly thereafter by disputes over chivalric accoutrements. First, Mandricardo takes issue with Rugiero wearing the same emblem as found on his newly acquired armor and the two knights contest the right to bear that coat of arms. Before they can take action, however, Gradasso intervenes to challenge Mandricardo over Orlando's sword and then actually comes to blows with his new travel companion (*OI* 3.6.45–54). There is something ludicrous about two knights attacking each other with elm and pine tree trunks in a brawl over a sword of unknown whereabouts, and in fact Rugiero walks away laughing.

The suspension of the fight thanks to the arrival of Brandimarte leads directly to another adventure. The knight recounts having learned from a soothsayer ("indovino") in Africa that the current owner of the sword is trapped among naiads in the nearby enchanted Laughing Stream (Fonte del Riso) (*OI* 3.6.53–56).[7] Unbeknownst to the knights, the wizard

---

[7] We are not privy to this encounter in the poem, but only to Brandimarte's encounter with King Agramante and, subsequently, Rugiero, in Biserta (*OI* 2.28.1–43).

Atalante had devised the enchantment specifically to entrap Orlando. While Mandricardo, who is excluded through a lottery, makes his way toward Agramante's camp, Brandimarte, Rugiero, and Gradasso will jointly undertake an adventure to liberate the Frankish paladin.

Although the knights carry the weapons, it is Brandimarte's wife Fiordelisa who is in command. In addition to acting as a guide through the various perils, she has also fashioned four garlands—for the three knights plus Orlando—in the shape of crowns that will nullify the enchantment. Just as Brandimarte is falling under the spell of the naiads, Fiordelisa slips one of the crowns upon his head and instructs him how to free the other knights (*OI* 3.7.33).

The *Storia dei paladini* replays the episode with some variations. Gradasso's account of his past efforts to attain Durlindana, for example, includes the admission that he "dissipated an entire treasure" in the process (8: 231), echoing the *Innamorato*'s opening reflection on the calamities resulting from the unbridled desire of great lords (*OI* 1.1.5). Mandricardo remarks that this dispute has effectively ruined their friendship (8: 231), underscoring the disastrous consequences of discord on a personal level and serving as a contrast to the indestructible bond between Brandimarte and Orlando reflected in the upcoming rescue. In addition, the use of tree branches rather than trunks as weapons perhaps lends greater verisimilitude to the action.

In recounting the appearance of Brandimarte and Fiordiligi upon the scene as well as the upcoming Fonte del Riso adventure, Lodico follows Boiardo's lead in underscoring the primacy of Fiordiligi while also adding details not present in the *Innamorato*. For example, he links the damsel's knowledge of how to construct the spell-breaking garlands back to an African hermit: "Through divine providence, a hermit from Africa had secretly revealed to the lady the virtue of those flowers that were a remedy for the spell" (8: 234). He does not say whether this hermit is the same character as the soothsayer who indicated Orlando's whereabouts to Brandimarte, but in either case this reference to a more familiar religious figure counters the overtly magical connotation of Boiardo's "indovino." In addition, the mention of providence as the ultimate guiding force prepares readers for the kind of divine intervention that will occur in the upcoming episodes derived from the *Orlando Furioso*.

In keeping with his tendency to add narrative detail, moreover, Lodico imagines that Brandimarte has not only fallen prey to the enchantment, as in Boiardo, but has also refused to listen to Fiordiligi's instructions. As a result, the damsel must use her ingenuity to save him: "While embracing him, she attached the garland to his helmet and tied another five to the hilt of his sword" (8:235). Beyond adding to the number of garlands,

Lodico accentuates Fiordiligi's already crucial agency in the adventure by demonstrating her quick thinking as well.

Although Agrippino does not include the Fonte del Riso adventure in *sera* 182, he prepares for it early in the play by adding an encounter that is not in his sources. Whereas both Boiardo and Lodico simply have Brandimarte refer in passing to a soothsayer he encountered in Africa, Agrippino actually stages a scene in which Brandimarte and Fiordiligi learn the whereabouts of Orlando and the means to liberate him. In the process, he alters the circumstances so that they have already left Africa behind and are travelling through Christian lands when they come across a "hermit" (Act 1, scene 8). This scenario is certainly more congruous—why, after all, would an African soothsayer be involved in the liberation of Orlando? But it also foreshadows God's later intervention through another religious figure (St John) to instruct another knight (Astolfo) how to free Orlando— this time from his own insanity (discussed in Chapter 9).[8]

Agrippino also modifies the role played by Fiordiligi. Boiardo had designated Brandimarte's beloved wife as the guide in this adventure in keeping with her role as a figure of wisdom throughout the *Innamorato*. In addition to instructing the knights, primarily Brandimarte, Fiordelisa had created four garlands in the shape of crowns with the power to break spells. Whereas these became six in the *Storia dei paladini*, as noted above, Agrippino imagines instead that Fiordiligi has received one garland along with instructions from the hermit during a tête-à-tête after Brandimarte's departure: "Hermit calls Fiordiligi, gives her a garland and says to give it to Brandimarte because it will break every enchantment" (Act 1, scene 8). Although Agrippino still depicts Fiordiligi as the key to the rescue mission's success, he transfers the practical knowledge about how to construct spell-breaking garlands to a hermit. In this way, Fiordiligi's special status remains intact while her association with magic becomes once removed. In addition, the switch to a single garland may evoke Angelica's spell-breaking ring that was passed from one knight to the next at Dragontina's garden.

Agrippino also enacts structural changes as well at this point in the narrative. Both the *Innamorato* and the *Storia dei paladini* go on to relate the Fonte del Riso adventure immediately following Ruggiero's encounter with the other knights. In *sera* 182, however, the episode is interrupted just as

---

8 Interestingly, despite this staged encounter with a hermit in Christian lands in Act 1, Brandimarte nevertheless later mentions an "indovino" in Act 3, scene 1, thereby directly echoing Boiardo's "uno indovino" (*OI* 3.6.56) and Lodico's "un indovino" (8: 232).

Ruggiero, Gradasso, and Brandimarte are heading to the fountain (Act 3, scene 1). The focus then shifts to Bradamante's chance encounter with a hermit who will treat her wounds (scene 2) and to the martial events taking place in and around Paris (scenes 3 and 4). The Fonte del Riso episode is thus postponed until Act 1, scenes 2–4, of the following evening. The fact that Agrippino nevertheless staged the adventure in the course of just three consecutive scenes indicates that he could have placed it at the end of *sera* 182 had he wished to do so. Breaking off the story at this point of heightened interest and delaying the liberation of Orlando no doubt creates suspense in quintessential Boiardan fashion. Yet it also provides a structural frame for the evening's play by returning to the epic, and thus agonistic, plot with which Act 1 began.

Sera 182 also contains a scene not announced in the evening's summary—and not even present in the sources—that is in contrast with both the enamorment of Ruggiero and Bradamante and the warfare surrounding their encounter. Just after Bradamante and Ruggiero have lost sight of each other while fighting off the ambush, the action switches to Angelica escaping from Carlo's camp (Act 2, scene 3). This direct staging of an action that was mentioned only retrospectively in Agrippino's sources reminds spectators that the mutual love of the two couples featured in this play is the exception to the many instances of unrequited desire for a fleeing or otherwise unattainable object. Angelica's flight also serves as a preparation for the next evening's play in which the princess continues to flee as she is first pursued by Rinaldo (Act 3, scene 2) and then fought over by Rinaldo and Ferraù (Act 3, scene 4). These events bring us to the section of the *Storia dei paladini* based on the *Orlando Furioso*. The next three chapters will therefore focus on the relation between Ariosto's poem, Lodico's prose, and Agrippino's dramatic scripts, beginning with the transformation of Orlando from *innamorato* to *furioso*.

Chapter 8

THE MADNESS OF ORLANDO (*SERA* 198)[1]

Introduction

When Boiardo opens his *Orlando Innamorato* with the shocking news that King Carlo's most dutiful paladin accomplished "stupendous feats" and "amazing labours" while under the influence of love, he warns readers not to be surprised to hear about Orlando in love since "no strong arm, no audacity, / no blade well-honed, no shield or mail, / no other power can avail, / for in the end Love conquers all" (*OI* 1.1.1–2). Orlando's infatuation leads him to forsake his duty not only to the emperor, but also to his wife Alda (his fiancée Aude in the French tradition) and to Christendom as a whole in a vain attempt to win over the wily princess of Cathay.

Yet an even more extreme fate befalls the paladin in the *Orlando Furioso*. In picking up the narrative threads of the poem that Boiardo left unfinished at his death in 1494, Ariosto famously announces his intention to tell something never before related in prose or verse: the hero's descent into madness because of love (*OF* 1.2). And the poet indeed makes good on his promise about midway through the poem. Upon learning about Angelica's love affair with the North African footsoldier Medoro, Orlando literally goes insane with jealousy. In losing his rational faculties, he also leaves behind his identity as a Frankish paladin and his very humanity in the process (*OF* 23.100–36).

One might expect that the play staging Orlando's madness, one of the most iconic episodes in both Italian literary history and Sicilian puppet theater, would take up most of the evening's action. In *sera* 198, however, Orlando's loss of his sanity is concentrated in the four scenes that conclude the play (Act 2, scene 6, and the three scenes of Act 3). Agrippino prepares for this climactic moment by interweaving the vicissitudes of other enamored characters: (1) Bradamante longing for her beloved Ruggiero; (2) Rinaldo seeking to

---

[1] The play translated and discussed in this chapter is found in *Copione* 14. To compare versions, see *serata* 202 in Mike Manteo's notebook 17.

challenge Orlando over Angelica; (3) the star-crossed lovers Isabella and Zerbino reuniting; and (4) Rodomonte pursuing Mandricardo for having abducted his beloved Doralice.

Translation

Evening 198

Bradamante arrives in Montalbano and sends Ippalca to deliver the horse Frontino to Ruggiero. Rodomonte encounters Ippalca and takes the horse away from her. Zerbino, falsely accused by Gabrina, is sentenced to death. Orlando liberates him. A great battle between Orlando and Mandricardo. Orlando arrives in the shepherd's hut where he hears the news about Angelica, goes insane, and throws off his weapons and armor.

Characters and props
Salardo
Orlando prepared for the scene of his madness
Various farmers
2 Horses
some animals
Two movable trees that mad Orlando chops down
Bed for the hut
1 Club for Orlando to fight Mandricardo
Anselmo, Pinabello's father
Pinabello, dead
1 Belt
Chains
Magonzesi captains
Ippalca, Bradamante's servant

Act 1°

Scene 1° Forest

Bradamante near Montalbano, she is undecided whether to enter the fortress or go to the Vallombrosa monastery to encounter Ruggiero. She sees her brother Salardo approaching and realizes she cannot get away because Salardo has seen her

Salardo   arrives, hugs his sister, and tells her that Carlo is still besieged by Agramante and that he was sent to gather troops, they enter Montalbano

2 Forest

Rinaldo   in search of Orlando in order to attain Angelica. He was in Brava but had not heard any news, he decides to search throughout the world just to find him

3 Montalbano

Bradamante, distraught that the encounter with her brother compelled her to enter Montalbano, decides to send the horse Frontino with Ippalca, daughter of her governess, to Ruggiero. She calls Ippalca (the latter arrives)

Bradamante   My trusted Ippalca, you will have to go to Vallombrosa where, as I told you, you will find my beloved, that is, Ruggiero, you will excuse my absence and tell him, however, that, when he is baptized, he will be able to come to Montalbano and we will get married, and you will give him the horse Frontino. If someone wants to take it away from you, tell him the name of its owner (Ippalca departs)

4 Forest

(Pinabello lies dead on the ground)
Zerbino and the old woman Gabrina

Zerbino   Cursed old woman, I am bound to accompany you, whereas I would gladly rid myself of this burden (he see the corpse). God, and who killed this man? If I knew, I would avenge him, especially if he was killed wrongly. Old woman, wait here while I look around the woods to find out something (he leaves)

Gabrina   While he is gone, I want to see if the dead man has something of value. She finds a belt and hides it, Zerbino returns and says he has not found anything, they go in search of lodging

5 Forest

Rodomonte and the Dwarf

Rodomonte   I cannot locate Doralice's abductor. What do I see? A woman is leading along a horse. If she were a knight, I would take it away from her. (Ippalca arrives.) Tell me, whose horse is this?

Ippalca	Don't develop a liking for it because you can't have it without a serious battle
Rodomonte	I wouldn't dare take it away from a woman. Do you want to give it to me?
Ippalca	I am not the owner, its owner is Ruggiero
Rodomonte	Heaven be praised that I'm not taking it away from a woman. I'm taking the horse and you will tell Ruggiero that Rodomonte, king of Algeria, took it. If he wants it, let him come and get it (he departs)
Ippalca	cries, goes to find Ruggiero

6 Forest

Zerbino and the old woman see a castle, they decide to ask for hospitality

7 Room of the Altariva castle

Count Anselmo, Pinabello's father

Anselmo	(crying) My son was found dead in a valley. I sent for his body to be brought, but I swear to avenge his death (arrival of Zerbino and the old woman)
Zerbino	We came to ask for hospitality, but what is happening here?
Anselmo	My son was found dead in a valley
Zerbino	imagines who it is (they hear of the arrival of the corpse) (two soldiers bring it)
Anselmo	(crying) Whoever discovers the murderer will have a great reward. They go to the funeral

8 Forest

Mandricardo in search of the killer of Alzirdo and Manilardo, keeping in mind the knight's characteristics. He travels keeping Doralice in his company

9 Room in the Altariva castle

Gabrina	decides to procure the reward. Anselmo arrives and she tells him that it's useless to search for your son's killer, he is in the fortress, the one you have hosted, and the proof is a belt which I've kept (she shows the belt)

Anselmo	This knight must be a friend of Rinaldo and, learning that my son was a Magonzese, killed him. Old woman, you may retire to your quarters, you will get the reward (the old woman departs). He calls the soldiers to arrest Zerbino in his sleep

10 Room

Zerbino arrested while asleep

Act 2°

1° Room in the Altariva castle

Anselmo	orders that the prisoner be sent to his death

2 Forest

	Orlando and Isabella near the castle
Orlando	Isabella, by now we are far from the cave that was a den of thieves, but look, I think someone is being led to his death. Wait here, I want to go and see what this is about

3 Walls

Soldiers	lead Zerbino to his death
Orlando	asks why they are leading him to his death
Zerbino	I am the son of the King of Scotland, I was hosted by Anselmo di Magonza at the castle of Altariva. His son was killed and, blaming me, he had me arrested during the night
Orlando	frees him, is attacked, and then kills everyone, including Anselmo. He takes the prisoner and departs. Gabrina takes the horse and runs off because she recognizes Orlando

4 Forest

Isabella	waits, Orlando and an armed Zerbino arrive
Zerbino	Heavens! Isabella is in the company of that knight
Orlando	Look, I freed this young man
Isabella	recognizes and embraces him, and relates how she was liberated (Mandricardo and Doralice arrive)

Mandricardo	(looking at Orlando) The features are those of that knight. Sir, I have been looking for you for a long time to avenge the death of two kings, Alzirdo and Manilardo
Orlando	It is true, but if you had known who I am, you would not have looked for me so hard. In any case, take the field. But you have no sword! How can you fight?
Mandricardo	Don't worry about that! With my presence alone I have scared away many men. Besides, if I have no sword it is because when I attained this armor I swore to win Durlindana from the knight who holds it, Orlando, who killed my father through treachery
Orlando	You lie! Here is the sword that killed your father and—to prove that I killed him fair and square—I will hang Durlindana right here and I will take a tree branch and then we will fight. He takes a piece of wood (they fight)
Orlando	and Mandricardo come to blows, they resume the fight, Mandricardo flees
Orlando	(to Zerbino) I take leave of you. I will take back my sword to go looking for him (he departs)
Zerbino	decides to follow Orlando

5 Forest

	Mandricardo and Doralice
Mandricardo	searches for Orlando. He sees the old woman on horseback and laughs (Gabrina arrives)
Mandricardo	Old lady, my horse is without a bridle. I will take yours and so you will race forward without a bridle until you break your neck
Gabrina	yells out, but Mandricardo gives her a push

6 Forest

Orlando	in search of Mandricardo. He quenches his thirst at a fountain, then looks at what is written on a tree (([The names of] Angelica and Medoro tied together with different knots))
Orlando	(laughs) My Angelica, trying to make me jealous, I know that under Medoro she meant to write Orlando. (He looks at another tree.) There's more writing but it is not from Angelica's hand. (He reads)

> Happy plants, green grass, clear water,
> Dark cavern and cooling, welcome shade
> Where the beautiful Angelica, who was born
> to Galafrone and loved by many in vain,
> Would often lie naked in my arms,
> For the comfort offered to me here,
> I, poor Medoro, cannot reward you
> In any other way than to forever praise you
> And to beseech every enamored gentleman
> And knights and damsels and every
> Person or villager or wayfarer
> Who arrives here, by their own agency or by chance,
> To say to the grass, to the shade, to the cave, to the river, to the plants,
> 'May the sun and moon be kind to you,
> And the choir of the nymphs, and may it be ensured
> That a shepherd never leads his flock [to you] to graze

Orlando   Who is this imposter who wrote this and who also imitated Angelica's handwriting? (Night has fallen, he sees a farmhouse, he calls, a farmer arrives) Orlando seeks shelter, they go inside

Act 3°

1° Hut with a bed

Farmer	You have eaten, here is your bed
Orlando	(gets in bed) Tell me, don't you have a better bed? One sleeps badly on this one
Farmer	And yet some time ago a nice couple came here and they slept in this bed, and they gave my wife a nice bracelet
Orlando	Let me see it
Farmer	calls for his wife and can show it himself
Orlando	Their names?
Farmer	Angelica and Medoro
Orlando	knocks down the bed
Farmer	flees
Orlando	leaves the hut

2 Forest with movable trees

Orlando   That treacherous woman betrayed me. He reads "Angelica and Medoro," chops down the tree. (He reads on another tree) "Happy plants, green grass...." (He chops the other tree) He begins to throw off his armor and weapons while shouting, farmers arrive, then flee. Orlando chases after them

3 Forest

Farmers   who are chased by Orlando
Orlando   directs his violence toward various animals

Comparative Analysis

Act 1 (scenes 1, 3, 5): "Bradamante arrives in Montalbano and sends the horse Frontino to Ruggiero via Ippalca. Rodomonte encounters Ippalca and takes the horse away from her."

As dicussed in the previous chapter, the newly enamored Bradamante and Rugiero were separated from one another during their combat in the final cantos of the *Innamorato*. Ariosto imagines that the two knights (in the meantime reunited, separated, and brought together again) lose sight of each other once more after Bradamante kills the treacherous Pinabello in the woods while Ruggiero puts an end to an evil custom at the traitor's castle. At the moment in the *Furioso* corresponding to the opening of *sera* 198, Bradamante unwittingly finds herself near her family's castle in Montalbano as she is on her way to reconnect with Ruggiero. Although, after some deliberation, she decides to continue on her journey without delay, her chance encounter with her brother Alardo leaves her no choice but to return home (*OF* 23.20–23).

Bradamante's sojourn at Montalbano under her parents' watchful eye will initiate a new phase of her trajectory: rather than an intrepid warrior on the battlefield, she now plays the part of a dutiful daughter confined within castle walls. Although she thereby loses the fierce independence we witnessed in both her earlier combat against Rodamonte and her enamorment of Rugiero, she nonetheless takes action indirectly by sending her beloved's horse Frontino to him along with a message via her nurse's daughter Ippalca. Unfortunately, her plan is foiled when the steed is abducted by none other than Rodomonte.

Although Ariosto does not press the point, it is ironic that Rodomonte has no qualms about stealing the horse of an absent fellow knight while he himself is angrily pursuing Mandricardo for having abducted his fiancée in his absence (*OF* 23.33–37). The irony is intensified if we recall that the knight on the receiving end of this affront is not only an African ally whose participation in the invasion of France was deemed essential to score any victory but also, as the reader knows, the very same knight Rodamonte had previously vowed to treat forevermore as his superior (discussed in Chapter 7).

The *Storia dei paladini* follows Ariosto's plot closely. Bradamante likewise intends to steer clear of her family home in order to avoid being detected since, as in the *Furioso*, she fears her mother "would prohibit her from departing once she arrived" (9: 137). In the subsequent encounter between Ippalca and Rodomonte, Ariosto had told readers that the maiden "flings at him no lack / Of menaces and insults and abuse" (*OF* 23.37). The *Storia dei paladini* dramatizes her diatribe by switching to direct discourse. The maiden first censures Rodomonte by calling him an "infamous thief" and then points out that "it is not fitting for an honorable knight to steal other people's belongings" (9: 138).

Sera 198 opens with three alternating scenes dedicated to Bradamante's return home and her failed attempt to send Frontino to Ruggiero (scenes 1, 3, and 5). In the first scene, she is near her family's castle in Montalbano. Whereas Agrippino's precedents had Bradamante decide to continue on her way to meet up with Ruggiero, the puppeteer leaves the female warrior still undecided which path to follow when her brother arrives on the scene (Act 1, scene 1). This indecision may prepare the spectator for the more passive role that she will play while at home. In addition, showcasing Bradamante's yearning for the absent Ruggiero at the start of the very evening in which Orlando will lose his rational faculties due to jealousy foreshadows the intense and persistent jealousy that this female knight will endure when she later (erroneously) believes that Ruggiero has abandoned her for Marfisa.

Agrippino also capitalizes on the encounter between Ippalca and Rodomonte to bring out the irony—or, more precisely, the hypocrisy—of the knight's illicit appropriation of something he desires. Act 1, scene 5, opens with Rodomonte searching for Doralice's abductor Mandricardo. This initially creates a parallel between the king of Sarza and the play's other three characters who are bent on finding their beloved: Bradamante, Orlando, and Rinaldo. Yet no sooner is his state of mind established than he switches to the role of abductor himself. While the reversal of roles is already present in the *Furioso* and *Storia dei paladini*, Agrippino accentuates the abruptness of Rodomonte's change of heart through his first-person speech: "I cannot locate Doralice's abductor. What do I see? A woman is leading along a horse. If she were a knight, I would take it away from her." The original Italian script renders even more clearly how swiftly this switch occurs since the only punctuation in the above utterance is a single comma.

Act 1 (scenes 4, 6, 7, 9, and 10); Act 2 (scenes 1–4): "Zerbino, accused falsely by Gabrina, is sentenced to death. Orlando liberates him. A great battle between Orlando and Mandricardo."

The Saracen Spanish princess Isabella and the Christian Scotsman Zerbino undergo various vicissitudes after having fallen in love despite their different faiths. The central part of their trajectory, while bringing extreme danger to both of them separately, also serves to underscore Orlando's dedication to acting on behalf of others prior to his madness. The paladin's intervention in their story begins when he saves a captive Isabella from being sold as a slave to the sultan in the East (*OF* 13.31). The damsel's warden at the time, an iniquitous elderly woman named Gabrina, not only escapes punishment but, due to a series of circumstances, ends up traveling under the protection of Isabella's beloved Zerbino.

When Zerbino and Gabrina stumble upon the corpse of the traitorous Pinabello in a forest, the old woman secretly steals the dead man's belt and then later accuses her escort of murder while they are guests in Pinabello's family castle.[2] As a result, Zerbino is apprehended in his sleep and condemned to die the following day. When Orlando happens to be passing by the site with Isabella, he hurries to prevent the execution, overcoming anyone who opposes him. Orlando thus not only single-handedly rescues Zerbino just as he had earlier rescued Isabella, but he also thereby becomes the one responsible for the couple's joyous reunion. Although the pair will later meet a tragic fate (Zerbino at the hands of Mandricardo and Isabella at the hands of Rodomonte), at this point in the story there is the provisional sense of a happy ending thanks to Orlando's civic-mindedness and knightly prowess.

Orlando likewise acts in an exemplary fashion in his next encounter preceding his insanity. While the paladin is still in the company of the happy couple, Mandricardo appears with Doralice (whom he had abducted earlier) and, upon recognizing Orlando's identity, accuses him of having treacherously killed his father Agricane. The outrageousness of this claim brings to mind instead Orlando's actual conduct during that fateful battle (discussed in Chapter 5). Yet we need not rely solely on memory since Orlando immediately gives another display of his chivalrous nature. He hangs his sword Durlindana upon a tree branch because he does not want to fight Mandricardo with an advantage in weaponry: "I wouldn't have it be mine any more / than yours during our combat" (*OF* 23.81).

---

[2] Pinabello had instead been justly killed by Bradamante (*OF* 22.97) for having earlier attempted to murder her by treachery (*OF* 2.66–76).

This courteous gesture not only recalls Orlando's encounters with Agricane in the *Innamorato* but also reminds us that until now his infatuation with Angelica has not prevented him from treating strangers in a praiseworthy manner.

The *Storia dei paladini* follows the sequence of events laid out by Ariosto with minor variations. One of these is to increase Orlando's agency in rushing to the rescue of Zerbino. In the *Furioso*, it is Isabella who, upon seeing the group, asks Orlando about their identity, thus spurring him on to action: "When all those crowds of people she had seen, / She asked the Count Orlando who they were" (*OF* 23.55). Orlando is somewhat slow to react since we were told two stanzas prior that he had already seen the group (*OF* 23.53), and he responds to her question with "I do not know" (*OF* 23.55) before heading down the mountain. By fashioning Isabella as the catalyst, at this moment, Ariosto is privileging the connection between the lovers over the exemplary action that the paladin is about to undertake. In the *Storia dei paladini*, by contrast, Orlando heads to the scene as soon as he sees the group without waiting for a prompt from his travel companion: "Now as soon as the paladin saw that group of people, he left the lady on the hill and descended to the plain to find out what was happening" (9: 140). The immediacy with which Orlando takes the initiative contributes to his characterization as a knight errant who seeks to uphold justice at all times.

The *Storia dei paladini* also gives Zerbino the opportunity to demonstrate heroic valor in his own defense. In the *Furioso*, Orlando single-handedly kills at least eighty men before the combat is over (*OF* 23.62). Ariosto makes a point to tell us that when Orlando finally approaches Zerbino, the latter, whose heart was trembling in his breast, would have prostrated himself before his rescuer had he not been tied to the nag transporting him (*OF* 23.62). By contrast, in the *Storia dei paladini*, Orlando kills just over twenty before helping to arm Zerbino, who then takes his revenge directly by killing more than eighty of those who were planning to summarily execute him (9: 141). As a result, both knights are the recipients of Isabella's high praise.

In *sera* 198, Agrippino devotes over twice as many scenes to the vicissitudes of Isabella and Zerbino as he does to the madness of Orlando. Zerbino first appears in the play still accompanying the odious Gabrina. Whereas various other characters in the surrounding scenes are seeking a beloved in vain, Agrippino underscores Zerbino's opposite problem of escorting someone against his will by having the knight tell the woman in first-person discourse: "Cursed old woman, I am bound to accompany you, whereas I would gladly rid myself of this burden" (Act 1, scene 4). This statement becomes ironic in light of the events that will soon unfold since it is Gabrina who rids herself of Zerbino through her false accusation.

Orlando's interactions with the couple, moreover, constitute the most centrally placed storyline of the evening, keeping the emphasis on the knight's unwavering chivalric behavior toward strangers prior to his insanity. Agrippino shows the paladin taking the initiative in his speech to Isabella: "But look, it seems to me that someone is being led to their death, wait, I want to go and see what it is about" (Act 2, scene 2). Not only does Orlando direct Isabella to look at what he sees, but he now also already understands the nature of the spectacle before him and seeks to uncover the motivation.

In the liberation scene itself, Agrippino's sequence of events departs from both the *Furioso* and the *Storia dei paladini*. Rather than attacking the crowd after hearing Zerbino's account, Orlando immediately unties the youth. In this way, it is Orlando who is attacked by the crowd and then kills them in response. Despite the fact that Zerbino is freed, he does not take part in the action. This may be because he was not wearing armor as he was being led to his death, but it would have been possible for the unarmed puppet to exit and be substituted with an armed version in order to follow the *Storia dei paladini*'s account of a joint effort. As it stands, the scene unequivocally showcases Orlando's heroism as he rescues the unjustly condemned prisoner.

Agrippino also adds small details during Orlando's encounter with Mandricardo that keep his stature high vis-à-vis his challenger. During the combat in both the *Furioso* and the *Storia dei paladini*, the knights switch from using their shattered lances as weapons to applying their bare hands in an all-out brawl. Ariosto likens them to "yokels" (*OF* 23.83), and Lodico, after having initially compared them to "furious lions," soon thereafter depicts them throwing punches like "madmen" (9: 142). Such debasement hints at the actual madness to come and the savage violence that Orlando will release as a result of it. Agrippino's audience, however, could not have been expected to imagine the two combatants on stage before them as anything less imposing than the splendidly armored knights that they were. After hanging up his sword, Orlando announces to Mandricardo that he will take up a tree branch (Act 2, scene 4). The spectators are thus invited to imagine that the "piece of wood" that Orlando wields represents something grander. While possibly also echoing the earlier fight between Mandricardo and Gradasso with tree branches for the right to possess Orlando's very same sword (discussed in Chapter 7), Agrippino does not lower the tone of the combat in his script.

In the course of the battle, however, Agrippino does enact a narrative twist that vividly separates the chivalric ethos of Orlando from the deficiencies of Mandricardo in this regard. Both the *Furioso* and the *Storia dei paladini* depict Orlando pulling the reins from Mandricardo's horse, thus causing the horse and rider to speed off into the distance. Agrippino, by contrast, depicts the Tartar ruler intentionally fleeing from his more valorous opponent in the heat of battle (Act 2, scene 4). Even if this new version was arguably simpler to stage, the puppeteer could have certainly found a way to spare Mandricardo this uncharacteristic moment of cowardice had he wished to do so.

Act 2 (scene 6); Act 3 (scenes 1–3): "Orlando arrives in the shepherd's hut where he hears about Angelica, goes insane, and throws off his weapons and armor."

Ironically, it is while searching for his opponent Mandricardo—rather than for his beloved Angelica—that Orlando learns that the princess has given her heart and body to another man. The paladin initially remains in denial, finding excuses for the names of Angelica and Medoro etched on trees and the written poem in which the latter explicitly states that Galafrone's daughter Angelica ceded her virginity to him. Eventually, however, Orlando is forced to face the truth when the shepherd who hosts him for the night tells him that Angelica and Medoro slept in the very same bed and shows him a bracelet left as a gift—the same bracelet, Ariosto tells us, that Orlando had previously gifted to the princess. Such irrefutable proof sends the paladin into such a fit of rage that he heads back into the woods where he loses his mind. In addition to destroying the trees bearing the names of Angelica and Medoro, he uproots other trees at will and savagely murders any human or animal unlucky enough to be within his grasp: "He hunted animals, and humans too" (*OF* 24.13).

Even though Orlando's case is extreme, Ariosto opens the following canto by asserting that the malady is not uncommon because love itself is a form of madness: "For what is love but madness after all, / As every wise man in the wide world knows?" (*OF* 24.1). A few stanzas later, moreover, he associates Orlando with Rinaldo by telling us that if the one is in a "furious and frenzied state," the other is "scarcely less insane" (*OF* 27.8). Rinaldo, in fact, having heard (erroneously) that Angelica was in the company of Orlando, has been consumed with jealousy (*OF* 27.9). Of late he returned to Paris to seek the couple but, having no success, he is compelled by his great desire ("gran disio") to continue his search (*OF* 27.10).

In the *Storia dei paladini*, the account of Orlando's *pazzia* (9: 143–47) likewise serves as an ominous precedent for Rinaldo's jealous quest. After having searched throughout Brava and spent a couple of days in Paris "tormented by jealousy" (9: 168), Rinaldo sets out once again on their trail. Whereas Ariosto had focused on the road or path ("la via") between Anglante and Brava (*OF* 27.12), locations previously associated with Orlando, the *Storia dei paladini* focuses instead on Rinaldo's "wandering through the woods" (9: 168), a situation reminiscent of his cousin's current dire circumstances.

Following the *Storia dei paladini*, Agrippino envisions Rinaldo in a single-minded pursuit of Orlando and Angelica as he travels through the forest. The puppeteer diverges from his precedents structurally, however, by staging this episode prior to Orlando's discovery of Angelica's so-called infidelity. Indeed, Rinaldo's decision "to search throughout the world" to find Orlando occurs in the second scene of Act 1. By presenting early in the play a knight aiming to wrest the princess of Cathay from a purported rival, Agrippino introduces the theme of jealousy that will later come to a climax with Orlando's madness. In this way, too, although Orlando does not appear until late in Act 2, right from the start of the evening we are reminded of his continued connection to the beautiful and heretofore elusive Angelica.

Agrippino prepares for the onset of Orlando's madness in the final scene of Act 2. As in the sources, the paladin is searching for Mandricardo to continue their combat over Durlindana when he first spies the names of Angelica and Medoro carved together with different knots on a tree and then reads the verses that the youth wrote in honor of his beloved (Act 2, scene 6). Agrippino appears to have followed the *Storia dei paladini*'s quotation (9: 144) rather than the *Furioso*'s original *ottava rima* verses (*OF* 23.108–9) when writing out Medoro's two-stanza poem.[3] Like Lodico, he omits the key word "voi" ("you") from the poem's final verse—rendering Ariosto's "Che non conduca a voi pastor mai greggia" (*OF* 23.109) as "Che non conduca a pastor mai greggia"—even though this omission renders the statement incomprehensible.[4]

Orlando's full realization of Angelica's amorous choices and his subsequent transformation into a wild beast are reserved for the three scenes of Act 3. Orlando remains in a state of denial until he visits the shepherd's hut that had housed the two lovebirds and finds himself in the same bed at the moment in which the shepherd and his wife supply irrefutable details of the romance

---

[3] It is not possible to determine this with certainty, however, without knowing what edition of the *Furioso* Agrippino had in hand. His minor divergences from the *Storia dei paladini* could have been due to his consultation of Ariosto's original.

[4] Agrippino also follows the *Storia dei paladini* in presenting the sixteen verses in one solid block rather than in two stanzas separated by line spaces. By contrast, for Medoro's prayer to the moon, which reproduces a stanza directly from the *Furioso*, he adds line spaces. It is true that there are also no line spaces for the verses quoted directly from the *Furioso* in *sera* 184, but this may be due to their short and fragmentary nature.

(in Act 3, scene 1). Whereas in the *Furioso* and the *Storia dei paladini* Orlando rushes out of the hut, Agrippino has the paladin show signs of rage right on the spot as he proceeds to knock over the loathsome bed. This act of violence thereby anticipates his destruction of the trees that bore the names of the lovers in the following scene.

The final two scenes of Act 3 are based on action rather than dialogue and are thus brief on paper. The paucity of the stage directions does not imply, however, a rapid denouement. On the contrary, if the continued performances of Orlando's madness in contemporary Sicilian puppet theater are any indication, each moment of the paladin's transformation is given due attention. A special puppet is prepared for the occasion so that Orlando can effectively throw off his armor, sword, and shield, one piece at a time, ending up about as naked as a puppet can get.[5] Agrippino's Cast of Characters specifies, in fact, that the Orlando puppet is "prepared for his madness." Props are also essential in this scene since Orlando's feral destructive streak is evidenced through his violence not only against the humans and animals that cross his path but also against the very trees in the forest. Accordingly, immediately following Orlando "prepared for his madness," the Cast of Characters continues with "various farmers," "2 Horses," "some animals," and "two movable trees that mad Orlando chops down."

After Orlando's protective stance toward the damsel Isabella, valiant rescue of the falsely accused Zerbino, and civility toward his challenger Mandricardo in Acts 1 and 2, his transformation into a madman arbitrarily attacking innocent humans, animals, and plants seems all the more like the fall of a tragic hero. In terms of dramatic visualization, the paladin's prior relinquishing of any material advantage over an opponent by carefully hanging his sword upon a tree branch is shockingly contrasted with his frenzied destruction of the trees themselves and reckless throwing away of his very sword, along with his shield and armor.

If in the penultimate scene of the play Orlando takes revenge on the trees that bear the names of the lovers that are offensive to him (substitutional violence), in the final scene he directs his rage against random farmers and then various animals (indiscriminate violence). The play's final stage direction ("He attacks some animals") brings home both the senselessness of his violence and the indifferentiation of his targets across the plant, human, and now also animal realms.

---

5 For videotaped examples of this episode in Sicilian *opera dei pupi* and other forms of theater, see the "Madness of Orlando" page on the eBOIARDO website (https://edblogs.columbia.edu/eboiardo/authors/ariosto/follia/).

Chapter 9

THE VOYAGE OF ASTOLFO TO THE MOON (*SERA* 203)[1]

Introduction

Although Ariosto relays Orlando's loss of sanity in painstaking psychological detail, he later reveals that the paladin's affliction is nothing less than divine retribution. After Orlando has spent three months wandering aimlessly and wreaking havoc wherever he goes, the period of punishment is over and God enlists Astolfo to restore his cousin's sanity. The English knight had already been a world traveler in the *Innamorato*, departing from Paris (discussed in Chapter 4) and reaching Cathay on horseback, then continuing on a circuitous route to the most disparate corners of the globe. In the *Furioso*, he travels not only by land and sea, but also by air, first upon a hippogriff that takes him to Africa, the entrance of hell, and the terrestrial paradise, and subsequently in a divine chariot that transports him to the moon where he will retrieve Orlando's wits.

Astolfo's aerial adventures constitute the core of *sera* 203. He appears in Act 1 descending from the sky on the hippogriff as he arrives in Nubia (Ethiopia), and he finds himself on the lunar surface by the final scene of Act 3.[2] His divinely orchestrated mission to retrieve Orlando's wits, however, is not the exclusive focus of the play. His adventures are interwoven with additional narrative threads that revolve around the theme of the quest: (1) Bradamante finally decides to leave her family home in Montalbano to seek out Ruggiero; (2) the knights Sansonetto and Oliviero are intent on searching for Orlando; and (3) Rinaldo, although not mentioned in the summary,

---

1 The play translated and discussed in this chapter is found in *Copione* 14. To compare versions, see *serata* 207 in Mike Manteo's notebook 18.
2 Although Nubia technically comprised southern Egypt and northern Sudan, lying north of the modern state of Ethiopia, it was also sometimes referred to as Ethiopia. Ariosto uses "Nubia" and "Ethiopia" interchangeably and Agrippino accordingly assumes their equivalence.

appears in one scene aiming to recover his horse Baiardo from Gradasso. Whereas Astolfo, following God's design, will succeed in restoring Orlando's sanity without having knowingly set out to do so, his peers are not as fortunate: Bradamante's reunion with Ruggiero will be obstructed and delayed until much later; Orlando's two friends Sansonetto and Oliviero are challenged, defeated, and imprisoned by Rodomonte; and Rinaldo simply wanders in vain. The juxtaposition of these various storylines in the play creates a contrast between the utter efficacy of divine intervention and the inherent difficulties of human undertakings.

Translation

Evening 203

Bradamante leaves Montalbano to find Ruggiero. Astolfo chases the Harpies away from Senapo's table, enters the infernal cavern, and listens to Lidia's story. Then, losing the bridle of the winged animal, he flies through the celestial gates and reaches the earthly paradise where he receives Orlando's wits from St John the Evangelist and sees wondrous things. Carlo leaves for Arles to besiege Agramante. Sansonetto and Oliviero are taken prisoner by Rodomonte at Isabella's bridge.

Characters
Lidia as an infernal spirit
Saint John
Enoch
Elijah
Hell
Paradise
Moon
Flasks
bladders
Dudone

Act 1°

1 Paris

Sansonetto   has heard about Orlando, he goes to see for himself

2 Montalbano

Bradamante   despairs over Ruggiero, changes her armor, takes Astolfo's lance, and departs

3 Isabella's Bridge

Sansonetto	taken prisoner by Rodomonte

4 Paris

Oliviero	distressed about Orlando, he decides to go and find out whether his brother-in-law's illness can be cured

5 Forest

Rinaldo	cannot find peace. Every day he has gone out to search for Baiardo and he believes that Gradasso has taken him

6 Isabella's Bridge

Oliviero	taken prisoner by Rodomonte

7 Forest

Astolfo	descends with the hippogriff and says he has flown all over the world and has arrived in the capital of Ethiopia, that is Nubia, and then enters the city

8 Nubia

Senapo	blind, he is distressed over the Harpies who do not leave him in peace. One hears shouts of "Long live Mars!" The arrival of a knight is announced
Senapo	asks his minister to accompany him, to bring him to meet this Mars in order to seek his grace
Minister	Here he is, this must be him arriving now (Astolfo arrives)
Senapo	Here I am at your feet, oh God Mars, have pity on me. I don't want my sight back but send away the Harpies
Astolfo	I am neither Mars nor God, but I promise to send away the Harpies and for this you must praise God who led me here. Have the table set
Senapo	gives the order, they go to the table
Harpies	(enter)
Senapo	with Astolfo. You see how the Harpies have ruined everything
Astolfo	remembers the horn and says: reset the table, everyone shut your ears, I will take care of the rest. The table is set and they go to sit down (the Harpies enter)
Astolfo	chases them with the sound of his horn, goes to get the hippogriff, and continues to pursue them

9 Forest

Harpies — are fleeing. Astolfo is upon the hippogriff blowing his horn. He sees that the Harpies rush down into an abyss, he ties the horse and enters

Act 2°

1 Hell

Astolfo — has entered trusting in the horn, and the place appears to be a hell. He sees a spirit approaching, he decides to strike it and rushes forward

Lidia — screams

Astolfo — Who are you and do you want to be praised in the world?

Lidia — Praises are not worth anything when your soul is in pain and particularly your incantations bother me. I will tell you, but do not interrupt, and when you are in the royal courts do not spare any effort in showing what is the fate of those women who are ungrateful to their husbands. I am Lidia, I am and was the daughter of the king of Lydia. A young man, being in my palace, fell in love with me, and in order to win me placed himself at the service of my father, and he subjugated many cities on behalf of my father; with so many victories that my father began to love the young man, called Alceste. The latter asked my father for my hand but I, who was thinking of others, gave him a negative reply. Offended, the young man made an alliance with the king of Armenia and waged war on my father, taking away almost all his lands. Then my father, having no more means of salvation, sent me to Alceste's camp because I was the cause of his ruin. When I arrived at the camp I deceived Alceste by promising to marry him and I had my father's lands returned, and so we prepared for the wedding, but I constantly invited Alceste to undertake great adventures in order to send him to his death, but I didn't succeed. Then I ran away with a lover of mine and Alceste died of a broken heart. I was then betrayed by my lover because he knew I was guilty, and murdered in his realm and condemned to this place

Astolfo — curses her and exits

2 Cave

Atlante — dying, says that Ruggiero's fate is sealed and since he has learned from the spirit that Ruggiero will have to fight Marfisa at Arles, he orders the spirit to make his grave there so that his own spirit will reveal to them that they are brother and sister

3 Forest

Astolfo   on the hippogriff that has walled up the cavern so as not to let the Harpies emerge (the reins fall). God, how to restrain the horse that flies away as it pleases, God help me!

4 Arles

Agramante, who has fortified his army in Arles, curses Discord and the arrival of Rinaldo

5 Garden

Astolfo   gets off the hippogriff, admires the place, sees that a man who inspires respect is approaching

St John   Welcome, Duke Astolfo, it is God who has brought you here, this is the place where Adam and Eve originated. I am John the Evangelist. You who come from the world do not know that Orlando has gone mad and that is why you are here. Come, first let's eat and then I will tell you everything

6 Paris

Carlo   leaves for Arles to besiege Agramante

Act 3°

1 Garden

Astolfo   and St John; Enoch and Elijah arrive

St John   Since God brought you here to restore the sanity of Orlando, whom God has forgiven, now we have to wait for the moon to get lower and together with St John you will ascend.[3] (The moon goes down, they stand side by side and rise up)
(Enoch and Elijah remain)

---

[3] Agrippino had originally attributed the declaration to Enoch, following the *Storia dei paladini*, but he then crossed out the patriarch's name and replaced it with that of St John, following the *Furioso*. He also changed the phrase "together with the prophet you will ascend" to "together with St John you will ascend," presumably at an earlier moment when the speaker was still Enoch. In the ensuing conversation as well, Agrippino initially wrote Enoch's name but then replaced it with that of St John. These changes capture the puppeteer in the process of navigating between Ariosto's original narrative and Lodico's prose retelling.

Scene 2 Paradise[4]

Trees, flasks, and bladders
St John and Astolfo arrive

Astolfo	What a delightful place, tell me, oh Evangelist, what is the meaning of these flasks, some of them full and others half empty?
St John	The ones that are half empty are the tears of lovers and the useless time spent in idleness of every sort, the full ones are men's desires, the empty ones belong to fleeting life (screams are heard coming out of the bladders)
St John	These are the ancient crowns of Assyria, Lydia, Persia, and Greece
Astolfo	And those garlands?
St John	This is the flattery that mortals show to those in power under the semblance of respect
Astolfo	And those dishes full of moldy soup?
St John	It is the alms that the rich give to the poor
Astolfo	And that bread?
St John	It is a poisoned bread that women give to libidinous husbands. There is the flower of wisdom, and there, as you see, that full flask contains Orlando's wits
Astolfo	How is it that a man loses his mind?
St John	Everyone in the world loses it, some for love, some for money, some for painting or astrology
Astolfo	I want to see mine, oh! here it is, why is it only half full?
St John	You, too, have lost half your mind, but by placing your nose there it will be restored. Now you will take Orlando's wits and also a flower that—applying it to the eyes of Senapo—will restore his sight, and then we will descend to the same place, and when you are in front of Senapo you will say that God punished him because he had denied Him

---

4 Although the dialogue of the previous scene indicates that Astolfo's destination is the moon, here the location is given as Paradise. Agrippino appears to be eliding the two. Orlando's wits are to be found on the moon in both Agrippino's sources and traditional Sicilian puppet theater. Alessandro Napoli notes, however, that the evening was commonly referred to as "Astolfo in Paradiso" in the Catanese tradition in reference to the earthly paradise (email message to author, November 14, 2022). For recent theatrical, musical, and artistic renditions of this episode, see "Astolfo on the Moon" on the eBOIARDO website (https://edblogs.columbia.edu/eboiardo/authors/ariosto/astolfo-on-the-moon/).

Comparative Analysis

Act 1 (scenes 7–9); Act 2 (scenes 1, 3, and 5); Act 3 (scenes 1 and 2): "Astolfo chases the Harpies away from Senapo's table, enters the infernal hole, and hears Lidia's story. Then, losing the bridle of the winged animal, flies through the celestial doors and reaches the earthly paradise where he receives Orlando's wits from St John the Evangelist and sees wondrous things."

In the *Orlando Furioso*, a hippogriff carries Astolfo from France to Ethiopia, where he encounters Senapo who, Ariosto tells us, is better known to his readers as Prester John (*OF* 33.106). Western European rulers, in fact, had been actively seeking this legendary Christian priest-king as an ally against Islamic invaders since the late twelfth century. In the *Furioso*, however, it is the Ethiopian sovereign who is in need of rescue.[5] Like Phineus in the story of the Argonauts, Senapo was struck blind and doomed to have all his meals polluted by the Harpies. In his case, however, these afflictions are part of God's punishment for his foolhardy attempt to scale a nearby mountain leading to the earthly paradise in order to subjugate its inhabitants (*OF* 33.110–111). In addition, God sent an angel to annihilate the hundred thousand men who had accompanied him.

Astolfo chases away the Harpies and pursues them to the cavernous entrance to hell, where he listens to Lidia's woeful tale about her ingratitude toward her former suitor. He next flies upward on the hippogriff as far as the earthly paradise, where he encounters St John and discovers that his journey there was divinely ordained in order to "rescue Christendom and Charlemagne / From present peril" (*OF* 34.56). After a repast at which the patriarch Enoch and prophet Elijah are also present, St John goes on to explain that God had punished Orlando with insanity because the paladin was so blinded by his illicit love for a pagan woman that he forgot his higher calling and even attempted to kill his cousin Rinaldo out of jealousy. (This transgression occurred in the context of Boiardo's Albraca episode.) St John reveals, moreover, that Orlando's three-month sentence is nearing completion and that Astolfo's fated mission to cure his cousin entails his travel to the moon (*OF* 34.62–67).

While Astolfo's principal task is to retrieve Orlando's wits and thus restore the paladin's identity as staunch defender of Christendom, he will also locate and inhale "a good portion" of his own brain previously lost due to his folly

---

5 For the historical and literary background of his character as well as his treatment by Ariosto, see Cavallo, *The World beyond Europe* 182–90 ("Prester John").

(*OF* 34.84–86). And the human faculty of reason is not the only thing lost on earth that reappears on the moon. The lunar valley is a veritable cosmic junkyard, littered with items of both a political and a personal nature, from politicians' favors and monarchs' crowns to the tears and sighs of lovers and even prayers to God and penitential vows (*OF* 34.73–81).

Notwithstanding the comedic and satiric overtones of the episode, the consequences of Astolfo's undertaking could not be more serious. Orlando's recovery of his sanity will effectively end his deviant Arthurian phase and realign him with the figure of the dutiful paladin of the Carolingian epic tradition. Together, Orlando and Astolfo will direct the counteroffensive resulting in the complete destruction of Biserta. Moreover, upon his return from the moon to the earthly paradise, the English knight also procures a herb that will restore Senapo's eyesight (*OF* 38.24). In return, the grateful priest-king will place at Astolfo's disposal a vast army that will prove instrumental in defeating Agramante's forces on north African soil (*OF* 38.28).

Although the *Storia dei paladini* closely follows the *Furioso*'s account of Astolfo's adventures, there are some variants worth noting. Whereas Ariosto had prefaced his introduction of Senapo by stating that the Ethiopian Christians and Saracens were constantly armed to defend their borders (*OF* 33.101), Lodico reports that the Christians "always had weapons in hand to defend their rights" (9: 203). The stated motivation for their armament thus shifts from a more material emphasis on territorial protection to the more abstract moral category of justice. Senapo's alleged sin, moreover, is reframed in a new narrative. Ariosto's sovereign had attempted to conquer the earthly paradise to subjugate its inhabitants because of his Satanic pride: "[he] became/As proud as Lucifer; daring to raise/his eyes against his Maker" (*OF* 33.109). In the *Storia dei paladini*, by contrast, "he had fought against virtue and had banished honesty from his realm, raising the image of Mohammad and demolishing the Christian religion" (9: 204). Whereas the poem had evoked the story of Lucifer's fall together with the construction of the tower of Babel in Genesis 11:1–9, the prose version seems more reminiscent of the episode of the idol constructed and worshiped by the Israelites in the desert in Exodus 32. The new backstory thus shifts the focus from a flawed character to a false belief. At the same time, God's ire is just as intense as in the *Furioso* and likewise extends beyond the perpetrator to his followers. Echoing Ariosto's report of the hundred thousand men killed for having accompanied Senapo on his military expedition, the *Storia dei paladini* claims that a celestial angel struck down the exact same number for their sin of idolatry: "This crime cost a hundred thousand lives, who in the same night were killed by a heavenly angel, because they had worshiped a false prophet" (9: 204).

In the *Storia dei paladini*, Astolfo likewise heads to the terrestrial paradise after having contained the Harpies within the infernal cavern. Yet whereas Ariosto had initially described this journey upward as the knight's own idea (*OF* 34.48), here Astolfo inadvertently loses hold of the reins, thus finding himself unable to direct the hippogriff's course, "staggering in the air" and "uncertain of his survival" (9: 208). Lodico immediately alerts the reader, moreover, that this apparent misfortune was instead a case of divine intervention: "That accident was the will of God, so that the animal flew until it brought him to where Adam and Eve had their origin." This addition to the narrative prevents readers from attributing any agency to Astolfo. There is no degree of curiosity or wanderlust that propels the knight upward, as in the *Furioso*, but exclusively divine will.

When in the *Storia dei paladini* St John explains God's punishment of Orlando to Astolfo, he leaves out the paladin's attempt to kill Rinaldo out of jealousy and focuses instead on his failing toward his king and the Christian Church: "He cared little about defending his lord and bringing peace to the persecuted Church" (9: 209). Although Lodico's St John speaks much less than Ariosto's counterpart, he makes a point to underscore both the justice of God and the gravity of the retribution: "God, very just judge, punished him in the most severe way" (9: 209).

Agrippino extends the account of Astolfo's adventures through all three Acts of *sera* 203 for a total of eight scenes. The English paladin initially appears on stage as the hippogriff brings him to Ethiopia (Act 1, scenes 7–9), and he then travels to Hell (Act 2, scenes 1 and 3), the earthly paradise (Act 2, scene 5; Act 3, scene 1), and the moon (Act 3, scene 2).[6] Although Agrippino generally follows the *Storia dei paladini* when the prose adaptation deviates from the *Furioso*, he also expands, omits, and modifies according to his own artistic vision and understanding of the narrative.

At the moment in which the hippogriff takes flight outside the entrance of hell, Agrippino attributes this action to an accident, as in the *Storia dei paladini*, rather than to Astolfo's own volition, as in the *Furioso*. Yet whereas the prose compilation had focused on the divine intention behind the supposed mishap, Agrippino concentrates all his attention on Astolfo's state of mind by conveying the knight's utter confusion and fear. And while divine will is no longer cited as the catalyst, God is now invoked by Astolfo as his protector: "God, how can I restrain the horse that flies off as it pleases, God help me!" (Act 2, scene 3). In addition to increasing the audience's emotional participation in Astolfo's distress and demonstrating the knight's reliance on God in a moment of need,

---

6 See footnote 4 for Agrippino's apparent merging of the moon with paradise.

this second-person address also foreshadows Astolfo's discovery that God is indeed very active behind the scenes in events concerning both himself and Orlando.

Agrippino makes St John much more circumspect, however, when it comes to relating Orlando's deviant behavior and God's subsequent punishment. As in Lodico's sources, the saint promises to tell Astolfo everything after their meal (Act 2, scene 5). Yet when the action returns to the terrestrial paradise at the opening of Act 3, St John simply tells Astolfo that "God brought you here to restore the sanity of Orlando, whom God has forgiven" (Act 3, scene 1). Since Agrippino often offers detailed explanations, at times adding to what he finds in the *Storia dei paladini*, it cannot be assumed that the inattention to Orlando's sin and punishment here is simply in the interest of saving time. By restricting the focus to God's forgiveness of Orlando and role in his recovery, Agrippino avoids dwelling on both Orlando's sins and God's responsibility for his subsequent madness.

Agrippino also tempers the account of Senapo's transgression and retribution. When St John instructs Astolfo to take back a flower (perhaps more visually appealing than a herb, as in his precedents) to restore Senapo's eyesight, he explains the motive for the priest-king's blindness: "God punished him because he had denied Him" (Act 3, scene 2). Senapo's alleged denial of God, while placing him in the negative category of a renegade, nonetheless avoids the more sensational actions undertaken by the Ethiopian king as well as the accompanying large-scale divine retribution befalling his subjects recounted in the *Furioso* and *Storia dei paladini*.

Act 1 (scene 2); Act 2 (scene 2): "Bradamante leaves from Montalbano to find Ruggiero."

Although Astolfo's travels are the most salient events of *sera* 203, Agrippino juxtaposes the sequence with other ongoing storylines, as noted above. This interlacing gives space to romance adventure just as the epic plotline of Agramante's war is moving toward its final climactic battle in Lampedusa (discussed in Chapter 10). The first of these narrative threads concerns the dynastic story of Bradamante and Ruggiero. The maiden is increasingly desperate because of her beloved's prolonged absence despite his earlier promise to reunite with her and get married. Rumors of his dalliance with Marfisa, albeit unfounded, prompt her to finally leave Montalbano to confront Ruggiero for having allegedly broken faith with her (Act 1, scene 2).

Although Ruggiero does not appear in the play, we do hear news of him when his former mentor Atlante, before dying, arranges to intervene from beyond the grave to stop the impending mortal combat between Ruggiero and Marfisa by revealing that they are long-lost twins (Act 2, scene 2).

Atlante's arrangement will thereby also bring an end to Bradamante's jealous rage via supernatural means, suggestively paralleling the cessation of Orlando's insanity via divine intervention. Yet whereas Orlando forgets Angelica as he recovers his identity as a dutiful paladin, Bradamante is destined to marry her beloved Ruggiero.

Act 1 (scenes 1, 3, 4, 6): "Sansonetto and Oliviero are taken prisoner by Rodomonte at Isabella's bridge."

In the *Orlando Furioso*, after Isabella tricks Rodomonte into decapitating her in order to avoid being raped, the remorseful warrior orders built a tomb, a fortress, and a nearby bridge upon which he can challenge approaching knights and eventually atone for his crime (*OF* 28.95–29.37). After tussling with mad Orlando (*OF* 29.39–48) and capturing Brandimarte (*OF* 31.63–75), Rodomonte is eventually defeated by Bradamante (*OF* 35.48–50). At this point, we learn that among the knights previously bested by Rodomonte were also Sansonetto and Oliviero. In just two verses, Ariosto gives the background story that explains how they happened to arrive at this perilous site: "When looking for Orlando they had gone, / The route they took (the straightest) led them here" (*OF* 35.53).

In the *Storia dei paladini*, Bradamante likewise comes upon the arms of Oliviero "who, having heard the previous day from his sons about the misfortune of his brother-in-law, had come to the bridge" (9: 213). Sansonetto, however, has been replaced by Dudone, who, we are told, "had also followed in the footsteps of the Marquis." Despite the substitution of one name, in both cases the information is likewise relayed quickly and in retrospect (within a single stanza of the *Furioso* and in the middle of a lengthy sentence of the *Storia dei paladini*). The narrative, at this moment, is more focused on the discovery of Brandimarte's armor.

Agrippino, by contrast, transforms the passing background reference in his sources into four separate scenes that take place in real time in the course of *sera* 203. In envisioning the scenes, the puppeteer reintroduces Sansonetto as the other knight besides Oliviero who is defeated by Rodomonte. Whereas the puppeteer generally relied on the *Storia dei paladini* when not citing poetry, his recourse to the original name suggests that he had an eye on Ariosto's version here. The actions of both knights also gain increased prominence through their placement, occupying four of the first six scenes. The play itself, in fact, opens with Sansonetto who "has heard about Orlando" and "goes to see for himself" (Act 1, scene 1).

The numerical progression of the four scenes creates a symmetrical pattern: 1, 3, 4, 6. In the intervening scenes, a desperate Bradamante seeks Ruggiero (scene 2) and a restless Rinaldo seeks Baiardo (scene 5). The vicissitudes of the two knights, moreover, are intertwined: Sansonetto and Oliviero in turn set out to seek Orlando in scenes 1 and 4, and are overcome by Rodomonte and taken prisoner in scenes 3 and 6, respectively. The quick succession of scenes shows that while there are knights who actively attempt to help the mad Orlando, they fail to achieve their goal despite their best efforts.

If we examine this sequence in the context of the surrounding plays, moreover, we discover that Agrippino was further developing structural changes enacted in the prose adaptation. Whereas in the *Furioso*, the events stretching from Rodomonte's encounter with Isabella to his defeat by Bradamante take place across seven cantos (28–35), the *Storia dei paladini* relates the events in three segments closely following each other in the course of only four chapters (9: 175–79, 190–91, 211–13). Agrippino, in elaborating the narrative by giving the two defeated knights their own scenes in real time, makes this addition part of a dramatic arc spanning four consecutive evenings.

Agrippino's habitual audience, therefore, would have experienced this action within a carefully designed cluster of plays involving Isabella's bridge. In *sera* 201, Rodomonte encounters and kills Isabella, erects a bridge in her honor, and then fights Orlando until they both fall into the river.[7] In *sera* 202, Rodomonte defeats Brandimarte and takes him prisoner. In *sera* 204, Bradamante puts an end to the peril by knocking Rodomonte off the bridge. *Sera* 203, therefore, serves to maintain the spectators' focus on the storyline while underscoring the king of Sarza's continuous threat to travelers. Such sustained treatment also builds up dramatic tension in anticipation of Bradamante's victory the following evening.

Act 2 (scenes 4 and 6): "Carlo leaves for Arles to besiege Agramante."

In *sera* 203, the Christian victory is foreshadowed not only by Astolfo's journey to the moon to retrieve Orlando's wits but also by Carlo's impending counterattack on Agramante's forces in the French coastal city of Arles. Agrippino creates a symmetry by first depicting Agramante having reinforced his army (Act 2, scene 4) and subsequently showing Carlo as he leaves Paris to besiege Agramante (Act 2, scene 6).

---

7 As in the *Storia dei paladini*, this occurs because the bridge collapses.

Although Agramante curses the arrival of Rinaldo in Act 2, scene 4, the Frankish knight has already left to search for Baiardo in the (correct) belief that Gradasso has abducted the horse (Act 1, scene 5). We recall that at the opening of the *Innamorato*, the king of Sericana had crossed Asia and Europe in order to attain Durlindana and Baiardo through his valor. In the course of the *Furioso*, however, he obtains both the sword and the horse fortuitously rather than winning them in combat. In the latter case, he surreptitiously appropriates Baiardo following a chance encounter. Rinaldo's search for Baiardo and Gradasso in *sera* 203 keeps this unresolved storyline in the foreground. Gradasso's loss of the coveted sword and horse five plays later will coincide with the conclusion of the combat that brings Agramante's war to a definitive end (discussed in Chapter 10).

Chapter 10

THE BATTLE OF THREE AGAINST THREE IN LAMPEDUSA (*SERA* 208)[1]

Introduction

Right from the grand council in which Boiardo's Agramante announced his plan to invade France, the North African king exemplified an overreaching ruler destined to lose his kingdom in a reckless attempt to acquire something beyond his reach. Boiardo had foretold, moreover, that the invasion of France would not only end in failure but would lead to the destruction of Biserta as well (*OI* 2.1.19). As Ariosto fulfills this prophecy in the final cantos of the *Furioso*, Agramante's original *aviditas dominationis* gives way to warfare based on religious difference.

In an episode that evokes the fall of Jerusalem in First Crusade chronicles, Biserta is destroyed above all thanks to the leadership of Orlando and Astolfo, the military support of Senapo's Ethiopians, and the direct intervention of the Christian God.[2] Indeed, God not only orchestrates the recovery of Orlando's wits and Senapo's eyesight (in the latter case securing an important ally for the Christians), as we have seen in the previous chapter, but enacts three additional miracles to help the Ethiopian army reach Biserta: the capture of the disruptive African winds inside a wineskin bag, the metamorphosis of stones to horses, and the transformation of leaves into ships (*OF* 38.29–30, 38.33–35, 39.26–29).

Although with the sack of Biserta Agramante has essentially lost both the war and his kingdom, the final outcome will be determined by a battle of Orlando, Oliviero, and Brandimarte against Agramante, Gradasso, and Sobrino on Lipadusa (the island of Lampedusa that lies between Sicily and Africa). This climactic three-on-three combat is the core of *sera* 208.

---

1 The play translated and discussed in this chapter is found in *Copione* 14. To compare versions, see *serata* 212 in Mike Manteo's notebook 18.
2 See Cavallo, *The World beyond Europe* 197–207 ("The Destruction of Biserta").

The play opens with Gradasso swept by a storm at sea to the shores of Lampedusa, where he is soon thereafter joined by Agramante and Sobrino (Act 1, scene 4). Preliminaries continue intermittently throughout Act 2, while the battle and its aftermath take up all of Act 3.[3]

While this final epic confrontation constitutes much of the play's action, there are two additional narrative threads that are carefully interwoven through the customary technique of *entrelacement*. The first, concerning Rinaldo, is present in all three Acts and spans from Act 1, scene 2, to the final moments of Act 3. The second, involving Ruggiero, begins in Act 1, scene 8, and is continued in Act 2, scenes 1 and 3. These narrative threads were developed in two separate chapters of the *Storia dei paladini*. In one chapter, Ruggiero's religious conversion during a shipwreck at sea and subsequent baptism are juxtaposed with the battle of Lampedusa (10: 18–33). In the following chapter, Rinaldo's release from his passion for Angelica during an allegorical combat in the Arden Wood is juxtaposed with the aftermath of the battle and Brandimarte's funeral in Agrigento, Sicily (10: 34–54). Only at the end of this chapter do all the storylines merge when Orlando, Rinaldo, and Ruggiero come together at a hermitage on an island not far from Agrigento. By reordering the narrative to juxtapose Rinaldo's and Ruggiero's storylines within the same play, Agrippino encourages spectators to associate the knights' respective transformations. While Rinaldo undergoes a moral conversion from a wayward pursuer of Angelica to a loyal paladin of Carlo, Ruggiero undergoes an explicitly religious conversion from a Saracen to a believer in the Christian God. Moreover, as discussed below, the nature of the latter's conversion will depart substantially from both the *Orlando Furioso* and the *Storia dei paladini*.

Translation

Evening 208

Rinaldo leaves Paris, fights against a monster in a forest, and drinks from the Fountain of Disdain. Gradasso challenges Orlando to a battle of three against three on the island of Lampedusa. The baptism of Ruggiero. The great battle of three against three. The death of Brandimarte, Gradasso, and Agramante. ~~The baptism of Subrino.~~ Rinaldo arrives in Lampedusa and finds Orlando. Subrino asks to be baptized.

---

3 For videotaped scenes from this extended episode by the Marionettistica dei Fratelli Napoli of Catania, see "Battle of Lipadusa" on the eBOIARDO website (https://edblogs.columbia.edu/eboiardo/authors/ariosto/lipadusa/).

THE BATTLE OF THREE AGAINST THREE IN LAMPEDUSA

Characters
a monster or wild beast or animal
a knight neither young nor old
1 Hermit
Ruggiero in a shirt [i.e., unarmed]
Malagigi disguised as a knight
Fountain

Act 1

Scene 1 Ship

Gradasso	was headed for Sericana, the storm pounded him and he landed on the island of Lampedusa

2 Room

Rinaldo	thinks about Angelica, calls Malagigi, and says he is crazy about Angelica
Malagigi	But how can that be? She loved you and you refused her, in any case, go rest. He conjures up Nucalone and learns from him that Angelica married Medoro and that Rinaldo drank from the Fountain of Disdain and then from the Fountain of Love and that Angelica is traveling through Spain
Malagigi	calls for Rinaldo and tells him everything
Rinaldo	Okay, I'm going to ask Carlo for permission and I'm going away

3 Paris

Carlo	has planned to divide among everyone the booty recovered in Arles (Rinaldo arrives)
Rinaldo	says that having learned that Gradasso has Baiardo, he wants to go to Sericana. Cladinoro, Carinda, and Guidone offer their assistance, but Rinaldo does not want their help and leaves. Everyone accompanies him out of Paris
Malagigi	(alone) calls Nucalone and tells him to take the shape of a monster and attack Rinaldo and then I will arrive

4 Beach

Agramante	and Subrino meet with Gradasso
Agramante	talks about the defeat and how Orlando has set fire to Biserta

Gradasso	Listen, for love of you I will issue a challenge to Orlando. Once he is dead, Carlo will be defenseless
Agramante	It is up to me to punish Orlando
Gradasso	You will challenge a fellow knight of his and we will be two against two
Subrino	You're not including me in the number because I'm old? We will fight three against three. They send a messenger to Biserta

5 Forest

Rinaldo	sees a monster along his path and fights it
Malagigi	is transformed and says you can't kill him, step aside
Malagigi	kills him
Rinaldo	Who are you?
Malagigi	Follow me and you will find out

6 Forest Fountain

Malagigi	and Rinaldo, who sees the fountain and drinks
Malagigi	You want to know who I am? Disdain (and he departs)
Rinaldo	falls asleep, then wakes up, no longer thinks about Angelica, and goes in search of Gradasso

7 Biserta

Orlando	is dividing the booty, the messenger arrives and proposes the challenge
Orlando	accepts and says that as soon as possible I will go to Lampedusa and say who the selected knights will be
Orlando	chooses Oliviero and Brandimarte, says that before going to the island they must put all their affairs in order

8 Ship in a storm

Ruggiero	and the kings that he freed. The storm is raging, Ruggiero removes his armor. Some throw themselves into the sea because the ship is in danger

9 Forest

Rinaldo	sees a knight along the road
Knight	Tell me, are you married?
Rinaldo	Yes

Knight	Then come with me, I will offer you a liquor. If you are able to drink it, your woman is chaste; if it pours out of your mouth, she has betrayed you
Rinaldo	I know that women are Eve's daughters. I will lose my peace of mind wanting to know what you propose. You drink your own liquor!
Knight	If I had known you before today, I would not be suffering for having wanted to know too much about women's secrets. Goodbye, knight!
Rinaldo	goes to embark

Act 2

1 Beach

Ruggiero	naked, falls unconscious, then regains consciousness, follows the path

2 Biserta

Orlando	leaves Astolfo and goes to the beach with Oliviero and Brandimarte to load the ship with supplies in order to go to Lampedusa. Brandimarte leaves Fiordiligi crying

3 Forest

Ruggiero	prays to the God of the Christians along the road
Hermit	Son, whoever tries to fool God is fooling himself, remember what you promised to Bradamante and Rinaldo
Ruggiero	kneels down, Father, have mercy, place me in God's grace
Hermit	Come to my hermitage and you will be instructed and baptized

4 Beach

Orlando	and his companions see a ship without a helmsman. Wait for me, I'll go and see
Orlando	departs and returns, says he found armor and the sword Balisarda that he had taken from Falerina. He gives the armor to Oliviero and the horse to Brandimarte, and he takes the sword for himself. They pass onto Lampedusa and he sends Brandimarte as an ambassador to see if, who knows, Agramante wants to be baptized, and to disclose who are the ones selected to fight

5 Ship

Rinaldo   tries to land on the island of Lampedusa

6 Forest

Gradasso, Agramante, and Subrino. Brandimarte arrives

Brandimarte   Agramante, Orlando is ready to return everything to you on the condition that you get baptized. I, too, was a pagan and in the new faith have found peace. You know that Orlando's name is terrible and no enemy of his has any hope of winning. Oliviero is the second knight selected and you know how much he is worth. I am the third.

Agramante   I challenged you to a battle and not to a sermon that is useful for women. Even though you betrayed Mohammad, I will not betray him. If Orlando is terrible, I have Gradasso here with me and Subrino is the third

Act 3

1 Beach

Brandimarte returns, they prepare for battle

2 Forest

	Encounter of the six knights
Orlando	wants to convert them, but gets nowhere
Agramante	chooses to fight Oliviero
Brandimarte	Subrino |

Orlando and Gradasso | they fight

Orlando	flees, stunned, and Gradasso pursues him
Brandimarte	stuns Subrino and goes to help Orlando
Oliviero	fights Agramante
Subrino	gets up and wounds Oliviero, sending him to the ground
Brandimarte	returns, fights Agramante. They engage in combat
Gradasso	arrives and kills Brandimarte. You see, the victory is ours
Subrino	There is still Orlando
Orlando	arrives, kills Agramante, stuns Subrino, kills Gradasso, and then throws himself upon Brandimarte
Brandimarte	Count, I place my Fiordiligi in your hands, he dies
Oliviero	laments, Rinaldo arrives
Orlando	embraces him, says he has arrived too late

Subrino   asks to be baptized
Orlando   has Oliviero, Subrino, and Brandimarte brought to Agrigento and sends the news to Astolfo

Comparative Analysis

Act 1 (scenes 1, 4, 7): "Gradasso challenges Orlando to a battle of three against three on the island of Lampedusa."

In accordance with the *Furioso*'s increasing attention to religious difference, even the East Asian king Gradasso is refashioned as an avowed enemy of the Christian faith. When he encounters Agramante and Sobrino on the island of Lipadusa following the destruction of Biserta, his proposal to kill Orlando in single combat is presented from a holy war perspective alien to Boiardo's original character: "Once he is dead, the Christian Church may be accounted as so many lambs for a hungry wolf" (*OF* 40.49). It is thus in the guise of a wolf seeking to devour the Church's helpless lambs that Gradasso spurs the defeated African king to further bloodshed.

When the *Storia dei paladini* brings Gradasso together with Agramante and Subrino on the island of Lampedusa, the king of Sericana likewise offers to challenge Orlando in a one-on-one duel. Yet rather than repeating Ariosto's reference to a hungry wolf devouring the defenseless lambs of the Christian Church, Gradasso's motivation is reframed as the recapture of Biserta: "Once I have removed him [i.e., Orlando] for you, the Christians will not be able to defend themselves for long and they will be forced to leave Biserta, thus you will have your ancient kingdom back" (10: 22). While adopting the grammatical structure of Ariosto's verses, the rewording of the dependent clause from "once he is dead" to "once I have removed him for you" shifts the emphasis from the overt act of killing Orlando to the more functional elimination of the threat to Biserta. By substituting the earlier holy war rhetoric with practical military strategy, the *Storia dei paladini* recaptures the secular spirit of Boiardo's original character.

The divergences between the *Orlando Furioso* and the *Storia dei paladini* present different options for Agrippino. Gradasso's declaration in Act 1, scene 4, appears to strategically combine both sources. The dependent clause "once he is dead" replicates Ariosto's brutally direct reference to Orlando "dead" in lieu of the more functional-sounding "removed" used in the *Storia dei paladini*. Nonetheless, the conclusion of the sentence, "Carlo will be defenseless," focuses exclusively on the Frankish emperor's inability to hold Biserta militarily without Orlando. The absence of Ariosto's subsequent reference to the destruction of the Christian Church thus maintains Gradasso's more secular outlook that the prose adaptation reintroduced.

Act 2 (scenes 2, 4, 6): "The great battle of three against three."

Ariosto's designation of Brandimarte and Oliviero as Orlando's fellow warriors further develops the shift to religious warfare. The poet underscores the Christian identity of Brandimarte by having the neophyte recall his own conversion in a vain attempt to convert Agramante prior to the final combat. Unlike the friendly conversation between Orlando and Agricane in the *Innamorato* but like the contentious discussions between warriors in many earlier Carolingian epics, Brandimarte's speech celebrates Christianity as the only true faith and denigrates Islam: "That Christ is God I recognized as true. / A dupe henceforth Mahomet seemed to me" (*OF* 41.39). Oliviero, for his part, has had only a minor role up to this point in the poem, but had been one of the protagonists of the *Chanson de Roland*, fighting and dying alongside his close companion Roland in the battle of Roncevaux. His reappearance at this critical moment imbues the upcoming combat with the aura of religious conflict that characterized that legendary battle.[4]

Although eschewing Ariosto's holy war rhetoric when relating Gradasso's proposal to challenge Orlando, the *Storia dei paladini* nonetheless conveys the religious import of the upcoming combat once all six knights have arrived on Lampedusa. On the Christian side, Orlando takes on greater prominence in the proselytizing effort. Whereas Ariosto had intimated that Brandimarte's attempt to convert Agramante was undertaken on his own initiative with the "permission of his commandant" (*OF* 41.37), now it is Orlando himself who sends Brandimarte "as an ambassador" (10: 27).

Brandimarte, for his part, not only explains that Agramante's conversion would have the practical political advantage of maintaining his kingdom, as in the *Furioso*, but more fully elaborates the beneficial effects on a personal, spiritual level:

> if you, lord, will experience for a single day what peace and comfort the true God gives to the spirit, you would not refuse to grant Orlando what he has asked of you. I lived in darkness for a long time and never felt that calm that I now feel, but when I recognized Mohammad to be false and Christ to be true, I despised the first and I adore the second as the creator of all things. (10: 28)

Lodico's Orlando subsequently underscores the battle's religious dimension in an address to his fellow warriors, positing "how much advantage the Church

---

4 For further parallels between the battle of Lipadusa and that of Roncevaux (via Pulci's *Morgante*), see Quint 79–82.

would gain by extinguishing the life of the two proud monarchs who have made the Christians miserable for such a long time" (10: 29). The paladin's speech keeps the focus on the religiosity of their mission by evoking God, His faithful ones, and the Church rather than Carlo and the Frankish empire. Orlando even tries to make another effort at persuasion just as the fighting is about to begin: "The count wanted to say something that would prevent the battle" (10: 30).

The *Storia dei paladini* also makes readers privy to the thoughts of the warriors on the opposing side. Although we are told that the souls of the "pagans" are too proud to heed Orlando's words, Subrino's following thoughts directed at his own king actually echo Brandimarte's earlier argument: "And you Agramante, who have not considered how powerful the God of the Christians is and how little fruit you have had up to now from the faith sworn to Mohammad, prefer to lose both peace and your empire by not worshiping the true God" (10: 29). Thus, while avoiding the menacing holy war rhetoric of Gradasso's proposal, as noted above, the prose adaptation nonetheless picks up on and expands the role of religion in a succession of moments preceding the combat.

Agrippino sets the stage for the battle in three alternating scenes in the course of Act 2 (scenes 2, 4, and 6). In the central scene in which Orlando sends Brandimarte as his ambassador, as in the *Storia dei paladini*, Agrippino includes the phrase "if, who knows, Agramante wants to be baptized" (Act 2, scene 4). Whereas the prose adaptation does not report any specific instructions on the part of Orlando, his statement here underscores that the proselytizing attempt is sincere and not perfunctory. In addition, Agrippino avoids the insults to the African king's current faith found in his sources and limits Brandimarte's autobiographical reference to the positive effect that the Christian religion had upon him: "I, too, was a pagan and in the new faith have found peace" (Act 2, scene 6).

As in the *Storia dei paladini*, Agrippino's Orlando makes a final attempt at converting his opponents himself as they face each other the next morning. This is indicated via stage directions rather than written first-person speech: "Orlando wants to convert them, but gets nowhere" (Act 3, scene 2). Yet whereas Lodico's Orlando had only wanted to say something but did not manage to speak, now the puppet theater audience would have been the direct witnesses to the improvised dialogue.

Act 3 (scenes 1 and 2): "The death of Brandimarte, Gradasso, and Agramante."

While determining the definitive outcome of Agramante's entire war, the three-against-three battle of Lipadusa shines the spotlight on the individual knights involved. Most shockingly, Ariosto imagines that Gradasso treacherously kills Brandimarte by lunging at him from behind while the latter is engaged in fighting Agramante (*OF* 41.99). Then, as if literally stabbing Brandimarte in the back were not sufficiently shameful, the king of Sericana then loses his courage in his final struggle of the poem. After watching Orlando kill Agramante, he is so overcome with fear—"he quailed, he blanched"—that he is unable to move (*OF* 42.10). He thereby becomes easy prey at the hands of his outraged opponent, who effortlessly pierces his side (*OF* 42.11). Thus, Ariosto's transformation of Gradasso entails not only a new antagonism toward Christianity, but also, in the end, his betrayal of the chivalric code and an abandonment of his customary bravery.

While Ariosto thereby condemns Gradasso to ignominy in the mind of his readers, the poet takes a step further and informs us of the divine judgment awaiting the other two warriors who died on the field. Agramante's soul descends to the underworld and is picked up by Charon (*OF* 42.9), the ferryman of Hades employed in Dante's *Inferno* to ferry the damned into hell. By contrast, Brandimarte's soul ascends to heaven amidst the sound of "angelic voices sweetly blend[ing] / With the celestial instruments they play" (*OF* 42.14).

Despite his grief, Orlando tends not only to Oliviero but also to Sobrino, likewise gravely wounded. Indeed, Ariosto makes a point to note that Orlando speaks kindly to his former opponent as though they were from the same family while the latter's "life was hanging by the merest thread" (*OF* 42.18–19). Orlando's new attitude prepares the reader for Sobrino's subsequent conversion that will occur after the episode of Brandimarte's funeral in Agrigento.

In the *Storia dei paladini*, Brandimarte's ascension into heaven receives even greater cosmic attention. In addition to the aural manifestation of his salvation ("music and songs were heard"), there is now also a visual component: "the whole island was seen shining with an unusual light" (10: 33). Even more spectacularly, Orlando now has the privilege of witnessing his friend's soul fly into the heavens. The prose adaptation remains silent, however, on the ultimate destiny of Agramante's soul after the king is beheaded by Orlando.

The *Storia dei paladini*, most notably, reverses the dynamic between Orlando and Sobrino in the aftermath of the battle. Whereas in the *Furioso* the almost lifeless Sobrino is the unresponsive recipient of Orlando's kindness, here it is Subrino who takes the initiative. Although he similarly lies gravely wounded, upon seeing Orlando, he offers his sword to the victorious paladin in a gesture of submission (10: 33). In response, Orlando simply has Subrino's wounds treated along with those of Oliviero without any indication of further dialogue or personal interest on his part.

In *sera* 208, the entirety of Act 3 is devoted to the battle of Lampedusa and its immediate aftermath. Although the episode is outlined without much first-person speech, Agrippino does depict Gradasso overconfidently boasting to Subrino after Brandimarte's death: "You see, the victory is ours." Subrino, who knows better, immediately corrects him: "There is still Orlando." And sure enough, in a whirlwind of martial activity, Orlando "arrives, kills Agramante, stuns Subrino, kills Gradasso, and then throws himself upon Brandimarte." Whereas in the *Furioso* and *Storia dei paladini* Brandimarte died before being able to pronounce the full name of his beloved wife, Agrippino's character is able to complete his final request to his friend ("I place my Fiordiligi in your hands") before expiring. Without any mention of the souls of the deceased warriors heading to either heaven or the underworld, Agrippino keeps the attention on human action and its consequences rather than divine judgment in the afterlife. This is not for the lack of technical means because it was customary, for example, to show an angel descending to accompany Orlando's soul to heaven following his death in Roncevaux. Yet the episode is not yet over and contains a development absent in the sources, as discussed below.

Act 3 (scene 2 continued): "The baptism of Subrino. Rinaldo arrives in Lampedusa and finds Orlando. Subrino asks to be baptized."

In the *Furioso*, after Brandimarte's funeral in Agrigento, Orlando travels with Oliviero and Sobrino to a nearby island inhabited by a hermit reputed to help people via miraculous means (*OF* 43.187). Orlando asks the "saint" to heal Oliviero who had been wounded and brought near to death while "fighting for the Faith and Christendom" (*OF* 43.191). The hermit first goes into a church to pray and then heals Oliviero miraculously by giving him "his blessing" (*OF* 43.192).

Sobrino's subsequent conversion to Christianity is related in the very next stanza:

> [...]; he decided to abjure
> Mahomet; scarcely could he bear to wait
> Christ to confess in all His living power.
> Thus, filled with faith and with a heart contrite,
> He begged admittance to our sacred rite.
>
> (*OF* 43.193)

Ariosto focuses the attention on both Sobrino's internal state of mind and his formal request for baptism, based entirely on having witnessed "so evident and great / A marvel" (*OF* 43.193).

The *Storia dei paladini* further develops the accounts of both Oliviero's healing and Subrino's conversion by adding supporting narrative details and dialogue. First, the hermit not only enters a church to pray, but he brings Oliviero inside with him and asks the paladin to confess his sins. After conferring absolution, the hermit then leaves to pray in solitude, returns to the group, and places his hand on the paladin's leg in an act of healing through physical contact. This more ritualistic and dramatic representation of the miracle has a noticeably more powerful effect on Subrino, whose conversion is now rendered in a first-person exclamation:

> Subrino, terrified by the power of the God of the Christians, exclaimed weeping: "Father, may it never be that, having seen the greatness of your God, I chose to retain my prior creed. I abdicate Mohammad and confess that your God is the true one, and mine is a liar; ensure that I too may become a follower of Carlo and the new faith" (10: 44).

Thus, while the *Storia dei paladini* omitted the holy war rhetoric in Gradasso's proposal to Agramante, its heightened attention to the Christian faith from the battle preliminaries right through to Subrino's conversion serves to reinforce the importance of religion in this phase of the narrative.

Sera 208 presents a significant modification at the conclusion of the battle of Lampedusa: Subrino spontaneously asks to be baptized before the knights even prepare to leave the island (Act 3, scene 2). This alters the dynamic of the narrative in two important ways. First, it partially counters all the death and destruction—in particular, the heartbreaking demise of Brandimarte—with an immediate positive outcome from the perspective of Agrippino's (presumably Christian) audience. This is the same narrative procedure that one finds in the *Chanson de Roland*, for example, when, after all the bloodshed on both sides, Marsile's widow, Queen Bramimonde of Zaragoza, spontaneously converts and asks to be baptized.[5] Second, this spontaneous conversion is decoupled from the miracle that had prompted Sobrino to embrace Christianity in both the *Orlando Furioso* and the *Storia dei paladini*. The focus thus shifts from Subrino's awe at the power of the Christian God to his rejection of the unbridled and ultimately destructive imperialism of the deceased king of Biserta. In this way, Subrino's conversion can be seen as the final and logical conclusion of his initial speech at the council

---

5 One may question how spontaneous it can be to convert after one's husband and people have been killed in battle. Nonetheless, from within the fictional world of the epic, this is presented as a strictly voluntary conversion in contrast to the mass conversions imposed by military force.

of Biserta in which he had praised the valor of the Christian warriors and advised Agramante against invading France (discussed in Chapter 6).

Agrippino had been so intent on linking Subrino's baptism to the outcome of the battle that he had originally written "the baptism of Subrino" in the summary preceding the play. Yet the presence of the saintly hermit was still necessary for this ritual action to occur. The words were thus crossed out and replaced with Subrino's request for the sacrament. The baptism itself will take place on a nearby island following Brandimarte's funeral in Agrigento in the subsequent play, *sera* 209.

Act 1 (scenes 2, 3, 5, 6, and 9); Act 2 (scene 5): "Rinaldo leaves Paris, fights a monster in a forest and drinks the water of disdain."

As Orlando, Oliviero, and Brandimarte prepare to defend Christendom in a final epic battle on the island of Lipadusa, Ariosto turns his attention to Rinaldo's amorous vicissitudes. The news of Rinaldo's infatuation with Angelica surprises Malagigi who had previously failed to lead his recalcitrant cousin into the willing arms of the Cathayan princess (discussed in Chapter 4). After conjuring up a demon informer, Malagigi learns not only that Angelica has given herself to the African Medoro but also that Rinaldo has fallen under the spell of the Fountain of Love (*OF* 42.34–37). When the necromancer conveys Angelica's latest news to Rinaldo, the paladin sets off in search of her, pretending that he intends instead to wrest Baiardo from Gradasso.

In the ensuing fantastical scene in the depths of the Arden Wood, an unknown knight defeats a monster that Rinaldo was unable to subdue on his own because of his erotic subjection to Angelica. The knight then leads Rinaldo to drink from the eros-squashing Fountain of Merlin and reveals his name to be Disdain (Sdegno). Rinaldo is unsure whether his savior was sent by Malagigi or God (*OF* 42.65–66), leaving it open as to whether the episode is to be understood within the sphere of magical enchantment in the original spirit of Boiardo's Twin Fountains or in the realm of religious miracle in keeping with the poem's recent divine interventions in the trajectories of Astolfo, Orlando, and Ruggiero (discussed further below). In either case, Rinaldo's release from his erotic subjection will eventually lead him to Lipadusa even though he will arrive only after the battle is over (*OF* 43.150).

On his way southward through Italy, Rinaldo is given the opportunity to test by magical means whether his wife has been faithful to him. After some reflection, he declines the chance to know more than is licit for both ethical and practical reasons. His moral argument goes back to God's prohibition in Genesis: "For God denies such certainty / More than to Adam He denied the tree" (*OF* 43.7). Ariosto develops, in fact, an analogy between husbands who should not want to know their wives' secrets and Adam who should not have tasted the prohibited fruit. Rinaldo's practical reason, on the other hand, is the risk of learning an unpleasant truth that could only bring him unhappiness given that, as he says, "Women are women, easy to beguile. / My wife's a woman" (*OF* 43.6).

Although Rinaldo singles out the weakness of women here, it would not be lost on the reader that the paladin himself had spent the latter part of the *Innamorato* and all of the *Furioso* until shortly before this moment chasing after Angelica while his wife remained home alone—not to mention his reputation as a womanizer in previous chivalric works. Following his refusal to test his wife's chastity, moreover, Rinaldo listens to two tales about jealous husbands that reinforce the view of human (and not just female) nature as easily corruptible. In the second tale, this point is poignantly driven home when a husband planning to kill his wife for adultery consents to being sodomized by an Ethiopian stranger in exchange for an opulent palace (*OF* 42.69–144).

In the *Storia dei paladini*, the battle of Lampedusa has already concluded when we learn that Rinaldo, unable to find news of Angelica, "presented himself to the necromancer Malagigi and disclosed his love" (10: 34). Indeed, the prose adaptation not only reorders the narration of events but also separates the two storylines through a chapter break. The unknown knight who subsequently rescues Rinaldo from his monstrous opponent is referred to by the narrator as "the unknown one" ("l'incognito") and "the stranger" or "foreigner" ("lo straniero") and likewise identifies himself as "disdain" ("lo sdegno") before disappearing (10: 36). Although Rinaldo is said to be astounded, he falls asleep without further ado. He is apparently too exhausted by the ordeal to ponder whether Malagigi's magic or God's divine force is responsible for his liberation.[6]

The *Storia dei paladini* likewise emphasizes certain aspects while omitting others in the episode of Rinaldo's refusal to drink from the chalice. The prose adaptation elaborates, for example, on the paladin's decision not to test his wife's chastity by adding further remarks on the fragility of women:

> It is enough for me to know that my wife is a woman, as soft and fickle as a fern leaf, and if there are faithful ones from the weaker sex, they are singled out and held in great veneration by us, and it would not be so if all women were of a single constitution. (10: 38)

---

6 Lodico's original edition explicitly identifies the stranger as Malagigi in a footnote (3: 680), absent in Leggio's version.

The expansion of Ariosto's single adjective "soft" ("molle") into the simile "pliable and fickle like a fern leaf" ("molle e volubile quanto una fronda") recalls the proverb "Woman is fickle like a feather in the wind" ("La donna è mobile qual piuma al vento") that was bantered by the notoriously inconstant Duke of Mantua in Giuseppe Verdi's *Rigoletto* (1851). Whatever the inspiration for Lodico's simile, it is worth noting that the *Storia dei paladini* steers clear of Ariosto's Biblical analogies when Rinaldo ponders his decision. Eschewing the *Furioso*'s lengthy reference to the divine prohibition against illicit knowledge in Genesis, the paladin reasons in purely practical terms: "Wanting to know more could be my ruination" (10: 38).

Agrippino, following the sequencing of the *Furioso* rather than that of the *Storia dei paladini*, turns his attention to Rinaldo prior to the three-against-three battle instead of after its completion. Unlike Ariosto, however, he does not relate the knight's story in one continuous narrative block but uses *entrelacement* to alternate between Rinaldo's various encounters and the preparations for the epic combat on the island of Lampedusa. Indeed, five of the nine scenes of Act 1 (scenes 2, 3, 5, 6, and 9) and an additional scene in Act 2 (scene 5) feature Rinaldo before he reaches the island near the very end of the play.

The enamored Rinaldo's first appearance in the play depicts him revealing his predicament to Malagigi (Act 1, scene 2). Whereas the *Storia dei paladini* had recounted Rinaldo's admission to his cousin by the more impersonal "he disclosed his love to him" (10: 34), Agrippino's Rinaldo declares that he is "crazy" ("pazzo") for Angelica. Recourse to that particular adjective underscores the parallel between his condition and that of Orlando. Although Rinaldo is not reduced to the same bestial level, he will nonetheless also have to be cured of his malady, in his case, by drinking from the Fountain of Merlin.

Whereas the *Furioso* advanced the idea that Rinaldo's fantastical adventure could have been the work of either Malagigi or God and Leggio's version of the *Storia dei paladini* left the entire question aside, Agrippino informs his audience from the outset that the wizard is in charge: "Malagigi (alone) calls Nucalone and says to take the shape of a monster and attack Rinaldo and then I will arrive" (Act 1, scene 3). The stage directions indicate, moreover, that Malagigi will disguise himself as the unknown knight before addressing Rinaldo: "Malagigi is transformed and says you can't kill him, step aside" (Act 1, scene 5).

Agrippino likewise refashions the subsequent narrative of the host who challenges Rinaldo to put his wife's faithfulness to the test. The Frankish paladin explains his refusal in the following way: "I know that women are Eve's daughters" (Act 1, scene 9). Whereas the *Storia dei paladini* had completely removed Ariosto's Biblical references, Agrippino brings back Genesis, albeit from a different angle. In acknowledging that women are susceptible to temptation, he turns to a figure who had not been named in his sources. By shifting the focus from Adam's illicit desire for knowledge to Eve's vulnerable nature, Agrippino also reconfigures the point of the Biblical analogy from a warning not to transgress by seeking prohibited knowledge to an explicit acknowledgment of human frailty—thus reinforcing the overriding theme of the episode.[7]

Even though Agrippino's Rinaldo alludes to the Biblical story by linking women to Eve, he does not replay the *Furioso*'s analogy comparing inquisitive husbands to Adam. Instead, he moves directly to a softer version of the *Storia dei paladini*'s projected scenario. While not completely ruining his life, putting his wife's chastity to the test could nevertheless cause him to lose his "peace of mind" (Act 1, scene 9).

If, at the opening of *sera* 208, Rinaldo is depicted as an Arthurian-style knight errant just as infatuated with Angelica as he was in the first canto of the *Orlando Innamorato* before drinking at the Fountain of Merlin, by the close of the evening—indeed, near the end of the final scene—he joins his companions on the island of Lampedusa as a stalwart Carolingian paladin. Agrippino thus not only develops a sense of simultaneity between Rinaldo's return to his senses and the decisive battle of three against three via interwoven scenes, but he also brings Rinaldo's deviant romance story back in line with the main epic plot at the conclusion of this momentous evening.

Act 1 (scene 8); Act 2 (scenes 1 and 3): "The baptism of Ruggiero."

In the *Orlando Furioso*, Marfisa converts to Christianity as soon as she learns that her father was Ruggiero di Risa and her mother the neophyte Galaciella. Her twin brother Ruggiero, however, delays his conversion in order not to appear disloyal to Agramante in the eyes of the Saracens. Even after learning that Agramante has abandoned the invasion and fled back to Biserta without

---

7 Although the *Storia dei paladini* includes only the first novella related by the jealous host, leaving out the second novella in which the adulterous wife catches her husband in an even more compromised situation, Agrippino could have read both in the original poem.

him, he still postpones his conversion to Christianity and heads back to Africa to support his political leader. It is only when he is shipwrecked at sea and in danger of drowning that he finally decides to convert. Ruggiero, in fact, fears that the shipwreck was Christ's revenge for his procrastination (*OF* 41.47). Remembering his previous promises to Bradamante and Rinaldo, Ruggiero now makes a new pledge directly to the Christian God:

> Four times, ten times, in penitence he said,
> If God would overlook these sins so black,
> If ever he set foot on land again,
> He would become a Christian there and then.
>
> (*OF* 41.48)

After Ruggiero vows likewise to never again draw his sword against the Christians on behalf of the Moors and to both serve Carlo and marry Bradamante, the narrator reports the immediate occurrence of a miracle (*OF* 41.49). Before the stanza is complete, we learn that "When he has promised this / His strength and his agility increase." By the following stanza, Ruggiero has arrived safely on shore. The narrator goes on to confirm to the reader that the knight's sole survival while everyone around him drowned was indeed the will of God (*OF* 41.51). And just in case Ruggiero had been in any doubt, before he goes a hundred steps, he encounters a hermit who confirms his sensation of divine intervention: "God has a long arm and reaches you / Just when you think He is less likely to" (*OF* 41.53).

Even though Ruggiero had originally intended to become a Christian for love of Bradamante, as his mother Galaciella had done for love of his father Ruggiero II and as was fairly common in the chivalric epic tradition, Ariosto draws attention to the fact that in the end the conversion follows a sacred rather than secular model. The hermit first addresses Ruggiero by calling out the words of Jesus to Saint Paul in Acts 9:4: "Saul! Saul! / Why do you persecute me?" (*OF* 41.53). The narrator further reveals that their encounter was not by chance, but that the hermit had received a vision from God the previous night explaining that Ruggiero would arrive ashore with His help and revealing the paladin's past and future in their entirety (*OF* 41.54). Before going on to instruct and baptize Ruggiero, the hermit rebukes him for not "submitting to the gentle yoke" of his own free will but turning to God only when "threatened with a lash / Which, as he feared, upon his back would crash" (*OF* 41.55). The metaphor of the lash, evoking compulsion under the threat of violence, reinforces the fact that the tempest was divinely orchestrated and that Ruggiero's life had indeed hung in the balance.

In the *Storia dei paladini*, Ruggiero, alone in the tempestuous sea while all those around him are drowning, understands the storm to be a divine response to his procrastination and duly repents: "Mindful of the many promises made to his beloved to leave Mohammad and adore Christ, he was assailed by severe repentance and recognized that the storm was his divine punishment." The prose adaptation then goes on to report Ruggiero's direct speech to God in words that recall the proposition outlined in Ariosto's above-cited verses: "'Oh God, you who govern your Christian people with justice,' the hero said out loud, 'I vow to receive baptism as soon as, strengthened by your power, I will be saved by touching the nearby shore'" (10: 26). As soon as Ruggiero proffers "these and other words of repentance," an "invincible power" propels the waves that carry Ruggiero safely to shore. The fact that Ruggiero reaches land in the space of the same sentence reinforces the sense that God heard the knight's promise and acted instantaneously.

As in the *Furioso*, Ruggiero soon thereafter encounters a hermit who remonstrates with him for his procrastination. Although the hermit does not reference the Biblical conversion of Saint Paul, he does remind Ruggiero of his promise to Bradamante and Rinaldo and confirms that the knight had indeed been brought to the brink of death: "Son, said that holy man, whoever tries to fool God is fooling himself. He had prescribed baleful death to you. Remember what you promised to Bradamante and lastly to Rinaldo, and, because a vain desire made you linger, I tell you that a few seconds later you could have lost your life" (10: 26). While the hermit has been forewarned of Ruggiero's arrival, as in the *Furioso*, in this case, the prophecy came not in a dream vision but through the actual visitation of an angel (10: 27). In addition, whereas in the *Furioso* the hermit does all the talking for the space of four stanzas (*OF* 41.53–56), in the *Storia dei paladini*, the hermit's above-cited reprimand is immediately followed by Ruggiero's statement expressing sincere repentance for his offence to God and entrusting himself to the hermit for help in attaining God's grace.

Agrippino substantially alters both the order and the nature of these life-changing events in a succession of three scenes occurring within Acts 1 and 2. The first scene is that of Ruggiero caught in a tempest at sea. While some passengers throw themselves into the sea to escape danger, Ruggiero removes his armor (Act 1, scene 8). The next time he appears on stage, he is shown falling unconscious upon the beach. He subsequently regains consciousness and begins to follow a path (Act 2, scene 1). There is no dialogue composed for either of these scenes. Following an intervening scene in Biserta in which Orlando and his companions prepare to leave for Lampedusa, Agrippino returns to Ruggiero for the climactic scene of his conversion (Act 2, scene 3).

It is only after Ruggiero has safely reached the shore and begun to walk along a path that his thoughts turn to God: "Ruggiero prays to the God of the Christians along the road" (Act 2, scene 3). In this way, rather than turning to God under compulsion when his life is in imminent danger, Ruggiero prays freely and of his own initiative after having survived the shipwreck. This removes the double discomfort of the Christian God orchestrating a shipwreck and pushing Ruggiero to the point of death to force him to convert and of Ruggiero fearing so much for his life that he seemingly makes a deal with God in order to survive.

There is another notable consequence of delaying Ruggiero's address to the Christian God until he has reached safety: the knight's prayer, rather than prompting divine intervention to save his life, leads instead to the appearance of the hermit. This gives the impression that Ruggiero's prayer is answered in the form of the instruction and baptism he will receive on the part of this saintly figure.

Agrippino develops the conversation between Ruggiero and the hermit to fit his revised version. The hermit's initial words to Ruggiero echo part of his speech in the *Storia dei paladini*: "Son, whoever tries to fool God is fooling himself, remember what you promised to Bradamante and Rinaldo" (Act 2, scene 3). Since, however, in this case, Ruggiero's embrace of Christianity is purely voluntary and not due to dire straits, there is no need for further remonstration on the part of the hermit. When Ruggiero in reply asks for his help in attaining divine grace (directly echoing the *Storia dei paladini*), the hermit invites the knight to undertake the next steps: "Come to my hermitage and you will be instructed and baptized" (Act 2, scene 3). The directness of the hermit's response indicates that he will immediately place Ruggiero in God's grace by instructing and baptizing him in the Christian faith.

By arranging the narrative sequence so as to stage Ruggiero's religious conversion in the same play as the magical-allegorical conversion of Rinaldo, Agrippino invites us to compare their trajectories. Both knights undergo a transformational experience that leads them to a better place mentally and spiritually. The fact that Rinaldo's recovery required the involvement of Malagigi in disguise but Ruggiero's conversion does not stem from any other motive than a sincere belief in the Christian God serves to put the agency of Ruggiero into even greater relief. The latter's situation thereby also aligns with Subrino's request for baptism which in Agrippino's script is spontaneous rather than a consequence of witnessing God's miraculous intervention.

The trajectories of Rinaldo and Ruggiero also invite comparison with that of Orlando. In drawing the *Furioso* to a close, Ariosto had suggestively evoked parallels in all three restorative situations: Orlando inhales the vial that restores his sanity, Rinaldo drinks water from a magic fountain to be free of his unruly passion, and Ruggiero is washed with the holy water of baptism to be cleansed of his sins. Agrippino arranges the narrative material from the *Furioso* and the *Storia dei paladini* so that the three storylines intertwine structurally and thematically throughout *sera* 208 before Orlando, Rinaldo, and Ruggiero are physically united on the hermit's island to witness further blessings (the miraculous healing of Oliviero and the actual baptism of Subrino) in the following evening's play.

CONCLUSION

As a puppeteer whose formation in Sicily coincided with *opera dei pupi*'s heyday, Agrippino devoted his life to reimagining the vicissitudes of the Paladins of France and to representing them on stage for primarily Italian-speaking audiences in the Americas, from his early years in Argentina to his almost two decades of performing nightly in New York City. Even though American society changed substantially in the decades following the closing of the Teatro Manteo in 1939, the passion that Agrippino's children felt for the tradition motivated them to bring their style of Catanese puppet theater to a wide variety of audiences right up to the death of Mike Manteo in 1989.

Each successive adaptation is both an interpretation of the previous material and a recipe for living in the present. Agrippino's stated aim was to remain faithful to his source, the *Storia dei paladini*, and yet in the very act of transporting action from the page to the stage, he recreated the chivalric stories according to his own Weltanschauung. As exemplary as I find the eight selections that I chose to translate and analyze, they are only a fraction of Agrippino's 265 extant plays in the Paladins of France cycle. It is, therefore, my hope that anyone who has made it to the end of this study will be inclined to further investigate Agrippino's "irreplaceable scripts" and to read (or perhaps reread with fresh eyes) the chivalric masterpieces that gave rise to them.

Appendix 1

LIST OF CHARACTERS[1]

1. Pagan captain in the army of Balaheim
2. Balaheim, mighty pagan giant, ruthless against all Christians
3. Christian captain with the army of Charlemane
4. Mamalock, pagan giant in the court of King Solatiello
5. Pagan captain with the army of Mamalock
6. Pagan captain with the army of Mamalock
7. Agolaccio, half brother of Orlando
8. Rinaldo (white armor) Second knight to Orlando, in the court of Charlemane. He was very strong and powerful. The white armor was used for festivities. He was also cousin to Orlando.
9. Morgante, he is an original, made in 1923. Morgante was a very strong pagan giant who was baptized a Christian.
10. Uggier il Danese, 4th knight in the court of Charlemane
11. Soriano, Christian king
12. Astolfo, cousin of Orlando, knight in the court of Charlemane
13. Pagan captain in the army of Balaheim
14. Rinaldo, in brass armor, used in battles.
15. Pagan captain in the army of Balaheim
16. Pagan captain in the army of Balaheim
17. Agrippo, knight in the court of Charlemane. Agrippo is one of the newest marionettes made by Papa in 1984
18. Alessandro, knight in Charlemane's court.
19. Zervino, knight in Charlemane's court.
20. Arismondo, pagan king of Trebisonda
21. Bradamante, sister of Rinaldo. Also a knight in the court of Charlemane. She was called "The Tiger of Montalbano."

---

[1] This is the title at the top of the type-written inventory of marionettes owned by the Manteo family in the 1980s. The spelling of names, including variations, follows the original five-page list.

22. Gabby, beggar. Was used in the earlier stories of Orlando when he was young.
23. Febbu, pagan giant, brother of Mamalock
24. Pagan captain in the army of Mamalock
25. Brandmarto, great warrior
26. Pagan captain in the army of Mamalock
27. Henchman
28. Malagigi, sorcerer. Cousin of Orlando and Rinaldo. He helped the Christians.
29. Bramadoro, pagan king of Persia
30. Guerino, detto meschino
31. Agramante, Pagan king of Besertta
32. Pagan captain
33. King Charlemane in armor
34. Christian captain
35. Pagan captain
36. Oliviero, 3rd knight in the court of Charlemane
37. Pagan captain
38. Count Gano, cousin of Charlemane. He was cunning and ruthless. He was the cause of many betrayals involving Orlando and Rinaldo with Charlemane.
39. Gandelino, son of Cladinoro
40. Carlo Martello, son of Agolaccio
41. Polindo, Christian knight
42. Pagan captain in the army of Mamalock
43. Christian knight
44. Guidone Salvaggio, son of Rinaldo
45. Pagan captain
46. Guido Santo, son of Bradamante
47. Pagan captain
48. Marguto, pagan giant
49. Carinda, daughter of Rinaldo
50. Rodomonte, powerful pagan
51. Christian knight
52. Ruggiero of the white eagle, husband of Bradamante
53. Pagan captain, in the army of Mamalock
54. Princess Viviana, wife of Alesandro
55. Princess Gilda, wife of Polindo
56. King Salatiello, pagan king of San Marchan
57. Pagan thief
58. Fulbia, queen of San Marchan

59. Orlando in white armor, 1st knight in Charlemane's court
60. Arcail, African slave freed by Zervino
61. Pagan giant Mataballa
62. Pagan thief
63. Devil Pluto
64. Ricardo Del Leone (Lion) Rinaldo's brother
65. Belingire, Christian knight
66. Ferrau, prince of Spain
67. Pagan thief
68. Christian captain
69. Christian soldier
70. Christian captain
71. Onofrio
72. Catarinella
73. Cladinoro, knight, son of Ruggire
74. Buovo Di Antona, soldier
75. Mondricardo, he kills Zervino
76. Orlando Furioso
77. Melissa, sister of Gilda
78. Carlomagno (Charlemane), King of France
79. Dragon
80. Pepinino, symbol of Sicilian puppetry. Pepinino is the joker, dancer, and comforter of kings and knights
81. Ponponia, lady of the court
82. Body ready to be dressed in armor
83. Rinaldo dressed in court clothing
84. Body to be dressed for next story
85. Devil named Nucalone
86. Milione, Christian soldier
87. Pagan head
88. Count Gano
89. Girado Di Fratta, Oliviero's grandfather
90. Alcina, Queen of all witches
91. Women's head
92. King Balante
93. Christian king
94. Pagan soldier
95. Subrino, pagan king
96. Christian captain
97. King Masiglio of Spain
98. Pope Silvestro

99. Pagan Giant Pirate (Pirate)
100. Pulicane, half dog/half man
101. Christian shepherd
102. Body to be dressed
103. Head of Pulicane
104. Lio-Fene of China
105. Gigilino of Africa
106. Balsabu, devil
107. Ginamo, brother of Count Gano
108. Pagan King Pinamonde
109. Christian King
110. Gorilla head
111. Head of Morgante
112. Head of pagan giant Burato
113. Christian soldier
114. Head of pagan King Gradasso
115. Head of Charlamane, king of France

Appendix 2

PAPA MANTEO'S MARIONETTES— CURRENTLY AT IAM[1]

#	Name	Description/Comments	Location
1	Pagan Captain	Army of Balaheim	IAM
4	Mamalock	Pagan Giant in the Court of King Solatiello	IAM
6	Pagan Captain	Army of Mamalock	IAM
7	Agolaccio	Half Brother of Orlando	IAM
9	Morgante	He is an original, made in 1923. Morgante was a very strong pagan giant who was baptized a Christian.	IAM
14	Rinaldo (in brass armor)	Used in battles	IAM—Currently on display at the museum
20	Arismondo	Pagan King of Trebisonda	IAM
23	Febbu	Pagan Giant, brother of Mamalock	IAM
29	Bramadoro	Pagan King of Persia	IAM
31	Agramante	Pagan King of Beserta	IAM
38	Count Gano	He was cousin to Charlemagne. He was cunning and ruthless. He was the cause of many betrayals involving Orlando and Rinaldo with Charlemagne.	IAM
39	Gandelino	Son of Cladinoro	IAM
47	Pagan Captain		IAM

(*Continued*)

---

1 This is the title at the top of the type-written inventory of marionettes donated to the Italian American Museum in 2010. The formatting reproduces the original two-page list.

#	Name	Description/Comments	Location
48	Marguto	Pagan Giant	IAM
50	Rodomonte	Powerful Pagan	IAM
53	Pagan Captain	Army of Mamalock	IAM
58	Fulbia	Queen of San Marchan	IAM
59	Orlando (in white armor)	1st Knight in Charlemagne's Court	IAM
63	Pluto	Devil	IAM
67	Pagan	Thief	IAM
78	Charlemagne	King of France	IAM
80	Pepinino	Symbol of Sicilian Puppetry. Pepinino is the joker, dancer, and comforter of kings and knights	IAM
85	Nucalone	Devil	IAM
88	Count Gano (only the head)		IAM
98	Pope Silvestro (only the head)		IAM
99	Pagan Giant	Pirate	IAM
100	Pulicane	Half Dog/Half Man	IAM
101	Christian	Shepherd	IAM
107	Ginamo (only the head)	Brother of Count Gano	IAM
111	Morgante (just the head)		IAM
118	Witch		IAM

Appendix 3
EXTANT PUBLICATIONS FROM THE LIBRARY OF AGRIPPINO MANTEO

Donated to the Italian American Museum of New York

Leggio, Giuseppe. *Il figlio di Ricciardetto, ovvero Guido Santo e i discendenti di Carlo Magno seguito alla rotta di Roncisvalle.* Vol. 1. Palermo: Leggio, 1907.
———. *Rinaldino ovvero l'Emulo di Guido Santo seguito a Dolores e Straniero Rinaldino.* Vol. 2. Palermo: Leggio, n.d.
———. *Trabazio.* The cover is missing, but *Storia di Trabazio imperatore di Costantinopoli e dei suoi valorosi figli Febo e Rosaclerio* was published by Leggio in Palermo in 1912 (Napoli in Pasqualino, *Rerum palatinorum fragmenta* 500).
Malfa, Giuseppe. *Uzeta il Catanese e Magilda di Catana.* Palermo: Leggio, n.d.

Privately Owned

Bulfinch, Thomas. *Charlemagne or Romance of the Middle Ages.* New edition with an explanatory introduction by Arthur Richmond Marsh. Boston: Lee & Shepard, 1903.
Leggio, Giuseppe. *Dolores e Straniero.* The front matter is missing, but *Dolores e Straniero ed Il prete rinnegato seguito al Guido Santo,* was published by Leggio in Palermo in 1899, 1907, 1922, and without a date (Napoli in Pasqualino, *Rerum palatinorum fragmenta* 500).
———. *Guido Santo.* The front matter is missing, but *Il figlio di Ricciardetto ovvero Guido Santo e i discendenti di Carlo Magno Seguito alla rotta di Roncisvalle* was published by Leggio in Palermo in 1912, 1920, 1922, 1928, and without a date (Napoli in Pasqualino, *Rerum palatinorum fragmenta* 500).
———. *Storia di Trabazio imperatore di Costantinopoli e dei suoi valorosi figli Febo e Rosaclerio.* Parte prima. Palermo: Leggio, 1912.
Lo Dico, Giusto. *Storia dei paladini di Francia.* Naples: Bideri, 1909. Giuseppe Leggio's expanded version bound together in three volumes.

Appendix 4

PALADINS OF FRANCE SCRIPTS IN THE HANDWRITING OF AGRIPPINO MANTEO

The notebooks followed by an asterisk are privately owned, while all others listed below were donated to the Italian American Museum of New York.

The "Copioni" set
Copione 3 (originally *Libro* 1): *Serate* 1–14*[1]
Copione 4 (originally *Libro* 2): *Serate* 16–27*
Copione 5 (originally *Paladini* 2): *Serate* 25–45*[2]
Copione 6 (originally *Paladini* 3): *Serate* 46–68
Copione 7 (originally *Paladini* 4): *Serate* 69–93*
Copione 8: *Serate* 92–107
Copione 9: *Serate* 108–128
Copione 10: *Serate* 129–146
Copione 11: *Serate* 147–164
Copione 12: *Serate* 165–180
Copione 13: *Serate* 181–195*
Copione 14 (originally *Paladini* 9): *Serate* 198–209
Copione 18 (originally *Paladini* 13): *Serate* 245–253
Copione 19 (originally *Paladini* 14): *Serate* 254–265
Copione 21: *Serate* 281–292

---

1 There are two notebooks titled *Libro* 1, Agrippino's original (with *serate* 1–15) and Johnny's copy (with *serate* 1–14). Since the latter was repurposed as *Copione* 3, I include it in this list of notebooks otherwise in Agrippino's handwriting. Both are privately owned.

2 Although the front cover also contains the number 3 twice in pen, the notebook could only have been *Paladini* 2. It would have been roughly the equivalent, however, to *Libro* 3.

Copione 22: *Serate* 293–304
Copione 23: *Serate* 319–330

Notebooks and plays missing from this set: 15–17 (*serate* 210–244); 20 (*serate* 266–280), and *serate* 305–318 between *Copioni* 22 and 23.

The "Libri" set
Libro 1: *Serate* 1–15*
Libro 1: *Serate* 1–14 (repurposed as *Copione* 3)*[3]
Libro 2: *Serate* 16–27 (repurposed as *Copione* 4)*
Libro 5: *Serate* 49–63*
Libro 6: *Serate* 64–79*
Libro 7: *Serate* 80–91*

The rest of the set is missing.

The "Paladini" set
Paladini 1: *Serate* 1–24*[4]
Paladini 2 (repurposed as *Copione* 5): *Serate* 25–45*
Paladini 3 (repurposed as *Copione* 6): *Serate* 46–68
Paladini 4 (repurposed as *Copione* 7): *Serate* 69–93*
Paladini 6: *Serate* 120–142*
Paladini 7: *Serate* 143–172*
Paladini 8: *Serate* 173–195*
Paladini 9 (repurposed as *Copione* 14): *Serate* 198–209
Paladini 13 (repurposed as *Copione* 18): *Serate* 245–253
Paladini 14 (repurposed as *Copione* 19): *Serate* 254–265

The rest of the set is missing.

Additional Notebooks Containing Select Episodes from the Paladins of France Cycle

La morte dei Paladini nella Roncisvalle: *Serate* 326–328
Untitled notebook (missing a cover) with ten plays based on the *Storia dei paladini*'s adaptation of the *Orlando Furioso*: *Serate* 1–10*

---

3 See footnote 1.
4 The notebook cover is missing, along with the summary and Cast of Characters for the first play.

Appendix 5

AGRIPPINO MANTEO'S SUMMARIES OF PLAYS IN THE PALADINS OF FRANCE CYCLE

This appendix contains 269 translated synopses from the *Copioni* set (including notebooks repurposed from the *Libri* and *Paladini* sets) and two synopses of plays that are extant in the *Libri* set but not in the *Copioni* set.[1] Where applicable, I have noted in parentheses additional extant versions in Agrippino's handwriting in the other two sets in order to facilitate a first-hand comparison across plays. A study of the variants would no doubt yield new insights into Agrippino's process of rewriting and revision from one set of scripts to the next.

In addition to the synopses, I have included the sparse comments in Agrippino's handwriting discussed in Chapter 2. I have also standardized the punctuation for greater ease of comprehension. Not included are revisions to the script (unless noted), temporal indications, or comments in handwriting other than Agrippino's.[2] My explanations are in brackets.

Libro 1 (equivalent of *Copione* 3): *Serate* 1–15 (139 pages)[3]

Sera 1°

Bernardo di Chiaramonte, Girardo di Frata, Morando di Riviera, and Raimondo advise Pipino to take a wife in order to produce an heir. The four barons arrive in Buda and marry Pipino to Berta *del gran piè* [of the big foot],

---

1 Four synopses lack accompanying plays, as noted below.
2 In addition, summaries of plays at the end of notebooks are skipped over when they are also available at the beginning of the following notebook.
3 Although it was actually Johnny's copy of *Libro* I that was repurposed as *Copione* 3, I draw the following summaries from Agrippino's original *Libro* 1.

they return to Paris. The conspiracy of Lisetta, with the help of Grifone, Spinaldo, and Tolomeo. Berta, abducted by four assassins, is tied up in the forest and then freed by Lamberto.

Sera 2°

Berta, who has set up a pavilion, sends Lamberto to sell it. Grifone di Magonza buys it and initiates a search for Berta. King Filippo goes to Paris to find Berta. The queen recognizes Lisetta. Pipino goes hunting with Filippo and the barons, gets separated from his companions, and happens to arrive at Lamberto's home. Berta and Pipino recognize each other. The barons go in search of Pipino.

Serata 3°

Filippo and his barons arrive at Lamberto's dwelling. Filippo recognizes Berta. Pipino returns to Paris and attacks the Magonzesi. A great battle in the squares of Paris. The Magonzesi flee. Lisetta is burned alive. The barons go to retrieve Berta. Grifone prepares an ambush and a great battle follows. The agency of Berta, death of Spinaldo and Tolomeo, escape of Grifone, and birth of Gano.

Sera 4°

The birth of Berta and the death of Berta *del gran piè*. Lanfroi and Olderigi, advised by Grifone, kill King Pipino. The escape of Carlo Magno. A great battle inside Paris between the French and the Magonzesi. The coronation of Olderigi. Carlo recovers in the abbey of Saint Omer. Morando di Riviera sets out in search of Carlo.

Sera 5

Carlo is recognized by the abbot. Morando arrives at the convent of Saint Omer where he finds Carlo, and together they leave for Spain. Galerana falls in love with Mainetto [i.e., Carlo in disguise] and reveals her love to him. Galafro announces a joust to marry off Galerana. Olderigi is upset because he cannot find Carlo. Ulieno, hearing about the joust, leaves for Spain.

Sera 6

Carlo receives arms from Galerana, he enters the tournament and outshines the others. The first stirrings of love between Carlo and Galerana.

The departure of the jousting knights. Galerana realizes that Mainetto is Carlo and is then baptized. Bramante encounters the jousters, rallies his army, and together with Polinoro besieges Zaragoza to attain Galerana, who refuses him. Arrogance of the emperor Bramante.

Sera 7°

Polinoro goes up to the city walls, challenges the Spaniards, and captures Ulieno, the Spaniards, and Galafro. Morando challenges Polinoro and is taken prisoner. Polinoro praises the old man's valor. Carlo called Mainetto receives arms from the queen of Spain. The first great battle between Mainetto and Polinoro. The pagan's offers. The second battle between Polinoro and Mainetto. The death of Polinoro. Carlo takes Durlindana.

Sera 8

Mainetto challenges Bramante; a great battle between the two adversaries; the night divides them. Bramante sends Morando to Mainetto to draw him to himself. Agolante sends Gualfrediano to help Bramante. Second battle between Bramante and Mainetto; Bramante stuns Mainetto and carries him away; the resumption of the battle; Bramante's death; destruction of the camp; liberation of the prisoners. Gualfrediano arrives in Zaragoza with Uggiero.

Sera 9

Ugiero becomes fond of Mainetto. Challenge between Mainetto and Gualfrediano and their reconciliation. Marsilio despises Mainetto. Ugicro discovers that Mainetto is Carlo and is then baptized. Ugiero wants to kill Marsilio, Morando stops him. Ugiero's feigned friendship with the Spaniards. Marsilio and his brothers are pleased about Ugiero and they plot how to kill Mainetto. Olderigi is still searching for Carlo.

Sera 10

Ugiero discovers the conspiracy of the queen and her children and warns Galerana about it. Carlo, Galerana, and companions escape. The Spaniards stab the bed, believing they are killing Carlo. They chase the fugitives and catch up with them at Malborgheto. Great battle of Ugiero against the Spaniards. Morando asks for help at the Calisfor castle. Carlo engages in a great battle. Defeat and escape of the Spaniards. Carlo and his companions head to Rome.

Sera 11

Carlo and his companions arrive in Rome where they find themselves in dire straits. Arrival of Cardinal Leone who alleviates their misery. In Lombardy, Carlo and his companions meet Bernardo di Chiaramonte, they then go to Bavaria and join Duke Namo, and they leave for Paris with troops. Bernardo di Chiaramonte encounters the Irish army and destroys it. Exploits of Milone d'Anglante.

Sera 12

Carlo's army arrives near the city of Lyon; the city's surrender. Carlo besieges Paris with the armies of Namo and Bernardo di Chiaramonte. Conspiracy of the citizens in favor of Carlo, great battle in the countryside outside Paris, exploits of Milone d'Anglante. Carlo kills Guerino and Lanfroi and takes Olderigi prisoner. Carlo enters Paris and kills Olderigi. Berta is introduced to him. Carlo appoints his counselors. Milone d'Anglante is made a top-ranking general. Girardo imprisons Emilio because of a dispute between them.

Sera 13

Girardo scorns the ambassadors and Carlo. The Spaniards go to Paris. Gano, Ginamo, and Manfrediano arrive in Paris and swear allegiance to Carlo. Coronation of Carlo and his marriage to Galerana. Amone and Ginamo fall in love with Beatrice. Gano befriends the Spaniards. Constantine asks for the hand of Berta. Carlo announces a tournament. Berta and Milone fall in love.

Sera 14

Tournament in Paris. Ugiero is knocked down by Bulogante. Amone knocks down the proud Spaniard. Falserone knocks down Amone; his arrogance and contempt for France. Carlo sends for Milone whom Rampaldo finds asleep. Berta by means of Ruggiero sends a garland to Milone. The latter enters the joust and topples the pride of the Spaniards. Ugiero marries Armelina. Amone and Ginamo ask for the hand of Beatrice.

Sera 15

Grand festive ball in Paris. Fresina invites Milone to dance and then with a stratagem locks him in Berta's private chamber. Milone takes Cupid's fruit, then, dressed as a woman, leaves Berta's room. Agolante prepares to wage war on Salatiello of Libya. The pope sends a cardinal to Paris because of Agolante's military preparations. The queen of Spain sends Durlindana to Agolante. Ginamo becomes friends with the cardinal.

Sera 16[4]

To pacify Amone and Ginamo, Carlo proposes a duel. Conspiracy of the Magonzesi to kill Amone. Ottone becomes aware of the conspiracy and reveals it to Carlo. Milone receives a slap from Ginamo. Fierce battle that Milone sustains against the Magonzesi. Carlo banishes Milone. The latter goes to abduct Berta, but when he is attacked, he kills Bernardo and Manfredonio. Escape of Berta and Milone.

Copione 4 (originally Libro 2): Serate 16–27 (117 pages)[5]

Sera 17

Milone kills a peasant and goes to Rome. Falcone di Magonza discovers the inn where Milone is staying and informs Ginamo. The latter informs Carlo. Gano leaves for Rome. He meets with Falcone and they treacherously arrest Milone and Berta, planning to take them to Paris. The pope, informed, reaches Gano and orders that Milone and Berta be brought back.

Sera 18

Astuteness of the pope to save Milone's life. Gano warns Carlo, the latter sends Ginamo to force the pope to kill Milone. Carlo's vision. Namo remonstrates with Carlo. Milone and Berta are absolved. Wedding of Berta and Milone, and their departure from Rome. A band of thieves kills Galisena's husband. Arrival of Milone and Berta. Milone takes the arms of the dead man and kills the thieves.

Sera 19

Milone engages in a great battle against three strong knights. A hermit predicts to Milone the birth of Orlando. In a ship Berta is abducted by the captain,

---

4 This summary, on the last page in the notebook, is written in block letters in different handwriting, presumably by one of Agrippino's children. I include it here because the page with the summary of *sera* 16 is missing from *Copione* 4 (*Libro* 2), which, however, contains the play itself.

5 As noted in footnote 4, the summary to *sera* 16 is missing in this notebook.

Raimondo. Milone engages in a great battle on the ship. Queen Lucietta announces a tournament. Duel between Amone and Ginamo. Berta kills Raimondo. The enchantress Giliana saves Milone.

Sera 20

Buovo di Agramonte arrives in Orsitania. He wins the tournament and marries Lucietta but first she is baptized. Gano has Beatrice's ring stolen. Galisena finds Berta, and together with a shepherd they go to a cave. Leone di Chiaramonte elected pope after the death of Adriano. Orlando's birth with a *scena in fondo* (deep stage). St Michael and the Fates give gifts to Orlando.

Sera 21

Because of a dream Milone abandons a pregnant Giliana. Buovo and Lucietta leave Rome. Birth of Malagigi and Viviano. Buovo attacked by the king of Portugal, he loses his children. Malagigi is taken by Merlin. Birth of Astolfo. Milone hears about the birth of Orlando from the hermit, then arrives in Risa [Reggio Calabria] and is welcomed by Rampaldo.

Sera 22

Milone instructs Ruggiero and his brothers, then under the name of Sventura [Misfortune] goes to Africa to fight in defense of Agolante. Birth of Rinaldo. Balante and Milone go to defeat Salatiello. Fierce battle in the Libyan countryside. Milone kills Argorante and Balciniano. Defeat of the army, surrender of Salatiello. Milone is made a general by Agolante.

Sera 23

Agolante encounters the Persian army and engages in a great battle. Exploits of Milone, who kills the terrible Manadoro. Agolante joins his army to Almonte's army and wages a great battle against the Tartars. The king of Tartaria challenges Agolante to a battle of five against five, and his challenge is accepted. Milone is the victor. The first exploits of Orlandino.

Sera 24

A merchant is charitable to Orlando by giving him clothing and food. Agolante returns to Biserta. Orlando is clothed in four colors by the merchants.

Tournament of the boys. Orlando defeats Oliviero who, feeling offended, slaps Orlando, who in return breaks his head. Rainieri has Orlando arrested and then helps him. Charles is crowned emperor by Pope Leo.

Sera 25

Carlo arrives in Sutri and is honored by Rainieri. Orlando beats up a beggar and takes away his food. The beggar, seeking revenge, deceives Orlando. The latter clobbers the porter and steals the bowl from Carlo's table. Rainieri confides in Namo that it is Orlando. Carlo interrogates Oliviero and tries to discover the identity of the little thief.

Sera 26

Orlando returns to Sutri and steals the bowl from Carlo's table. He knocks to the ground the knight who tries to arrest him and then flees. Carlo's dream. Orlando steals the bowl from Carlo for the third time. Namo and Ugiero follow him. Berta, brought before Carlo, is kicked by him. Orlando pursues Carlo while clubbing his assailants. Berta and Milone are forgiven.

Sera 27

Ruggiero leaves for Africa, arrives at the court of Guarnicre, and falls in love with Claudiana. Milone is recognized in Africa and is treacherously arrested. The love between Ruggiero and Claudiana. The latter is baptized. Ruggiero hears about the imprisonment of Milone and rushes to Biserta, and, like a new Achilles, enters the city. He engages in a great battle, stuns Agolante and others, and frees Milone.

Sera 28[6]

Ruggiero leaves Milone and returns to Africa where he abducts Claudiana. He is attacked by pirates on the high seas. He engages in a great battle and loses Claudiana, who is saved by another ship. Ruggiero arrives in Sicily where he kills two giants. Milone arrives in Paris. Guarniere leaves for Rome with his army. Birth of Cladinoro.

---

6 This notebook contains the summary of *sera* 28, but not the play itself.

Copione 5 (originally *Paladini* 2): *Serate* 25–45 (pages numbered until page 73)[7]

25

Agolante unites his army with that of Almonte and undertakes a great battle against the Tartars. The king of Tartaria challenges Agolante to a battle of five against five, and his challenge is accepted. Milone is the victor. The first exploits of Orlandino in Sutri. Agolante leaves to join Troiano.

26

Agolante returns to Biserta with Troiano. Orlando is clothed in four colors by the merchants. He defeats Oliviero who, feeling offended, slaps him. Orlando in return breaks his head. Orlando is arrested and then helped by Rainiere. Charles is crowned emperor by Pope Leo.

27

Carlo arrives in Sutri and is honored by Rainieri. Orlando beats up a beggar and takes away his food. The beggar deceives Orlando. The latter clobbers the porter and steals the bowl from Carlo's table. Rainiere confides in Namo that it is Orlando.

28

Orlando returns to Sutri and steals the bowl from Carlo's table. He knocks to the ground the knight who wants to arrest him and flees. Carlo's dream. Orlando steals Carlo's bowl for the third time. Namo and Ugiero follow him. Berta, brought before Carlo, is kicked by him. Orlando pursues Carlo while clubbing his assailants. Berta and Milone are forgiven.

29

Ruggiero leaves for Africa, arrives at the court of King Guarniere, and falls in love with Claudiana. Milone is recognized in Africa and is treacherously arrested. Ruggiero hears about it and rushes to Biserta, and, like a new Achilles, enters the city, stuns Subrino and Agolante, frees Milone, and flees.

---

7 The overlap in the numbering of three plays (25–27) between *Copioni* 4 and 5 is due to the fact that the former was originally in the *Libri* set and the latter was originally in the *Paladini* set (cfr. *serate* 23–28 of *Copione* 4 [*Libro* 2] and *serate* 25–30 of *Copione* 5 [*Paladini* 2]).

30

Ruggiero leaves Milone and returns to Africa where he abducts Claudiana; he is attacked by pirates on the high seas, undertakes a great battle, and loses Claudiana who is taken by another ship. Ruggiero arrives in Sicily where he kills two giants. Milone arrives in Paris. Birth of Cladinoro. Guarniere with his army leaves to besiege Rome.

31

Guarniere besieges Rome. Milone is sent to help the Pope, great battle outside Rome. Milone kills Guarniere, defeat of the pagan army. Ginamo by means of the ring [falsely] demonstrates to Amone that he is the true father of Rinaldo. Namo goes to Darbena. Rinaldo's impulse to defend his mother.

32

Beatrice arrives in Paris where she slaps Ginamo. A great council in Biserta. Subrino is sent on an exploratory mission. Solemn oath of Ginamo and Beatrice. Tournament in Risa won by Ruggiero, who recognizes Subrino. Departure of Almonte and Galiacella to besiege Risa.

33

Almonte and Galiacella besiege Risa, a hermit predicts to Almonte his demise. Almonte challenges Ruggiero, who first defeats four kings and then sends Almonte to the ground twice. Third combat between Ruggiero and Almonte, the latter is defeated. Galiacella is bested by Ruggiero and taken into the city where she is baptized.

34

Horrendous betrayal by Beltramo, but first he is slapped by Galiacella because he asks for her love. Salatiello refuses to take part in the betrayal against Ruggiero. The city of Risa is in flames. The death of Ruggiero, Rampaldo, and Milonetto; the imprisonment of Galiacella; the destruction of Risa.

35

The death of Beltramo, birth of Ruggiero and Marfisa, and death of Galiacella. Carlo hears about Ruggiero's death and mourns him greatly. Malagigi pursues the magical arts and receives Merlin's wand. Rinaldo kills a lion.

36

Rinaldo kills the giant Scarivante and frees Beatrice, then arrives at the enchantment of Malagigi and Sibiliana. Agolante arrives in Risa. Rinaldo receives weapons from Malagigi and vows to kill the traitor Ginamo.

37

Almonte treacherously captures the castle of Serra. Agolante sends Balante as ambassador to Carlo, great miracle in Paris, baptism of Balante. Great battle in Aspromonte, defeat of the Christians.

38

Carlo sends Milone to Rome. Rinaldo leaves Brava and goes in search of adventure. An encounter between the army of Milone and that of Almonte, they engage in battle. Defeat of Almonte at the hand of Milone. Balante returns to Risa, great duel between Balante and Corbano, death of the latter.

39

Carlo sends Namo as an ambassador to Risa, Namo kills a griffin and fights with the son of Balante. Battle in Aspromonte. Girardo captures the castle of Serra. Great battle between Almonte and Milone. Almonte breaks his weapons and sword, death of Milone, battle between Almonte and Donchiaro, flight of Almonte. Orlando and Astolfo escape from the seminary.

40

Almonte arrives at the fountain and trembles, believing Ruggiero has come back to life. Carlo finds Almonte and undertakes a great battle against him. Orlando, warned by an Angel, finds his uncle about to die and rescues him by killing Almonte. Ugiero at the Serra Castle is defeated by Don Chiaro.

41

Agolante sends an ambassador to Carlo. Dispute between Orlando and Donchiaro. Great battle between the Christians and the Africans, battle between Orlando and Agolante. Astolfo falls under the spell of Voltiera. Death of Agolante and Ulieno, defeat of the pagan camp.

42

Vision of Orlando, who then kills a giant and frees Astolfo. Don Buoso marries Alerina. Carlo cedes Risa to Agolante's wife. Troiano besieges Vienna. Ruggiero Vassallo, sent on an exploratory mission, sustains a great battle against Troiano's troops.

43

Ruggiero Vassallo is defeated by Troiano. Girardo and his army attack the camp and are forced to flee by Troiano. Carlo comes to Girardo's aid. Rinaldo learns from Malagigi how to attain Baiardo, then he finds Clarice and falls in love and on her behalf demonstrates his valor. Rinaldo becomes friends with Isoliero.

44

Rinaldo tames Baiardo, wins the shield of love, and gets into a terrible fight with a knight who, defeated, tells Rinaldo an unpleasant story. Rinaldo attains Tristano's lance, then he and Isoliero fight against the knights of Galerana. Rinaldo abducts Clarice.

45

Rinaldo pursues the chariot that whisks away Clarice and encounters a shepherd who is consumed with love, then together they go to the temple for advice. Rinaldo and Florindo arrive in Vienna. Florindo is knighted by Carlo. Rinaldo kills Atlante and acquires Frusberta, he kills a Magonzese and undertakes a great battle against Orlando.

Copione 6 (originally *Paladini* 3): *Serate* 46–68 (pages unnumbered)

46[8]

Carlo sets out to attack the camp of Troiano, who demonstrates his valor. The latter stuns Orlando and Donchiaro. Rinaldo and Florindo enter the fray, Rinaldo shows his valor and undertakes a great battle against Troiano. Orlando attacks Troiano again, death of the pagan. Rinaldo attacks the pavilions, defeat of the pagan camp. Carlo enters Vienna victorious.

---

[8] The summary and Cast of Characters can be found on a loose page inserted at the end of the notebook, but the play itself is at the beginning.

47

Rinaldo reveals himself to Carlo and challenges Ginamo and avenges the offense by killing the traitor. Ginamo, before dying, confesses his treachery. Amone embraces his wife and children. Orlando falls in love with Alda. War between Girardo and Carlo, Donchiaro kills Ruggiero, Uggiero kills Balante.

48

Orlando challenges Donchiaro. Rinaldo challenges Girardo. The latter's imprisonment. Peace between Girardo and Carlo. Wedding of Gano and Berta with a sumptuous scene at the temple. Crinzia out of jealousy follows her husband. Because of the darkness, the husband, believing Crinzia to be a wild boar, shoots an arrow and kills her. A moving scene and very popular with the public.

49

Rinaldo and Florindo arrive in a forest where Rinaldo fights against a knight who, after his defeat, narrates the demise of Crinzia. Rinaldo and Florindo go to the enchantment of Euridice, they kill Mambrino's men on the high seas, and they reach Francardo's pavilion. The battle that awaits them. Francardo's death. Rinaldo kills Chiarello and Costantino.

50

Brunamonte kills Beltrino, Caldiva escapes. The latter encounters Rinaldo and Florindo, and she leads them to Brunamonte. Rinaldo kills the terrible giant, then together with Florindo defeats Floriana's knights in a field. The love between Rinaldo and Floriana.

51 (cfr. sera 49 of Libro 5)

Rinaldo abandons Floriana. She sends her knights to arrest him, but they are defeated. Floriana tries to kill herself; the sorceress Medea saves her and takes her to the Island of Pleasure. Rinaldo and Florindo are separated during a storm. Florindo is saved by Scipione, whom he subsequently recognizes as his father.

52 (cfr. sera 50 of Libro 5)

Don Buoso arrives in Paris with his dog. Gano treacherously has Don Buoso killed; the dog reveals the crime. The first exploits of Bradamante; she kills a knight and acquires his weapons. She meets Berlinghieri and challenges him. They recognize each other. At Risa a knight tries to possess Alerina and, when rebuffed, offers his son. Alerina strangles him and flees.

53 (cfr. sera 51 of Libro 5)

Carlo besieges Frata, a great battle follows. The prowess of Bradamante. The challenge between Orlando and Don Chiaro and the retreat of the two armies. The first battle between Orlando and Don Chiaro, demonstrating their equal valor. The second battle between Orlando and Don Chiaro. The latter is deprived of his weapons in the course of the combat.

54 (cfr. sera 52 of Libro 5)

The final battle between D. Chiaro and Orlando. The death of D. Chiaro. The destruction of the army of Girardo, who flees to Africa and gives himself over to Mohammad. The birth of Guidone and Carinda. Oliviero rebels against Carlo. The latter sends Orlando to lay siege to Vienna.

55 (cfr. sera 53 of Libro 5)

Duel between Oliviero and Orlando. Alda saves Oliviero, who returns to Carlo. Orlando beseeches Rinaldo to ask Alda's hand in marriage on his behalf. Great duel between Orlando and Fieramonte, death of the latter. Rinaldo and Bradamante leave for Paris; on the way they kill two giants.

56 (cfr. sera 54 of Libro 5)

Orlando and Alda's wedding. A tournament in Paris. Carlo elects his paladins. Clarice despises Rinaldo out of jealousy. Rinaldo kills Anselmo of Magonza and undertakes a great battle against the Magonzesi. Orlando and Bradamante defend Rinaldo. The latter slashes Gano's face and is banished.

57 (cfr. sera 55 of Libro 5)

Rinaldo enters the valley of pain and is saved by Malagigi. Mambrino kidnaps Clarice. Florindo is attacked by Mambrino's men. The arrival of Rinaldo, who undertakes a great battle. Rinaldo and Florindo recognize each other. Rinaldo, aided by Malagigi, reaches the camp, undertakes a great battle against Mambrino, and rescues Clarice.

58 (cfr. sera 56 of Libro 5)

Malagigi obtains Carlo's pardon of Rinaldo. Carlo returns to Paris. Orlando and Astolfo ask Carlo for Clarice's hand on behalf of Rinaldo. Carlo gives Rinaldo the territory of Montalbano. Gano besieges Paris but subsequently regrets it. Carlo forgives Gano thanks to Orlando.

59 (cfr. sera 57 of Libro 5)

Gano's treachery in an attempt to kill Rinaldo and Florindo. A battle of the Magonzesi against each other because of the darkness of night. Rinaldo attacks Gano's army. A battle between Bradamante and the paladins. The banishment of Rinaldo and Gano.

60 (cfr. sera 58 of Libro 5)

Buovo asks Carlo for help and is refused. Astolfo offers to help his uncle and leaves. Balante besieges Orsitania. Viviano challenges the knights of Orsitania and takes them captive. A battle between Buovo and Viviano; Buovo is in danger and is rescued by Malagigi. Malagigi and Viviano recognize each other.

61 (cfr. sera 59 of Libro 5)

Malagigi challenges Abalante's knights. Buovo attacks the army. The arrival of Astolfo's forces which support Buovo's warriors. After a great battle Balante cedes defeat to Buovo. Astolfo destroys the pagan camp. Buovo and Lucietta recognize each other and their children. The baptism of Abalante.

62 (cfr. sera 60 of Libro 5)

A joust in Numizia. Rinaldo kills Febur, Mambrino's brother, and abducts Olinda. The latter is happy to know that Florindo is the son of a king. Galinferno reaches Rinaldo and attacks. Rinaldo is in danger and is saved by Florindo. Rinaldo kills Galinferno. Florindo marries Olinda. The baptism of King Sorillo. Rinaldo leaves Numizia, defeats Ternaù, and becomes a thief.

63 (cfr. sera 61 of Libro 5)

Rinaldo and Ternau steal money from Gano, killing Bernardo. In defense of Luniella, Rinaldo kills Crapasso, Francardo's father. Carlo forgives Gano and with a great army leaves for Sommidoro. Ricciardetto kills the giant Ternaù.

64 (cfr. sera 62 of Libro 5)

Carlo besieges Sommidoro. A great battle between Rinaldo and the Magonzesi. The paladins fight against Rinaldo. Orlando disguised as Florindo defends Rinaldo. Rinaldo and his brothers escape through an underground passage. Orlando storms the castle. Carlo has Sommidoro destroyed.

65 (cfr. sera 63 of Libro 5)

Rinaldo is attacked in a forest by thieves who, recognizing him, accept him as their leader. Carlo goes to Orsitania and receives forces from Buovo. He then goes to Gascony and attacks Mambrino's camp. A great battle between Orlando and Mambrino. Carlo enters the city.

66 (cfr. sera 64 of Libro 6)

Malagigi advises Rinaldo to attain the helmet of Mambrino. The latter challenges the paladins and takes them prisoner. The captivity of Carlo. Bradamante attacks Alceo. Rinaldo confronts Mambrino and rescues Carlo. The death of Mambrino and Alceo.

67 (cfr. sera 65 of Libro 6)

Carlo attacks Mambrino's camp. Rinaldo rushes to the scene with Bradamante. The destruction of the army. Malagigi kidnaps Mambrino's treasure. The wedding of Rinaldo and Clarice. Carlo returns to Paris. The construction of the castle of Montalbano via Malagigi's magic.

68 (cfr. sera 66 of Libro 6)

Carlo learns from Gano how Rinaldo built the castle. Carlo sends Orlando and then goes himself to visit Montalbano. The council of Dama Rovenza, who then besieges Paris with her army. Rovenza takes Astolfo, Ugiero, and Oliviero prisoner. A battle between Orlando and Rovenza.

Copione 7 (originally *Paladini* 4): *Serate* 69–93 (pages unnumbered)

69 (cfr. sera 67 of Libro 6)

The birth of Giovone, Rinaldo's son. Malagigi and Rinaldo steal Rovenza's treasure and set her ships on fire. Rinaldo kills Caradoro. Rinaldo leaves Montalbano with the army and his brothers to fight against Baldassore. Malagigi's deception to the detriment of the pagans.

70 (cfr. sera 68 of Libro 6)

Rinaldo, with the help of Malagigi, kills Baldassore, the father of Rovenza. He undertakes a great battle against the pagans and destroys the army. Rinaldo takes over Monfalcone. Orlando, the paladins, and the entire army go out to battle against Rovenza. She chases them away through her own valor. Rinaldo and Bradamante enter the battle.

71 (cfr. sera 69 of Libro 6)

A great battle between Rovenza and the Christians. The prowess of Bradamante, who causes Rovenza to flee. Rinaldo goes into battle against Rovenza, he is in grave danger and is saved by Orlando. Tuttofuoco asks Malagigi for the secret of his art. An infernal struggle between Malagigi and Tuttofuoco. Malagigi is in danger. The death of Tuttofuoco.

72 (cfr. sera 69 of Libro 6)

Carlo, advised by Gano, promises a prize to the knight who succeeds in killing Rovenza. Malagigi arrives in Monfalcone. Carlo attacks Rovenza's army. Rinaldo kills Feragraffo. The withdrawal of Carlo due to the presumed death of Rinaldo. The death of Dama Rovenza. The destruction of the army.

73 (cfr. sera 70 of Libro 6)

Gano attacks Rinaldo with ten thousand Magonzesi and Tebaldo in order to steal from him. The death of Tebaldo. Gano goes to Brava and complains to Orlando. Carlo besieges Montalbano. Rinaldo and Bradamante attack Gano's pavilion. Rinaldo wounds Carlo, Orlando rushes to the scene. A great battle between Orlando and Rinaldo.

74 (cfr. sera 71 of Libro 6)

The first and second battle between Orlando and Rinaldo. Peace between them because of Gattamogliere's arrival. Carlo honors the pagan. A great battle between Rinaldo and Gattamogliere. Rinaldo receives four wounds. Malagigi heals Rinaldo.

75 (cfr. sera 71–72 of Libro 6)

The second battle between Rinaldo and Gattamogliere, Rinaldo is in danger and is healed by Malagigi. The third battle between Rinaldo and

Gattamogliere. Malagigi saves Rinaldo from certain death, then he learns that a strong enchantment protects the giant. He goes to the field and receives Durlindana from Orlando.

76 (cfr. sere 72–73 of Libro 6)

Rinaldo receives Durlindana and challenges Gattamogliere. A great battle between the two rivals. The death of the giant. Gano flees and causes the army to flee. Salinarte besieges Rome. Moriante besieges Orsitania. Peace between Carlo and Rinaldo. Buovo fights his way across the field and enters Orsitania.

77 (cfr. sera 73 of Libro 6)

Agolaccio with his sword becomes the leader of Gattamogliere's army. The death of Buovo and Lucietta. The conquest of Orsitania. Salimarte leaves Rome, goes to Orsitania, and challenges Agolaccio. A great battle between the two rivals, Agolaccio's victory. Great lamentation for the death of Buovo and Lucietta. Orlando and Rinaldo leave for Orsitania.

78 (cfr. sere 73–74 of Libro 6)

A great battle between Orlando and Agolaccio and between Rinaldo and Salimarte. The death of the pagan. The baptism of Agolaccio. The conquest of Orsitania. The Barbassore of Russia announces a tournament to marry off Rosetta. The first exploits of Cladinoro, who kills a terrible snake in Soldanella.

79 (cfr. sere 74–75 of Libro 6)

Cladinoro arrives in Russia and wins the first day of the joust by defeating Lo Scapigliato [the Disheveled One]. The secret love affair between Cladinoro and Rosetta. Cladinoro, awakened by a page, defeats Lo Scapigliato a second time and is attacked, then flees. Lo Scapigliato marries Rosetta and departs to lay siege to Paris.

80 (cfr. sera 75 of Libro 6)

Lo Scapigliato destroys the monk's castle. The death of Baccaldo, then he besieges Paris and sends someone to threaten Carlo. Lo Scapigliato reaches the city walls, challenges the paladins, and takes them prisoner. Rosetta of Russia, being pregnant, tries to hide from her father's eyes. Cladinoro seeks adventure.

81 (cfr. sera *76 of* Libro *6)*

Gano obtains Carlo's forgiveness and goes to Paris. He has a conversation with the pagan who advises him to attack Paris. Rinaldo, alerted by Orlando, leaves Montalbano together with his brothers and Bradamante. He arrives near Paris and encounters Catello. The death of the giant. Rosetta is discovered to be pregnant and is imprisoned. Gandellino is born.

[Given that the summaries of *serate* 82 and 83 are missing from *Copione* 7, I am including below the summaries of *serate* 80 and 81 from the *Libri* set to fill in the narrative gap. Because of the different arrangement of the narrative material in these two sets, these two summaries should be considered approximations rather than exact equivalents of the missing material.]

Libro 6, *sera* 80[9]

Scapigliato attacks Paris.[10] Rinaldo and Bradamante attack the pavilions and free the paladins, then go beneath the city walls. Bradamante kills Astasaro. Rinaldo fights Scapigliato and is in danger, to the delight of Gano. Rinaldo kills Scapigliato, the defeat of the pagans. Mambriano leaves for Paris to satisfy his mother, a storm causes him to lose his ships, he saves himself inside a barrel and is nursed back to health by Carandina.

Libro 7, *sera* 81

Carandina brings Rinaldo to Monte Faggio A great battle between Rinaldo and Mambriano, the pagan is in danger and is defended by others. Mambriano resumes the battle but then flees. Rinaldo enjoys Carandina. Mambriano returns to Bitinia. Polindo flees and is devoured by a beast. Mambriano gathers his men and leaves for Montalbano. Orlando and Astolfo, following a dream, set off in search of Rinaldo.

---

9 *Libro* 6 ends with *sera* 80's summary and Cast of Characters, but the actual play is found at the opening of *Libro* 7 (minus Act 1, scenes 1–6, due to missing pages).
10 Scapigliato's attack on Paris is also staged in *sera* 80 of *Copione* 7.

Copione 7 (originally *Paladini* 4): *Serate* 69–93 (continued)

84 (cfr. sera *82 of* Libro *7[11])*

A great battle between Orlando and two pagans. Astolfo chases Androsilla. Orlando kills a snake. Astolfo is taken prisoner and then freed by Orlando. The death of Andronio. Orlando goes to Fulvia's castle. Bulogante attacks the castle in order to capture Orlando. The latter kills the giant Alfrano. Cladinoro rescues Carmenio and Androsilla. Bulogante has a wall built to shut in Orlando.

85 (cfr. sera *83 of* Libro *7)*

Mambriano besieges Montalbano. Malagigi hears how Carandina tied up the spirits and he leaves for the Island of the Faggio [beech tree]. Mambriano sends an ambassador, Bradamante's reply. The first battle outside the castle of Montalbano. The arrival of Carlo. Bradamante kills Tearco. Bradamante sends Sinadoro and Policardo in exchange for her brothers.

86 (cfr. sera *84 of* Libro *7)*

The imprisonment of Ugiero and Dudone. Malagigi in disguise reaches the island of Monte Faggio. The necromancer falsely recounts his origin and then reveals himself to Rinaldo. He leads the knight off the island and sets fire to Carandina's desk. A great battle near Montalbano. Mambriano captures the paladins.

87 (cfr. sera *85 of* Libro *7)*

The battle near Montalbano continues. Rinaldo's arrival bolsters the spirits of the Christians, and he frees Carlo and Oliviero. Mambriano flees. Sinadoro rescues Amone. Malagigi fabricates ships to chase Mambriano. Orlando is comforted by an angel at Fulvia's castle. Feburro kills Teude and rescues Orlando. The wedding of Fulvia and Feburro in Piraga.

---

11 Whereas the refashioning of narrative materials in the previous plays had brought *Libro* 6 and *Copione* 7 (*Paladini* 4) from two to five plays apart, the deliberate jump in the numbering between *serate* 76 and 80 in *Libro* 6 makes the sets only two plays apart for the remainder of *Libro* 7 and *Copione* 7.

88 (cfr. sera 86 of Libro 7)

Orlando leaves Piraga in order to punish Meonte. He kills Fulicano and rescues a woman and a youth. He frees Sinadoro and sets fire to the temple of Mars. Sinadoro narrates the misfortune of Namo and Ottone. The death of Meonte and the destruction of his men.

89 (cfr. sera 87 of Libro 7)

Marfisa kills Miriante of Persia. She undertakes a great battle and is proclaimed the empress. Nisballe finds his father with an army. The siege of Utica and a great battle. The capture of Filomede. The people of Utica elect Namo and Ottone as their captains. Rinaldo arrives in Calidonia and attacks Mambriano's camp. A great battle. The capture of Carminiano.

90 (cfr. sera 88 of Libro 7)

Rinaldo frees King Carminiano. Mambriano sentences Gano to death as a traitor. Gano promises to deny Christ and betray Rinaldo. A deadly battle that befalls the pagans. Rinaldo frees the Sultan in exchange for Ugiero. The deceptions of Malagigi.

91 (cfr. sera 89 of Libro 7)

Mambriano orders the paladins to be hanged. Malagigi has the tower removed and rescues the prisoners. Mambriano kills the wizards in his army. Pinamonte becomes infatuated with Bradamante, who plays a dirty trick on him. Truce between Rinaldo and Mambriano, who sends for reinforcements.

92 (cfr. sera 90 of Libro 7)

Pinamonte, in order to demonstrate his gallantry, dances with Bradamante. Carminiano's baptism. Ottone and Namo embrace their grandson and son. The conquest of Utica. Orlando, because he is pious, rescues the city from the flames. Nisballe is crowned king of Utica. The Garamanti besiege the city of Utica. A great battle. The valor of Astolfo, who takes Cleofasto prisoner.

93 (cfr. sera 91 of Libro 7)

Astolfo recklessly puts himself in danger of dying, but the enemy spares him. Filomede is condemned by Timocrate as a traitor. A truce between Alifarne and Orlando. The arrival of Argillo and Pinagora onto the field and the proposal of a challenge between Orlando and Pinagora. Gariante, in order to avenge Teude, treacherously kills Feburro.

Copione 8: *Serate* 92–107 (141 pages)[12]

Sera 92

A great battle of Orlando against Argillo and Pinagora. Orlando's victory. Peace between Alifarne and Ascarione. Orlando reveals himself to the Africans. The wedding of Nisballe and Saporilla. Orlando leaves to help Fulvia. Carandina abandons the island and falls prey to the giant Arpia, who makes her his paramour. End of the truce and resumption of the battle between Rinaldo and Mambriano. The death of Pinamonte.

Sera 93

The battle continues near Calidonia. Malagigi's deceptions. Defeat of the pagan camp. Mambriano's escape. Carminiano offers himself to Rinaldo. Mambriano hangs a goatherd. Rinaldo follows Mambriano and frees a goatherd, then finds Mambriano asleep. Fierce duel between Rinaldo and Mambriano. Carandina escapes from the castle. Rinaldo kills a lion and resumes his battle against Mambriano. Carandina saves Mambriano who surrenders to Rinaldo. Arpia's death.

Sera 94

A storm throws Orlando onto a beach, where he and his companions are invited by a woman to sleep in a castle. Astolfo, Argillo, and Pinagora are taken prisoner by seven giants. Orlando attempts to free his companions and confronts the giants, and he runs into danger. Cladinoro arrives in time to help Orlando. The death of sixteen giants. The liberation of Astolfo and his companions.

Sera 95

Carinda is taken prisoner by treachery. Cladinoro kills two giants and many thieves and then frees Carinda, with whom he falls in love after he realizes she is a woman. Medea takes Carinda away from Cladinoro. Fulvia is informed about Orlando's arrival. A fierce battle near Piraga.

---

12 Although the first two plays of *Copione* 8 have the same number as the final two plays of *Copione* 7 (*Paladini* 4), the action is consecutive.

The death of Gariante by Sinadoro's hand. Another battle outside Piraga. A wounded Argillo is sent back to town.

Sera 96

The battle outside Piraga rages on. Galafrone attacks the city walls. The wounded Argillo fights off the pagans. Timocrate arrives. The death of Galafrone. Sinadoro and Timocrate attack the pavilions. The defeat of the Spanish army. Marsilio's flight. A victorious Orlando enters Piraga. Grandonio leaves to avenge the Spaniards, encounters Marsilio, and is wounded by Bianciardino's ambassador. Peace between Marsilio and Orlando. Sinadoro falls in love with Fulvia.

97

The wedding of Sinadoro and Fulvia. Rinaldo arrives in Utica with the paladins, then leaves for Piraga together with the nobles. Rinaldo fights against Ginisbaldo in a forest. He defeats him and frees many knights. Ginisbaldo invites Rinaldo to Monte Fegro. Licomene and his companions kill Marlimante, Ginisbaldo's brother, luring him into a trap. Licomene dons Marlimante's armor to make himself the master of Malaspina.

Sera 98

Ginisbaldo treacherously takes prisoner Rinaldo with all the paladins. Licomene, disguised as Marlimante, frees Agolaccio and the other paladins. Rinaldo, freed by Pulima, reaches Ginisbaldo and hangs him. Balzaba employs deception. Rinaldo, believed to be Ginisbaldo, fights against all the paladins. Malagigi saves him and punishes the wizard.

Sera 99

Licomene and Pulima's wedding. Rinaldo and the paladins leave Granata. A tournament in Piraga. Grandonio tries to disrupt it, but Rinaldo punishes him. Orlando in disguise fights Rinaldo and knocks off his helmet. Rinaldo is recognized by everyone. Giovone is attracted to Floria. Astolfo's jealousy.

Sera 100

The wedding of Giovone and Floria. The departure of the paladins for France. Nine giants invade Italy. Carlo leaves Paris to honor Rinaldo. Orlando and his companions are honored in Valenza. Baldiana, having escaped from San Severino, asks for help in Valenza. Rinaldo and Orlando free Nocera. Death of the giant Maglio. Cladinoro kills Armanto and frees Rosetta. A great battle between Cladinoro and Gradasso, the latter intends to marry Rosetta.

Sera 101

Carlo besieges Benevento. Moriante imprisons the paladins. Orlando sends Rinaldo and Bradamante to Benevento. Rinaldo kills Dardo and together with Bradamante destroys the army. Cladinoro leaves Russia after the wedding of Gradasso and Rosetta. Duel between Rinaldo and Moriante. The first exploits of Ruggiero, who kills two giants and frees Claudiana. The second battle between Rinaldo and Moriante. Atlante creates an enchantment at Monte Carena in order to protect Ruggiero.

Sera 102

Bradamante challenges Moriante and they undertake a great battle. Orlando hears about Moriante's deception from a woman, tricks the giant, takes him away from the walls, and kills him. He enters the city and undertakes a great battle, putting himself in danger. Carlo wants to send reinforcements. Gano opposes the idea. Rinaldo slaps Gano and goes to help Orlando. The arrival of other giants who attack. Rinaldo kills Moriante. Orlando kills Altofasso. Rinaldo kills Saltamonte. The death of Floria. Giovone challenges Altobrando with Durlindana and kills him. The flight of Atripaldo and Antifor.

Sera 103

Orlando and Rinaldo reach Atripaldo and Antifor near Capua and kill them. Agolaccio marries Baldiana. Carinda frees an enchantress. Cladinoro sees the image of Carinda in a fountain. Guidone Selvaggio leaves Media, his first exploit. Carlo sends the four paladins to defend Fedelsmonda. Oliviero falls in love. Orlando kills Scarabaglia and Rinaldo Tilofarne. Defeat of the pagan camp.

Sera 104

Rinaldo uses cunning to benefit Oliviero. The baptism of Fedelsmonda and her marriage to Oliviero. Victory celebration in Paris for the arrival of the four paladins. Leonida refuses to dance with Rinaldo's family.

Rinaldo kidnaps Leonida. Orlando goes after them. A great battle between Orlando and Rinaldo. Malagigi's tricks. Rinaldo stuns Orlando and goes to look for Leonida.

["End of the first volume" is written following the play.]

Second Volume

Sera 105   1[13]

Carinda is honored by Lucina, to whom is presented Ardelio, who tells her of his misfortune. Carinda promises to help him and they leave together. Orlando brings back Leonida. Ricciardetto slaps Gano. Orlando does battle inside Paris and is banished together with Astolfo. Oliviero and Ricciardetto kill two giants, the third surrenders to Astolfo. Rinaldo encounters Altabianca. Orlando frees Anziano [Elderly Man]. Guidone is invited to the Perilous Forest.

Sera 106   2

Orlando liberates Gerbina by killing two knights. Guidone arrives at the Perilous Forest and successfully crosses the first bridge and attains a garland. Rinaldo finds Oliviero and Ricciardetto with Astolfo and together they go to Denmark. Orlando arrives in Denmark. Peace between Orlando and Rinaldo. Guidone is victorious at the second bridge and acquires the shield that he loses at the third bridge. Orlando and the paladins fight the serpent of Denmark, placing themselves in danger. Orlando kills the serpent by throwing a column at him.

Sera 107   3

Dalinda demonstrates in words and deeds her great admiration for the count. The wedding of Anziano and Gerbina. Carlo forgives the paladins thanks to Malagigi. Rinaldo drinks the water of Lethe and forgets Leonida. Malagigi reveals his identity to his relatives, then goes to Paris and gets money out of Carlo and Gano by killing a fake serpent.

---

13. As noted in Chapter 2, between *sera* 105 and *sera* 195 (the plays that mark the opening and conclusion of the *Storia dei paladini*'s second volume), Agrippino generally provides an additional number (from 1 to 91) following the number of the play. Since the plays outnumber the chapters, however, this numbering to the right of the play does not correspond to the chapter number of the prose adaptation.

Copione 9: Serate 108–128 (169 pages)

Sera 108   4

The arrival of the paladins in Paris and their departure for their respective states. The treachery of Gano, who advises Marsilio to scorn Carlo. Marsilio attains Orifiamma thanks to Gano. Rinaldo, warned by a fugitive, reaches the Spaniards. He undertakes a great battle and wins back Orifiamma. He then goes to Carlo, remonstrating with him and taking the flag to Montalbano.

109   5

Rinaldo goes to Asia and arrives in Trebisonda [Trebizond] where the wizard Araspase abducts Astilacuore. Rinaldo, with the help of Sabina, destroys the enchantment and frees Astilacuore. Araspase abducts Astilacuore a second time. Sabina shows Rinaldo how to free her. Girardo heads for Italy to wage war against Carlo. Gano sends spies to denounce Rinaldo.

Sera 110   6

Rinaldo uses an herb to make the wizard Araspase fall asleep and then frees Astilacuore, their amorous encounter. Rinaldo, discovered by Lucreziano, is arrested and condemned to the amphitheater of the lions. Malagigi, disguised as Jupiter, frees him. Girardo gets help from Desiderio and they leave for Vienna with the army.

Sera 111   7

Girardo and Desiderio besiege Vienna. A great battle follows. The capture of the city. The escape of Fedelsmonda, whose sons are abducted by two sorceress friends. Carlo besieges Vienna. Gano goes to Lombardy. Desiderio abandons Girardo. Fedelsmonda, unable to find her sons, enters a cave to do penance.

Sera 112

Carlo attacks Vienna. Orlando takes Girardo prisoner. Carlo forgives him because he swears loyalty. Carlo besieges Pavia. A great battle follows. Desiderio declares his obedience to Carlo once again. Ferraù departs from Spain to kill Orlando and Rinaldo. Giunetto, Rinaldo's son, is armed by Don Trico. He escapes from Montalbano. A great battle near Chiusi. The arrival of the army of Ildebrando. Carlo is in danger and is found by Giunetto.

Sera 113

Adalgiso and the Greeks besiege Carlo in Chiusi. Rinaldo encounters Ferraù. The latter defeats Rinaldo's brothers and wounds Bradamante. A battle between Rinaldo and Ferraù. The latter, defeated, surrenders to Rinaldo. Carlo attacks Adalgiso's camp. The arrival of Rinaldo in Carlo's camp. The death of Adalgiso, the victory of Carlo. A battle between Orlando and Rinaldo.

Sera 116[14] 12

A solemn hand-kissing ritual in Paris. Ferraù, instructed by Astolfo, clobbers Gano. Rinaldo's great battle against the paladins. Carlo banishes Rinaldo. Arimando attempts to have his son killed. Rinaldo adopts Morbello, who later calls himself Malaguerra, and takes him to Montalbano. Ferraù returns to Spain.

Sera 117 13

Rinaldo encounters Tremontes and hears about the siege of Villabella and departs with Malagigi. Rinaldo in Villabella kills Babusso and destroys the army. Carlo besieges Villabella. Rinaldo, disguised as Babusso, takes the paladins prisoner. Gano's offer to the fake Babusso to hang the paladins. Carlo's fright over the supposed death of the paladins.

Sera 118 14, vol. 2° (cfr. 120 of Paladini 6)

A great battle between Orlando and Rinaldo, the latter discloses his identity. Rinaldo presents himself to Carlo and is forgiven. The arrival in Paris of the giant Burato, who fights all the paladins. Departure of the four paladins for Alexandria where, having arrived, Ugiero is wounded by an arrow and saved by the white fairy.

Sera 119 15, vol. 2° (cfr. 121 of Paladini 6)

The four paladins enter Alexandria in disguise. Orlando attempts to kill Astiladoro. The four paladins are in danger and are saved by Burato. The latter flees from Alexandria, joins the four paladins, and is baptized. Arlete besieges Paris with Astiladoro and captures Carlo and the paladins.

---

14 The script passes directly to *sera* 116, skipping two numbers.

Sera 120   16, vol. 2° (cfr. 122 of Paladini 6)

The four paladins are caught in a fierce storm on the high seas and lose Burato. The latter is miraculously saved. He arrives in Paris and challenges Arlete, whom he kills after a great battle. Astiladoro flees and joins King Carbone. Burato besieges Astilaga. The four paladins arrive in Paris, then depart for Astilaga. Oranio is saved by Florinda who, because she has fallen in love with him, proposes to liberate the prisoners.

Sera 121   17 (cfr. 123 of Paladini 6)

Oranio and Florinda free Carlo and the paladins. The latter kill the guards and leave the castle. Astiladoro attacks Burato's camp. Carlo arrives with the paladins; they are in danger. The arrival of the four paladins. The death of Astiladoro. The destruction of Astilaga. Charles baptizes the people of Alexandria.

Sera 122   18 (cfr. 124 of Paladini 6)

A festive ball in Paris. The treachery of Gano. Rinaldo's great battle against the paladins, Carlo banishes him. Orlando slaps Gano and then slaps Carlo and undertakes a great battle inside Paris. Carlo banishes him. Orlando at the Belvedere bridge kills Antifor di Barossia and dons his armor. Mourning in Paris for Orlando's presumed death.

Sera 123   19 (cfr. 125 of Paladini 6)

Orlando attacks Arcario di Cesarena's camp and undertakes a great battle. Peace between Costantino and Arcario. They besiege Paris with a great army. Orlando, disguised as Antifor, takes Carlo and the paladins prisoner. Gano offers Paris to the supposed Antifor. Alda speaks to Orlando who is believed to be Antifor and then goes to Montalbano to call upon Rinaldo. The latter leaves for Paris with Bradamante.

Sera 124   20 (cfr. 126 of Paladini 6)

Rinaldo arrives in Paris and challenges the supposed Antifor. A great battle between Orlando and Rinaldo and their recognition of each other. The liberation of the prisoners. The death of Arcario and Costantino. Destruction of the pagan camp. Orlando and Rinaldo reach the fugitives, undertake a great battle, and free three paladins who had been captured. Escape of the pagans because Astolfo falls asleep.

Sera 125   21 del vol. 2° (cfr. 127 of Paladini 6)

Orlando and Rinaldo arrive in Cordia and find it besieged by the Algazar. They present themselves to Balante and then attack the enemy camp. Duel between Rinaldo and the Algazar. Rinaldo is victorious thanks to Durlindana. A Magonzese denounces Orlando and Rinaldo and is thrown from the balcony. Balante's baptism. The sorceress Angiolina goes to Paris to abduct Alda.

Sera 126   22 vol. 2° (cfr. 128 of Paladini 6)

Spells of the sorceress Angiolina, who abducts Alda with an enchanted pavilion and takes her to Geometria. Alda slaps Corbolas. Carlo and the paladins arrive at the Pleasure Castle and are taken prisoner by Angiolina. Dudone besieges Geometria. Balante departs with Orlando and Rinaldo to free Alda.

Sera 127   23 vol. 2° (cfr. 129 of Paladini 6)

Rinaldo kills a giant and rescues a woman. He arrives at the Pleasure Castle and is captured by Angiolina. Rinaldo clobbers Gano. Orlando frees Rinaldo. The enchantments and tricks of Malagigi. An infernal struggle between Malagigi and Angiolina. The death of the sorceress.

Sera 128   24 (cfr. 130 of Paladini 6)

Malagigi liberates the paladins and goes to Geometria. Carlo attacks the city. A great battle follows. Orlando kills Corbolas. The capture of the city. Carlo banishes Rinaldo and Malagigi. Orlando is taken prisoner in a castle. Malagigi's spells. Rinaldo frees Orlando who, together with Oliviero, Ugiero, and Astolfo, leaves for Jerusalem.

Copione 10: Serate 129–146 (166 pages)

Sera 129   25 (cfr. 131 of Paladini 6)

Pipino, Carlo's son, instigated by Gano, kills Baldovino, Ugiero's son. Carlo has him shut up in a room. Iorio, led by an innkeeper, is attacked by thieves; overpowered, he flees and hides atop a tree. The thieves compete for the prey by shooting arrows into the tree. Iorio arrives in Marseille, where he surprises Sardonio and Policasta in the midst of a conversation. Iorio, believed to be Sardonio, escapes with Policasta who at the inn realizes that he is not Sardonio.

Sera 130   26 vol. 2° (cfr. 131 of Paladini 6)

Pipino, instigated by Gano, attempts to kill Ugiero but is killed by the paladin. Carlo sentences him to death. Rinaldo is opposed. Carlo sends Ugiero to prison. Iorio is attacked by thieves on a beach and taken prisoner, then sold to the sultan. Rinaldo, in spite of Carlo, keeps Ugiero company in prison. Policasta arrives in Genoa and presents herself to Brunaldo.

Sera 131   27, vol. 2° (cfr. 132 of Paladini 6)

Marsilio besieges Paris. King Braviero captures Carlo and all the paladins with his enchanted voice. Ugiero is freed and is counseled by the white fairy who reveals Braviero's deception. He challenges the pagan and kills him. Marsilio frees Carlo and the paladins. Carlo forgives Ugiero.

Sera 132   28, vol. 2° (cfr. 133 of Paladini 6)

Brawl between Gano and Rinaldo. Rinaldo's great battle against the Magonzesi and the paladins. Carlo banishes him. Orlando compels him to leave. Fulminauro sends [a messenger] to Paris to ask for the hand of Armelina, Gano's daughter. Rinaldo defeats four giants and, disguised as Altubrando, captures the paladins. A battle between Rinaldo and Orlando. Rinaldo abducts Armelina by taking her from Bella Dea [Beautiful Goddess].

Sera 133   29, vol. 2° (cfr. 134 of Paladini 6)

Malagigi's spells. Rinaldo challenges Rinaldo-disguised-as-Altubrando and kills him, freeing the paladins, and then obtains Carlo's forgiveness.[15] Armelina and Fulminauro's wedding. Uriella, sent to marry Balcaus, flees with Meleagro. Balcaus, who feels mocked, gathers the army to wage war against Salmanarte. Morbello (also called Malaguerra) beats D. Trico with a club.

134   30, vol. 2° (cfr. 135 of Paladini 6)

Balcaus's army encounters that of Salmanarte. They fight a great battle and Balcaus is killed. Aquilante, crowned king, kills two giants and captures Salmanarte and others. Meleagro betrays Uriella because of his love for

---

15 Malagigi has asked the demon Nucalone to impersonate Altubrando so that Rinaldo may defeat him and thereby win back Carlo's favor.

Rosana, but he is duly punished. Grifone challenges Aquilante. A great battle between the two brothers; the night stops their fighting.

Sera 135   31 volume secondo (cfr. 136–137 of **Paladini 6**)

Another fierce battle between Grifone and Aquilante. The white fairy and the black fairy stop the battle and explain their origin to the two brothers. Grifone and Aquilante find Fedelsmonda. Aquilante defeats Sinibaldo and makes his beloved undress. The two brothers arrive in Paris and challenge the paladins. Oliviero embraces his sons. Rosana arrives in Paris.

Sera 136   32 vol. secondo (cfr. 137 of **Paladini 6**)

Rinaldo arrives in Paris. Morbello falls in love with Rosana, he asks for arms and is refused. Malagigi shows Morbello how to win Meleagro's arms. Morbello goes to the enchantment, takes the arms, wins the joust, attains Baiardo, and flees. Rinaldo, Orlando, and others pursue him. Iorio visits his father.

Sera 137   33 vol. secondo (cfr. 138 of **Paladini 6**)

Malaguerra steals Durlindana from Orlando. He kills a lion and goes on a pilgrimage. Astolfo, Rinaldo, and the others fall into the enchantment of Uriella. Malaguerra, informed by Malagigi, overcomes many obstacles and destroys the spell. The death of Meleagro. Malagigi exhorts Carlo to declare Malaguerra the victor. Carlo honors him and promises him Rosana.

Sera 138   34 vol. 2° (cfr. 139 of **Paladini 6**)

Astolfo steals Durlindana from Malaguerra. Orlando kills Baleastro and Pirronte and frees Iorio. Ferraù kills Mocrante, arrives at the castle, and praises the count. Astolfo defeats a Catalan and hears about the beauty of Argonetta from him, then goes to win her over. Malagigi steals Durlindana from Astolfo.

Sera 139   35 vol. 2° (cfr. 140 of **Paladini 6**)

Astolfo is captured by Gioroante. Cladinoro hears about the adventure of the three bridges in the Perilous Forest. He bravely fights the enchantment and wins, taking the shield. Marsilio besieges Andropeo. Astolfo's squire falls in love with Argonetta and is captured. Argonetta's death. Orlando receives Durlindana from Malagigi.

Sera 140   36 vol. 2° (cfr. 141 of **Paladini** *6)*

Marsilio attacks the Belviraggio castle. Andropeo kills Azio and Pireo. Malaguerra defends Marsilio and kills Andropeo, then he fights against the Spaniards because he is disobeyed. Gandellino learns of his origin from an enchantress. He defeats Agolaccio and Baldovino and attains Brigliadoro. A great battle between Cladinoro and Gandellino. Cladinoro loses his shield. A battle between Orlando and Gandellino.

Sera 141   37 vol. 2° (cfr. 142 of **Paladini** *6)*

Pulima encounters Orlando and tells of her misfortune. The count defends her against Grandonio. Agolaccio undertakes a duel against Cartalone and kills him. A great battle between Grandonio and Gandellino. Grandonio's imprisonment. Scilarco challenges Orlando's knights. He undertakes a first and second battle against Baldovino and is killed.

Sera 142   38 vol. 2° (cfr. 143 of **Paladini** *7)*

Marsilio and his brothers are taken prisoner at the Beautiful Bridge. Peace between Orlando and Grandonio. The latter goes to the camp, challenges Pitargo, and is taken prisoner. Orlando and his companions leave to free Astolfo, and they encounter Sinadoro, whose help Orlando refuses. Orlando arrives in the Spanish camp, arrives at the Beautiful Bridge with his companions, kills Gioroante and Pitargo, and frees the prisoners.

Sera 143   39 vol. 2° (cfr. 144 of **Paladini** *7)*

Baldino tries to abduct Rosana. In Piraga, Orlando baptizes Cleonte Novello. Gano abducts Rosana on behalf of Baldino, but then tries to keep her for himself. Malaguerra meets a fugitive, attacks the Magonzese camp, and kills Baldino. The latter reveals the betrayal before he dies. Malaguerra arrives in Pontieri and attacks, Gano flees. Berta cedes Rosana to Malaguerra.

Sera 144   40 vol. 2° (cfr. 145 of **Paladini** *7)*

Guidone finds the shield. A great battle between Cladinoro and Guidone. Cladinoro regains the shield. Malaguerra goes to Paris where he wounds Baldovino and kills Buovo di Magonza. A simulated peace between Gano and Malaguerra. Gano attempts to have Malaguerra apprehended during the night.

The latter, because he is awake, discovers the treachery and wounds Gano, who is then believed dead. The paladins attack Malaguerra. Orlando, Agolaccio, and Gandellino accompany him outside Paris.

Sera 145   41 vol. 2° (cfr. 146 of Paladini 7)

Carlo orders the arrest of Orlando. A fierce battle inside Paris between Orlando and the Magonzesi. Carlo is arrested. Orlando leaves Paris. Malaguerra besieges Paris with his men. He challenges the paladins and captures them together with Carlo. He takes them to Montalbano, locks them in a prison, and takes away the keys.

Sera 146   42 vol. 2° (cfr. 147 of Paladini 7)

Arrival of Rinaldo in Montalbano. He goes to find Malaguerra and frees Carlo with the paladins. Malaguerra bites Carlo's hand and is locked in prison. Malaguerra's plot against Carlo. Rinaldo swears to kill him and goes in search of him. Malagigi saves Malaguerra by compelling him to flee.

Copione 11: Serate 147–164 (162 pages)

Sera 147   43 vol. 2° (cfr. 148 of Paladini 7)

Malaguerra hears from a dwarf about the misfortune of Pigmalione, king of Macedonia, and goes to present himself to the king. Bradamante convinces Rinaldo to forgive Malaguerra. Orlando, Gandellino, and Agolaccio arrive in Montalbano. Malaguerra kills the serpent and cures Pigmalione of his blindness. Festivities in Macedonia. Malaguerra's departure for an unknown destination.

Sera 148   44 vol. 2° (cfr. 149–150 of Paladini 7)

Malaguerra is thrown by a storm to the shores of Trebisonda, where he is welcomed by three enchantresses. Soldanella becomes his favorite. Because of a vision Malaguerra abandons Soldanella and flees to Trebisonda where he hears about the misfortune of Polinarda and Odoardo. He goes to the square and challenges Ipparco, whom he kills after a great battle. Tirendo and his brothers besiege Trebisonda and force Arimondo to hand over Malaguerra to them.

Sera 149   45 vol. 2° (cfr. 151 of **Paladini** *7)*

The emperor Arimondo's betrayal: he has Malaguerra arrested during the night. The people rebel and restore him to his earlier high status. The five kings enter Trebisonda to kill Malaguerra. The innkeeper goes in search of Rinaldo and meets Orlando and his companions, who offer to save Malaguerra. They encounter Rinaldo, Oliviero, and Bradamante, and together they hurry to Trebisonda.

Sera 150   46 vol. 2° (cfr. 152 of **Paladini** *7)*

Arimondo has the five Armenian kings poisoned. Malaguerra, at the table, believing himself to be likewise poisoned, kills Arimondo and undertakes a great battle. Odoardo treacherously wounds him from behind. The arrival of Rinaldo and companions, who undertake a great battle. The prowess of Baiardo. Rinaldo kills Odoardo. Malaguerra discovers the identity of his parents. Malagigi saves Malaguerra. Eremete and Carossa attack Trebisonda. Gandellino kills Carossa and receives praise.

Sera 151   47 vol. 2° (cfr. 153 of **Paladini** *7)*

The paladins attack the Armenian camp. Rinaldo kills the giant Eremete. Victory of the Christians. The capture of Eraclina, who becomes Malagigi's wife. Coronation of Malaguerra. Gandellino goes in search of his father. The paladins arrive in Paris. The departure of Angelica and Argalia for Paris. Gradasso hears about Sibilla's enchantment and goes to attain Samson's armor.

Sera 152   48 (cfr. 154 of **Paladini** *7)*

Gradasso at the enchantment of Sibilla, fights four giants, cuts down the tree, attains Samson's armor, and vows to acquire Durlindana and Baiardo. The Spaniards arrive in Paris and attempt to mock Rinaldo, who gives a worthy answer. Angelica arrives in Paris. Great *scena in fondo* [deep stage]. Orlando and others fall in love with Angelica. Gradasso gathers his troops in order to attain Baiardo and Durlindana.

Sera 153   49 (cfr. 154–155 of **Paladini** *7)*

Carlo makes fate decide who will fight first against Argalia. Malagigi tries to rape Angelica and remains a prisoner. Astolfo is defeated by Argalia. A great battle between Ferraù and Argalia. Ferraù kills the four giants and negotiates with Argalia. Argalia and Angelica flee. Astolfo finds Argalia's lance. A great battle between Guidone and Cladinoro. Carinda finds her wounded brother.

Sera 154   50 (cfr. 156 of Paladini 7)

Carinda finds Cladinoro and they engage in a great battle as strangers. Their recognition of each other. Lucina saves Guidone. A joust in Paris. Grandonio defeats Ugiero and Oliviero and scorns Carlo. Astolfo wins the joust with Argalia's lance. The treachery of Gano, the pride of Astolfo who engages in a great battle against the Magonzesi. Carlo imprisons him. Rinaldo drinks at the Fountain of Disdain.

Sera 155   51, vol. 2° (cfr. 156–157 of Paladini 7)

Angelica drinks at the Fountain of Love, she finds Rinaldo asleep and he rejects her. Ferraù finds Argalia and, after a great battle, kills him. A great battle between Orlando and Ferraù over Angelica. Fiordispina stops the battle. Cladinoro and his companions fight against six knights and then disperse. Carlo sends Rinaldo to help Marsilio. A great battle between Gandellino and Guidone Selvaggio.

Sera 156   52, vol. 2° (cfr. 158 of Paladini 7)

Rinaldo arrives to give help to Marsilio and together they go to Barcelona. A great battle between Christians and Pagans.[16] A battle between Rinaldo and Gradasso. Rinaldo kills Balorza. Alfrera takes Ferraù prisoner. Rinaldo is challenged by Gradasso and accepts, then each takes his leave. Angelica returns to Cathay and frees Malagigi in order to attain Rinaldo.

Sera 157   53 (cfr. 158–159 of Paladini 7)

Malagigi speaks to Rinaldo, who rejects Angelica's love. Malagigi plays a trick on Rinaldo. The latter fights the fake Gradasso and is distanced from Spain. Orlando rescues a boy and acquires a book, hears from a monster

---

16 More precisely, Gradasso's forces attack both Marsilio's Saracen troops and the Christian troops headed by Rinaldo that Carlo sent to help defend the neighboring Spanish kingdom.

where Angelica can be found, kills the monster, and heads to Albracca. Believing that Rinaldo has fled, Gradasso joins forces with the Spaniards to march on Paris.

Sera 158   54, vol. 2° (cfr. 159–160 of* Paladini *7)

Orlando arrives at the Bridge of Death, kills Zambardo, is caught in a net, and is freed by another giant whom he then kills. Angelica refuses to marry Agricane. Gradasso besieges Paris. Carlo, incited by the paladins, attacks Gradasso's army. A great battle between Christians and pagans. Carlo, informed of the danger, mounts Baiardo and is taken prisoner by Gradasso, along with the other paladins. Baiardo wounds Gradasso.

Sera 159   55 (cfr. 160–161 of* Paladini *7)

The battle outside Paris continues. Gradasso returns to the battle and takes Oliviero and Ugiero prisoner. Astolfo, freed by the people, challenges Gradasso with Argalia's lance and defeats him. Liberation of the paladins. Orlando falls victim to the spell of Drogantina. Rinaldo, invited to Angelica's garden, flees in order not to hear of her.

Sera 160   56 (cfr. 161–162 of* Paladini *7)

Rinaldo arrives near a castle where he fights a giant and is taken prisoner by trickery. An elderly woman tells him her story and he is thrown into Marchino's tomb, where he is in grave danger. In the end, with Angelica's help, he kills the serpent and the inhabitants of the castle along with the two giants. Astolfo leaves Paris and goes in search of Rinaldo, taking along Baiardo. He arrives in Sacripante's camp and his offer of service is rejected. He defeats Brandimarte and then Sacripante.

Sera 161   57 (cfr. 162 of* Paladini *7)

Astolfo and Brandimarte go to the enchantment of Drogantina. Brandimarte, captured by Grifone and Aquilante, drinks the water of oblivion. Astolfo reaches Cathay. A lion guides Carinda to Lucina's tent. Gandellino kills a giant and frees Poliso. Agricane attacks Albracca. Astolfo fights upon arriving in Agricane's camp and is taken prisoner. Agricane appropriates Baiardo.

Sera 162   58 (cfr. 163 of* Paladini *7)

Sacripante approaches Albracca with his army, sees the battle, and demonstrates his valor. Wounded by Agricane, he retreats within Albracca. Agricane enters with his men. The wounded Sacripante pushes back the Tartars. Rinaldo hears about the enchantment of Drogantina from Fiordiligi, defeats a giant and two griffins, reads about the treachery of Truffaldino, and vows to avenge Albarosa. He attains Rabicano, kills a Centaur, and loses Fiordiligi.

Sera 163   59 (cfr. 164 of* Paladini *7)

Archeloro abducts Alda and kills her knights, then takes Poliso and Agolaccio prisoner. Malisa and Silvanella go in search of knights. Angelica leaves the fortress of Albracca to seek help, happens to arrive at the prison where Fiordiligi is being held, and hears about Drogantina's enchantment. Angelica escapes thanks to her ring.

Sera 164   60 (cfr. 165 of* Paladini *7)

Angelica frees Orlando and his companions and returns to Albracca with the reinforcements. Truffaldino arrests Sacripante and Torindo. Orlando attacks Agricane's army. He arrives at the fortress and is compelled by Truffaldino to defend him. Malisa takes Bradamante and her companions to the castle of Archeloro, where they are captured. Silvanella encounters Gandellino and goes to Archeloro's castle.

Copione 12: Serate 165–180 (161 pages)

Sera 165   61 (cfr. 166 of* Paladini *7)

Gandellino is taken prisoner by Archeloro. Orlando challenges Agricane. King Galafro, along with many troops commanded by Marfisa and a giant, arrives at Albracca and engages in battle. A truce between Orlando and Agricane. Orlando scatters the Tartar army. Agricane with a simulated flight lures Orlando to a distant spot where they fight until nightfall. Each knight recounts his love for Angelica. Out of jealousy they return to fighting. Agricane's death.

Sera 166   62, vol. 2° (cfr. 167 of* Paladini *7)

The battle outside the fortress of Albracca continues. Destruction of the Tartar camp. Rinaldo frees Prasildo and Fiordiligi. Malisa leads

Carinda to Archeloro's castle. Silvanella leads Cladinoro. Meeting of the two lovers. Archeloro flees from Carinda and is killed by Cladinoro. Recognition of Cladinoro and Gandellino. A great battle between Rinaldo and Marfisa. Galafro injures Rinaldo. Marfisa turns against Galafro. Peace between Rinaldo and Marfisa.

Sera 167 63 (cfr. 168 of Paladini *7)*

Fiordiligi is abducted by a deceitful hermit. Brandimarte, attacked by three giants, is defended by Orlando. The release of Sacripante and Torindo. The latter goes over to Marfisa's camp. Rinaldo challenges Truffaldino and fights against Grifone and other knights. The woman freed by Orlando and Brandimarte tells the story of the old man Folderico. Fiordiligi falls into the clutches of a savage. Brandimarte frees her. Orlando receives a horn and a little book from a woman. Astolfo goes to Marfisa's camp seeking Rinaldo.

Sera 168 64 (cfr. 169 of Paladini *7)*

Orlando overcomes the enchantment of Morgana. Cladinoro and his companions arrive in Paris. A great battle between Orlando and Rinaldo. The death of Truffaldino. A battle between Orlando and Marfisa and their truce. Orlando and Rinaldo resume their battle, both demonstrating their valor. The night brings their fighting to a halt.

Sera 169 65 (cfr. 170 of Paladini *7)*

Angelica, knowing that Rinaldo is on the battlefield, is assailed by great desire. She asks the count for a favor and obtains it. A great battle between Orlando and Rinaldo. Angelica sends the count to Orgagna. Orlando comes to a bridge, fights four knights, and frees Origilla. The latter then steals his horse. Rinaldo and his companions leave Marfisa's camp. Rinaldo fights a giant and is believed dead.

Sera 170 66 vol. 2° (cfr. 171 of Paladini *7)*

A grand council held by Agramante to defeat Carlo. Grifone and Aquilante are taken prisoner at the Bridge of Roses. Mandricardo goes to Circassia to avenge his father. Rodomonte refutes the king of Garamanta's speech. The latter, before dying, explains how to find Ruggiero. Orlando frees Grifone and Aquilante, kills a giant, and heads for the enchantment of Falerina.

Sera 171   67, vol. 2° (cfr. 172 of Paladini 7)

Orlando destroys the enchantment of Falerina and attains the sword Balisarda. A great battle between Sacripante and Marfisa. Brunello steals Angelica's ring, Sacripante's horse, and Marfisa's sword. Sacripante leaves for Circassia. Carlo builds up his defenses. Rodomonte departs from Algiers.

Sera 172   68 (cfr. 173 of Paladini 8)

Rodomonte, caught in a tempest, loses many ships. He lands in Monaco and destroys the army of Arcimbaldo. The arrival of Bradamante and Desiderio. Battle between Bradamante and Rodomonte. Orlando, at the enchantment of Morgana, kills Aridano and catches hold of the fairy, but first struggles with suffering. He frees Rinaldo and his companions, but leaves behind Ziliante.

Sera 173   69 (cfr. 174 of Paladini 8)

Rinaldo and his companions are captured by Balisardo. Brunello steals Orlando's sword and horn. Orlando finds Origilla and retrieves Durlindana. He challenges Balisardo and is taken captive. Brandimarte kills Balisardo. Gano invites the Spaniards to fight against the Christians. The treachery of Origilla, who denounces Orlando to Monodante.

Sera 174   70 (cfr. 175 of Paladini 8)

Orlando goes to free Ziliante. He encounters Fiordiligi and Baldino. He goes to the enchantment of Morgana and then takes Ziliante back to Monodante. The recognition of Brandimarte by his father. Astolfo falls into the enchantment of Alcina. Rinaldo joins Ottachiero. He arrives in Monaco and finds the battle raging. A battle between Bradamante and Rodomonte. Rinaldo fights Rodomonte and puts him to flight.

175   71 (cfr. 176 of Paladini 8)

The battle continues between Christians and pagans. A battle between Rinaldo and Rodomonte. The captivity of Dudone. The arrival of Carlo's army. Cladinoro puts Rodomonte to flight. Defeat of the pagans. Brunello arrives in Biserta. Joust ordered by Agramante. Ruggiero takes up arms and demonstrates his valor. Bardulasto treacherously wounds Ruggiero and is killed. Rinaldo drinks at the Fountain of Love. Marfisa besieges Montalbano.

Sera 176   72 (cfr. 177 of Paladini 8)

A great battle outside Montalbano. Salardo's capture. Orlando and Brandimarte flee with Angelica. Torindo sets fire to Albracca and pursues Orlando. Brandimarte kills Torindo. A battle between Rodomonte and Ferraù. Brunello, sentenced to death, is freed by Ruggiero. The latter is dubbed a knight by Agramante.

Sera 177   73, vol. 2° (cfr. 178 of Paladini 8)

Orlando kills the Lestrigons and frees Angelica. Brandimarte frees Fiordiligi. Orlando goes to Cyprus. Brandimarte cedes his own arms to Marfisa, finds the deceased Agricane, takes his arms, and kills Barrigazzo. Joust in Cyprus. Orlando fights against Grifone and Aquilante. Constanzo plays a trick on the count to make him leave.

Sera 178   74 (cfr. 179 of Paladini 8)

Brandimarte, at the enchantment of Febosilla, kills two giants, kisses the serpent, and frees Doristella from the fairy. He attains the enchantment of his armor. Doristella narrates her story. Brandimarte kills many thieves and takes Fuggiforca prisoner. Theodore besieges Dolistone. Brandimarte attacks Teodoro's camp. Fiordiligi discovers her parents and marries Brandimarte, then they leave for France.

Sera 179   75 (cfr. 180 of Paladini 8)

Brandimarte lands in Africa, challenges the knights of Biserta, and fights against Agramante, then together they hunt down wild beasts. Agramante, reprimanded by a minister, orders their departure for France. Mandricardo fights Gradasso, kills Malapresa, and attains Hector's armor. Gradasso and Mandricardo happen to arrive at the mountain of the ogre and they rescue Lucina.

Sera 180   76 (cfr. 181 of Paladini 8)

Angelica drinks at the Fountain of Disdain and begins to hate Rinaldo. A great battle between Orlando and Rinaldo over Angelica. Carlo divides them. Angelica's escape and another battle between Orlando and Rinaldo. Ferraù and Rodomonte take Malagigi and Viviano prisoner. Carlo goes to Montalbano with his army and promises to give Angelica to whichever of the two cousins is more valiant in battle. Rinaldo meets his daughter Carinda. Destruction of the army of Marsilio, who curses Gano for having incited him to war.

Copione 13: *Serate* 181–195 (135 pages)

Sera 181   77 *(cfr. 182 of* **Paladini** *8)*

The battle outside Montalbano between Christians and Spaniards rages on. Agramante arrives in Montalbano and sends Pinadoro to the field where he is defeated by Orlando. He descends with his men and engages in combat. The valor of Rinaldo. Both armies are in danger. Ferraù loses Argalia's helmet, finds the count, and praises Rinaldo. Orlando indignantly returns to the field and fights against Ruggiero. Atlante, in order to save Ruggiero, makes Orlando succumb to his enchantment.

Sera 182   78 *(cfr. 183 of* **Paladini** *8)*

The battle below Montalbano continues, the arrival of Gradasso and Mandricardo, defeat of the Christians. Ruggiero fights against Rodomonte to defend Bradamante, the enamorment of Ruggiero and Bradamante. Martasino treacherously injures Bradamante. Ruggiero defends her. Battle between Mandricardo and Gradasso, Brandimarte divides them

Sera 183   79 *(cfr. 184 of* **Paladini** *8)*

Ruggiero, Brandimarte, and Gradasso go to the enchantment of the Naiads. Brandimarte frees Orlando. Great battle between Orlando and Gradasso, a dwarf separates them. Great combat outside Paris, arrival of Cladinoro and Carinda. Brandimarte and Orlando attack the tents and free the prisoners. Fiordispina falls in love with Bradamante. Great battle between Rinaldo and Ferraù for Angelica.

Sera 184   80 *(cfr. 185 of* **Paladini** *8)*

Great battle between Bradamante and Sacripante. Argalia appears to Ferraù, the latter swears to attain Orlando's helmet. Battle between Rinaldo and Sacripante. Angelica escapes and is restored to health by a deceitful hermit. Bradamante is honored by Fiordispina. Ricciardetto, believed to be Bradamante, enjoys the love of Fiordispina. Rinaldo leaves to gather troops. Bradamante encounters Pinabello and promises to help him.

Sera 185   81 (cfr. 186 of **Paladini *8)***

Pinabello betrays Bradamante by throwing her down into a cave. Bradamante is welcomed by Melissa who takes her to the tomb of Merlin, from whom she hears about her descendants. Bradamante seizes the ring from Brunello, takes Atlante prisoner, frees Ruggiero, and then loses him because of the winged horse. Isoliero sets Brunello free.

Sera 186   82 vol. 2° (cfr. 187 of **Paladini *8)***

Polinesso's plot to deceive Ariodante. Ginevra is condemned, Lurcanio makes the accusation, Dalinda is handed over to the executioners. Rinaldo is carried by a storm to Scotland. He frees Dalinda and hears the story about Ariodante and Ginevra. Rinaldo kills Polinesso who confesses his treason before dying. Ariodante marries Ginevra.

Sera 187   83 (cfr. **sera *188 of* Paladini *8)***

Ruggiero arrives on the island of Alcina, finds Astolfo transformed into a myrtle bush, and hears from him the evil deeds of the fairy. Ruggiero, infatuated with Alcina, remains under her spell until he is freed by Melissa. While fleeing he comes up against a huge obstacle. Melissa destroys the enchantment. Angelica falls into the hands of the people of Ebura. Orlando dreams about Angelica in danger and leaves Paris.

Sera 188   84 (cfr. **sera *189 of* Paladini *8)***

Orlando listens to the story of Olimpia and Bireno. He challenges Cimosco, is attacked, undertakes a great battle, and kills Cimosco after having lost his horse due to a gunshot wound. A battle inside Dordrecht, the liberation of Bireno. Ruggiero sees Rinaldo's army, arrives in Ebura, battles the orca, and frees Angelica. Bireno abandons Olimpia for a new love.

Sera 189   85 (cfr. **sera *190 of* Paladini *8)***

Olimpia is captured by the people of Ebura. Angelica escapes from Ruggiero thanks to her possession of the ring. Orlando kills the orca and frees Olimpia, from whom he hears about her misfortune. Odorico, in love with Isabella, sends Almenio away and undertakes a great battle against Corelo. Isabella escapes but is joined by Odorico, thieves capture Isabella. Orlando falls under the spell of Atlante where Ruggiero later arrives. Angelica frees

Orlando and others. Battle between Orlando and Ferrau. Astolfo receives the horn and the book from Longistella [Logistilla].

Sera 190   86 (cfr. sera 190 of Paladini 8)

Ferraù obtains Orlando's helmet, the latter kills Alzirdo and defeats Manilardo, then inside a cave hears about Isabella's misfortunes and kills the wicked mob. Bradamante succumbs to the enchantment of Atlante. Fiordispina, condemned to death, is saved by thieves. Agrimarte kills the thieves and marries Fiordispina and adopts her baby, calling him Idramoro. Oberto kills Bireno.

Sera 191   87 (cfr. sera 191 of Paladini 8)

Mandricardo abducts Doralice. Astolfo takes Caligorante prisoner. Grifone and Aquilante fight against the giant Orrillo. Astolfo by means of the book kills Orrillo. Agrimarte's brother kills Fiordispina. Agramante attacks Paris. Rodomonte enters from the Seine River and starts a fire. Gandellino pushes back Rodomonte. Rinaldo arrives with the army and reinforces the Christians.

Sera 192   88 (cfr. sera 192 of Paladini 8)

The battle outside Paris continues. Rinaldo kills Dardanello, son of Almonte. Cloridano and Medoro search for the corpse of Dardanello. Death of Cloridano. Angelica tends to the wounded Medoro. Grifone, near Damascus, finds Origilla with the vile Martano and together they enter Damascus. Joust in Damascus. Martano demonstrates his cowardice. Grifone wins the joust.

Sera 193   89 (cfr. sera 193 of Paladini 8)

Origilla and her lover steal Grifone's arms, the latter is arrested. Norandino condemns him to death. Grifone frees himself and undertakes a great battle. Aquilante punishes Martano and Origilla. Joust in Damascus, conflict between the people and Marfisa. Astolfo defeats Grifone and Aquilante, they recognize each other. Marfisa sets off with Astolfo and his companions, a storm carries them to Laiazzo.

Sera 194   90 (cfr. sera 194 of Paladini 8)

Marfisa and her companions land on the island of Laiazzo. Marfisa kills nine knights and fights against Guidone Selvaggio. Marfisa advises him to escape and they do flee, but first they undertake a great battle against the women. Astolfo saves them thanks to the sound of his horn. Marfisa leaves her companions and encounters the old woman Gabrina. Marfisa defeats Pinabello and forces his ladylove to undress.

Sera 195   *91 (cfr.* **sera** *195 of* **Paladini** *8)*

Sansonetto and his companions happen upon the castle of Pinabello. Marfisa defeats Zerbino and hands over the old woman to him. Astolfo destroys Atlante's enchantment. Ruggiero finds Bradamante and together they go to the castle of Altaripa. Ruggiero fights against Grifone and his companions. Bradamante kills Pinabello. Astolfo acquires the winged horse, that is, the hippogriff.

End of the second volume [following Act 3, scene 4]

I believe that this final scene is also written in the next script, take note that it belongs to the third volume. The second volume ends with the third scene.

Copione 14 (originally *Paladini* 9): *Serate* 198–209 (unnumbered pages)[17]

Sera 198

Bradamante arrives in Montalbano and sends Ippalca to deliver the horse Frontino to Ruggiero. Rodomonte encounters Ippalca and seizes the horse from her. Zerbino, falsely accused by Gabrina, is sentenced to death. Orlando liberates him. A great battle between Orlando and Mandricardo. Orlando arrives in the shepherd's hut where he hears the news about Angelica, goes insane, and throws off his weapons and armor.

Sera 199

The incursions of mad Orlando. Odorico is handed over to Zerbino, who gives him old Gabrina, who is then hanged. Zerbino collects Orlando's arms. Mandricardo takes possession of Durlindana. A great battle between Zerbino and Mandricardo. The death of Zerbino. Rodomonte encounters Mandricardo. A great battle between the two adversaries. A messenger from Agramante separates them. Ruggiero rescues Ricciardetto from being burned

---

17 Despite skipping over two numbers, *sera* 198 directly picks up the action that concluded *sera* 195. Confirmation of this is the fact that in Mike Manteo's notebook 17 the consecutive *serate* 201 and 202 correspond to *sera* 195 and *sera* 198, respectively.

at the stake. They go to Aldigiero's castle and hear about the misfortune of Malagigi and Viviano.

Sera 200

Aldigiero, Ruggiero, and Ricciardetto, in the company of Marfisa, liberate Malagigi and Viviano. Mandricardo defeats Ricciardetto and his companions. A great battle between Marfisa and Mandricardo and between Rodomonte and Ruggiero. Malagigi stops the battle. Mandricardo, Rodomonte, Ruggiero, and Marfisa make their way across Carlo's camp. Thanks to the arrival of his troops, Agramante orders an assault and a great battle follows. Carlo flees inside Paris. Discord in Agramante's camp. Ruggiero challenges Mandricardo, Rodomonte also challenges Mandricardo, Agramante entrusts them to fate.

Sera 201

Marfisa finds Brunello and carries him off to hang him. Rodomonte leaves the battlefield because of Doralice. Sacripante follows him. Rodomonte kills Isabella and then erects a bridge in her honor. Orlando throws Rodomonte into the river. Orlando's madness. The ruin of Angelica and Medoro, great duel between Ruggiero and Mandricardo. The Tartar's death. Ruggiero is wounded. Brunello's death. Bradamante welcomes Ippalca and hears news about Ruggiero. The arrival of Rinaldo in Montalbano.

Sera 202

Rinaldo leaves for Paris with family members. Guidone Selvaggio encounters Rinaldo. He fights against Viviano, Salardo, and his brothers, and defeats them. A great battle between Rinaldo and Guidone Selvaggio, their recognition of each other. Brandimarte is taken prisoner by Rodomonte at the bridge dedicated to Isabella. Rinaldo attacks Agramante's camp with the assistance of Carlo. A battle between Gradasso and Cladinoro, Guidone and Ferraù. Destruction of Agramante's camp and his escape. A great duel between Rinaldo and Gradasso. The latter finds Baiardo and leaves for Asia.

Sera 203

Bradamante leaves Montalbano to find Ruggiero. Astolfo chases the Harpies away from Senapo's table, enters the infernal cavern, and hears Lidia's story. Then, losing the bridle of the winged animal, he flies through the celestial gates and reaches the earthly paradise where he receives Orlando's wits from St John the Evangelist and sees wondrous things. Carlo leaves for Arles to besiege Agramante. Sansonetto and Oliviero are taken prisoner by Rodomonte at Isabella's bridge.

Sera 204 7[18]

Astolfo departs from paradise, arrives in Nubia, and cures Senapo's blindness. Bradamante defeats Rodomonte at Isabella's bridge, then sends the horse to Ruggiero and challenges the most valorous knights in Agramante's camp. She defeats Serpentino, Grandonio, and Ferrau, then fights against Marfisa and then against Ruggiero. The battle of the two armies. A great battle between Ferraù and Cladinoro. Astolfo goes to besiege Biserta with the Nubian army.

205 8

The battle outside Arles between Christians and pagans continues. Bradamante and Ruggiero leave the battlefield. Marfisa follows them. A great battle between Marfisa and Bradamante and then between Ruggiero and Marfisa. Atlante makes them embrace as siblings. Bradamante and Marfisa arrive in Carlo's camp. The baptism of Marfisa. Astolfo with the Nubian army arrives outside Biserta and attacks the city. Astolfo captures Bucifaro, who is then exchanged for Dudone.

Sera 206 9

A duel with daggers between Ruggiero and Rinaldo. Agramante, deceived by the fake Rodomonte, breaks the pact. A battle between Christians and pagans. The Spaniards flee. Astolfo frees Oliviero, Sansonetto, and Brandimarte. Orlando regains his senses. Dudone is sent to hire soldiers and obtain horses.

Sera 207 10

Agramante, now defeated, intends to kill himself; he then sets out to sea, but loses his ships in a storm. Orlando attacks Biserta where a great battle follows. Orlando climbs the city walls, enters Biserta, and sets it on fire.

---

18 Beginning with *sera* 204, the seventh play drawn from the *Storia dei paladini*'s third volume, Agrippino once again provides additional numbering that continues right up to the final play of the cycle (*sera* 330).

Dudone captures several pagan kings. Ruggiero fights against Dudone and frees the prisoners. Agramante lands near Biserta where he sees the flames and continues to the island of Lampedusa with Subrino.

Sera 208 11

Rinaldo leaves Paris, fights against a monster in a forest, and drinks from the Fountain of Disdain. Gradasso challenges Orlando to a battle of three against three on the island of Lampedusa. The baptism of Ruggiero. The great battle of three against three. The death of Brandimarte, Gradasso, and Agramante. ~~The baptism of Subrino.~~ Rinaldo arrives in Lampedusa and finds Orlando. Subrino asks to be baptized.

Sera 209 12

Orlando leads his companions to Agrigento and pays his final respects to Brandimarte in a grand funeral. They reach the hermitage and find Ruggiero. The baptism of Subrino. Rinaldo promises his sister to Ruggiero. Orlando and his companions arrive in Paris. Cladinoro meets Ruggiero. Tournament in Paris. Astolfo with his lance defeats Rinaldo and Malagigi. The latter explains the deception. Leone sends [a messenger] to ask for Bradamante's hand in marriage.

Sera 210[19]

The wedding of Cladinoro and Carinda. The arrival of Leone's ambassador in Paris. Amone and Carlo deny Bradamante to Ruggiero. The latter sets out to kill Leone. Costantino besieges Belgrade where a great battle takes place. Ruggiero fights in defense of the Bulgarians and kills a nephew of Costantino. Leone admires Ruggiero's valor. Bradamante is confined inside Roccaforte.[20]

[Copioni 15–17 are missing.]

---

19 The summary and Cast of Characters for *sera* 210 are at the end of this notebook, but the play itself would have been in the missing *Copione* 15.

20 In the absence of *Copione* 15, I include the following *Storia dei paladini* chapter summary in order to complete the material derived from the *Orlando Furioso*: "Ruggiero is taken prisoner by Leone, to whom he swears his loyalty. Ruggiero fights against Bradamante using Leone's insignia. Won over by Ruggiero's intense suffering, Leone cedes him Bradamante, and together with Melissa they go to Paris. Wedding of Ruggiero and Bradamante. Death of Rodomonte" (vol. 10 index, corresponding to pages 55–71).

APPENDIX 5 271

Copione 18 (originally *Paladini* 13): *Serate* 245–253 (pages unnumbered)

245 48

Rinaldo and his companions enter Jerusalem. The first day of the joust won by Paraninfo. Rinaldo falls in love with Leandra. The second day of the joust. Rinaldo takes part, kills Paraninfo and other knights. Leandra falls in love with Rinaldo. In order to demonstrate his valor, he challenges one hundred knights. The Sultan sends fifty. Rinaldo wins and longs for Leandra. The Sultan has a building constructed. Rinaldo knocks it down.

246 49

Leandra's love for Rinaldo makes Panfilo jealous. The latter proposes that Rinaldo must fight against a hundred knights. Rinaldo engages in a great battle but, attacked from all sides, is defended by Orlando and his companions. The destruction of the traitors. A messenger from Gano denounces the four paladins to the Sultan. Leandra reveals the treachery to Rinaldo. The escape of the four paladins with Leandra.

247 50

Orlando, Rinaldo, Oliviero, and Ugiero are led by Leandra to the Monfalcone castle; they kill the inhabitants. The Sultan besieges Monfalcone. The four paladins attack, undertaking a great battle. The Sultan captures the fortress thank to an underground route. The death of Leandra. The four paladins, hard-pressed by a storm, flee to the Castle of the Wolf.

Sera 248 51

Rinaldo and his companions kill the assassins at the Castle of the Wolf. Gano besieges Montalbano. Astolfo comes to the aid of those inside the fortress and attacks the Magonzesi with the help of the family of Montalbano. Amone sends messengers to find Rinaldo. The Sultan lays siege to the Castle of the Wolf and begins the assault. The four paladins repel the pagans by throwing rocks. The count Armonito and king Sanacarigi reach the camp. After a great battle Rinaldo kills the count Armonito.

249 52

Sanacarigi hears about the death of his brother and challenges Rinaldo. The latter, with Durlindana, fights the pagan, whom he kills after a great battle and danger to himself. Two of Rinaldo's men arrive in the Sultan's camp, then send a letter to the four paladins. Gano leaves the field and sends help to Carlo. The Spaniards unite with the Sultan. Carlo marches toward the Castle of the Wolf with a great army. The pagan vanguard near Bethlehem meets up with Carlo's army and they engage in a great battle.

250   53

Balante leads Ricciardetto to the Castle of the Wolf. The liberation of the four paladins. The desperation of the Sultan who announces a grand prize to anyone who brings him Rinaldo. The two armies engage in a great battle. Nightfall puts a halt to the hostilities. The second field battle in which Orlando and Rinaldo kill many pagans. The Spaniards flee. The capture of Jerusalem, captivity of the Sultan.

251   54

Feraba's first exploits. He learns of his origin from his mother and leaves for France. He undertakes a great battle out of love for a lady and listens to Filidora's story. Feraba challenges Ascalione but first kills his two children. The death of Ascalione. A great battle between Feraba and Cidaldano and their peace. Feraba besieges Rome and takes the city after a great battle. Captivity of the pope.

252   55

Ottavio and Bellisaria come to the aid of Rome. The pope baptizes Filidora. Carlo leaves Jerusalem because of the arrival of Tiburzio. Ottavio's army encounters the pagan one and they engage in a great battle. An abducted Bellisaria is liberated by the prince Adamaro. Ottavio's army arrives in Rome. Feraba goes to meet it and engages in a great battle. Feraba, defeated, flees to the Veneto. Rome is freed together with the pope.

253   56

Carlo arrives in Venice. Feraba leaves Venice and sets up camp near Montalbano. The sultan of Babylon besieges Jerusalem. Feraba takes Ugiero and Tiburzio prisoner. A great battle between Olivero and Feraba. The latter, defeated, is baptized. Ottavio's army arrives. Feraba marries Filidora. Feraba's army is baptized.

Copione 19 (originally *Paladini* 14): *Serate* 254–265 (pages unnumbered)

254   57

Carlo's vision in Rome. He arrives in Jerusalem and finds it besieged. A fierce battle between Christians and pagans. Carlo leaves for Mecca after the defeat of the sultan. Rinaldo is separated from his army by a storm and led to the island of Delphi. He topples the golden idol and kills the priests. Adriano goes to Delphi with his army. Rinaldo attacks Adriano's army and a great battle takes place.

255   58

Rinaldo attacks Adriano's camp. During the battle a twenty-day truce is established. Adriano sends for the ferocious Minotaur. Carlo arrives in Constantinople and finds the city in the hands of the Saracens. He attacks and, after a great battle, regains it and delivers it to Ottavio. Carlo leaves for Paris. Rinaldo ends the truce, challenging Adriano. The latter asks for another two days. Rinaldo grants his request.

256   59

A great duel between Rinaldo and Adriano. Rinaldo is attacked by the minotaur and is in grave danger. The death of the minotaur. Peace between Adriano and Rinaldo. The baptism of Adriano. Rinaldo comes to the aid of Prester John and kills many knights. The brave African Zenone arrives to defend Delfico. A great battle in which Rinaldo kills Zenone, but is hit by a rock and believed dead.

257   60

Rinaldo, healed by Malagigi, attains victory over Delfico. Rinaldo takes leave of Prester John. He arrives in one of Gano's cites and destroys it, then he besieges Paris with Adriano's army and Malagigi's infernal one. Disguised as grand vizier, Rinaldo challenges the paladins and takes them prisoner. He engages in a great battle against Oliviero and then reveals his identity. Oliviero pretends to be defeated. Gano is happy because of the presumed danger to Paris.

258   61

Gano plots against the paladins and sends money to Rinaldo, believing him grand vizier. Rinaldo, thanks to Malagigi's magic, shows the paladins hanged. Carlo's fright. Rinaldo goes once again to fight the paladins. Gano refuses to fight. Carlo is rejected by Rinaldo, to the disappointment of Gano. The latter invites the Persians to besiege Montalbano. Orlando hears about the death of the paladins. Rinaldo learns of the siege of Gascony. Malagigi deceives Gano in order to bring the Persians to Paris.

259   62

The Persian army goes to Paris to join the supposed vizier. Orlando arrives in the presence of Carlo and challenges the vizier. A great battle between Orlando and Rinaldo. The two cousins recognize each other. Gano dressed as a Jew and with a miter on his head is sent to the camp. Rinaldo tries to kill him. Malagigi saves him. Gano is forgiven for Orlando's sake.

260   63

Malagigi tries to deceive the Amostante. Gano sends a letter to the Amostante advising him to flee. Rinaldo challenges the Amostante and kills many knights. A great field battle. The death of Adriano. Rinaldo kills the giant, Orlando kills the Amostante. Victory of the Christians. Rinaldo returns to Montalbano. Gano is forgiven and returns to Paris. Prester John sends two cardinals to Rinaldo.

261   64

The arrival of Prester John's messengers in Paris. Gano derides Rinaldo's greatness. Sumptuous banquet held by Gano in Paris. Malagigi works his magic on all the food. A battle of Rinaldo against Gano and the Magonzesi. Rinaldo goes to Montalbano. Gano plots against Orlando. The latter wants to kill the traitor but Oliviero saves him. Orlando leaves Paris.

262   65

Orlando arrives in a monastery. He kills two giants. The third, Morgante, becomes a Christian. Morgante dons armor and equips himself with a clapper. The abbot narrates the valor and exploits of Milone. The abbot recognizes Orlando. Morgante and Orlando leave the convent. On the way they learn of the infamy of Gano and arrive at Manfredonio's camp where they engage in a great battle. Orlando kills Lionetto.

263   66

Meridiana challenges Manfredonio's knights. She engages in a great battle against Orlando and is defeated. An affray in Paris. Rinaldo fights against the Magonzesi and is banished. Rinaldo, Oliviero, and Dudone go in search of Orlando. The Saracen Brunoro takes the abbot Chiaramonte prisoner. Rinaldo arrives and kills Brunoro. The abbot recognizes Rinaldo. Rinaldo kills a dragon and rescues a lion.

264   67

Rinaldo and his companions go to Carrara and rescue Forisena from the serpent. The love affair between Oliviero and Forisena. Corbante's baptism. Meridiana challenges Orlando. Caradoro asks Corbante for help. Rinaldo and his companions go to defend Caradoro. Forisena's death. Rinaldo and his companions get lost in the forest and are protected by Malagigi.

265   68

Rinaldo and his companions reach Caradoro. Oliviero falls in love with Meridiana. Orlando challenges Rinaldo. Morgante takes Dudone prisoner. A great battle between Orlando and Rinaldo. Gano's treachery. Orlando and Rinaldo recognize each other. Morgante frees Dudone and throws Manfredonio into the river, then goes to set fire to the pavilions. The great battle that follows. Meridiana forgives Manfredonio and has him leave.

266[21]   69

The love between Oliviero and Meridiana. Erminione, instigated by Gano, besieges Paris and Montalbano with a great army. Astolfo goes to Montalbano, takes Leonfante prisoner, then liberates him. Mattafolle captures the paladins. Rinaldo, Orlando, and their companions take leave of Caradoro and depart. Morgante remains in Meridiana's custody.

[*Copione* 20 is missing.]

Copione 21: *Serate* 281–292 (pages unnumbered)
281   84

Malagigi with Antea and companions arrive at the enchantment of Creonta, but first Astolfo fights against Liombruno and is defeated. Creonta's death. Antea recovers her empire. Scuffle between Astolfo and Rinaldo. Astolfo leaves his companions, his horse is stolen; he kills the thieves and regains

---

21 The summary and Cast of Characters for *sera* 266 are at the end of this notebook, but the play itself would have been in the missing *Copione* 20.

his horse. Orlando goes in search of Astolfo. The valor of Astolfo in Carniglia. Orlando kills Chiaristante. Calavrione, the Veglio's brother, goes to besiege Paris. Grifonetto goes to besiege Montalbano.

282 85

Rinaldo, guided by Filiberta, arrives in Carniglia and challenges the supposed Galliano. A great battle between Orlando and Rinaldo. Peace between the two cousins. Dudone arrives in Carniglia and narrates the siege of Paris. Rinaldo and his companions arrive in Villafranca. Rinaldo kills a buffoon and a lion and undertakes a great battle against Diliante. Guidone in a village hears about Satuante's infamy and promises to liberate the village.

283 86

Gano's treachery. Aldinghieri kills Diliante. Guidone goes to kill Satuante. He fights against a giant and is caught in a spell. Orlando arrives in Paris with the army. Gano flees from his companions and goes to Grifonetto's camp. Aldinghieri goes to find Girardo. Gano kills Aldinghieri in an ambush. Girardo arrives and embraces his son and hurls himself at the Magonzesi. Gano flees.

284 87

Girardo reaches Paris and compels Carlo to avenge Aldinghieri. Peace between Carlo and Calavrione. Carlo and Calavrione besiege Pontieri. Rinaldo fights against Arpalista, whom he sends to Orlando missing an arm. Gano is defeated by Arpalista. Challenge between Arpalista and Calavrione. The death of both. Gano is forgiven and goes to find Rinaldo. Rinaldo departs from Saliscaglia.

285 88

Rinaldo finds Gano and forgives him, then fights against the strong Fuligatto who, after Spinaldo's death, becomes a Christian. Rinaldo and Fuligatto destroy Dulivante's men. Antea's council. She gathers troops to avenge her father. Marsilio refuses to join Antea because of Galerana's death. Antea continues toward France with the two giants Gattabriga and Fallabacchio.

286 89

Antea besieges Paris. A great challenge between Orlando and Antea. The two giants attack Paris. Malagigi uses deceit to cause Gattabriga and

Fallabacchio to burn to death. A great battle between Christians and pagans. Antea leaves the battle to defend her people. Peace between Antea and Carlo. Antea arrives at the inn where Guidone happens to be staying. She hears about the wizard who steals women. She dresses in feminine clothing and goes to kill the wizard.

287 90

Antea kills Satuante. She fights against a giant and frees Guidone. A battle between Fuligatto and Guidone. Fuligatto's death. Guidone defeats Rinaldo's brothers in a battle. A great battle between Rinaldo and Guidone and their recognition of each other. Rinaldo arrives in Paris. Guidone fights the Magonzesi and the paladins. Orlando and Rinaldo make him leave. Gano's plot. Rinaldo's battle against the Magonzesi. A horse race is being organized in Paris and Gano advises that Rinaldo should not be admitted. Malagigi prepares a hoax.

288 91

Rinaldo and Malagigi in disguise and Baiardo pretending to be lame are allowed to pass by Ugiero, and they arrive in Paris where the supposedly lame horse is entered into the race. A Magonzese discovers Rinaldo's secret and is killed. The horse race. Baiardo wins. Rinaldo takes the prize and flees. Carlo pursues him. Malagigi's enchantment. Rinaldo's banishment. A jester presents a portrait to Carlo, who falls in love and thinks about how he can attain Bellisarta.

289 92

Carlo crazy about Bellisarta. Orlando discovers the secret. Orlando and Rinaldo disguised as merchants steal the damsel from King Ussanoro of Napel. Rinaldo kills Ussanoro. Rinaldo, infatuated with Bellisarta, tries to attain her. A fierce battle between Rinaldo and Orlando. Rinaldo stuns Orlando and carries off the lady. The count's desperation over Rinaldo's action.

290 93

The death of Bellisarta. Carlo goes to Montalbano. He finds the woman dead and reproaches Rinaldo. Rinaldo banishes Carlo from Montalbano. Orlando refuses to besiege Montalbano. Carlo consults Gano about punishing

Rinaldo. The latter goes to Paris and is treacherously arrested and sentenced to the gallows. Malagigi's deceptions. The liberation of Rinaldo.

291 94

Rinaldo leads his troops to attack Paris and fight against the Magonzesi, then starts a fire. The paladins assault Rinaldo. A great battle between Orlando and Rinaldo. The latter sees the danger and returns to Montalbano. Orlando besieges Rinaldo but, persuaded of the treachery, makes peace with Rinaldo and reproaches Carlo. Return to Paris. Marsilio invites the Great Khan and others to go to Paris. Gano proposes to Carlo the boasting ritual of the paladins.

292 95

Astolfo and Orlando make offers to Rinaldo. The latter rejects them. Malagigi offers Rinaldo his assistance and hears of his approaching ruin. The boasting ritual of the paladins. Rinaldo scorns Carlo and everyone. His last banishment. Rinaldo takes up thievery, he steals from the Spaniards and two cardinals. Carlo prepares to lay siege to Montalbano. Rinaldo honors the Great Khan, a *scena in fondo* (deep stage).

Copione 22: *Serate* 293–304 (pages unnumbered)

293 96

Carlo besieges Montalbano and invites Orlando to challenge Rinaldo. The count relinquishes all assumed offices and challenges Rinaldo. A terrible battle between the two cousins. Rinaldo stuns Orlando and is attacked by the paladins. Orlando and Rinaldo challenge each other at Merlin's Rock. The last battle between Orlando and Rinaldo and their reconciliation. Rinaldo welcomes the paladins into Montalbano.

294 97

Malagigi leads Carlo inside Montalbano but, scorned by Carlo, burns his craft and abandons the castle to lead a solitary life. The wizard Solerte, a friend of Gano, partially destroys Montalbano but dies in the process. Astolfo threatens Gano and leaves for London. Rinaldo's painful separation from his troops. Rinaldo, overcome by hunger, drains blood from Baiardo as sustenance.

295   98

Rinaldo's abject poverty. He intends to kill Baiardo but, prevented by his affection, falls asleep and dreams of Malagigi who indicates a subterranean passage to him. Rinaldo encounters a herdsman who helps him. Rinaldo escapes with his family. The herdsman deceives Carlo and Gano. Don Trico intends to burn Carlo's tents, encounters the herdsman, and hears about Rinaldo's escape. Carlo orders the rest of the castle destroyed. Rinaldo takes refuge in Tremogna. Gano's desperation.

296   99

Rinaldo welcomes Don Trico and part of the army in Tremogna. The death of Amone. Astolfo leaves London with the army to go to Montalbano. Guidone leaves for Montalbano with the Bulgarian army. Rinaldo attacks Carlo's camp and takes Gualtiere prisoner and plans to hang him. Orlando saves him. Sorganello leaves to help Rinaldo. Rinaldo submits to Carlo. Gano strips him of his arms on stage. Rinaldo departs as a pilgrim, leaving his family as hostages.

297   100

Orlando, remorseful for not having defended Rinaldo, takes his sword and goes to join him. An emotional reunion between the two cousins. Carlo has Baiardo thrown into the river, but the animal escapes. Rinaldo follows Baiardo and finds Malagigi, to whom he narrates his misfortune. Astolfo arrives in Montalbano with his army and finds it destroyed. The arrival of Guidone with his army and that of Sorganello, the three united armies besiege Paris. Guidone challenges the paladins and takes them prisoner. Carlo believes that Guidone is Rinaldo and wants to execute his family by hanging. Orlando shows Carlo the danger and goes to fight Guidone.

298   101

A great battle between Orlando and Guidone, each demonstrating his valor. Nightfall halts the combat. Astolfo leaves the field, taking the paladins to London. Astolfo's mother sends a warning to Orlando. The latter goes to London where Astolfo locks him in prison. Rinaldo follows the road toward Damascus. Astolfo leaves London to besiege Paris again.

299   102

Astolfo is challenged and defeated by Aresteno. The latter offers Ramondo, Adriano's son, to Astolfo. Guidone is treacherously taken prisoner by Sormano. Ramondo besieges Arborea together with Astolfo. Ramondo kills Sormano. Guidone's liberation. Astolfo besieges Paris. The queen frees the paladins. Carlo and Gano attack Astolfo's camp. Guidone takes Carlo prisoner. Ramondo takes Gano prisoner. Guidone undertakes a great battle.

300   103

Gano is sentenced to death but is freed by Orlando just before he is hanged. Ramondo goes in search of Rinaldo and, together with Don Trico, finds Rinaldo Aquilotto against whom he wages a great battle. Peace between the two, who united go in search of Rinaldo. Carlo sends Orlando and others to Damascus. Rinaldo kills a beggar and is arrested. The Khan recognizes Rinaldo.

301   104

The first day of a joust in Damascus. The valor of Rinaldo Aquilotto, who wins the first day. The second day of the joust. The arrival of Orlando and his companions in Damascus. Costantino Selvaggio demonstrates his valor. Rinaldo punches Astolfo, takes up arms, defeats Costantino, Oliviero, and others, and wins the second day. The Khan reveals Rinaldo's enemies. Costantino demonstrates his honesty and earns Rinaldo's esteem.

302   105

Rinaldo wins the third day of the joust. Costantino marries the daughter of the Great Khan. Rinaldo has Orlando make a tribute payment. The emperor of Trebisonda besieges Cascai. Trionfalante asks the Great Khan for help. Rinaldo comes to Trionfalante's defense, encounters the army of Sorganello, and, not recognizing him, fights against him. Rinaldo attacks the army of Trebisonda with the assistance of Trionfalante. The great battle that follows, suspended because of nightfall.

303   106

Rinaldo attacks the army of Trebisonda with the help of Trionfalante. Imprisonment of the emperor of Trebisonda who, in order not to be in the hands of the enemy, kills himself. Rinaldo is crowned emperor.

Arming of the pagans to fight Rinaldo. The latter asks Carlo for help. A council in Paris where Gano's will prevails. Dudone expresses outrage and truthfulness. He abandons Carlo to go to Rinaldo's defense.

304 *107*

Rinaldo sends Costantino as the vanguard. He encounters Balano's army and is destroyed. Dudone goes to Bulgaria. Balano encounters the army of Rinaldo. The latter, invited to a meeting, does not reach an agreement. Rinaldo attacks Balano's camp and finds himself in danger. The arrival of Ramondo, Aquilotto, and Don Trico. The defeat and escape of Balano. Rinaldo returns to Trebisonda. Ramondo is sent to Rome.

305[22] *108*

Ramondo is propelled to Constantinople by a tempest at sea. Ottavio offers his assistance and that of his son Ansuigi, then they go to Rome. The pope sends Ramondo to Paris. Gano persuades Carlo to refuse help to Rinaldo and sends Angolino to stop Ottavio's progress. Ansuigi kills Angolino. A plot in Paris. Astolfo frees Rinaldo's brothers who, attacked by the Magonzesi, engage in a great battle and flee to Trebisonda. Carlo wants to destroy London. Orlando's forthright reply.

Copione 23: *Serate* 319–330 (pages unnumbered)

319[23] *12[2]*

Orlando, lost, encounters Organtino and from [...] they engage in a great battle. They recognize each other. He arrives at the Taran castle and fights against Rucometteno's army. Taken prisoner, he is freed by Balanetto. Rinaldo comes to the aid of Organtino. Destruction of the pagan camp. Gano returns to Paris. Orlando in Brava. Fargotto is sent as an ambassador to Carlo in order to recover Rinaldo's family.

320 *123*

Twenty-two kings leave for Paris to obtain Clarice. They land in Marseille, then arrive in Brava. Dudone is slapped by Orlando and abandons his companions. The twenty-two kings, in the company of Orlando, arrive

---

22 The summary of *sera* 305 is on the last page of *Copione* 22.
23 *Serate* 305–318 are missing.

in Paris. Carlo refuses to free Clarice. The sovereigns visit the prison. The death of Clarice and a great funeral with a grandiose *scena in fondo* [deep stage] never done before in Marionette theaters. Come and you will see for yourselves.

321 124

Balano and the kings reach Trebisonda. Rinaldo leaves his crown and arms to Ramondo, first breaking his sword, and then departs as a pilgrim. Gano sends men to kill Rinaldo. Guidone, attacked by the Magonzesi, is in danger. Perinda arrives and demonstrates her valor. The destruction of the Magonzesi. Perinda and Guidone fall in love and together go to Babylon. Perinda encounters Antea and fights against her, to her great peril. Guidone fights Antea. Perinda resumes the battle and kills Antea. Ricciardetto and Riccardo set out in search of Rinaldo.

[Following the Cast of Characters]
N.B. This is a beautiful evening, please study it well and it will have a great effect, just as the fire in the middle of the room has a great effect because nobody does it, so that even though it may seem that they don't say anything, the public is moved by it. I ask the young lady to devote her attention to Antea and Perinda. Anger, laughter, and calm give a beautiful color and also create a portrait; my congratulations, if it succeeds, and that of the public, accept my sincerity.

322 125

Guidone and Perinda, attacked by animals, separate. Perinda arrives in Persia, then goes in search of Guidone. She arrives at the Cursed Castle, kills two giants, and is treacherously captured. Orobante besieges Santarco to avenge Antea. A pilgrim steals the hilt of Rinaldo's sword. Ricciardo and Ricciardetto are attacked by four giants in a castle. Ricciardo's death. Ricciardetto's captivity. Rinaldo arrives in Santarco. He takes up arms and defeats the camp by killing Orobante.

323 126

A lion kills the false pilgrim. The Magonzesi believe it is Rinaldo and bring him to Paris. Balano sends for the body believed to be that of Rinaldo. The paladins go to Trebisonda. Balano and the kings besiege Paris. Fargotto, elected ambassador, threatens Carlo and the paladins. Gano's answer and Fargotto's counter-answer. Astolfo is beaten with a club by mistake. Orlando goes to Balano's camp. Gano attacks and is arrested by Orlando. Carlo frees Rinaldo's sons because of the people's threats. He goes to the camp and makes peace with Balano. Decision to have Montalbano rebuilt. Gano is released.

N.B. A bit of succinctness in speaking because the scenes are necessarily numerous, to shorten later the monotonous scenes regarding Montalbano.

324   127

The paladins visit the new Montalbano and return to Paris. Astolfo reproaches Orlando. Gano, elected plenipotentiary, arrives in Zaragoza. Courtesies used by the Spaniards. The latter invite Gano under the carob tree. Gano explains to the Spaniards how to kill the paladins. Threatened by a storm, he escapes to the palace together with the Spaniards. Gano returns to Paris where on behalf of the Spaniards he invites the paladins to Roncevaux.

325   128

The paladins get ready to leave for Roncevaux. Rinaldo, as a pilgrim, sees the military preparations of the pagans, then retreats to a cave. Carlo leaves Paris. Rinaldo, warned, leaves the cave, finds Astarotte and receives arms and Baiardo and together they go to free Ricciardetto. The paladins enter the valley. Oliviero discovers the betrayal. Orlando resolves to die with all the paladins. Astolfo steps forward first and demonstrates his valor, but is treacherously killed by Grandonio.

326   129 (cfr. 326 in **Roncisvalle***)*

The battle of Roncevaux continues. Rinaldo arrives at the castle and frees Ricciardetto by killing the giants, and together they head for the valley. Ugiero opens the way with his sword and flees from the valley, all the while following the battle. Agolaccio, Sansonetto, Berlinghieri, and others die. The grief of Orlando who, wanting to avenge everyone, hurls himself against the pagans in a fierce combat. Baldovino enters the fray. The pagans flee from him. Orlando kills Falserone.[24]

---

24 The original name is crossed out and replaced by Falserone in different handwriting. In the play, Orlando kills Falserone in Act 1, scene 6.

327   130 (cfr. 327 in **Roncisvalle**)

The great battle in Roncevaux continues. Rinaldo kills a knight who wants Baiardo. Orlando hears about the betrayal from Buiaforte. Baldovino encounters Orlando, who calls him a traitor. Baldovino tears off his insignia and rushes into battle against the pagans. Oliviero, wounded by treachery, becomes blind. Orlando leads him into the heart of the conflict. The death of Oliviero. Orlando blows his horn for the first time. The death of Baldovino. Orlando's grief. The death of Grandonio.

328   131 (cfr. 328 in **Roncisvalle**)

Orlando blows his horn for the second time. The death of Grifone, Aquilante, and others. Orlando blows his horn for the third time and begins to bleed. Carlo has Gano arrested and then heads to the valley. The arrival of Rinaldo and Ricciardetto. The death of Buiaforte, cut in two by Rinaldo. The defeat of all the pagans. Marsilio's escape. Orlando led out of danger, cuts a rock to test Durlindana, then dies comforted by an Angel.

N.B. I wanted to write in Rinaldo who embraces his children, but it would be better to have them die first as the book says.

329   132

Carlo, headed for the valley, encounters Terigi. The latter recounts the betrayal and dies. Carlo enters the valley where he sees the dead paladins and he curses the place. He finds Orlando, Rinaldo, and his companions. A great miracle, Orlando offers Durlindana to Carlo. Attack on Zaragoza. Carlo kills Balugante. Marsilio is captured. Rinaldo finds Bianciardino inside a sack. Turpino hangs Marsilio and Bianciardino. Carlo has Gano apprehended and heads to Paris. The Sultan besieges Jerusalem and captures it, Ansuigi escapes.

330   133

Gano is taken to Paris and handed over to the people, then quartered by four horses. Rinaldo departs as a pilgrim. Ricciardetto, crowned emperor, marries Balano's daughter. Alda becomes a nun. The death of Turpino and Namo. Guidone is elected head paladin. Rinaldo withdraws to the convent of Saint Omer. Plot by the masons. The death of Rinaldo and his miracle.

End of the Paladins [following the conclusion of the play]

Appendix 6

SELECT CHARACTERS FROM THE PALADINS OF FRANCE CYCLE

Agolante—North African king who invaded Calabria in the *Aspramonte*, grandfather of both Agramante (via his son Troiano) and Rugiero/Ruggiero (via his daughter Galaciella/Galaziella)

Agramante—King of Biserta (Tunisia); commands rulers of other African states

Agricane—khan of Tartary (Mongol Empire); father of Mandricardo

Alceste—hapless suitor of Lidia, princess of Lydia (western Asia Minor)

Alcina—enchantress; Boiardo locates her north of the Caspian Sea, Ariosto on an East Asian island

Alda—Orlando's wife

Almonte—North African warrior; Agolante's son and Galaziella's brother

Amone—Frankish paladin; father of Ranaldo/Rinaldo, Bradamante, and Ricciardetto

Angelica—daughter of Galafrone, king of Cathay; sister of Argalia

Anselmo di Altaripa—Pinabello's father

Aquilante—son of Oliviero, twin brother of Grifone, raised in Constantinople

Argalia—son of Galafrone, king of Cathay; brother of Angelica

Astolfo—son of Ottone, king of England; cousin of Orlando and Ranaldo/Rinaldo

Atalante/Atlante—North African wizard and guardian of Rugiero/Ruggiero

Baiardo—horse belonging to Ranaldo/Rinaldo, coveted by Gradasso

Balugante/Bolugante—brother of Marsilio, king of Spain, and of Galerana, empress of the Franks

Beltramo—treacherous brother of Rugiero/Ruggiero II (di Risa, i.e., Reggio Calabria)

Bradamante—Frankish paladin; beloved of Rugiero/Ruggiero and sister of Ranaldo/Rinaldo

Brandimarte—beloved of Fiordelisa/Fiordiligi; born in the Far Away Islands (northern Russia); kidnapped and raised at Castle Wild, near Samarkand, Uzbekistan

Branzardo di Bugia—African king

Brunello—North African thief; originally serves the king of Fez, becomes the king of Tingitana

Carlo/Carlomagno—emperor of the Franks; married to Galerana

Clarice—wife of Ranaldo/Rinaldo

Doralice—princess of Granada, beloved of Rodamonte/Rodomonte; becomes Mandricardo's lover

Dragontina/Drogantina—enchantress from Media (northern Iran)

Falerina—enchantress in charge of the enchanted Garden of Orgagna (possibly in Turkmenistan)

Falsirone—brother of Marsilio, Balugante/Bolugante, and Galerana

Feraguto/Ferraù—nephew of Saracen King Marsilio of Spain

Fiordelisa/Fiordeligi—beloved of Brandimarte; from the Syrian city of Laodicea (Latakia); kidnapped and raised at Castle Wild, near Samarkand, Uzbekistan

Fiordespina/Fiordispina—Spanish Saracen princess, King Marsilio's daughter

Gabrina—an evil elderly woman who guards Isabella and then betrays Zerbino

Galaciella/Galiziella—daughter of an Amazon warrior and the African king Agolante; wife of Ruggiero II; mother of Rugiero/Ruggiero and Marfisa

Galafrone—king of Cathay; father of Angelica and Argalia

Galerana—king Marsilio's sister, Carlomagno's wife

Gano di Maganza/Magonza—Carlomagno's treacherous adviser; Orlando's stepfather

Garamanta, king of—African king and astrologer

Gradasso—king of Sericana (southeast Asia)

Grandonio—king of Morocco

Grifone—son of Oliviero, twin brother of Aquilante, raised in Spain

Grifone di Magonza—treacherously wounds Rugiero/Ruggiero during the African invasion of France

Ippalca—Bradamante's servant sent to deliver Frontino to Ruggiero

Isabella—princess of Galicia, beloved of the Scottish prince Zerbino

Lidia—princess of Lydia (ancient kingdom in Anatolia); currently a shade Astolfo encounters in hell

Logistilla—fairy; virtuous stepsister of the evil fairies Morgana and Alcina

Malabuferso—African king, sent to search for Rugiero/Ruggiero

Malagise/Malagigi—Carolingian counterpart to the Arthurian wizard Merlin; cousin of Ranaldo/Rinaldo

Mandricardo—son and heir of Agricane di Tartaria
Marfisa—warrior queen from the East; designated as Ruggiero's twin sister by Niccolò degli Agostini in a continuation of the *Orlando Innamorato*
Marsilio—king of Spain
Medoro—North African foot soldier in Agramante's army, marries Angelica
Morgana—enchantress, Alcina's sister
Nucalone—demon serving the Christian necromancer Malagise/Malagigi
Oliviero—Frankish knight; Orlando's friend and brother-in-law
Origille/Origilla—devious woman who beguiles Orlando on his way to the garden of Orgagna
Orlando—Carlomagno's nephew, in the Italian literary tradition born in Sutri (north of Rome)
Pinabello—son of Anselmo of Altaripa
Ranaldo/Rinaldo—Frankish knight from Montalbano (Montauban, Provence)
Ricciardetto—Bradamante's brother (identical twin according to Ariosto)
Rodamonte/Rodomonte—king of Sarza (Algeria)
Rugiero/Ruggiero—son of Rugiero/Ruggiero II (of Reggio) and Galaciella/Galaziella, raised in the Atlas Mountains (northern Africa)
Rugiero/Ruggiero II (of Reggio)—knight from Reggio Calabria, marries Galaciella/Galaziella
Sacripante—King of Circassia (in the Caucasus)
Saint John—Astolfo's guide during journey to the moon; inhabits the Earthly Paradise
Sansonetto—neophyte Christian, governor of Jerusalem
Senapo—Christian ruler of Ethiopia, also called Nubia; the legendary Prester John
Serpentino della Stella—son of Balugante/Bolugante
Sobrino/Subrino—North African king and advisor to Agramante
Torindo—Turkish king; Marfisa's ally during the war at Albraca
Troiano—King Agramante's father; King Agolante's son
Turpino—archbishop and warrior in Carlomagno's army
Zerbino—Scottish prince, beloved of the Galician princess Isabella

Appendix 7

MANTEO FAMILY GENEALOGY

Agrippino Manteo (April 1, 1884–August 1, 1947) and his wife, Caterina Golino (June 14, 1884–May 17, 1963), had five children:

Ida, also called Agata, Adelaida, Agatina, Aida (1905–1994)
Mike, also called Miguel, Michele, Michael (1910–1989)
Dominic, also called Domingo, Domenic, Dom, Leo (1911–1985)
Ritz, also called Agrippino II and Pino (1916–1956)
Johnny, also called Giovanni (1921–1939)

Of Agrippino and Caterina's numerous descendants, those mentioned in the context of the family's theatrical activities (Chapter 1) are as follows:

Susie Bruno (b. 1939), daughter of Ida Manteo and Angelo Grillo, wife of Joe Bruno
Joanne Lauria (b. 1942), daughter of Ida Manteo and Angelo Grillo, wife of Vincent Lauria
Pino (Agrippino) Manteo (1932–2018), son of Mike and Mary Manteo
Dolores Amoriello (1935–2019), daughter of Dominic Manteo and Frances Vidal, wife of Rick Amoriello

WORKS CITED

Adler, Lois. "The Manteo Family's Sicilian Puppets." *TDR: The Drama Review* 20.2, American Theatre Issue (June 1976): 25–30. http://www.jstor.org/stable/1145053.
Allaire, Gloria. *Andrea da Barberino and the Language of Chivalry*. Gainesville: University Press of Florida, 1997.
Amico, Donata. *"Teatrar narrando": L'Opera dei pupi catanese. Le "serate" di Raffaele Trombetta (1882–1928)*. Quaderni dell'Associazione Peppino Sarina, "Le tesi del Premio Dottor Burattino" 7. Bergamo: Junior, 2008.
Andrea da Barberino. *I reali di Francia*. Volume 1: *Richerche intorno ai* Reali di Francia *per Pio Rajna seguito dal libro delle storie di* Fioravante *e dal* Cantare di Bovo d'Anona. Volume 2: *I reali di Francia*. Critical edition edited by Giuseppe Vandelli. 2 vols. Bologna: G. Romagnoli, 1872–1900. Collezione di opere inedite o rare dei primi tre secoli della lingua. https://catalog.hathitrust.org/Record/000114640.
———. *The Royal House of France*. Trans. Max Wickert. https://www.yumpu.com/en/document/read/16187489/the-royal-house-of-france-outriders-poetry-project/200
Ariosto, Ludovico. *Cinque Canti: Five Cantos*. Translated by Alexander Sheers and David Quint. Berkeley: University of California Press, 1996.
———. *Orlando furioso*. Edited by Lanfranco Caretti. c1966. 2 vols. Turin: Einaudi, 1992.
———. *Orlando furioso*. Translated by Barbara Reynolds. 2 vols. London: Penguin Books, 1973.
Baird, Bil. "Orlando Furioso: The Flower of Chivalry." In *The Art of the Puppet*. New York: Macmillan, 1965. 118–29.
Bell, John. *Strings, Hands, Shadows: A Modern Puppet History*. Detroit: The Detroit Institute of Art, 2000.
Boiardo, Matteo Maria. *Historia imperiale attribuita a Ricobaldo tradotta da Matteo Maria Boiardo*. Edited by Andrea Rizzi and Antonia Tissoni Benvenuti. Novara (Italy): Interlinea, 2019.
———. *Orlando Innamorato*. Translated by Charles S. Ross. West Lafayette, IN: Parlor Press, 2004.
———. *"Orlando Innamorato" di Bojardo – "Orlando furioso" di Ariosto, with an essay on the romantic narrative poetry of the Italians*, Memoirs and Notes by A. Panizzi. 9 vols. London, William Pickering, 1830–1834. https://catalog.hathitrust.org/Record/001226767.
———. *Orlando Innamorato di Matteo M. Bojardo rifatto da Francesco Berni*. 4 vols. Società tipografica de' Classici Italiani, 1806. https://catalog.hathitrust.org/Record/009707368.
———. *Orlando Innamorato*. Edited by Riccardo Bruscagli. Turin: Einaudi, 1995. 2 vols.
Caparrotti, Laura. "La dinastia dei pupari d'America." *Oggi*. March 17, 1997. 27.

Carocci, Anna. "Metamorfosi del tema dell'esilio: tradizione, rivoluzione e continuità dai romanzi cavallereschi all'opera dei pupi." *World Epics in Puppet Theater*. Edited by Jo Ann Cavallo. *AOQU* 4.2 (2023), forthcoming.

———. *Il poema che cammina: La letteratura cavalleresca nell'opera dei pupi*, Palermo: Edizioni Museo Pasqualino, 2019.

Cavallo, Jo Ann. "Boiardo and Ariosto in Contemporary Sicilian Puppet Theater and the Tuscan-Emilian Epic *Maggio*." *Modern Language Notes* 133.1 (2018): 48–63.

———. "Boiardo's Eastern Protagonists in Giusto Lodico's *Storia dei paladini di Francia*." In *Boiardo sconfinato: citazioni epiche, liriche e storiche dalle fonti classiche agli adattamenti noveceteschi*, edited by Jo Ann Cavallo and Corrado Confalonieri. *Parole rubate* 23.1 (June 2021): 135–64.

———. *Boiardo's "Orlando Innamorato": An Ethics of Desire*. Rutherford, NJ: Fairleigh Dickinson Press; London: Associated University Presses, 1993.

———. "Encountering Saracens in Italian Romance Epic and Its Folk Performance Traditions." In *Teaching Medieval and Early-Modern Cross Cultural Encounters across Disciplines and Periods*, edited by Lynn Shutters and Karina Attar. New York: Palgrave Macmillan. 2014. 159–78.

———. "The Ideological Battle of Roncevaux: The Critique of Political Power from Pulci's *Morgante* to Sicilian Puppet Theatre Today." In *Luigi Pulci in Renaissance Florence and Beyond*. Eds. James K. Coleman and Andrea Moudarres. Turnhout: Brepols, 2017. 209–32.

———. "Malaguerra: The Anti-State Super-Hero of Sicilian Puppet Theater." *AOQU (Achilles Orlando Quixote Ulysses). Rivista di epica* 1 (July 2020): 259–94.

———. *The Romance Epics of Boiardo, Ariosto, and Tasso: From Public Duty to Private Pleasure*. Toronto: University of Toronto Press, 2004.

———. "Six Characters in Search of a Puppeteer: Sicilian *Opera dei pupi*." In *Bodies of Enchantment: Puppets from Asia, Africa, Europe and the Americas*. Eds. Jill Baird and Nicola Levell. Museum of Anthropology at the University of British Columbia, Vancouver. 124–41.

———. "Where Have All the Brave Knights Gone? Sicilian Puppet Theater and the Tuscan-Emilian Epic *Maggio*." *Italian Culture* 19.2 (2001): 31–55.

———. *The World beyond Europe in the Romance Epics of Boiardo and Ariosto*. Toronto: University of Toronto Press, 2013.

Clinton, Audrey. "Old World Puppets Find New Friends." *Newsday (Suffolk Edition)*. February 18, 1963. 42. https://www.newspapers.com/image/717496187. Accessed February 7, 2022.

Coad, Luman. "Carter Family Marionettes. Celebrating Four Decades." *The Puppetry Journal* 66.1 (fall 2014): 2–3.

Colford, Paul D. "The Treasure of Papa Manteo." *Newsday*. August 24, 1983. 120. https://www.newspapers.com/image/703826533. Accessed February 7, 2022.

Cremante, Simona. "Entra Angelica (*Orlando innamorato*, Ii)." *Studi italiani* 1.2 (1995): 5–17.

Crimi, Giuseppe. "Dalle *Memorie* di Giuseppe Crimi scritte intorno al 1924." In Li Gotti, *Il teatro dei pupi*. 161–67.

Crooks, Salle. "Benefit Set for Dying Sicilian Art." *Star-Gazette (Elmira, New York)*. June 15, 1976. 4. https://www.newspapers.com/image/277813948. Accessed February 7, 2022.

Cuticchio, Mimmo. *Pina Patti Cuticchio. Una vita con l'Opera dei Pupi*. Ed. Mimmo Cuticchio. Palermo: Associazione "Figli d'Arte Cuticchio," 2000.

WORKS CITED

De Nonno, Tony. *It's One Family, Knock on Wood*. Brooklyn, NY: De Nonno Productions, Incorporated, 1982.

Engels, Mary. "Hart Hails Puppet Theater at Reception." *Daily News*. April 1, 1987. 123. www.newspapers.com/image/492021320. Accessed February 6, 2022.

———. "Manteo Puppets Come to Isle." *Daily News*. February 8, 1987. 697. https://www.newspapers.com/image/492079249. Accessed February 6, 2022.

———. "Museum's Annex Making History." *Daily News*. September 17, 1989. 462. www.newspapers.com/image/466954101. Accessed February 6, 2022.

Fay, Hope. "Your New York—And Mine." *The Brooklyn Daily Eagle*. September 15, 1933. 26. https://www.newspapers.com/image/59985751. Accessed on February 6, 2022.

"Festival Italiano." *Newsday (Suffolk Edition)*. September 24, 1977. 63. https://www.newspapers.com/image/711022011. Accessed February 13, 2022.

Fressola, Michael. "Opera dei pupi: Manteo Marionettes a Unique Experience." *Staten Island Advance*. April 19, 1987.

Gold, Donna Lauren. "Plucky Puppets Are the Stars in One Man's Family." *The Smithsonian*. August 1983. 68–73. http://www.personalhistory.org/wp-content/uploads/2017/03/smithsonian_manteo-puppeteers.pdf.

Greene, Mabel. "This Show a Family Affair." *The [New York] Sun*, February 14, 1933.

Harris, Neil. "L'avventura editoriale dell'*Orlando innamorato*." In *I libri di Orlando innamorato*, edited by Riccardo Bruscagli. Modena: Panini, 1987. 35–100.

———. *Bibliografia dell'*Orlando innamorato. 2 vols. Modena: Panini, 1988–91.

Jean, Elsie. "Members of Luna Park Party to See Papa Manteo's Marionettes." *Brooklyn Times Union*. May 29, 1933. 15. https://www.newspapers.com/image/576116171. Accessed February 6, 2022.

Kalcik, Susan. "Old Ways in the New World: Gifts to America." *Festival of American Folklife*. Smithsonian Institute, Washington, DC, 1976. 12–13.

———. "Orlando in America." *Puppetry at the Smithsonian*. Ed. Jeffrey LaRiche. Smithsonian Folklife Program. June 1980. 11–14.

Kelly, Lora. "Box Office Receipts? Pshaw! All for Art, but Sans Temperament." *The Cleveland Plain Dealer*. April 2, 1916.

Kinoshita, Sharon. *Medieval Boundaries: Rethinking Difference in Old French Literature*. Philadelphia: University of Pennsylvania Press, 2006.

Kline, Polly. "Bay Ridge Revives Old-Time Puppetry." *The Brooklyn Daily Eagle*. January 21, 1963. 4. https://www.newspapers.com/image/541761317. Accessed February 6, 2022.

"Knights of Old Find Modern Audience." *Newsday (Nassau Edition)*. March 14, 1969. 100. https://www.newspapers.com/image/713995782. Accessed February 7, 2022.

Kramer, Albert. "Sharing a heritage." *Daily News*. March 29, 1979. 659. https://www.newspapers.com/image/483871547. Accessed February 7, 2022.

Lagnado, Lucette. "From a Musty Workshop, a Renaissance of Puppet Wizardry." *Brooklyn Spectator*. April 11, 1979.

LaRosa, Paul. "Hey, Pinocchio! Meet Papa Manteo's Raimondo." *Daily News*. November 21, 1979. 363. https://www.newspapers.com/image/484751162. Accessed February 7, 2022.

Li Gotti, Ettore. *Il teatro dei pupi*. Florence: Sansoni, 1957.

Lodico, Giusto. *Storia dei paladini di Francia cominciando dal Re Pipino sino alla morte di Rinaldo*. 3 vols. Naples: Bideri, 1909.

———. *Storia dei paladini di Francia cominciando da Milone conte d'Anglante sino alla morte di Rinaldo.* 4 vols. Palermo: Gaudiano, 1858–1860.

———. *Storia dei paladini di Francia cominciando da Re Pipino fino alla morte di Rinaldo.* Edited by Felice Cammarata. Catania: Clio-Brancato, 1993 (vols. 1–9); and Brancato, 2000 (vols. 10–13). Reprint of 1970–71 edition, edited by Felice Cammarata, based on Giuseppe Leggio's extended edition first published in 1895–1896.

"Luna Fascinates Children." *Brooklyn Times Union.* June 7, 1933. 3. https://www.newspapers.com/image/577541611. Accessed February 7, 2022.

McCormick, John, with Alfonso Cipolla and Alessandro Napoli. *The Italian Puppet Theatre: A History.* Jefferson, NC: McFarland, 2011.

McMahon, Jane. "Puppet Art Thrives through Four Generations." *The Daily Item.* April 24, 1979. 17. https://www.newspapers.com/image/715657863. Accessed February 7, 2022.

McPharlin, Paul. *The Puppet Theater in America. A History 1524–1948.* c1949. Boston: Plays Inc., 1969.

———. *Puppetry 1939. An International Yearbook of Puppets and Marionettes.* Vol. 10. Detroit: Puppetry Imprints, 1939.

Maffi, Mario. *Gateway to the Promised Land Ethnic Cultures on New York's Lower East Side.* New York: New York University, 1995.

Majorana, Bernadette. *Pupi e attori. Ovvero l'opera dei pupi a Catania. Storia e documenti.* Biblioteca teatrale. Memorie di teatro/20. Bulzoni, 2008.

Mandell, Jonathan. "Soap Opera of the Dolls. A Legacy of Wood and Blood." *New York Newsday.* August 7, 1991. 49, 56–57, 73.

Manteo, Mike. *The Diary of the Manteo's.* Unpublished manuscript. Privately owned.

"Manteos Arrive on Broadway." *Daily News.* April 27, 1938. 53.

Milburn, Terry. "Pull New Hits with Old Puppets." *Daily News.* July 21, 1963. 138. https://www.newspapers.com/image/459819950. https://www.newspapers.com/image/459819950. Accessed February 6, 2022.

Morgan, Leslie Zarker. "From Roland to Orlando: French Charlemagne Tradition and Its Development in Italy." *Teaching the Italian Renaissance Romance Epic.* New York: Modern Language Association, 2018. 41–55.

Murrin, Michael. *History and Warfare in Renaissance Epic.* Chicago: University of Chicago Press, 1994.

Napoli, Alessandro, ed. *Immaginare Ariosto in Sicilia: Orlando e Peppininu, Astolfo e Rodomonte.* Gli archivi di Morgana 12. Palermo: Associazione per la conservazione delle tradizioni popolari, 2009.

———. "The Fratelli Napoli Puppet Company: The Catanian Opira from 1921 Until Today." In John McCormick, *The Italian Puppet Theater: A History.* 232–48.

———. *Il racconto e i colori: "Storie" e "cartelli" dell'Opera dei Pupi catanese.* Palermo: Sellerio, 2002.

National Endowment for the Arts. NEA National Heritage Fellowships. "Mike Manteo." 1983. https://www.arts.gov/honors/heritage/mike-manteo.

Pasqualino, Antonio. *L'opera dei pupi.* Palermo: Sellerio, 1977.

———. "Il repertorio epico dell'opera dei pupi." *Uomo e cultura* 2, no. 3–4 (1969): 59–106.

———. *Rerum palatinorum fragmenta.* Ed. Alessandro Napoli. Palermo: Edizioni Museo Pasqualino, 2018.

Pollock, Arthur. "Agrippino, Ida, Mike, Leo, Pino and John Manteo, with Their Shining Puppets, Give a Show at the Nora Bayes." *Brooklyn Daily Eagle.* Thursday, April 28, 1938. 12. https://www.newspapers.com/image/52682864. Accessed February 6, 2022.

Ponte, Giovanni. *La personalità e l'opera del Boiardo*. Genoa: Tilgher, 1972.
Porta, Pietro. *Gente di Sarina. Il burattinaio Peppino Sarina e le comunità del Tortonese e dell'Oltrepò pavese nella prima metà del Novecento*. Diakronia, 1997.
———. "Riti e miti del Gano, dall'Opera dei pupi a Peppino Sarina." *L'epica cavalleresca e il teatro di animazione nell'Italia settentrionale*. Conference proceedings edited and published by the Associazione Peppino Sarina, 1999. 14–20.
Praloran, Marco. *"Maraviglioso artificio": Tecniche narrative e rappresentative nell'*Orlando innamorato. Pacini Fazzi, 1990.
Pulci, Luigi. *Morgante: The Epic Adventures of Orlando and His Giant Friend Morgante*. Translated by J. Tusiani, introduction and notes by Edoardo A. Lèbano, Bloomington: Indiana University Press, 1998.
"Puppets in Garage." *The Brooklyn Daily Eagle*. December 30, 1933. 6. https://www.newspapers.com/image/686042559. Accessed February 6, 2022.
Quint, David. "The Death of Brandimarte and the Ending of the *Orlando furioso*." *Annali d'Italianistica* 12 (1994): 75–85.
Ross, Charles S. "Boiardo and the Derangement of Epic." *Orlando Innamorato*, by Matteo Maria Boiardo, translated by Charles S. Ross. West Lafayette, IN: Parlor Press, 2004. l–lxiv.
Rousseau, Victor. "A Puppet Play which Lasts Two Months." *Harper's Weekly* 3 (October 1908): 15–16.
Rushdie, Salman. *The Enchantress of Florence: A Novel*. New York: Random House, 2008.
Schonberg, Harold C. "Marionette Mix of Fun and Tradition." *The New York Times*. January 20, 1984. C3.
Singer, Mark. "Opera dei Pupi." *The New Yorker*. September 17, 1979, 154–57, 164.
Staub, Nancy Lohman. "The Manteo Family Sicilian Marionette Theatre Finds a Home." *Puppetry Journal* 40.2 (1988): 3–4.
Sunderland, Luke. *"Bueve d'Hantone/Bovo d'Antona*: Exile, Translation and the History of the Chanson de geste." In *Rethinking Medieval Translation: Ethics, Politics, Theory*, edited by Emma Campbell and Robert Mills. Cambridge, UK: D. S. Brewer, 2012. 226–42.
Tasso, Torquato. *Rinaldo*. Translated by Max Wickert, New York: Italica Press, 2017.
Tolan, John V. *Saracens: Islam in the Medieval European Imagination*. New York: Columbia University Press, 2002.
Villoresi, Marco. "Le donne e gli amori nel romanzo cavalleresco del Quattrocento." *Filologia e critica* 23 (1998): 3–43.
———. *La letteratura cavalleresca: Dai cicli medievali all'Ariosto*. Rome: Carocci, 2000.
Walker, Danton. "Thoughts While Trying to Get a Sun Tan." *Daily News*. July 26, 1938. 28. https://www.newspapers.com/image/421870012. Accessed February 6, 2022.
Zampese, Cristina. *"Or si fa rosa or pallida la luna": La cultura classica nell'*Orlando innamorato. Lucca: Pacini Fazzi, 1994.

INDEX

Adam (character) 183, 187, 206, 208
Adler, Lois 3n3, 7n12, 8, 12, 17n23, 20, 24, 25, 26n29, 34, 40, 41
Agolaccio (character) 135
Agolante (character) xxii, 134, 139, 151, 156
Agostini, Niccolò degli 112
Agramante (character) xxii, 66, 131, 131n2, 132, 135–42, 139n3, 146, 147, 149–51, 153, 154, 160, 164, 180, 183, 186, 188, 190, 191, 193–96, 198–205, 208
Agricane di Tartaria (character) 29, 33n38, 35n44, 69, 106, 111–21, 112n3, 124–29, 128n12, 130n13, 131, 136, 143, 144, 147, 154, 172, 173, 200
Alardo (character) (see Salardo [character])
Alceste (character) 182
Alcina (character) 61
Alda (character) 65, 106, 121, 163
Alexander of Macedonia 139, 139n4, 156
Alfrera (character) 76, 93, 95
Almonte (character) 118, 134, 135
Alzirdo (character) 133, 166, 168
Amadigi (B. Tasso) 120n7
Amico, Donata xxin2, 50n15, 142n7
Amoriello, Dolores 29, 32, 34
Andrea da Barberino 58n27, 139n3
Angelica (character) xxiv, 16, 23, 32, 33, 34n40, 40, 61, 65, 66, 69, 70, 73, 74, 78–80, 82, 86, 87n11, 87n13, 88–92, 97, 106–13, 119–21, 124–28, 131, 136, 137, 143–45, 152, 161–65, 168, 169, 173, 175, 176, 189, 194, 195, 205–8
    arrival in Paris 73

Angelica innamorata (Brusantini) 61n32
Anselmo di Altaripa (character) 166, 167
Antaeus (character) 127
Antea (character) 51
Anthony, Vincent 34
Aquilante (character) 115, 132, 136–38, 145, 146
Archeloro (character) 112, 113, 121, 122n8
Archilao/Archiloro (character) 113, 122, 122n8, 124
Argalia (character) 69, 73, 78, 88, 91, 92, 98, 108
Ariosto, Ludovico xxiv, 29, 32, 39, 40, 41n3, 43, 47, 61n32, 65–69, 70n5, 140, 162, 163, 170, 173–76, 179, 185n5, 186, 187, 189, 193, 199, 200, 202, 203, 205–10, 212
Armida (character) 73
Aspramonte (anonymous poem and Andrea da Barberino prose version) 139
Aspremont (anonymous) 139, 159n4
Astolfo (character) 67, 69, 91–107, 109, 128, 161, 179–88, 190, 193, 197, 205
    Gradasso (character) and, duel between 91
    voyage to the moon 179
Atalante/Atlante (character) 135, 147, 160, 182, 188, 189

Baiardo (horse) 73–76, 80, 93n3, 94, 96, 98–100, 103, 105, 108, 112, 115, 120, 147, 150, 180, 181, 190, 191, 195, 205
Baird, Bil 8n13, 9n14, 13, 17, 26n29, 40, 41, 58
Balaheim/Balahiem/Balahim/Balaìm (character) 29, 30, 32

Balisarda (sword) 197
Balugante/Bolugante (character) 69, 74–77, 82, 83n9, 84–86, 95, 97, 99
battle of Lampedusa (see also battle of Lipadusa) 193, 194, 202, 204, 206
battle of Lipadusa (see also battle of Lampedusa) 200n4, 201
battle of Roncevaux xxi, 47, 51, 53, 66n1, 86, 104n10, 200n4
Bay Ridge Theater 29
Bell, John 17
Beltramo (character) 151
Berni, Francesco 71, 72, 83n9, 85n10, 87n13, 88n14, 89, 95n5, 100n9, 105, 109n13, 122n9, 123, 125, 127, 128, 139n5
Berta (character) 58, 59
Boiardo, Matteo Maria xxiv, 29, 35n44, 39, 65, 66n1, 66n3, 67, 68, 70n5, 71–73, 76n5, 81n6–7, 82n8, 85n10, 87n13, 88n14, 89, 90, 95n5, 97n6, 99, 100n7, 101–3, 105, 109–12, 117n5, 118n6, 121, 122n9, 123–27, 128n12, 129, 139n3, 140–43, 145–47, 153n3, 154, 156–60, 161n8, 163, 185, 193, 199, 205
Bradamante (character) 34, 47, 134, 147–55, 156n4, 157–59, 162–65, 170, 171, 172n2, 179, 180, 188–90, 197, 209–11
Bramadoro (see Brandimarte (character))
Bramimonde of Zaragoza (character) 204
Brandimarte (character) 69, 115, 128, 149, 151, 153, 159n7, 160–62, 161n8, 189, 190, 193, 194, 196–205
Branzardo di Bugia (character) 132, 133, 139
Brunello (character) 137
Bruno, Joe 26, 30
Bruno, Susie xxiii, 3n1, 5n7, 8, 14n18, 18n24, 22, 26, 30, 32n37, 34, 35, 50
Brusantini, Vincenzo 61n32
Bufano, Remo 17, 20

Canino, Nino 142n7
Capuana, Luigi 6
Carinda (character) 153, 195

Carlo/Carlomagno (character) 48, 50, 52, 53, 65, 67, 69, 70, 73, 75–77, 79–82, 84–91, 93–99, 100n8, 101–6, 114, 122, 131–35, 138, 146, 147, 149, 150, 152–57, 162, 163, 164, 180, 190, 194–96, 199, 201, 204, 209
Carocci, Anna 9n15, 22, 39n1–2, 49, 50n15–16, 65, 75n4, 88
Carter, Chris 34
Carter, Stephen 34
Catherine Street theater 36
Chanson de Roland (anonymous) 111n2, 200, 204
Charlemagne (character) (see also Carlo/Carlomagno [character]) xxi, xxii, 16, 21, 32, 35n44, 48n10, 58, 185
Cinque canti (Ariosto) 39, 61n32
Cladinoro (character) 149, 153, 195
Clarice (character) 51
Constantine (emperor and/or character) xxi, 42, 43, 58, 59
Copioni set 44, 45n8, 46
  Copione 12, 55, 68, 69
  Copione 4 (originally Libro 2) 57
  Copioni 5–7 45
  Copioni 9–13 45
Coppola, Francis Ford 28
Cremante, Simona 87n12
Crimi, Gaetano 4n4–5, 5n6–7, 6, 12, 49, 50n15, 88n14
Crimi, Giuseppe 3, 4, 4n5, 5n7–8, 7, 50
Crimi, Peppe (see Crimi, Giuseppe)
Crimi, Peppino (see Crimi, Giuseppe)
Croce, Marcella xxin2
Cuticchio, Mimmo 73

Daniforte (character) 149, 151, 152
Dante Alighieri 202
De Nonno, Tony 14n19, 35
Dolce, Lodovico 31n35
Doralice (character) 164–68, 171, 172
Dragontina/Drogantina (character) 93, 96, 97, 106–9, 121, 132, 161
Dudone (character) 138, 146, 189
Duke of Mantua (character) 207
Durlindana (sword) 73–76, 80, 98, 147, 152, 168, 172, 176, 191

INDEX 299

Elijah (character) 180, 183
Elmira Free Academy 28
Enchantress of Florence, The (Rushdie) 74
Engels, Mary 36
Enoch (character) 183n3, 185
entrelacement technique 194, 207
Este, Ercole I d' 112, 147
Ethnic Folk Arts Center 33
Eve (character) 187, 197, 208

Falerina (character) 132, 137, 138, 145, 146, 197
Falsirone (character) 95
Febosilla (character) 69
Feraguto/Ferraù (character) 69, 75, 80, 93, 95, 108, 162
Fiordelisa/Fiordiligi (character) 151, 152, 160, 161, 197, 198, 203
Fiordispina (character) 69
Frontino (horse) 164, 165, 170, 171

Gabrina (character) 164–68, 172, 173
Galaciella/Galiziella (character) 151, 156, 208, 209
Galafrone/Galafro (character) 73, 87, 88, 112, 114, 118, 122n8, 123, 124, 131, 143, 169, 175
Galerana (character) 102, 103
Game of Thrones (television series) 16
Gandellino (character) 112, 113, 120, 149
Gano di Maganza/Magonza (character) 51–53, 69, 76, 77, 82–86, 91, 95, 96, 98–101, 104–6
Garamanta, king of (character) 132, 133, 135, 136, 138–42
Gerusalemme Liberata (T. Tasso) 4, 73
Giglio, Sandrino 25
Gish, Dorothy 17
Gold, Donna Lauren 17, 21, 24, 41n3
Gradasso (character) 66, 69, 73–76, 80, 81n6, 87, 91–99, 100n9, 101–6, 108, 111, 114, 122, 128, 131, 147–49, 160, 162, 180, 181, 191, 193–96, 198–205
  Astolfo (character) and, duel between 91
  Astolfo's defeat of 91, 101, 105
  battle between Mandricardo and 149, 152, 153, 159, 174
Grandonio (character) 74, 75, 93, 95

Grasso, Angelo 6
Grasso, Giovanni (ca. 1792–1863) 6
Grasso, Giovanni (1873–1930) 6
Great Tournament in Damascus (puppet play) 29
Greene, Mabel 6, 10, 12, 13, 16, 17, 21, 27, 40
Grifone (character) 115, 132, 136–38, 145, 146
Grifone di Magonza (character) 149
Guidone (character) 51, 195

harpies 180–83, 185, 187
Hector of Troy (character) 69, 127, 151, 156
Henson, Jim 28, 33n38, 34
Hercules (character) 127
Here Come the Puppets (Henson) 33n38
Herodotus 139n4
hippogriff (winged horse) 179, 181–83, 185, 187
Homer xxiii
Hunter, Derick 26

Inferno (Dante) 202
Ippalca (character) 164–66, 170, 171
Isabella (character) 33, 164, 167, 172–74, 177, 180, 181, 189, 190
It's One Family, Knock on Wood (De Nonno) 14n19, 15, 35

John the Evangelist, St (character) 180, 183–85, 187, 188

Kalcik, Susan 12n17, 20, 28
Kinoshita, Sharon 87n11

Lauria, Joanne 25
Leggio, Giuseppe xxi, 22, 39, 39n2, 43, 48, 58, 70, 71, 100n8, 140, 141, 207
Leopard, The (Tomasi di Lampedusa) 74
Levin, Meredith 27n30
Libri set 45–47, 55–57
  Libro 1 (*Copione* 3) 43, 45, 48, 54, 58
  Libro 2 (*Copione* 4) 45, 55–57
  Libro 6 45, 46n9, 47, 55
  Libro 7 46, 55–57
Lidia (character) 180, 182, 185
Life of Genovefa, The (puppet play) 24
Livy 139n4

Lodico, Giusto xxi, xxiii, 31n35, 39n1–2,
    43, 65, 71, 75n4, 76n5, 81n6, 82,
    83n9, 85n10, 87, 88, 97n6, 100–2,
    105, 107, 108, 110n14, 120–23,
    127, 128, 140, 141, 144, 157, 158n6,
    159, 161n8, 174, 186–88, 200, 201,
    206n6
  Boiardo's and Ariosto's poetry in 67
  Renaissance poems refashioned by 39
Lord of the Rings (film series) 16

Macbeth (Shakespeare, performance of) 18
Maffi, Mario 27n30
Majorana, Bernadette xxin2, 4n4–5,
    5n6–7, 6n10–11
Malabuferso (character) 133, 135, 136
Malagise/Malagigi (character) 70, 87,
    97, 108, 109, 195, 196, 205, 206n6,
    207, 211
Malaguerra (character) 75n4
Mamalock/Mammaloc (character) 31–33
Mancuso, Enzo 41n4
Mandell, Jonathan 3n3, 12n17, 17, 21
Mandricardo (character) 29, 69, 131, 132,
    136, 143, 144, 147–50, 152, 153, 159,
    160, 164, 166, 168, 171, 172, 174–77
Manilardo (character) 166, 168
Manteo, Adelaida (see Manteo, Ida)
Manteo, Agata (see Manteo, Ida)
Manteo, Agatina (see Manteo, Ida)
Manteo, Agrippino xxii, xxiii, xxiv,
    3n1–2, 5n7, 8n13, 9n14, 17, 20,
    22, 41n3, 43, 44n6, 45, 47, 49n13,
    50–52, 57, 58, 70n5, 71, 72, 74, 81,
    84–86, 88, 90, 91, 101–7, 109, 112,
    120, 121, 123–29, 132, 142–46, 154,
    157n5, 158, 159, 161, 163, 171, 173,
    174, 176n3–4, 177, 183n3, 184n4,
    187–90, 194, 199, 201, 203–5, 207,
    208, 210, 211
  apprenticeship 4
  Boiardan and Ariostan material
    in scripts of 67
  comments in the margins of his
    scripts 50
  early life 3
  as an electrician 9
  immigration to Argentina 7
  legacy of 20
  in Little Italy 19
  mentors and models 6
  in New York City 8
  reading from script 14
  recourse to poetry from *Orlando
    Furioso* 68
  recourse to poetry from *Orlando
    Innamorato* 68
  scripts, composition of 49
Manteo, Agrippino II (see Manteo, Ritz)
Manteo, Aida (see Manteo, Ida)
Manteo, Caterina 7, 8, 10, 12, 13
Manteo, Dom (see Manteo, Dominic)
Manteo, Domenic (see Manteo, Dominic)
Manteo, Domingo (see Manteo, Dominic)
Manteo, Dominic 8, 10, 12, 22, 24, 26, 32,
    34, 56n23
Manteo, Giovanni (see Manteo, Johnny)
Manteo, Ida 3n3, 7, 12n17, 22, 24, 25, 34,
    35, 42
Manteo, Johnny 8, 10–12, 14n18, 15,
    20n25, 45, 54
Manteo, Leo (see Manteo, Dominic)
Manteo, Michael (Agrippino Manteo's son)
    (see Manteo, Mike)
Manteo, Michael J. (Agrippino Manteo's
    great-grandson) 3n2, 14n18
Manteo, Michele (Agrippino Manteo's
    father) 3
Manteo, Michele (Agrippino Manteo's
    son) (see Manteo, Mike)
Manteo, Miguel (see Manteo, Mike)
Manteo, Mike 5, 8, 9, 10n16, 12n17, 13,
    20n25, 21n26, 22–26, 28, 29, 33n38,
    35n44, 36n45, 37, 41–44, 47, 49n13,
    53, 55, 56, 56n25, 58, 58n28, 59,
    61, 73n1, 91n1, 111n1, 131n1, 147n1,
    163n1, 179n1, 193n1, 213
  scripts copied by 59
Manteo, Pino (Agrippino Manteo's
    grandson) 14n18, 24–26, 36, 61
Manteo, Pino (Agrippino Manteo's son)
    (see Manteo, Ritz)
Manteo, Ritz 7n12, 8, 10–12, 16, 22,
    56n23
Manteo, Signor 19
Manteo family, members of 8

Manteo Sicilian Marionette Theater 22, 36
Marfisa (character) 51, 112, 113, 122,
  122n9, 123, 135, 143, 144, 171, 182,
  188, 208
Marsilio (character) 53, 66, 75, 77, 81, 82,
  84, 85, 95, 97, 134, 151
Martasino (character) 149, 151, 155
Martoglio, Nino 6
McCormick, John xxin2
McPharlin, Paul 7n12, 17, 18n24, 20, 21, 37
Medoro (character) 69, 163, 168–70, 175,
  176, 195, 205
Metamorphoses (Ovid) 108
Monti, Augusto 31n34
Morgana (character) 68
Morgante (Pulci) 39, 51n18, 105n11, 200n4
Murrin, Michael 139n4

Napoli, Alessandro xxin2, 30, 30n33,
  48n11, 49, 49n12, 49n14, 50n16,
  51n17, 53n20, 70n6, 97n6, 104n10,
  120n7, 141n6, 184n4
Napoli, Marionettistica dei Fratelli
  xxiin3, 194n3
Nora Bayes Theatre 18
Nucalone (character) 70, 97, 109, 195, 207

Old Bay Ridge Theater 27
Oliviero (character) 53n20, 92, 93, 95, 98,
  99, 104, 134, 149, 150, 179–81, 189,
  190, 193, 196–200, 202–5
opera dei pupi xxi, xxii, 16, 19, 41, 49, 67,
  146, 213
Origille/Origilla (character) 132, 137,
  138, 145, 146
Orlando (character) xxii, 11, 16, 23, 29,
  31–34, 40, 52, 53, 65–69, 73, 74,
  76, 77, 80, 83, 86, 96, 99, 107–10,
  114–20, 122, 128–30, 132, 135–38,
  144–48, 152, 153, 159, 160, 162,
  163, 167–80, 183, 186, 188–90,
  193–96, 198–202, 205, 207, 210, 212
  Agricane and, duel between 111–15,
    121, 124–28
  Angelica and 176
  Astolfo and 193, 197
  Brandimarte and 160
  Bridge of Roses episode 146
  God's punishment of 185, 188, 189
  Gradasso challenging 199
  Isabella and 167
  madness of 163
  Mandricardo and 164, 174
  Rinaldo and 91, 98, 171
  Sobrino/Subrino and 202, 203
  victim of Drogantina 93, 106
  Zerbino liberated by 164, 172
Orlando Furioso (Ariosto) xxiv, 29, 32,
  33, 39, 40, 41n3, 43, 47, 65, 66n3,
  68–71, 71n7, 111n2, 112, 131n2,
  140, 157, 160, 162, 163, 170, 171,
  173, 174, 176, 177, 179, 183n3,
  185–91, 193, 194, 199, 200, 202–4,
  206–8, 210, 212
Orlando Innamorato (Boiardo) xxiv, 32, 39,
  65, 66n3, 67, 68, 70–72, 80–84, 86,
  87n13, 88, 90, 95n5, 98, 100, 101,
  104, 106, 108, 109, 111n2, 115n4,
  121, 126–29, 131, 131n2, 138,
  140–42, 145, 147, 154–56, 159–62,
  170, 173, 179, 191, 200, 206, 208
ottava rima poetry xxii, 49, 68, 70, 85,
  87–90, 105, 127, 139n3, 176
Ovid xxiii, 108

Paladini di Francia (scripts) 42
Paladini di Francia (title erroneously
  attributed to Ariosto) 41
Paladini notebooks 45–47, 45n8
  Paladini 1 45
  Paladini 2–4 45
  Paladini 4 (*Copione* 7) 45, 47
  Paladini 6–8 45
Paladins of France cycle 39
  composed by Agrippino 47
  dates recorded in 54
  prior to 58
  relation to *Storia dei paladini di Francia* 48
  scripts containing 43
  sources of 39
Panizzi, Antonio 71, 71n7
Parisi, Antonio 16
Pasqualino, Antonio xxin2, 16, 16n20,
  33n38, 39n2, 48n11, 50n16, 51n17,
  104n10, 112n3, 120n7, 123n11
Perinda (character) 51
Phineus (character) 185

Pinabello (character) 47, 165, 166, 170, 172n2
Pinadoro (character) 151
Pipino (Pippin III) (king of the Franks and character) 48, 58, 59
Poliferno (character) 114
Pollock, Arthur 18
Ponte, Giovanni 139n4
Porta, Pietro 16n20, 31n34, 104n10
Praloran, Marco 81n7
Prester John (see Senapo [character])
"primitive" legends 43
Pulci, Luigi 39, 51n18, 105n11, 200n4
Puppet Players Studio 17
Puppetry (McPharlin) 20

Rajna, Pio 58n27
Rampaldo di Risa (character) 151
Ranaldo/Rinaldo (character) 39, 53, 53n20, 73, 74, 76, 77, 82–86, 94, 97, 99, 108–10, 132, 134, 138, 149, 150, 162, 163, 165, 167, 175, 176, 179–81, 185, 190, 191, 194–98, 205–11
    arrives in Lampedusa 203
    Carlomagno's persecution of 52
    infatuation with Angelica 205
    leaves Paris 205
    Orlando and 69, 83, 91, 93n3, 98, 149, 171
    returning from exile 53
    Ruggiero and 212
    speech expressing desperation 69
Reali di Francia (Royals of France) cycle 42, 58, 58n27, 59
Reighard, Catherine 17
Reynolds, Barbara 71
Ricciardetto (character) 53, 93, 94, 94n4, 103
ricordini 49
rifacimento of the *Orlando Innamorato* (Berni) 71, 72, 83, 89, 105, 122, 125, 128
Rigoletto (Verdi) 207
Rinaldo (T. Tasso) 39
Rodamonte/Rodomonte (character) 131–33, 135–37, 139–43, 147–50, 153, 153n3, 155–57, 164–66, 170–72, 180, 181, 189, 190
    king of Garamanta and 138
    Sansonetto and Oliviero taken prisoner by 189

Roland (character) 200
Roland and His Friends (puppet play) 28, 29
Roncisvalle (script) 53
Rosana (character) 75
Rosetta (character) 74, 76
Ross, Charles S. 71, 82n8
Rossi, Cesare 6
Rousseau, Victor 16n21
Ruggiero II (of Reggio) (character) 209
Rugiero/Ruggiero (character) 112, 132, 134–39, 147–66, 156n4, 170, 171, 179, 180, 182, 188, 190, 194–97, 205, 208–12
Rushdie, Salman 74

Sacripante (character) 69, 131, 136, 143, 144
Salardo (character) 164
Salatiello, African king (character) 31n35, 33
Samson (character) 74, 76, 80
Sansonetto (character) 179, 180, 189, 190
Sarg, Tony 17, 18
Scionte, Joseph 16
scripts (see Paladins of France cycle)
Senapo (character) 180, 181, 184–86, 188, 193
Serpentino della Stella (character) 74, 75, 95
Shakespeare, William 19
Sheffer, Isaiah 32n37
Sibilla (character) 74, 75, 80
Silvanella (character) 113
Smithsonian Folklife Program 28
Sobrino/Subrino (character) 133, 134, 139, 193–95, 198, 199, 201–4, 211
Staten Island Institute of Arts and Sciences (SIIAS) 36
Statius 139n4
Staub, Nancy 28n32, 33n38, 34, 36
Storia dei paladini di Francia (Lodico) xxi, xxii, xxiii, xxiv, 4, 16, 22, 31, 34, 37, 39–43, 47, 48, 50, 53, 58, 65, 67–72, 74, 81–87, 90, 99–102, 104, 106–9, 112, 120–22, 126, 127, 129, 140–42, 144–46, 154, 156–58, 160–62, 171, 173–77, 183n3, 186–90, 194, 199–202, 204, 206–8, 208n7, 210–13
Storia di Guido di Santa Croce (Catanzaro) 30, 30n33

Tasso, Bernardo 120n7
Tasso, Torquato 4, 39, 73
Teatro Manteo 8, 13, 16, 213
Thalberg, Irving 17
Thebaid (Statius) 139n4
three-on-three combat 193
Tomasi di Lampedusa, Giuseppe 74
Torindo (character) 135
Tornello, Agata 3
Troiano (character) 118, 133–35
Trombetta, Raffaele 50n15, 88n14
Turpino (character) 149, 150, 154

Ugiero/Uggiero (character) 92, 93, 98, 134, 149
Uldano (character) 114

Verdi, Giuseppe 207
Villoresi, Marco 87n11, 139n3
Virgil xxiii

Webb, Hartwell M. 27
Wickert, Max 58n27

Zampese, Cristina 139n4
Zerbino (character) 33, 164–68, 172–74, 177

www.ingramcontent.com/pod-product-compliance
Lightning Source LLC
Chambersburg PA
CBHW021136230426
43667CB00005B/132